David Harvey

Antipode Book Series

General Editor: Noel Castree, Professor of Geography, University of Manchester, UK
Like its parent journal, the Antipode Book series reflects distinctive new developments in radical geography. It publishes books in a variety of formats – from reference books to works of broad explication to titles that develop and extend the scholarly research base – but the commitment is always the same: to contribute to the praxis of a new and more just society.

Published

David Harvey: A Critical Reader
Edited by Noel Castree and Derek Gregory

Working the Spaces of Neoliberalism: Activism, Professionalisation and Incorporation
Edited by Nina Laurie and Liz Bondi

Threads of Labour
Edited by Angela Hale and Jane Wills

Life's Work: Geographies of Social Reproduction
Edited by Katharyne Mitchell, Sallie A. Marston and Cindi Katz

Redundant Masculinities? Employment Change and White Working Class Youth
Linda McDowell

Space, Place and the New Labour Internationalism
Edited by Peter Waterman and Jane Wills

Spaces of Neoliberalism
Edited by Neil Brenner and Nik Theodore

Forthcoming

Neo-liberalization: States, Networks, Peoples
Edited by Kim England and Kevin Ward

Cities of Whiteness
Wendy S. Shaw

The South Strikes Back: Labour in the Global Economy
Rob Lambert and Edward Webster

David Harvey

A Critical Reader

Edited by Noel Castree and Derek Gregory

Blackwell
Publishing

© 2006 by Blackwell Publishing Ltd

BLACKWELL PUBLISHING
350 Main Street, Malden, MA 02148–5020, USA
9600 Garsington Road, Oxford OX4 2DQ, UK
550 Swanston Street, Carlton, Victoria 3053, Australia

The right of Noel Castree and Derek Gregory to be identified as the Authors of the Editorial Material in this Work has been asserted in accordance with the UK Copyright, Designs and Patents Act 1988.

First published 2006 by Blackwell Publishing Ltd

1 2006

Library of Congress Cataloging-in-Publication Data

David Harvey : a critical reader / edited by Noel Castree and Derek Gregory.
  p. cm. — (Antipode book series)
Includes bibliographical references and index.
ISBN–13: 978–0–631–23509–5 (hardcover: alk. paper)
ISBN–10: 0–631–23509–4 (hardcover: alk. paper)
ISBN–13: 978–0–631–23510–1 (pbk.: alk. paper)
ISBN–10: 0–631–23510–8 (pbk.: alk. paper)
1. Geography—Philosophy. 2. Social sciences. 3. Harvey, David, 1935– I. Castree, Noel, 1968– II. Gregory, Derek. III. Title. IV. Series.

G70.D379 2006
910'.01—dc22   2005013795

A catalogue record for this title is available from the British Library.

Set in 10/12.5 pt Sabon
by The Running Head Limited, 70 Regent Street, Cambridge CB2 1DP
Printed and bound in India
by Replika Press

The publisher's policy is to use permanent paper from mills that operate a sustainable forestry policy, and which has been manufactured from pulp processed using acid-free and elementary chlorine-free practices. Furthermore, the publisher ensures that the text paper and cover board used have met acceptable environmental accreditation standards.

For further information on
Blackwell Publishing, visit our website:
www.blackwellpublishing.com

Contents

Notes on Contributors

Trevor Barnes is Distinguished University Scholar and Professor of Geography at the University of British Columbia, Vancouver, Canada, where he has been since 1983. His recent work is about geography's postwar quantitative revolution and based upon oral histories.

Bruce Braun teaches political and environmental geography at the University of Minnesota. He is the author of *The Intemperate Rainforest: Nature, Culture and Power on Canada's West Coast* (University of Minnesota Press, 2002) and the co-editor with Noel Castree of *Remaking Reality: Nature at the Millennium* (Routledge, 1998) and *Social Nature: Theory, Practice, Politics* (Blackwell, 2001). He is currently working on the politics of biosecurity.

Alex Callinicos is a Professor of Politics at the University of York, UK. His recent books include *Equality* (Polity, 2000), *An Anti-Capitalist Manifesto* (Polity, 2003) and *The New Mandarins of American Power* (Polity, 2003).

Noel Castree is a Professor in the School of Environment and Development at Manchester University, UK. He is author, mostly recently, of *Nature: The Adventures of an Idea* (Routledge, 2005) and has written numerous essays on Marxist theory. He is co-editor of *Antipode: A Journal of Radical Geography* (published by Blackwell).

Marcus Doel is Professor of Human Geography at the University of Wales, Swansea. He has written numerous essays on the work of Deleuze, Guattari and Derrida and is author of *Poststructural Geographies: The Diabolical Art of Spatial Science* (Edinburgh University Press, 1999).

Derek Gregory is Distinguished University Scholar and Professor of Geography at the University of British Columbia at Vancouver. His previous publications include *Geographical Imaginations* (Blackwell, 1994) and *The Colonial Present: Afghanistan, Palestine, Iraq* (Blackwell, 2004); he is also co-editor of the *Dictionary of Human Geography* (Blackwell, 2001) and the interdisciplinary journal *Society and Space*. His current research centres on the 'war on terror' and Arab cities under military occupation.

Nancy C. M. Hartsock is Professor of Political Science at the University of Washington. She is the author of *Money, Sex, and Power: Toward a Feminist Historical Materialism* (Northeastern University Press, 1984) and *The Feminist Standpoint Revisited and Other Essays* (Westview Press, 1998) and numerous articles. She is currently at work on a book on the processes by which women are included in and excluded from the world economy.

Bob Jessop is Director of the Institute for Advanced Studies and Professor of Sociology at Lancaster University, UK, and is best known for his contributions to state theory and critical political economy. His latest book is *The Future of the Capitalist State* (Polity, 2002).

Cindi Katz is Professor of Geography at the Graduate Center of the City University of New York. She is author of *Growing Up Global: Economic Restructuring and Children's Everyday Lives* (University of Minnesota Press, 2004).

Eric Sheppard is Professor of Geography, with adjunct appointments in the Interdisciplinary Center for Global Change and American Studies, at the University of Minnesota. He has co-authored *The Capitalist Space Economy* (with T. J. Barnes, Unwin Hyman, 1990) and *A World of Difference* (with P. W. Porter, Guilford, 1998), co-edited *A Companion to Economic Geography* (with T. J. Barnes, 2000) and *Scale and Geographic Inquiry* (with R. B. McMaster, Blackwell, 2004), and published 90 refereed articles and book chapters. Current research interests include the spatiality of capitalism and globalization, environmental justice, critical GIS, and contestations of neoliberal urbanization.

Nigel Thrift is Pro-Vice Chancellor for Research, Professor of Geography and a Student of Christ Church at Oxford University, and an Emeritus Professor of Geography at Bristol University, UK. His main research interests are in international finance, cities, non-representational theory and the history of time. His recent publications include *Cities* (with Ash Amin, Sage Publications, 2004) and *Knowing Capitalism* (Sage Publications, 2004).

Melissa W. Wright is Assistant Professor in the Departments of Geography and of Women's Studies at the Pennsylvania State University. She has conducted research along the Mexico–US border, particularly in Ciudad Juarez, since the early 1990s. She has published articles in geography, anthropology, feminist studies and cultural studies, and co-edited *Geographies of Power: Placing Scale* (with Andrew Herod, Blackwell, 2002).

Sharon Zukin is Broeklundian Professor of Sociology at Brooklyn College and the Graduate Center of the City University of New York. Author of *Loft Living* (Rutgers University Press, 1989) *Landscapes of Power* (University of California Press: 1991) and *The Cultures of Cities* (Blackwell, 1995) she has published, most recently, *Point of Purchase: How Shopping Changed American Culture* (Routledge, 2003).

1

Introduction: Troubling Geographies

Derek Gregory

There is something troubling about geographies . . .

Harvey 2000c

Destinations

David Harvey's work can be read in many ways, but whatever else it may be, it is surely both an affirmation and a critique of the power of geographical knowledges. The plural is deliberate. Although Harvey's early writings traced and extended the frontiers of a formal if necessarily fuzzy Geography, he came to realize that geographical knowledges cannot be confined to any one discipline. They are produced in multiple locations, inside and outside the academy, and they shape multiple publics, for good and ill.[1] If 'geography is too important to be left to geographers', as Harvey has repeatedly claimed, he has also insisted that the potency of geographical knowledges does not reside in the accumulation of data in inventories or gazetteers, or even in their selective diffusion through the corridors of power and the circuits of the public sphere. It resides, rather, in the use of ideas – if you prefer (and Harvey does prefer), concepts and theories – that produce a systematic and ordered representation of the world that is sufficiently powerful to persuade others of its objectivity, accuracy and truth. When I describe Harvey's work as an affirmation of the power of geographical knowledges, I do so because he insists that geography matters, that it makes a difference to critical analysis, and because he believes that concepts of space, place

---

[1] See David Harvey, 'Cartographic identities: geographical knowledges under globalization', in his *Spaces of Capital: Towards a Critical Geography* (Edinburgh: Edinburgh University Press, 2001) pp. 208–33; idem, 'Geographical knowledges/Political powers', in John Morrill (ed.), *The Promotion of Knowledge* (*Proc. British Academy*, 122 (2004)) pp. 87–115.

and landscape unsettle and dislocate mainstream social theory to such a degree that they open up altogether different perspectives on the world. And I describe it as a critique because the development of Harvey's project has distanced him from concepts whose purchase is limited by the calculus of spatial science or whose provenance lies in Continental European philosophy, and because his purpose is to invest the emancipatory potential of other concepts in the materialization of a truly human geography.

This introduction is a rough guide to Harvey's project, written in the first instance for those who may be unfamiliar with the details of his work, and I will argue that his writings in their turn provide a sort of guidebook to the turbulent landscapes of modern capitalism. Not only is there a spatial systematics to his project, a series of itineraries shot through with critical recommendations and evaluations, but there is also something panoramic, selective and authoritative about his view of the world. This is not an unassailable position, however, and the perils of proceeding like this were underscored by one of Harvey's favourite novelists, Honoré de Balzac, when he introduced the *Comédie humaine*. 'The author who cannot make up his mind to face the fire of criticism', he wrote from Paris in 1842, 'should no more think of writing than a traveller should start on his journey counting on a perpetually clear sky.' Fortified by that observation, I propose to map some of Harvey's routes (and roots), and provide some critical signposts to other paths and other destinations that are explored in more detail in the chapters that follow.

Co-ordinates

While it would be a mistake to collapse Harvey's work into a single journey, two key texts frame his project and reveal a remarkably consistent template: *Explanation in Geography* and *The Limits to Capital*. These are usually read as opposing contributions, separated by the transitional essays of *Social Justice and the City* that recorded Harvey's movement from spatial science to historical materialism. This is a perfectly valid interpretation, but for all the differences between them, I think that there are also a number of revealing continuities.[2]

---

[2] For a cogent contextual reading of the transition, see Trevor Barnes, 'Between Deduction and Dialectics: David Harvey on Knowledge', this volume; for further discussion of the continuities that span it, see Eric Sheppard, 'David Harvey and Dialectical Space-Time', this volume.

Explanation in Geography, published in 1969, was written against the background of two revolutions. The first was the 'Quantitative Revolution' that convulsed geographical inquiry in the 1960s. This is a shorthand expression (a misleading one at that) for a concerted movement away from traditional regional geography towards a formal spatial science. The study of world regions as building blocks in a global inventory was criticized for its reduction of geographical inquiry to a mundane exercise in compilation and cartography, and in its place a new geography equipped with properly scientific credentials was to be devoted to the search for generalizations about spatial organization in both nominally 'human' and 'physical' domains. Harvey was no observer standing on the sidelines. He occupied a central place in the experimental reconfiguration of the field, and had made several avant-garde contributions to spatial analysis.[3] That spatial science was self-consciously experimental bears emphasis; much of this work was highly speculative, inquisitive, pragmatic, and conducted with little or no awareness of (or even interest in) wider philosophical and methodological issues. If *Explanation in Geography* can be read as an attempt to provide a warrant for those endeavours, however, it also sought to retain the flexibility required by their frontier character. For Harvey insisted on a 'vital' distinction between philosophy and methodology. He claimed not to be concerned in any direct way with philosophical arguments about the 'nature' of geography (though he plainly had views about it) or with the ways in which philosophers of science had established criteria for what he called 'sound explanation'. His focus was on the application of these criteria to geographical inquiry, on the 'logic of explanation', which prompted him to distinguish between 'those aspects of analysis which are a matter of logic and those aspects that are contingent upon philosophical presupposition'.[4]

But it was not possible to uncouple philosophy and methodology as conveniently as this implied. Indeed, Harvey's entire project was based on a central philosophical claim. He rejected the tradition of exceptionalism that

---

3 See, for example, David Harvey, 'Theoretical concepts and the analysis of land use patterns', *Ann. Ass. Am. Geogr.* 56 (1966) pp. 361–74; idem, 'Geographical processes and point patterns: testing models of diffusion by quadrat sampling', *Trans. Inst. Br. Geogr.* 40 (1966) pp. 81–95; idem, 'Some methodological problems in the use of the Neyman Type A and negative binomial probability distributions in the analysis of spatial series', loc. cit., 43 (1968) pp. 85–95; idem, 'Pattern, process and the scale problem in gegraphical research', loc. cit., 45 (1968) pp. 71–7.

4 David Harvey, *Explanation in Geography* (London: Edward Arnold, 1969) pp. 3–8.

could be traced back to Kant's foundational distinction between different knowledges, and which had received its canonical disciplinary statement in Hartshorne's *The Nature of Geography* in 1939, because he believed that the division had both marooned Geography and History outside the mainstream of scientific progress and also separated them from one another. Unlike the sciences that organized the world into categories on the basis of logical classifications (equivalence, similarity, affinity), and which thus allowed for replication and generalization, Geography and History were supposed to be predicated on physical classifications: that is, on observations of phenomena that occurred together, as singular and unique constellations in either space or time. Against this, Harvey focused on the delineation of a recognizably scientific method, grounded in the philosophy of science in general and positivism in particular, that could underwrite the search for an order (in spatial structure and sequence) beneath the particularities of place. The sense of 'grounding' was crucial: Harvey's project was a foundational one, anchored in bedrock, and he rejected what he called 'extreme' versions of logical positivism precisely because they claimed that knowledge 'could be developed independently of philosophical presuppositions'. The approach that he outlined in *Explanation* derived from Braithwaite, Carnap, Hempel, Nagel and other philosophers of (physical) science who had established the deductive-nomological model as what he termed 'the standard model of scientific explanation'.[5] Again, standardization was essential: for Harvey, like most of his contemporaries, there was only one ('the') scientific method capable of sustaining the production of systematic and generalizable geographical knowledge.

Explanation was about more than the projection of these methods onto the terrain of geographical inquiry. Its conceptual fulcrum was space, which Harvey identified as 'the central concept on which Geography as a discipline relies for its coherence'. But for this coherence to be realized, he argued, a double transformation was necessary: space had to be transformed from the planar categories of Euclidean geometry, and its materializations had to be transformed by process ('the key to temporal explanation'). From the very beginning, therefore, one of Harvey's central concerns was to establish the connection between spatial structure and process. The issue had emerged out of his doctoral research on agricultural change in nineteenth-century Kent, a study in traditional historical geography, but Harvey subsequently

---

[5] Ibid., pp. 8, 29–30. This is the only explicit reference to positivism in the whole book but despite Harvey's hostility to these 'extreme' versions of logical positivism, *Explanation* – like most of spatial science more generally – was fully consistent with the protocols of positivism.

reformulated the question in the lexicon of modern location theory. If, as now seemed likely, it was simply impossible to infer generative process from geometric form, then how could a process-based geography be developed? Although he never put it quite like this, how could History and Geography be convened within a plenary, integrated – in a word, unitary – science of terrestrial change? Harvey's principal methodological objective in *Explanation* was to identify modes of spatial analysis that would displace the conventional conception of space as a 'container' (absolute space), and build from but ultimately transcend other geometries of spatial form by setting them in motion. At the time, Harvey took this to be a matter of translation, a means to move between Euclidean (form) and non-Euclidean (process) languages, but the more important point is that processes of geographical transformation were at the very heart of Harvey's project from the outset.[6]

Harvey would later describe Bhaskar's prospectus for a non-positivist social science as a work of 'intimidating difficulty and intensity', but one might say the same of *Explanation*. I was reading Geography at Cambridge when it was published, and even for someone being expertly schooled in spatial science, locational analysis and systems theory it was an unusually demanding text. But it was also unsatisfactory, not least because I was also being taught an historical geography that took Harvey's central question – geographical transformation – with the utmost seriousness, but which also required a close engagement with the empirical, in the field and the archive, that modulated its theoretical dispositions and advanced an analysis of the dynamics of space-economies and landscapes in substantive terms. 'By our theories you shall know us', Harvey had concluded, but I had become drawn to an historical geography that was less about knowing 'us' – forming the disciplinary identity that, to my surprise, still haunted

---

6 'A study of process is not the prerogative of the historical geographer alone', he had written two years earlier, and yet 'an unfortunate gap has developed between the scholarly studies of the specialist historical geographers . . . and the analytical techniques of human geographers concerned with contemporary distributions': David Harvey, 'Models of the evolution of spatial patterns in human geography', in R. J. Chorley and Peter Haggett (eds.), *Models in Geography* (London: Methuen) pp. 549–608: 550. The emphasis on process explains both Harvey's admiration for and his distance from one of the architects of the modern discipline of Geography, Alexander von Humboldt (1769–1859). Harvey clearly admires the systematicity of Humboldt's project, most evident in the multi-volume *Cosmos*, but insists on the need to transcend Humboldt's Kantian view of geographical knowledge 'as mere spatial ordering [to be] kept apart from the narratives of history': David Harvey, 'Cosmopolitanism and the banality of geographical evils', *Public Culture* 12 (2000) pp. 529–64: 554.

Harvey at the very end of *Explanation* – than it was about knowing the world. In fact, he later attributed the limitations of the book to its preoccupation with language, and distanced himself from the formal language systems that structured spatial analysis in favour of ordinary language systems capable of capturing the substance of social practices. You could see the problem in the closing chapters of *Explanation*, where the systems to be modelled remained spectacularly unidentified, so many empty boxes to be tied together, and where their geography had all but disappeared. It had been a long journey down the yellow brick road, and I was left with the uncomfortable feeling that there was nothing behind the wizard's curtain.

As Harvey was soon to remind his readers, however, Marx had warned that there was no royal road to science. *Explanation in Geography* had been written against the background of another revolution of sorts, one that animated the academy but which also filled the streets: the anti-war and civil rights movements in the United States and the events of May 1968 in France, Germany and elsewhere in Europe. Harvey confessed that he had been so preoccupied with methodological issues that he had been more or less detached from these events, and they find no echo in the austere pages of *Explanation*. But soon after its publication, and coinciding with his move from the UK to the United States, Harvey began to explore the ethical and political dimensions of geographical inquiry that had been suspended during his ascetic pilgrimage through the philosophy and methodology of science. His initial forays were recorded in the essays that compose *Social Justice and the City*. This was a much more subversive book than *Explanation* and it had much more of an impact inside and outside the discipline. Harvey gave a lecture based on one of the early essays in the book to an undergraduate conference I attended at Bristol, and the effect was electric. There is always something thrilling about Harvey's performances – I've never seen him read from a prepared text let alone a series of overheads or slides – but this was more than a matter of style: the intellectual apparatus, the political passion and the urban texture were all a long way from the abstracted logics of *Explanation*. Later essays widened the gap, until it must have been difficult for many readers to believe that the two books had been written by the same author. Harvey's denunciation of the trivial pursuits of spatial science (the 'clear disparity between the sophisticated theoretical and methodological framework we are using and our ability to say anything really meaningful about events as they unfold about us') and his exuberant endorsement of the power of historical materialism ('I can find no other way of accomplishing what I set out to do') fused to shock what was one of the very last disciplines in the English-speaking world to take Marx's writings with the seriousness they deserved. And yet, despite Harvey's desire to spark a 'revolution in geographical thought', he continued to insist on the importance of science (though he now defined it in different terms and understood it as an intrinsically social practice) and reaffirmed the need to provide systematic theorizations of space and spatial transformations (though he now insisted 'there are no philosophical answers to philosophical questions that arise over the nature of space – the answers lie in human practice').[7]

Social Justice was only a bridgehead; Harvey knew he needed to do much more work on Marx. I choose my words with care: the object of his studies, and of the various reading groups and courses in which he was involved, was Marx not Marxism. 'I wanted to see how far I could get', he explained, 'from within the framework laid out in Marx's *Capital, Theories of Surplus Value*, the *Grundrisse*, and some of the ancillary writings on political economy.'[8] It took him the best part of a decade, and the result was *The Limits to Capital*, published in 1982. This emphasized two central dimensions. First, echoing his earlier insistence on systematicity, Harvey argued that Marx's visionary contribution was 'the capacity to see capitalism as an integrated whole', as a dynamic and dialectical totality. Harvey's previous attempts to exorcise the demons of fragmentation through appeals to systems theory (in *Explanation*) and structuralism (in the coda to *Social Justice*) had been as diffuse as they were formalistic, but he now grounded his arguments in a focused and forensic rereading of Marx's critique of political economy. The discipline, rigour and clarity of Harvey's exposition have been noted by many commentators, though, as I will explain later, these qualities are not universally admired![9] Second, reinforcing his focus

---

7 David Harvey, *Social Justice and the City* (London: Edward Arnold, 1973; Oxford: Blackwell, 1998) pp. 13, 17, 128. The pathbreaking effect of *Social Justice* was recognized by an appropriately forward-looking conference commemorating the twentieth anniversary of its publication: see Andy Merrifield and Erik Swyngedouw (eds.) *The Urbanization of Injustice* (London: Lawrence and Wishart, 1996).

8 David Harvey, 'Retrospect on *The Limits to Capital*', *Antipode* 36 (2004) pp. 544–9: 544; see also Alex Callinicos, 'David Harvey and Marxism', this volume.

9 It is a measure of the rigour of Harvey's exegesis that it should have attracted the equally rigorous commentaries published in the 'Symposium on *The Limits to Capital*: Twenty years on', *Antipode* 36 (2004): the essays by George Henderson, 'Value: the many-headed hydra' (pp. 445–460) and Vinay Gidwani, 'The Limits to Capital: questions of provenance and politics' (pp. 527–543) in particular are models of serious, scrupulous intellectual engagement, and there are (sadly) precious few books in the field that could attract or sustain such consideration. See also Bob Jessop's careful excavation of *Limits* in 'Spatial Fixes, Temporal Fixes and Spatio-Temporal Fixes', this volume.

on spatial transformations, Harvey argued that Marx's analysis of the dynamics of capitalism as a mode of production, in contradistinction to the pinhead formulations of neoclassical economics, was predicated on (that is, assumed and depended on) the production of a differentiated and integrated (urbanized) space-economy.[10] This was a contribution of unsurpassed originality. The spatial problematic remained latent within Marx's own corpus, and none of the (very few) writers who had thus far registered the production of space under capitalism – including most prominently Henri Lefebvre – had integrated its turbulent landscapes within the logics of capital accumulation.[11] While Marx prioritized time (in the labour theory of value) and historical transformation (in the creative destruction of successive capitalisms) – these were the limits to *Capital* in Harvey's title – Harvey showed that the volatile production of space was at once the solution (or 'spatial fix') and dissolution of capitalism (hence the limits to capital).

If Harvey had shown how space could be built into the framework of historical materialism, as what Perry Anderson has called 'an ineliminable element' of its deductible structure, this was not the last word on the matter, and Harvey never presented it as such (quite the opposite); in fact, he considers the third-cut theory of crisis to be the least satisfactory part of his argument. I know many geographers who were dissatisfied by the closing chapters of the book too, not least because they had expected a detailed reconstruction of the uneven geographies of capital accumulation and circulation. But two decisions had foreclosed that possibility: Harvey's determination to stay close to Marx's own writings rather than trace the subsequent advances of Marxist political economy or economic geography more generally (there are scattered commentaries on some key contemporary controversies, but these are usually relegated to the footnotes); and Harvey's decision to divest the argument of its complicating 'historical content' and instead present his theorizations as a series of 'empty boxes' (his term). These are both serious limits to *Limits*, to be sure, and yet even

---

[10] This is not the only difference between neoclassical economics and historical materialism, of course. I remember Harvey being taxed at a conference by a cocksure critic who insisted on the superior analysis afforded by the neoclassical trinity of land, labour and capital. Turning to the board where he had developed a complex circuit diagram in the course of his presentation, Harvey showed that the categories he had worked with were landlords, labourers and capitalists. His rejoinder was unforgettable: 'You are telling us you are happier dealing with things than with people.' The emphasis on social relations (and hence on social change) is of vital importance to Harvey's project.

[11] See my discussion of Harvey and Lefebvre in *Geographical Imaginations* (Oxford: Blackwell, 1994) pp. 348–416.

on these reduced terms the scale of the task is such that I sympathize with Harvey when he wryly notes the common tendency 'to criticize texts for what they leave out rather than appreciate them for what they accomplish'.[12]

In a thoughtful commentary on these questions, Trevor Barnes records how much he admired *Social Justice* for its 'unfinished quality' – the sense of Harvey arguing not only with others but with himself – whereas *Limits* seemed to him to be preoccupied by a 'search for definitiveness' and a sense of closure.[13] In this too, *Explanation* echoes in *Limits*. But when I suggest that the connections between the two provide the foundations for Harvey's subsequent work, I do not mean to imply that the development of his project has been fully formed around them. Science and systematicity, space and transformation have remained its watchwords.[14] But, as I now want to show, Harvey has also used them to illuminate other paths that have opened up new views over new landscapes.

Directions

Two new directions seem most significant to me, one conceptual and the other substantive. Although Harvey has continued to remain close to Marx's critique of political economy, he has also registered the importance

12 David Harvey, *The Limits to Capital* (Oxford: Blackwell, 1982; London: Verso, 1999); idem, 'Reinventing Geography' (interviewer: Perry Anderson), *New Left Review* 4 (2000) pp. 75–97; idem, 'Retrospect'.

13 Trevor Barnes, '"The background of our lives": David Harvey's *The Limits to Capital*', *Antipode* 36 (2004) pp. 407–413.

14 The absence of any consideration of Harvey's work from a collection of essays on social theory and space – edited by two geographers – is bizarre (especially when one considers some of the other subjects of their critical acclaim): see Mike Crang and Nigel Thrift (eds.) *Thinking Space* (London: Routledge, 2000). Harvey's focus on 'space' has been unwavering, and its centrality is confirmed by his 'Space as a Keyword', this volume. That said, another, looser thematic can be traced through his project: 'nature'. Although this too is a keyword for both Geography and historico-geographical materialism, Harvey accords it much less systematic discussion. The model of science set out in *Explanation* was derived from a particular reading of the physical sciences, but the question of nature remained submerged in Harvey's work, breaking the surface only in a clutch of essays on population and ecology (in which Marx sees off Malthus) and in a section of the Paris studies (where Harvey provides a tantalizingly brief account of aesthetic and scientific appropriations of a distinctively urban 'nature' in Haussmann's Paris). It receives its most sustained treatment in his *Justice, Nature and the Geography of Difference* (Oxford: Blackwell, 1996). See Bruce Braun, 'Towards a New Earth and a New Humanity', this volume.

of other writings, notably the luminous *Eighteenth Brumaire of Louis Napoleon*, that were more attentive to the significance of cultural and social relations. I suspect that the vivid prose of the *Eighteenth Brumaire* helped renew Harvey's interest in narrative as a means of conveying the sense that, as Marx famously put it in that pamphlet, 'people make history, but not just as they please nor under conditions of their own choosing', and perhaps it also played a part in his newfound interest in the capacity of the modern novel to capture the urban condition. 'I find myself most deeply impressed', Harvey wrote in *Consciousness and the Urban Experience*, by 'those works that function as both literature and social science'.[15] The finest writings to flow from Marx's pen (and Engels's too) have that same extraordinary power to evoke as well as explain. In addition, Harvey has provided a rereading of the account of primary ('primitive') accumulation found in the first volume of *Capital*, where Marx traced the erasure of non-capitalist economic forms, the supercession of petty commodity production and the final emergence of wage-labour as the dominant modality of the capitalist economy. In *Limits*, Harvey had mapped the circuits of expanded reproduction with precision – the dispersed and distributed exploitation of living labour – and, like Marx, had relegated primary accumulation to the formative stages of the transition from European feudalism to capitalism. But Harvey has since recognised the continued salience of primary accumulation, which – precisely because the process is ongoing – he prefers to call 'accumulation by dispossession', and he has shown how its violent predations are insistently inscribed within contemporary globalizations.[16]

These developments have done more than advance Harvey's project in a conceptual register, for they have also involved a series of substantive considerations that has considerably widened and deepened the scope of his historico-geographical materialism. The *Eighteenth Brumaire* was the date in the French revolutionary calendar when Bonaparte staged his coup d'état in 1799, and Marx drew an ironic parallel between the original mobilization and its 'farcical' repetition by Bonaparte's upstart nephew, Louis Napoleon, in 1851. The subsequent tensions between imperial spectacle and

---

[15] David Harvey, *Consciousness and the Urban Experience* (Oxford: Blackwell, 1985) p. xv.

[16] See Nancy Hartsock, 'Globalization and Primitive Accumulation', this volume. Cf. Michael Perelman, 'The secret history of primitive accumulation and classical political economy,' *The Commoner* 2 (2001); Massimo De Angelis, 'Marx and primitive accumulation: the continuous character of capital's 'enclosures',' loc. cit.; Werner Bonefeld, 'The permanence of primitive accumulation: commodity fetishism and social constitution', loc. cit. These essays are all available at http://www.thecommoner.org.

the spectacle of capital provided the epicentre for Harvey's study of Second Empire Paris, originally published as an extended essay in *Consciousness* and recently reissued as *Paris, Capital of Modernity*. The revised version is studded with additional images, many of them drawn from contemporary photographs and prints, but Harvey's interest in cultural forms is most visible in the mirrors he places between Baudelaire's attempts to capture the fugitive traces of modernity, 'the transient, the fleeting, the contingent', and the whirlwind world of Marx's capitalist modernity where 'all that is solid melts into air'. The same analytic is evident in Harvey's critique of *The Condition of Postmodernity*, where the lessons of the *Eighteenth Brumaire* and Second Empire Paris are invoked to draw the contours of modernism and capitalist modernity. But Harvey's primary purpose there is to establish a connection between the volatile cultural formations of postmodernism (in architecture, art, cinema and fiction) and the basal emergence of a new regime of flexible or post-Fordist accumulation. Beginning in the early 1970s, he argued that the logics and disciplines of flexible accumulation had recomposed the circuits of expanded reproduction, and that this was not only coincident with but also causally implicated in the rise of postmodernism as a cultural dominant.[17] There are passages in the book that seem to tremble on the edge of a discussion of primary accumulation, but Harvey was clearly unaware of its contemporary (and contemporaneous) significance. Since then, he has argued with others that 'accumulation by dispossession became increasingly more salient after 1973, in part as compensation for the chronic problems of overaccumulation arising within expanded reproduction'. Harvey's belated awareness of the continuing significance of what Marx had called a 'reserve army of labour' is inseparable from the army of reservists that was called up after 9/11 to serve on the frontlines of American Empire in Afghanistan, Iraq and elsewhere in the world, and the connection he makes between the two armies enriches the critique of the global couplings of neoliberalism and neoconservatism that he provides in *The New Imperialism*.[18]

[17] David Harvey, 'Paris, 1850–1870', in *Consciousness* op. cit., pp. 62–220 and revised and reissued as *Paris, Capital of Modernity* (New York: Routledge, 2003); idem, *The Condition of Postmodernity: An Enquiry into the Origins of Cultural Change* (Oxford: Blackwell, 1989). For a discussion of the trope of 'mirroring' that I use here, see Meaghan Morris, 'The man in the mirror: David Harvey's "Condition" of postmodernity', *Theory, Culture and Society* 9 (1992) pp. 253–279; Gregory, *Geographical Imaginations* op. cit., pp. 398–400. But see my cautionary remark on mirroring below, p. 17.

[18] David Harvey, *The New Imperialism* (Oxford: Oxford University Press, 2003) p. 156.

These developments are of great interest, but they raise two issues of considerable moment. First, in the pursuit of these other paths, how far have the co-ordinates Harvey established in the trajectory from *Explanation* to *Limits* continued to guide his project? Can his work still be read through the same grid? Second, in extending the conceptual and substantive boundaries of his project, to what degree has Harvey integrated the theoretical with the empirical? What is the connection between these registers? These questions provide the framework for the rest of this chapter.

Ariadne's Threads

Science and systematicity, space and transformation: the four threads that I have suggested guide Harvey through the labyrinth of capitalism. The first two enable him to map its logic and reveal the structures of capital accumulation that persist into our own present. The last two enable him to set its geographies in motion and show how the dynamics of capitalism are embedded in its turbulent spaces. I will consider each in turn.

Harvey's interest in Paris was aroused by the year he spent in the French capital in 1976–7. He had planned to spend his time learning more about the debates that were taking place in French Marxism, but he ended up becoming less and less interested in them and 'more and more intrigued by Paris as a city'. Soon he began to wonder how 'the theoretical apparatus in *The Limits to Capital* [might] play out in tangible situations'. The model for his investigations was Carl Schorske's account of late Habsburg Vienna. Harvey was captivated by what he saw as Schorske's extraordinary ability to convey 'some sense of the totality of what the city was about through a variety of perspectives on material life, on cultural activities, on patterns of thought within the city'. This was precisely his own problem: 'How can some vision of Paris as a whole be preserved while recognizing, as Haussmann himself so clearly did, that the details matter?' In a later essay, incorporated within the extended version of the Paris study, Harvey even describes Walter Benjamin's Arcades Project – the multiple files in which the Marxist critic sought to re-present Paris as the capital of the nineteenth century – as an unfinished attempt to tease out 'persistent threads that bring together the whole and render some vision of the totality possible'. But the priority Harvey accords to seeing Paris as a totality is brought into boldest relief in his celebration of what he calls Balzac's 'synoptic vision'. The novelist's greatest achievement, so Harvey argues, was his ability 'to get beneath the surface appearance, the mad jumble, and the kaleidoscopic shifts' of early nineteenth-century Paris; to 'penetrate the labyrinth' and 'peel away the fetishism' imposed on its inhabitants through the circulation of commodities; and to reveal Paris as 'a product of constellations and clashes of class forces'. For Harvey, Balzac's analytic successfully exposed 'at the core' of the city 'the utter emptiness of bourgeois values' based on the calculus inscribed in fictitious forms of capital. I don't think it fanciful to read this as a wish-image for Harvey's own project; the same language reappears in his own renditions. But these are of course modelled directly on Marx; Harvey's purpose is to show how 'the fiction of the commodity' came to reign supreme in Second Empire Paris, and how Haussmann's grandiose schemes exercised in the name of the Emperor were instrumental in transforming the capital city into the city of capital.[19]

The same thematics reappear in Harvey's critique of *The Condition of Postmodernity*. Postmodernism is in many ways the antithesis of Harvey's predilections: it revels in fragmentation, he says, wages war on totality (the phrase is Lyotard's) and thumbs its nose at any metanarrative that might bring it to order. For all its apparent novelty, however, he insists that it is not exempt from 'the basic rules of a capitalist mode of production', and he invokes them to discipline and domesticate its excesses. Postmodernism is supposed to express and even enforce the logics of flexible accumulation, and Harvey recapitulates some of the key arguments from *Limits* to theorize the transition from one regime to another. 'Re-reading [Marx's] account in *Capital*', he says, produces a 'jolt of recognition': 'It is not hard to see how the invariant elements and relations that Marx defined as fundamental to any capitalist mode of production still shine through, and in many instances with an even greater luminosity than before, all the surface froth and evanescence so characteristic of flexible accumulation'. The depth model is constantly in play, in *Condition* and elsewhere, to explain how the 'underlying logic of capitalism' can account for a postmodernism that 'swims in the fragmentary and the chaotic currents of change as if that is all there is'. Against this, but repeating the metaphor in a different register, Harvey maintains:

> There are laws of process at work under capitalism capable of generating a seemingly infinite range of outcomes out of the slightest variation in

[19] Carl Schorske, *Fin-de-siècle Vienna: Politics and Culture* (New York: Random House, 1981); Harvey, 'Reinventing Geography' op. cit.; idem, *Paris* op. cit., pp. 17–18, 33, 35–6, 51, 102. The essay on Balzac was written after the main study was completed, but it brings out the organizing architecture of Harvey's investigations with clarity and concision. Harvey's Paris studies are set in the context of his studies of other cities and his general analysis of the urban condition in Sharon Zukin, 'David Harvey on Cities', this volume.

initial conditions or of human activity and imagination. In the same way
that the laws of fluid dynamics are invariant in every river in the world,
so the laws of capital circulation are consistent from one supermarket to
another, from one labour market to another, from one commodity production system to another. (p. 132)

Echoing both *Explanation* and *Limits*, Harvey insists that it is possible to
derive 'laws of process' and to theorize the turbulent transformation from
one regime of accumulation to another in a systematic manner.[20]

In *The New Imperialism* Harvey turns to a different 'regime change' – the
war in Iraq – but he sees this too as a surface expression of something much
deeper. In one of the closing chapters of *Condition* he had insisted on the
continuing importance of historical materialism, but in subsequent essays
he had raised the bar to claim that its insights into political economy had
become steadily more acute. *Limits to Capital* was 'now even more deeply
relevant to understanding how a globalizing capitalism is working'.[21] In
The New Imperialism, accordingly, he seeks 'to uncover some of the deeper
transformations occurring beneath all the surface turbulence and volatility'.
He invokes the analysis of the production of a capitalist space-economy and
the dynamics of a spatial fix within the circuits of expanded reproduction
that he had developed in detail in *Limits*, but he now complements this with
a delineation of 'the iron laws within the contingencies of accumulation by
dispossession'. His central focus is on the United States: indeed, he writes
from within the belly of the beast and, for that matter, from New York, 'the
empire state' itself. Within the United States, Harvey argues, the intercut
projects of neoliberalism and neoconservatism have consistently attempted
to solve what he diagnoses as 'chronic problems of overaccumulation of
capital through expanded reproduction' by reactivating, intensifying and
introducing radically new means of accumulation by dispossession. The two
circuits are not antagonistic but dialectically intertwined; so too are internal
politics and external expansion. It is politically more expedient 'to pillage
and debase far-away populations' than to attempt domestic reforms, but
the imperial projects of neoliberalism produced 'chronic insecurity' within
the United States. Harvey argues that the neoconservative response to this
predicament has been to repatriate the culture of militarism and violence
by strengthening the national security state, activating a nationalist rhetoric of 'homeland', and appealing to a religious fundamentalism to exorcize

[20] Harvey, *Condition* op. cit., pp. 44, 179, 187–8, 343.
[21] See also David Harvey, 'The difference a generation makes', in his *Spaces of
Hope* (Edinburgh: Edinburgh University Press, 2000) pp. 3–18.

demons at home as well as abroad. If 9/11 was a moment of opportunity for neoconservatism, therefore, and the Iraq war the most visible and violent realization of privateering, this was made possible – in all sorts of ways, internal and external – by the 'creative destruction' previously wrought by neoliberalism. In Harvey's analysis, these twin politico-economic projects fold in and out of each other, and privatization and militarism are the two wings of a vulture capitalism fighting to restore class power to the richest strata at home and to plunder markets abroad.[22]

In none of these studies does Harvey's analysis of the systematics of capitalism congeal into a static architecture; it remains a resolutely *historical* geography (or historico-geographical materialism). The interest in space and transformation runs like a red line through all his texts. In the extended Paris essays, for example, it becomes clear that Balzac's artistic and critical achievement is all the more impressive to Harvey because his novels reveal the machinations of capital in the city through a sort of spatial dynamics. He is particularly appreciative of the ways in which the 'spatial rigidities' in the early novels yield to a much more malleable view of space in which the spatiality of Paris is rendered as 'dialectical, constructed and consequential'. I've said the same about Harvey's own investigations, where the 'rigidity' of the opening sections and their stylized reconstructions of the geometry of

---

[22] Harvey, *Imperialism* op. cit., pp. 1, 17, 87–136, 135, 188, 193; idem, 'Neoliberalism and the restoration of class power', available at http://www.marxsite.com/updates.htm.; idem, *A Brief History of Neo-Liberalism* (Oxford: Oxford University Press, 2005). In *Limits* Harvey had noted the links between 'inner' and 'outer' transformations in periodic attempts to stabilize capitalism, and the intimate relations between colonialism, imperialism and 'primitive accumulation' (pp. 436–8), but (like Marx) he placed these sutures in the past rather than the present. Cf. Retort, 'Blood for oil?' *London Review of Books* 28, 8 21 April 2005: 'We are not the first to think Marx too sanguine in this prognosis. In fact, it has turned out that primitive accumulation is an incomplete and recurring process, essential to capitalism's continuing life. Dispossession is crucial to this, and its forms recur and reconstitute themselves endlessly. Hence the periodic movement of capitalism outwards, to geographies and polities it can plunder almost unopposed. (Or so it hoped, in the case of Iraq.)' That outward movement is propelled by environmental catatrophe as well as military violence. Vulture capitalism also feeds off earthquakes, hurricanes and tsunamis, and Naomi Klein's suggestive sketch of 'the rise of a predatory form of disaster capitalism' as a sophisticated form of contemporary colonialism reveals another dismal axis of accumulation by dispossession: 'The rise of disaster capitalism', *The Nation*, 2 May 2005. This intersects, at least in outline, with Harvey's discussions of the production of nature.

the class-divided city gradually yields, often in close proximity to his reflections on Baudelaire and Benjamin, to a fluid sense of the fleeting encounters and multiple spheres that made up the geographies of everyday life in Second Empire Paris. Harvey shows how the 'rationalization' of urban space under the sign of modernity depended on the mobilization of finance capital – on a new prominence for money, credit and speculation – that installed spaces as commodities and, on the other side of the coin, displayed commodities in spaces as the centre of Paris was increasingly given over to the conspicuous commodification of bourgeois social life. There are countless accounts of the reshaping of the capital during the Second Empire, of course, but what distinguishes Harvey's *geography* of Paris from Colin Jones's *biography* of the same city (for example) is its refusal to reduce space to a stage or setting. Harvey's interlocking thematics are intended to spiral together, as he says himself, 'to set the space in motion as a real historical geography of a living city'. Most other studies display Paris as possessive, Haussmann's Paris, a geometric arena and an abstract space of Reason, in which straight lines are drawn on maps, avenues are blazed through tenements, and a grand plan is inexorably materialized. But Harvey shows Paris to have been an insurgent city not only during the commotions of 1848 and the Commune of 1870–1 but also in the creative destructions and the no less creative accommodations to them that animated the spaces of the city in the intervening years.[23]

'Creative destruction' arises out of crises within the circuits of capital accumulation; it marks the sites of rupture between fixity and motion within the tense and turbulent landscape of capital. In *Condition* Harvey continues to work with the concept, and within the first twenty pages Second Empire Paris appears as an epitome of capitalist modernity. But his 'experimental punchline' of the book was the introduction of the supplementary concept of time-space compression. Creative destruction disrupts the sedimentations and stabilities that inhere within the meanings, routines and expectations that usually attach to 'place', he argues, but this experience of dislocation in all its particularity is threaded into more generalized

---

[23] Harvey, *Paris* op. cit., pp. 41, 105; Gregory, *Geographical Imaginations* op. cit., pp. 221–2; Colin Jones, *Paris: Biography of a City* (London: Allen Lane, 2004). Readers who are unpersuaded by Harvey's reading of Balzac's urban geography will find an instructive comparison in the cartographic 'plottings' of Balzac's novels in Franco Moretti, *Atlas of the European Novel 1800–1900* (London: Verso, 1998) pp. 87–101. Moretti's central claim is that 'specific stories are the product of specific spaces' and, indeed, that 'without a certain kind of space, a certain kind of story is simply impossible (p. 100). But even as Moretti connects stories and spaces he has to separate them, and so renders the spaces of Paris as pre-given to (rather than produced through) their representations.

processes of time-space compression. Harvey explains that the term is intended to signal 'processes that so revolutionize the objective qualities of space and time that we are forced to alter, sometimes in quite radical ways, how we represent the world to ourselves'. He uses the word 'compression', he continues, because the development of capitalism 'has been characterized by speed-up in the pace of life, while so overcoming spatial barriers that the world sometimes seems to collapse inwards upon us'. There is a trace of spatial science in this – of its preoccupation with the 'friction of distance', and with changing lapse rates and distance-decay curves – but only a trace. Harvey has not forgotten his critique of spatial science, and he repeats his rejection of the view 'that there is some universal spatial language independent of social practices'. Instead, he insists that 'spatial practices derive their efficacy in social life only through the structure of social relations within which they come into play'. In contradistinction to the geometric abstractions of spatial science, therefore, time-space compression functions as a sort of conceptual switch; its origins lie in the circuits through which the rotation time of capital is reduced and its sphere of circulation is increased, while its effects are registered in parallel and serial circuits of cultural change. Harvey provides an argumentation-sketch, which is suggestive but plainly not intended to be definitive, to demonstrate that revolutions in the capitalist production of space, from the European Renaissance through the Enlightenment to the long nineteenth century, were wired to revolutions in the representation and calibration of time and space. This narrative effectively prepares the ground for Harvey's central charge against postmodernism. If crises of capital accumulation are articulated (not, I think, merely mirrored) by crises of representation, time-space compression is the crucial process that mediates the double transition from Fordism to flexible accumulation and high modernism to postmodernism. Seen thus, postmodernism is at once the cultural logic and the cultural landscape of late capitalism.[24]

One of Harvey's most dramatic images of time-space compression was his rendition of 'the shrinking globe', and the stream of commodities and images cascading into the cities of the global North to be cannibalized into the hybrid cultures of postmodernity. But it was a curiously monotonic map. It planed away the variable geographies of time-space compression, and it discounted the contrary possibility of time-space expansion. Yet

---

[24] Harvey, *Condition* op. cit., pp. 222–3; 240; cf. Gregory, *Geographical Imaginations* op. cit., pp. 398–9; Frederic Jameson, *Postmodernism, or the Cultural Logic of Late Capitalism* (Durham: Duke University Press, 1991). Harvey also connects postmodernism to neoliberalism in his *Brief History* op. cit.

for many people the world had become much larger. These experiential variations were inflected by class and gender; as the artist Barbara Kruger pointedly observed, 'the world is a small place – until you have to clean it'. They were compounded by racialization. 'The globe shrinks for those who own it', Homi Bhabha noted, but 'for the displaced or the dispossessed, the migrant or the refugee, no distance is more awesome than the few feet across borders or frontiers.'[25] Harvey's willingness to recognize the significance of differences other than those produced through capitalism's grid of class relations has become a lightning rod for criticism. Most commentators agree that the multiple, material discriminations that arise from gender, sexuality, racialization, and other cultural and social markings that cannot be reduced to the impositions of capital demand a much more sustained discussion.[26] But Harvey's blindness to the geography of these variations derived as much from within his critique of capitalism as from without. It was, I think, his focus on expanded reproduction that directed his gaze inwards, to the global North and its metropolitan conjunctions of flexible accumulation and postmodernism. In *The New Imperialism*, however, the new emphasis on accumulation by dispossession turns Harvey's gaze outwards. The process is not confined to the global South, of course, and the pursuit of American Empire involves securing 'the exaction of tribute from the rest of the world', so it is important not to lose sight of the chains yoking North and South. But Harvey is now sensitive to the localization of some of the 'most vicious and inhumane' incidents of accumulation by dispossession in some of 'the most vulnerable and degraded regions' on the planet.

Harvey diagrams this global sphere as an insurgent space, its places and regions stripped and taken in the most violent of ways, racked by a chronic disjunction between what he identifies, following Giovanni Arrighi, as territorial logics of power that pivot around fixity and capitalist logics of power that require fluidity. There is something unsatisfactory about this polarity, because the twin logics of power need not confound each other: they may on occasion reinforce one another. It is not necessary to accept

[25] See Doreen Massey, 'Power-geometry and a progressive sense of place', in Jon Bird, Barry Curtis, Tim Putnam, George Robertson and Lisa Tickner (eds.) *Mapping the Futures: Local Cultures, Global Change* (London: Routledge, 1993) pp. 59–69; Cindi Katz, 'On the grounds of globalization: a topography for feminist political engagement', *Signs* 26 (2001) pp. 1213–34: 1224–5; Derek Gregory, *The Colonial Present: Afghanistan, Palestine, Iraq* (Oxford: Blackwell, 2004) pp. 252–56.

[26] Rosalyn Deutsche, 'Boys town', *Environment and Planning D: Society and Space* 9 (1991) pp. 5–30; Melissa Wright, 'Differences that Matter', this volume.

Zygmunt Bauman's characterization of liquid modernity and its 'planetary frontierland' to realize that territorial logics of power can be terrifyingly mobile; and Harvey has himself shown how molecular processes of capital accumulation are shot through with a tension between fixity and motion. Within this force-field, one of the pinions of Harvey's argument is that the contemporary crisis of overaccumulation within the global North is being resolved at the expense of the global South. The spatio-temporal solution is axiomatic: 'Regional crises and highly localized place-based devaluations emerge as the primary means by which capitalism perpetually creates its own "other" in order to feed upon it.' In the present conjuncture, however, and the other pinion of Harvey's argument, the resolution of this structural crisis has produced creative destruction with a vengeance, as the violence of accumulation by dispossession has been aggravated by territorial logics of power turned outwards and visited on those 'others' by the military violence of aggressor states.[27]

Achilles' Heels

The consistency and clarity of Harvey's project is at once his strength and weakness. The continuities that I have identified do not make Harvey's work predictable. He has repeatedly introduced theoretical and thematic innovations, and his writings have moved in a spiral as he reactivates and revises concepts from earlier studies and puts them to work in later ones. That last verb is significant; Harvey's project is not a mechanical repetition of Marx. Those who think it is should read him carefully rather than skim the references. He sees his work as an endless dialectic between reflection and speculation that is designed to produce new understandings, and when I read Harvey I often feel 'I've never thought of it like that before.' This doesn't mean I always agree with his arguments – disagreement and debate are vital moments in the production of knowledge – but it is a mistake to underestimate his capacity to surprise.[28] Similarly, the clarity of Harvey's exposition may make his analysis seem straightforward, but that is just the conceit of hindsight: once a trail has been blazed, it's much easier to follow.. There is no doubt that his explanations are astonishingly assured – as Nigel

[27] Harvey, *Imperialism* op. cit., pp. 77, 151, 173; cf. Zygmunt Bauman, 'Reconnaissance wars of the planetary frontierland', *Theory, Culture and Society* 19 (2002) pp. 81–90; idem, 'Living and dying on the planetary frontierland', in his *Society Under Siege* (Cambridge: Polity, 2002) pp. 87–117.

[28] Cf. Harvey, *Consciousness* op. cit., p. xvi.

Thrift says, 'Harvey knows what he knows'[29] – but they are rarely simple. To paraphrase Lévi-Strauss, Harvey has a gift for replacing a complexity you don't understand with a complexity you do. The art of explanation lies not in simplicity but in intelligibility.

None of this exempts Harvey's work from critique and criticism. The most common complaints revolve around his commitment to Marxism and metanarrative; we are supposed to have gone beyond both of them. Put like that, these observations are as uninteresting as they are unproductive. They close down debate by combining a Whiggish promotion of the present with a Kuhnian model of knowledge production: or, in the plainer prose of George W. Bush, 'I think we agree, the past is over.' Well, no. This is yet another reason to disagree with the President, and I much prefer William Faulkner: 'The past is not dead. It is not even past.' I want to restate these objections in radically different terms, therefore, and to consider two sets of questions that touch Marxism and metanarrative but also pirouette more suggestively around the relationship between the theoretical and the empirical. The first concerns the space of Harvey's discussion: whom does he recognize as interlocutors? If all knowledge is situated, as Donna Haraway insists (and Harvey certainly admires her work), and if in consequence we need to enter into conversations and form solidarities with those who occupy other positions, who are Harvey's others? The second concerns the space of Harvey's world: how can he discover so much order within it? If the world doesn't come as clean as you can think it, as A. N. Whitehead almost said (and Harvey holds his work in high regard too), and if in consequence we need to recognize and respect the diversity and variability of life on earth, what worlds are lost in Harvey's explorations?[30]

Harvey's circle of theoretical reference is tightly drawn, and this invests his project with an unusual purity. This has two sources. First, Harvey's work goes forward on the foundations of a classical Marxism, on a creative rereading of Marx's own writings, and he has shown little interest in postclassical controversies within historical materialism. In failing to consider these contemporary debates, however, he runs the risk of ignoring the predicaments that brought Western Marxism (in particular) into being in the first place. Second, Harvey's suspicion of work outside the perimeters of historical materialism has become steadily more pronounced. In his later writings, for example, he repeatedly invokes Heidegger only to dismiss him. Irredeemably tarnished by his proximity to German fascism, Heidegger's

---

[29] Nigel Thrift, 'David Harvey: A Rock in a Hard Place', this volume.
[30] For Harvey on both Haraway and Whitehead, see his *Justice, Nature* op. cit.

contribution is reduced to a series of arch-conservative renditions of 'place' and 'dwelling'. His profound influence on deconstructions of what Timothy Mitchell calls the 'world-as-exhibition', on radical critiques of modernity, on debates over the production of nature: all go unremarked. Much the same is true of Foucault. Harvey turns his fire again and again on Foucault's dismal squib on 'heterotopia' – which I too find deeply problematic and, in places, frankly objectionable – but even if Foucault only interests Harvey for what he has to say about space (which seems a needlessly flattened reading: what of bio-politics?) how is it possible to say so little about *Birth of the Clinic* or *Discipline and Punish*? And how can Harvey constantly reduce the material spaces that recur in so many of Foucault's studies to mere metaphors? These examples could be multiplied many times, from economic geography through feminism to postcolonialism and beyond. I am not of course saying that Harvey ought to have read everything; there are enough essays in our field weighed down by the excess baggage of bibliomania. And I'm not looking for a grand synthesis, which I think neither possible nor desirable. I am simply dismayed by Harvey's marginalization of contributions that speak to his own concerns. You might object that his project is directed towards the construction of historico-geographical materialism, and that this explains the excision of authors outside the traditions of Marxism. This would not account for his lack of interest in debates within Marxism in any case, but like Perry Anderson, I believe that historical materialism is not compromised by a careful acknowledgement of work outside Marxism; it requires it.[31]

Harvey's circle of geographical reference is also circumscribed. Most of his work has been concerned with Europe and North America, and in his interview with Anderson he conceded that this was a 'real limitation': 'For all my geographical interests, [my work] has remained Eurocentric, focused on metropolitan zones. I have not been exposed much to other parts of the world.'[32] This is more than an empirical matter, and reducing places outside the global North to exotic suppliers of the empirical, to so many instances

---

[31] What Anderson actually wrote was this: 'Maximum awareness and respect for the scholarship of historians outside the boundaries of Marxism is not incompatible with rigorous pursuit of a Marxist historical inquiry; it is a condition of it': Perry Anderson, *Passages from Antiquity to Feudalism* (London: Verso, 1971) p. 9. This is a particular version of the more general argument that can be derived from Anderson's accounts of the uneven development of historical materialism: see his *Considerations on Western Marxism* (London: Verso, 1976) and *In the Tracks of Historical Materialism* (London: Verso, 1983).

[32] Harvey, 'Reinventing Geography' op. cit.

and exceptions to be shipped back to the metropolitan *ateliers* in which High Theory is fashioned, only compounds the problem. For it is a profoundly theoretical matter. The issue is by no means confined to Harvey; it bedevils Euro-American social theory at large including, as its qualifier suggests, Western Marxism.[33] And it assumes a particular force in studies of globalization, where J. K. Gibson-Graham has objected to the 'rape script' that represents global capitalism as transcendently powerful and inherently spatializing. This works to reduce non-capitalist forms of life to feminized sites to be mastered by capitalist modernity: passive places carried off in the virile embrace of His-tory, silent victims waiting to be victimized. Now I know that Harvey would be horrified if these characterizations were applied to his work; *The New Imperialism* is an impassioned attack on the global plunder of neoliberalism and neoconservatism. Nevertheless, Vinay Gidwani has argued that Harvey theorizes within the epistemic space of capitalism's universal history, and 'writes back dispersed geographies of life into the expansionist narrative of capital's becoming – as variations in a singular, relentless process of capitalist development'.[34] Gidwani was commenting specifically on *Limits*, but I'm not convinced that the accent on accumulation by dispossession in *The New Imperialism* would fundamentally revise this judgement. Harvey's analysis remains at a high level of abstraction, and he pays more attention to political events within the United States than to the multiple ways in which accumulation by dispossession is implemented and resisted elsewhere in the world. The places that he enumerates – Afghanistan, Argentina, Chile, China, India, Iraq and the rest – become so many signs of something else, and while Harvey knows that the world does not exist in order to provide vignettes of our theorizations of it, one still aches for a recognition of the committed journalists to whom he dedicated *Social Justice*, of the novelists and essayists he invokes in his Paris studies, and of the role of critical ethnographies in grounding, worlding and denaturalizing the violence whose contours he maps with such clinical precision.[35] In his *Brief History of Neo-Liberalism* Harvey

---

[33] David Slater, 'On the borders of social theory: learning from other regions,' *Environment and Planning D: Society and Space* 10 (1992) pp. 307–27.

[34] J. K. Gibson-Graham, 'Querying globalization', in *The End of Capitalism (As We Knew It): A Feminist Critique of Political Economy* (Oxford: Blackwell, 1997) pp. 120–147; Gidwani, 'Questions' op. cit., p. 528.

[35] Here I am indebted to the brilliant discussion provided by Gillian Hart, 'Denaturalizing dispossession: critical ethnography in the age of resurgent imperialism', Paper prepared for *Creative Destruction: Area Knowledge and the New Geographies of Empire*, Center for Place, Culture and Politics, City University of New York, April 2004.

does pay closer attention to uneven development and to variations in neo-liberal programmes beyond the United States, but even here his analyses of (for example) China or Mexico remain at an aggregate, macro-level. Although Harvey explicitly acknowledges that the violence of neoliberalism is registered within the integuments of everyday life, the fractured spaces of experience, how such a promissory note is to be redeemed through his own way of working remains unclear.[36]

To meet these criticisms would require a different way of theorizing, a different way of working the theoretical and the empirical, that would disrupt the plenary ambitions of Harvey's project. These cannot be laid at the door of historical materialism, however, which Terry Eagleton insists 'is not some Philosophy of Life or Secret of the Universe, which feels duty bound to pronounce on everything from how to break your way into a boiled egg to the quickest way to delouse cocker spaniels'. He once described Harvey's encyclopedic propensities as 'comically ambitious'. (This is the same man, it should be said, who proclaimed on the jacket of *The Condition of Post-modernity* that 'those who fashionably scorn the idea of "total" critique had better think again'.)[37] And yet Harvey constantly reasserts the scope and systematicity of his project through a restatement of its logic: everything is assigned to its proper place (apart from the eggs and the spaniels). Again, this is not peculiar to him. Major social theory is always architectonic. Its constructions move towards completion, and in their most imperious forms they seek not only to order the partially ordered but also to display the whole world within a self-sufficient grid. It never works out quite like that, but to unlearn these privileges requires an openness to what Cindi Katz calls theory in a minor key: to theorizations that are situated, partial, incomplete, and constantly muddied by what she describes as 'the messy entailments of indeterminacy'.[38]

This is the crux of the critique of Harvey's project. He used to repeat Pareto's artful remark about Marx's words being like bats: 'you can see in them both birds and mice'. But Harvey's own writings sometimes lose this suppleness. I think at one pole of his dogged rendering of the princi-

---

[36] Harvey, *Brief History* op. cit.

[37] Terry Eagleton, *After Theory* (London: Allen Lane, 2003) pp. 33–4; idem, 'Spaced out', *London Review of Books*, 24 April 1997.

[38] Cindi Katz, 'Messing with "The Project"', this volume; see also her critique of my own work, 'Major/minor: theory, nature, politics', *Annals of the Association of American Geographers* 85 (1995) pp. 164–8. For a critical discussion of Harvey's ontology in a different register, see Marcus Doel, 'Dialectical Materialism: Stranger than Fiction', this volume.

ples of dialectics as a series of numbered (and numbing) propositions, and at the other of his global cartography of economic and political power with its centres, hierarchies and peripheries.[39] To be sure, Harvey at his best isn't like this at all; and yet the concern runs throughout thoughtful commentaries on his work. This is about more than the poetics of prose or the mechanics of metanarrative. It is, at its heart, about ontology: about the concatenations of ordering and disordering that make and unmake our world, and about particular places that are not passively caught up in general processes that 'play out' within them. Ultimately it is about geographies that are even more troubling than Harvey allows them to be.

Beginnings

In several recent interviews, Harvey says he has come full circle – from a childhood when much of the map of the world was still coloured red by the British Empire to a late modern world ravaged by the blood-red rise of an American Empire. But he has also brought many of us full circle with him. His work spans more than forty years, and it has traversed the space of more than forty disciplines. It stands as an enduring testament to the power of a geographical imagination: one that is intellectually rigorous, ceaselessly critical, and inspired by a deep concern for the human condition. Harvey may not be an activist, but he is keenly aware of the active power of ideas to shape the world in which we live and die.[40] This is why he attaches so much importance to teaching – and he has supervised or co-supervised some of the most creative geographers working in our field today – and to writing. Travelling with him is always demanding, and I suspect that Don Mitchell speaks for many of us when he suggests that this arises not only from

---

[39] Harvey, *Justice, Nature*, op. cit; pp. 48–57; for a critique of the global cartography of *The New Imperialism* that emphasizes the ambiguities and contingencies of power, see John Allen, 'Arm's length imperialism', *Political Geography* 24 (2005) pp. 531–541.

[40] This may seem surprising, given Harvey's political commitment and passion, but he has repeatedly said that he is not an activist. He has been drawn into struggles in the places where he has lived and worked – he was involved in a number of campaigns over housing in Baltimore, for example, but his (avowedly peripheral and largely academic) involvement in a labour dispute at Cowley (Oxford) was evidently a bruising experience: see *Justice, Nature* op. cit., pp. 19–23. For a full discussion of these and related issues, see Noel Castree, 'The Detour of Critical Theory', this volume.

the man's astonishing intellectual agility but also from the provocation, the open invitation, to go beyond the bounds. Reading Harvey, he says, is an exercise in being convinced and then engaging in the hard task of working out why you shouldn't be so convinced.[41] Moreover, as I've tried to show, the journey is never predictable. Even when Harvey returns to familiar sites – to science and geography, to space and the city, and to capitalism – there is a freshness about his apprehensions that constantly challenges those of us who travel with him to see them differently. This is an open invitation to critical reading, to critical debate – and, above all, to the unfolding of a critical geographical sensibility adequate to a world of such volatility and violence.

Acknowledgements

I am grateful to Noel Castree, Michael Dear, Jim Glassman, Ron Johnston, Don Mitchell, Allan Pred, Matt Sparke and Elvin Wyly for many helpful conversations on the way to a first draft of this essay, and for then commenting on it with generosity and insight.

[41] Don Mitchell, pers. comm., 23 April 2005.

2

Between Deduction and Dialectics: David Harvey on Knowledge

Trevor Barnes

On the one hand, I develop a general theory, but on the other, I need
to feel this rootedness in something going on in my own backyard.

Harvey 2000d: 94

Twentieth-century philosophy is littered with change-of-heart philosophers,
philosophers who start their intellectual life believing in one idea, but end
it believing in something quite different. Ludwig Wittgenstein is a paradigm example. Although writing much of his doctoral dissertation at first
behind the lines and later on the front while serving in the Austrian artillery
during the First World War (Monk 1990: chs. 6 and 7), his two Cambridge
University examiners, Bertrand Russell and G. E. Moore, judged Wittgenstein's thesis 'a work of genius' (quoted in Monk 1990: 272).[1] Published in
1918 as *Tractatus Logico-Philosophicus* (1961), his dissertation provided
a seemingly definitive justification of logical positivism. Framing it as the
picture theory of meaning, Wittgenstein argued that meaningful propositions possess the same form as facts of the world. In contrast, propositions
about other propositions, such as those found in philosophy, were, according to him, without sense, they were senseless. And statements that went
beyond the latter, including propositions found in moral philosophy, metaphysics and aesthetics, were not merely senseless but nonsense. So confident
was Wittgenstein that he had written the last word in philosophy that he
abandoned the discipline for the next ten years, becoming a primary-school
teacher in Trattenbach, rural Austria, albeit not without complaints from
both parents and students (Monk 1990: ch. 9).[2] It was perhaps just as well,
then, that in 1929 Wittgenstein returned to philosophy. In an unlikely
epiphanal moment on a train journey to Swansea accompanied by the
Italian Cambridge economist Piero Sraffa, Wittgenstein realized he could
not keep the senseless and the nonsense out of philosophy. In Norman

Malcolm's (1958: 69) account of Wittgenstein's Pauline experience in that railway carriage, 'Sraffa made a gesture familiar to Neapolitans and meaning something like disgust or contempt, by brushing the underneath of his chin with the outward sweep of the fingertips of one hand.' That moment was pivotal. It made Wittgenstein realize that meaningful propositions came in all shapes and sizes, and could not be restricted to the prison house of the picture theory of meaning. So began Wittgenstein's later philosophy turning on ordinary language, culminating in the posthumous publication of *Philosophical Investigations* in 1953, and the seeming renunciation of his previous staggering 'work of genius'.[3]

In interviews, and in his autobiographical essay, David Harvey (1997a, 2000d, 2002b) has never identified his own train-to-Swansea epiphanal moment,[4] but like Wittgenstein, he made a dramatic intellectual about-face sometime in the late 1960s and early 1970s. There is a break between Harvey's early work concerned with applying formal natural scientific methods to geographical questions, and exemplified by his celebration of the hypothetico-deductive method in *Explanation in Geography* (1969a), and his later work that applies dialectical materialism and associated with a move to Marxism found first in *Social Justice and the City* (1973a). In this chapter, I am concerned with the nature of that epistemological break. I am interested in how the early Harvey differs from the later one, what might explain such difference, and whether connections exist between the two halves of Harvey's intellectual life.

The same general questions are raised about Wittgenstein. How they have been addressed, I will argue, is useful for understanding the parallel issue for Harvey. The usual interpretation of Wittgenstein is of an epistemological rupture, a disjunction between the earlier *Tractatus* and the later *Philosophical Investigations*. Allan Janik and Stephen Toulmin in their book *Wittgenstein's Vienna* (1973), however, were the first to offer a more complex interpretation, arguing that while there were differences there were also significant continuities between Wittgenstein's early and late philosophies. They suggest the purpose of the *Tractatus* was not to rule out philosophical questions, or those of morality, metaphysics and aesthetics, but to point to their unreserved importance, and then taken up in a different form in *Philosophical Investigations*. Janik and Toulmin are able to offer this more complex rendering because of their particular sensibility towards knowledge. They are less interested in knowledge as a series of disembodied ideas, and clever moves in logical space, than in knowledge stemming from lives lived in the materiality and contingency of real places like *fin-de-siècle* Vienna where Wittgenstein grew up. For Janik and Toulmin the particular combination of people, things and ideas in Vienna at that end-of-century

moment that coalesced around issues of moral belief, metaphysical speculation about the nature of reality, and judgements about aesthetic form, left
a deep impression on Wittgenstein, shaping a lifetime intellectual agenda.
By following an historical and sociological approach to knowledge, Janik
and Toulmin find and trace connections not apparent from examining only
Wittgenstein's texts that by themselves appear radically at odds. This will
also be my approach in understanding the break in Harvey's work. As far as
possible, I will try to read his intellectual trajectory as found in his various
texts against the context of a set of historical, sociological and especially
geographical factors.

The chapter is divided into four sections. First, I discuss briefly the idea
of intellectual rupture, and set it within the context of the wider and now
burgeoning literature of the sociology of scientific knowledge. This is followed in the rest of the chapter by a grounded interpretation of David
Harvey's writings on knowledge from their beginning in the mid-1960s
(he completed his PhD at Cambridge University in 1962) through to the
present, but focusing especially on the late sixties and early seventies when
the break occurs. In the second section, I review his work on the natural
scientific explanatory model, setting it alongside the period he was at Cambridge as a student, and later at Bristol as a lecturer. In the third section, I
turn to his writings on Marxism and dialectical materialism, reading them
in relation particularly to his move to Baltimore in 1969. The last section
serves as an extended conclusion, and makes the argument implicit in the
epigraph that Harvey's different general theories of knowledge in part
reflect his rootedness in different geographies, in his different 'backyards'.
But this is no simple relation. There is a tension between his ambition to
realize the general and his aspiration to remain at the local making the
relation complex and messy. It is a life lived, as was Wittgenstein's, and contains ruptures and continuities.

On Rationality, Intellectual Breaks, and the Sociology of Scientific Knowledge

> I have never conceived of geography . . . as a fixed field of study . . .
> but [one that] should be changed according to individual and collec-
> tive needs, wants, and desires.
>
> Harvey 2002b: 164

In the standard rationalist account that in the past dominated discussions
of epistemology, and in some quarters still does, there is nothing messy

about knowledge. It is straightforward. Knowledge is acquired through rational inquiry ensuring commensurability and progress. Rational knowledge is brought under a common set of rules that allows comparison and thereby resolution of conflict and discrepancy (commensurability), and is cumulative in that new knowledge advances old knowledge (progress). For example, Isaac Newton famously said in a letter to his rival Robert Hooke, 'If I have seen farther it is by standing on the shoulders of Giants' (quoted by Gleick 2003: 98). Newton's metaphor speaks to both attributes of rationalism. Because of its rational foundation, Newton assumes his knowledge is a continuation of, that is, commensurate with, his predecessors (the 'Giants'), such as Copernicus, Kepler and Galileo. The iron rod of rationalism makes stable the human tower which Newton thinks he stands atop. Without rationality, it would be a Tower of Babel. Further, the elevated position afforded by rationality allows Newton to gain greater knowledge – 'to see further' – than his predecessors. It is progress.

Once a researcher embarks on rational inquiry, as on a conveyor belt, s/he is led inexorably and smoothly to new and improved knowledge. No breaks, no hesitations, no reversals. Sometimes researchers are misled, and engage in irrational inquiry, such as Newton in his secret experiments with alchemy (Gleick 2003). But in those cases, sociological reasons can be found to explain the error.

Against this rationalist view of commensurability and progress that makes knowledge acquisition appear a technical exercise to be completed by people in white coats, there has emerged over the last forty years a radical alternative associated with writings in the sociology of scientific knowledge. Arguing against commensurability, and the idea of progress, this body of work emphasizes the gaps and fissures, the blind alleys and dead ends, the points where rationality does not hold up, and is augmented by additional contingent factors. As Richards (1987: 201) writes, there has emerged 'a new respect for scientists, not as impersonal automata, but simply as human individuals participating in a culture common to all'. This alternative approach is not slick or heroic or triumphal – Mary Hesse (1980: 30) says it has been 'a notorious black spot for fatal accidents' – but it begins to make sense of apparent intellectual about-faces of the kind that David Harvey (and Ludwig Wittgenstein) appear to have made.

The literature of the sociology of scientific knowledge is vast and sprawling, and there is no single agreed-upon approach (Hess 1997). Three points from that literature are useful for my purposes. First, openings, breaches and cracks are normal in intellectual inquiry. Kuhn's (1962) work made the critical difference here. Disputing both commensurability because of the value-laden nature of theory, and progress because different approaches are incommensurable (they are like Gestalt shifts), Kuhn thought science was propelled by a series of intellectual revolutions, 'paradigm changes', each of which formed distinct, separate and partly incomparable worlds of inquiry. While Kuhn saw such revolutions as large scale and occurring infrequently, and while he later backtracked on the radical nature of his position, the damage to the rationalist model of unbridled progress was done. Kuhn opened the door to conceiving intellectual change as messy, hesitant, fractured and unresolved. Harvey's switch from logical deduction to Marxian dialectics, therefore, is not an irrational raving, akin to Newton attempting to transmute base metals into gold, but just the kind of break that we should expect. It is how intellectual inquiry is done.

Second, scientific practices are connected to changing social practices. The social, though, is not present in rationalist accounts. Humans there, to use Hilary Putnam's (1981: 7) image, are presented as isolated 'brains in vats', disembodied, and disembedded from society. In the sociology of science view, however, knowledge never arrives from pure brainpower. It is the outcome of grounded practice. Scientists are not faceless organs of scientific rationality, but real people with particular kinds of socially defined bodies, histories, skills and interests. Furthermore, those characteristics make a difference to the kind of knowledge produced. For example, that Harvey grew up during the Second World War, went to Cambridge University during the late 1950s and early 1960s, and was at Bristol University for much of the 1960s, shaped the writing of *Explanation in Geography*. The book was not a bolt out of the blue, nor the distillation of a pure form of rationality measured drop by drop on to the page, but arose in large part from the social practices of Harvey living at a particular time and place. That said, Harvey and his texts are never fully translucent, completely determined products. Lives and books are complicated, possessing their own agency, always resisting any final definitive statement. One must be open to individual creativity, contingency and even inscrutability. There is no single methodological template to achieve such an end, but exemplars exist such as Shapin's (1994) work on Robert Boyle or Janik and Toulmin's (1973) and Monk's (1990) on Wittgenstein. These authors negotiate successfully social context and individual biography, determination and contingency, the transparent and the opaque

Finally, sociologists of scientific knowledge stress that acquiring and disseminating knowledge is a local activity, and in contrast with the supposed universality suggested by the rationalist account. Joseph Rouse (1987: 72) says scientific knowledge stems from scientists moving 'from one local knowledge to another rather than from universal theories to their particular instantiations'. 'Local knowledge' takes a variety of connotations, however (Barnes 2000). My emphases are the geographical ones of place, and movement across space. Both have received increasing prominence from both sociologists of science (Shapin 1998a) and geographers (Livingstone 2003) who argue that they are active components shaping the very nature of knowledge produced. Places are conceived not as hermetically sealed sites, static and self-contained, but porous, dynamic and open-ended, defined as much by their relationships with other places and spaces as by internal characteristics (Massey and Thrift 2003; Barnes 2004). Given this broad conception, I will suggest that for Harvey places like Cambridge and Bristol, or Baltimore and Paris, become for him at different periods crucial 'truth spots', to use Thomas Gieryn's (2002) term, in working out his theories of knowledge. By this term, I mean places in which particular languages of explanation and validation are accepted as the 'truth' and acted on accordingly. In making my wider argument, I am not asserting place determinism, however. Places and their relation with other spaces are only one influence along with others that produce knowledge (but which are ignored by rationalism that presumes the 'view from nowhere' (Shapin 1998a; Livingstone 2003)).

The Deductive David Harvey

> I doubt if anything satisfactory will emerge in the way of general theory until the year 2000 AD or so.
>
> Harvey 1969b: 63

After 486 pages of dense and unadorned philosophical exposition, *Explanation in Geography* rallies at its end with a call for practical action. It is not exactly a charge to mount the barricades, but, within the context of a 1960s English provincial university (*Explanation* was written at Bristol University), it perhaps came to the same thing. Harvey exhorts us 'to pin up on our study walls . . . the slogan . . . "By our theories you shall know us"' (Harvey 1969a: 486).

The type of theory for which Harvey hopes geographers will be known is the natural scientific kind, or at least the kind that philosophers of science think natural scientists pursue. Much of *Explanation* is about taking classic statements in the philosophy of science made by people like Richard Braithwaite, Rudolph Carnap, Carl Hempel and Ernest Nagel (see the disproportionate amount of space each respectively occupies in *Explanation*'s index), and showing they are relevant to geography. The focus on geography is crucial. *Explanation* represents Harvey's commitment to the discipline, which continues throughout his later books.[5] *Explanation* is about geography *tout court*, human as much as physical, and was written less to change the world than to change the discipline. The problem with the discipline for Harvey is not the questions geographers ask, but the methodology they use to answer them. No one is spared, not even the person Harvey considers one of the greatest twentieth-century geographers, Carl Sauer. At the end of his long essay in *Models in Geography* (1967a) Harvey retheorizes Sauer's historical writings on evolution and landscape change, reinscribing them in the form of 'a synoptic model system' (1967a: 596).[6] Harvey (1967a: 597) says about his attempt to modernize Sauer:

> We are not dressing up a simple elegant statement in scientific jargon, but genuinely trying to lay bare elements in reality which for too long have remained hidden from our gaze ... An understanding of the principles and potential of model building may not be a 'sufficient' condition for a *Renaissance* in geographic research; but that we can be certain without such an understanding the 'necessary' conditions for that *Renaissance* will not be fulfilled.

So, what are those necessary conditions? They revolve around the deployment of scientific theory (Harvey 1967b), bringing into play traditional philosophy of science including its ideas about laws, logic, the hypothetico-deductive method and verification. Let me draw out some general features.

Perhaps the most important is that it is theoretical. As a theme, it dominates both Harvey's early papers as well as *Explanation*. He writes, 'Theory transforms the hallmark of a discipline ... It provides systematic general statements which may be employed in explaining, understanding, describing, and interpreting events' (Harvey 1969a: 75). The keyword is 'explaining'. For Harvey (1967b: 211), 'the quest for an explanation is the quest for theory'. That is why he wanted to update Carl Sauer. Only theory could 'lay bare elements in reality which for too long have remained hidden from our gaze'.

Of course, not any old theory will do. It must be scientific, and it is defined by him by four features. First, by mathematics, and represented in *Explanation* by the more than 100-page review of pure mathematics, geometry and probability ('Part IV'). 'Theory ultimately requires the use of mathematical languages', he writes (Harvey 1969a: 76). Second, by a set of precisely defined terms and concepts with clear inference rules connecting them (Harvey 1972f: 33). The precision is important because, as Harvey (1969b: 64) says, 'The one thing we cannot afford ... is ... intellectual laziness which regards it as unnecessary and foolish to try to eliminate vagueness and ambiguity in our conceptual apparatus.' And clear inference rules are necessary because they 'ensure the complete certainty as to the *logical* validity of the conclusion' (original emphasis, Harvey 1969a: 9). Third, by clear rules of verification. On the one hand, there is the abstract calculus of theory, couched in precisely defined concepts, the relationships among which are defined by formal logic. On the other, there is a messy, irregular world represented by measurement and empirical observation. The task of verification is to assess the relation between the observed empirical world and the abstract theoretical world. This is never easy, but if the rules are successfully applied, explanation is achieved. 'Explanation is regarded as a formal connection ... between factual statements and more general "theoretical" statements' (Harvey 1969a: 10). And fourth, by rationality. Harvey (1969a: 19) writes, 'This book [*Explanation*] is concerned with rational explanation', and this then enables achievement of its other ends like progress, objectivity and universality. These four features turn mere speculations into scientific theories. They represent a foolproof method. Follow them, Harvey says, and success is guaranteed. No wonder he wanted his slogan pinned to the wall. Like all believers, he was intent on spreading the word.

But there were other reasons as well, and ones which go to the sociology of knowledge. Central is the wider context in which Harvey carried out his work. It is unclear how aware Harvey was at the time of its role. After all, his epistemological position, as he says in *Explanation*, 'ignores explanation as an *activity*, as a *process*' (original emphases, Harvey 1969a: 9). That is, it ignores scientific practice, including presumably Harvey's own. But my argument is that wider forces bearing on Harvey cannot be ignored, and were as important in shaping his work as his own ferocious energy, singular concentration and painstaking brilliance.

Cambridge University of the late 1950s and early 1960s forms the immediate intellectual context for the deductive David Harvey. It was during exactly that period that the 'terrible twins' of British geography, Dick Chorley and Peter Haggett, were together in the Department of Geography (Chorley joined in 1958 and stayed for the remainder of his career, while Haggett joined a year earlier, staying until 1966 when he moved to Bristol as Professor of Urban and Regional Geography, and joining Harvey who was hired there in 1961). Chorley and Haggett were responsible for first-year laboratory teaching, where they introduced quantitative analysis 'to do with statistical methods, matrices, set theory, trend surface analysis, and network analysis' (Chorley 1995: 361). Harvey as a graduate student was the course's first demonstrator, i.e. teaching assistant. Also important at Cambridge (Harvey 2002b: 165) was a young lecturer, an historical demographer, Tony Wrigley, who introduced Harvey to Auguste Comte's positivism, and more generally to nineteenth-century thought including Marx's.[7] Wrigley's philosophical approach and Haggett and Chorley's emphasis on 'scientific methods' were then 'enmeshed' by Harvey in his 1962 doctoral dissertation, 'Aspects of agricultural and rural change in Kent, 1815–1900' (2002b: 165).

The broader point is that the Department of Geography at Cambridge during the period Harvey was a student, and later a young lecturer at Bristol, was a 'truth spot'. That is, it was one of an initially small number of sites in Europe and North America, and which by the mid-1960s included Bristol, where geographical practices were remade in the likeness of natural science in a movement dubbed 'the quantitative revolution' (Barnes 2001, 2004). That revolution was to move the discipline from the dark ages of its ideographic past to the dazzling promise of a nomothetic future. As a young, bright, ambitious student interested in ideas, Harvey inevitably was caught up in the change even though it went against the grain of his 'strong "Arts" background' (Harvey 1969a: v). Indeed, it may have been that Arts background that made him move away from his earlier sometimes fumbling attempts at quantitative analysis to the later philosophical and discursive treatment found in *Explanation*.[8] Whatever the precise reason, being at Cambridge during the late fifties and early sixties made a difference.

It made a difference in other ways too. The general intellectual culture of his student cohort was highly critical of Britain's social rigidity and traditionalism, and desirous of modernization. Clearly, this was not confined only to Cambridge. The dissatisfaction was found widely, reflected in writings, for example, of 'the angry young men' such as John Osborne and Alan Sillitoe. Harvey (2002b: 164) writes:

> Mine was the generation that spawned the *Footlights Review* that became *That Was The Week That Was* – a television show that mercilessly ridiculed the ruling class as well as almost everything else that might be regarded as 'traditional' in British life. Cambridge was populated by an intellectual elite, and if something was seriously wrong with the state of Britain (and many thought there was), then this elite was surely in a position to do something about it. The modernization of Britain was firmly on the agenda, and a new structure of knowledge and power was needed to accomplish that task.

Explanation did not attempt single-handedly to modernize Britain. But it provided a 'new structure of knowledge' to a hitherto unbending and conservative discipline, geography, which like Britain in the late 1950s and early 1960s was in desperate need of shaking off the confining shackles of its past and modernizing. Harvey, as part of that Cambridge intellectual elite, was 'in a position to do something about it', which he did. As he says, there was 'the idea that we could break out of tradition . . . There was a modern geography waiting to be constructed and we were the ones who could do it' (pers. comm.).

That idea of the modern is important. It connects to his later interest in modernity, and fascination with its sites of emergence such as Paris. It is also bears on his politics. In this earlier period, that politics turned on what he calls 'socialist modernization . . . backed by technological efficiency' (Harvey 2002: 165). Exactly the same politics lay behind the election in 1964 of the British Labour Party under Harold Wilson, partly resting on the catchphrase 'the white heat of the technological revolution' (an expression coined by Wilson the previous year). Increased technological efficiency, rational planning and progressive social change would unfold in a new Britain, a modern Britain, which broke the old conservative order. Specifically, the Labour Party at both local and national level moved quickly towards rational planning and progressive social ends. The National Economic Plan inaugurated in 1965 contained an explicit mandate to counter regional inequality by setting up Regional Economic Councils with the power to engage in physical and social planning (and lay behind the emergence of the Regional Studies Association established in 1967).

Within this context, *Explanation* was the kind of book that we might expect to emerge. While it is not a 'how-to' planning book, it drew its spirit in part from the wider changes in political and planning ethos that swept Britain during the 1960s. As Harvey (2002b: 166) says now: 'For those of us involved in geography [during the 1960s], rational planning (national, regional, environmental, and urban) backed by "scientific" methods of enquiry seemed to be the path to take.' *Explanation* was Harvey's contribution to those 'scientific methods of enquiry'. While not overtly political, it is nevertheless a thoroughly political text. It was Harvey's contribution to modernizing Britain, and associated politics.

The early Harvey, like the early Wittgenstein, put forward and justified a theory of knowledge based upon some form of positivism. My argument is that the epistemologies both men put forward are not the precipitates of rationality, the rationalist view, but are integrally connected to the social, cultural and political contexts, including the places in which they lived. That said, Harvey and Wittgenstein are not mere dupes of their context. Harvey's dissertation on the hop industry in Kent, for example, was historical, resting not on quantitative methods but on qualitative ones, in this case an entire summer spent in the archives devoted to reading nineteenth-century local newspapers (Harvey 2002b: 156). Gravity models and Lösch are mentioned, but the thesis is certainly no mirror of Haggett's (1965) *Locational Analysis* (see Harvey's 1963 paper that derives from the thesis). Harvey asserted his own agency, and was not some 'place-holder'. Indeed, he says now that the dissertation 'underlies' his later Marxist writings about 'the circulation of capital and the spatial and temporal dynamics of global and local relations' (Harvey 2002: 159). The point is that linking lives lived and intellectual production is messy and complex (never effortless as supposed by rationalism). This is amply demonstrated in Harvey's second life to which I now turn.

The Dialectical David Harvey

> We reach out dialectically (rather than inward deductively) to probe uncharted seas from a few seemingly secure islands of concepts.
>
> Harvey 1985a: xvi

Harvey (2002b: 167) submitted the manuscript of *Explanation* to Edward Arnold publishers in 1968. It was not the year to write a book about the virtues of rational conduct and the beneficence of science and technology, however. That year the world was convulsed by a sometimes savage irrationality, and skewered by a sometimes malevolent science and technology. Martin Luther King was assassinated in a Nashville motel in April, there was almost a revolution in Paris in May (as well as in other cities around the world during the same year), in June Robert Kennedy was shot, killed by Sirhan Sirhan at the Democratic Party Convention in California, and throughout 1968 science and technology in the form of B-52 bombers, helicopter gunships and Agent Orange were used by the US military to worsen the lot of people in Vietnam rather than to improve it.

In 1969, Harvey moved to Johns Hopkins University in Baltimore. It was a crucial relocation. The decision to join Hopkins Department of Geography and Environmental Engineering even now seems slightly eccentric, if not inscrutable, given the Department's main research specialty was waste management. It was also perhaps not the best place to become a Marxist, which is what Harvey did shortly after arriving. During the 1950s, George Carter, the Chair of the then Department of Geography at Hopkins, turned in his colleague Owen Lattimore to Senator Joseph McCarthy who immediately put him on his list of 205 names of Communist Party members (Harvey 1983).

As Harvey shifted towards Marxism after arriving in Baltimore, he became increasingly critical of his earlier work. In a wickedly funny reply to Stephen Gale's (1972) review of *Explanation* in the uprightly serious *Geographical Analysis*, Harvey (1972e: 323) said he was at a 'disadvantage' because he had 'never read' his own book and furthermore had 'no intention of doing so now'. What he was reading was Marx. The pivotal essay also appearing in 1972 and reprinted as the opening chapter in the 'Socialist formulations' section of *Social Justice and the City* was 'Revolutionary and counter-revolutionary theory and the problem of ghetto formation' (Harvey 1972c, 1972i). Even now, it is an extraordinary read. Harvey finds there his writing voice – pungent, passionate, precise and persuasive – which then rarely deserts him. There are no more 'technical blemishes' (Harvey 1969a: v), no more straining for positivist objectivity and political disinterestedness.

On the one hand, the 1972 essay appears as a repudiation of *Explanation*, and his earlier conception of theory and method (also see Harvey 1989b: 212–13). In a now well-known paragraph, Harvey (1972c: 6) wrote:

> [Geography's] quantitative revolution has run its course and diminishing marginal returns are apparently setting in as . . . [it] serve[s] to tell us less and less about anything of great relevance . . . There is a clear disparity between the sophisticated theoretical and methodological framework which we are using and our ability to say anything really meaningful about events as they unfold around us . . . In short, our paradigm is not coping well.

On the other hand, and implied by the last sentence, the essay points to a different approach, a new paradigm. But this is a more radical conception of paradigm than envisioned by Kuhn (1962), who thought that basic terms like theory, or law, or verification, would retain their meaning, as well as forms of scientific reasoning such as deductive logic. Harvey's idea, however, is more an alteration in what Ian Hacking (2002) calls a 'style of reasoning'. Fundamental concepts like theory, or reasoning, or even explanation are different in different styles. Harvey's purpose in his essay is to present a new style of reasoning, a Marxist one, that revises basic explanatory terms like theory, and introduces a new method, dialectical materialism.

In particular, Harvey's aim was to create 'revolutionary theory', a theory 'validated through revolutionary practice' (Harvey 1972i: 40). Unlike his previous approach in which theory is verified by formally connecting logic and empirical evidence, revolutionary theory is verified by bringing a new (revolutionary) world into being (see also Harvey 1973a: 12). Revolutionary theory changes social practices such that they call forth the reality that the theory anticipates. For example, a revolutionary theory of the ghetto provides both a set of new categories to uncover the social relations that produce the ghetto, and a set of revolutionary practices that eliminate ghettos altogether. The theory is validated by being 'productive', by changing social practices to bring about a ghetto-less world. Perhaps because of this conception, Harvey subsequently had a difficult time 'testing' his theories empirically. Many of his 'proofs' are not couched in terms of classical verification, or even use data or evidence that Harvey has collected.[9] Instead, his 'proofs' are a ghostly presence, the ghost not of the past but of a future not yet realized but desired. The issue of validation for him, therefore, is less one of truth or falsity than finding theoretical knowledge that changes the world for the better.

Informing this different conception of theory is a different style of reasoning, dialectical materialism. It is briefly mentioned in the 1972 article (1972c: 7), is elaborated in the last chapter of *Social Justice*, and then runs throughout his subsequent writings. Dialectic is defined as an opposition that propels change. In broad terms, it involves the forces of flux, flow and process butting up against what Harvey calls 'permanences' – structures, organizations, institutional dogma (1996a: 7–8). For a time permanences resist the forces of flow, but not forever. Sooner or later, resistance is overcome, and flux takes hold until new permanences arise. And new permanences must arise because life in a world of continual flux is impossible (1996a: 7). Materialism is important because the dialectic plays out in the world of material and social relations, the economy. Those relations for a period are organized into 'permanences', such as feudalism or capitalism, but over time even they are eroded by forces of flow, manifest, for example, as intermittent socio-economic crises. In particular, the dialectic embodied in material and social relations generates opposition, undermining permanence, taking the form under capitalism, say, of working-class revolution, or in geography of revolutionary theory.

This is a very abstract rendering. But it rarely takes this form in Harvey's writings. His best-known representation of dialectical materialism is his geographical theory of capital accumulation (1985a: ch. 1). Capital is always on the move, ready to make an extra buck, intent to annihilate space by time. But in order to make that move, to earn that extra buck, to annihilate space, capital first needs to be fixed in place, set within a 'structured coherence' of a particular location. Here is the dialectic: a tension between spatial flow and spatial fixity that then impels the changing geography of capitalism.

The dialectic also bears on theorizing and knowledge. Revolutionary theorizing relies on a dialectic creating a tension between stable concepts that enable us to understand the capitalist world in which we live, and a set of as yet unformed ones that anticipate a better world that has still not arrived. This partly explains Harvey's fascination with bat-like words, oxymoronic terms, that assert and deny at the same time – 'concrete abstraction', 'creative destruction', 'symbolic capital'. They are a means to bridge the world in which we live and the world in which we want to live. In his paper about ghetto-formation, his revolutionary theory was the means both to explain ghettos as they exist under capitalist urbanization – a theory that was solid and stable – and to envisage and bring about future cities in which ghettos do not exist – a theory that was labile and pliable in its imaginings.

Practising dialectics is enormously difficult, and Harvey would probably say that he has not always succeeded (he says he sometimes finds himself 'longing for the easy simplicities of faith of the Pentecostals, the certitudes of positivism, or the absolute of dogmatic Marxism': 1996a: 3). Further, as I will suggest below, the dividing line between deduction and dialectics in Harvey's work is not always hard and fast; there are continuities as well as disjunctions. To understand this complex relationship between his different knowledges, as with Wittgenstein, it is necessary to read that relation against Harvey's life, and the places in which it is lived.

Coming to America was critical. Specifically, Harvey's move from Bristol to Baltimore was formative. Baltimore 'had gone up in flames' the year before Harvey (2002: 169) arrived. Civil rights issues were paramount, and made literally concrete to Harvey when he slept on the pavement outside the Black Panthers' Baltimore headquarters to protect that organization from potential violence following the police killing of its leader, Fred Hampton, in December 1969 (Harvey 2002b: 170). The Vietnam War was reaching new crescendos of violence (President Nixon's secret campaign to bomb Cambodia began in 1969), sparking widespread university campus protest resulting in the killing of four students at Kent State University in May 1970. Yeats seemed to have got it right. 'Things fall apart', and 'Mere anarchy is loosed upon the world.' If ever there was a period when flux and instability reigned, it was then. Even the Beatles, whose inspiration Harvey (1969a: ix) acknowledges in *Explanation*, broke up.

Perhaps this is where the other side of the dialectic enters. To make sense of the 'blooming, buzzing, confusion' of his new home, living on the 'fall line' (Harvey 2002b: 150), living during the Fall, Harvey turned to Marx who provides a set of categories, a theory, to make sense of it all. This doesn't explain why Marx, though, because there were alternatives. In geography, there was the behavioural perspective that by the early 1970s was morphing into the humanistic approach including phenomenology, existentialism and symbolic interactionism (Ley and Samuels 1978), and even within radical geography, anarchism and various forms of non-Marxist socialism were on offer.

The 'Why Marx?' question is probably another 'inscrutable' case, overdetermined. There are contextual factors, though, which partially explain. Radical geography was beginning in the United States. The first issue of

Antipode: A Radical Journal of Geography was published at Clark University, Worcester, Massachusetts, in the same year Harvey started at Hopkins. Harvey was a frequent visitor to Clark, and presented his 'Revolutionary and counter-revolutionary' paper at a special session at the 1971 Boston AAG organized by Dick Peet who taught at Clark (Peet 2002). Again this does not explain exactly why Marx. In fact, Peet (2002) says it was Harvey who introduced him to Marx.

> I was quite friendly with David Harvey at the time, and I'd become editor of *Antipode* in 1970, and David had been here already a couple of times by that time . . . Anyway, he said to me, 'You've got to read Marx'. And I said, 'But I've tried and I've failed a couple of times already', and he said, 'I don't care'. He said, 'Don't read *Capital*. Get a book on Marx and read it'. And so, in the early 1970s, I started reading Marx, and bit-by-bit I put together an overall theoretical perspective on Marxian structural-type theory.[10]

There were also his colleagues and graduate students at Johns Hopkins, many of whom were interested in Marx (for a full listing see Harvey 2002b: 168–73). In an interview with the *New Left Review* Harvey says:

> [T]he initiative came from graduate students who wanted to read *Capital* – Dick Walker was one of them – and I was the faculty member who helped organize it. I wasn't a Marxist at the time, and knew very little of Marx . . . The reading group was a wonderful experience, but I was in no position to instruct anybody. As a group, we were the blind leading the blind. That made it all the more rewarding.
>
> (Harvey 2000d: 80)

Again, while Harvey's graduate students undoubtedly influenced him, it seems unlikely they were *the* determining force. After all, Tony Wrigley introduced Harvey to Marx when Harvey was still a student.

Another factor is clearly political. At some point, Harvey realized that *Explanation* failed as a political text.[11] The positivism it advocated was unable to achieve his political goals, which were thrown into sharp relief by the events of 1968, and later by his own move to Baltimore. In order to cope, a more radical, a more explicitly political, line was needed. Marx. Only Marx provided 'secure islands of concepts' to 'reach out' into the troubled waters that surrounded Harvey, making sense of what was going on, and providing the possibility for propitious political change (Harvey 1985a: xvi).

Perhaps no water was more troubled for Harvey than his newly adopted city of Baltimore. 'The travails of Baltimore have formed the backdrop to my theorizing', he writes (Harvey 2002b: 170). Baltimore is a constant in Harvey's Marxist theorizing from his beginning work on revolutionary theory through to his millennial writing on utopias (Harvey 2000a: ch. 8). 'A city deeply troubled by social unrest and impoverishment' (2002b: 169), Baltimore for Harvey functioned in a similar way to Manchester for Engels. The comparison is especially germane given that Harvey's initial empirical work along with his first US graduate student, Lata Chatterjee, drew upon Engels in understanding the dynamics of Baltimore's housing markets (Chatterjee and Harvey 1974). Furthermore, even Harvey's paper on revolutionary theory and its use of dialectical materialism was in part a working out of his project to understand Baltimore. Subsequently, Baltimore was the site in which he developed other of his theoretical ideas, for example about postmodern nostalgia and aestheticization of place (1989b), gentrification and redevelopment (1992a), and the foibles of capitalist urban planning (2000a). In fact, it is an interesting experiment to think how Harvey's theorizing would have been different had he stayed in Bristol, or moved elsewhere in the United States.

Scott Fitzgerald said, 'there are no second chances in America'. This is belied by David Harvey's life. Coming to America provided the impetus to a second theory of geographical knowledge based upon Marx and dialectical materialism. This move, I suggested, is linked to the larger social context in which Harvey was embedded, the places in which he lived and studied, and the spaces through which he moved. These are not all determining, making the shift inevitable and transparent. Harvey exercises his own agency, which adds contingency and complication. And this is certainly seen in the very relationship between the two halves of Harvey's knowledges.

David Harvey: Between Deduction and Dialectics

> My long standing belief (indeed, what had my whole career as an academic geographer been about?) [is] that geographical knowledges are not outside theory and that the usual dichotomy between universality and general theory, on the one hand, and geographical particularity and incomparable specificity, on the other hand, is a false distinction.
>
> Harvey 2002b: 183

It would be easy to conclude that David Harvey mark I and David Harvey mark II are not the same person: the first the committed positivist scientist, the second the committed dialectical Marxist. But lives, even intellectual lives, are not like that. We carry around our geographies and histories. This is the import of the sociology of science and its concern with lives lived (and seen in Janik and Toulmin's 1973 book). We never begin from scratch, from a *tabula rasa*. Nor do we live outside our geographies and histories, behaving as rational automata following universal logic wherever it leads. Charles Darwin (1974: 68) might say that, 'my mind has become a kind of machine for grinding general laws out of a large collection of facts.' But the biographical evidence tells another story.

I have argued in this chapter that the story of Harvey's own life, his geography and history, is intermingled with his intellectual one. As a result, earlier themes and concerns re-emerge, palimpsest-like, in later work. We can take the ideas out of Harvey – which explains why he is concerned about becoming a 'globalized . . . viable commodity' (2002b: 160) – but we can't take Harvey out of his ideas.

While there are certainly sharp differences between the two Harveys, there are also continuities, for example his commitment to geography, to politics and, perhaps most germane here, to theory. Intellectual inquiry for him means theoretical inquiry. The origin of that inclination in large part derives from his early experiences in geography and its ideographic heritage that produced an intellectually stultifying discipline. He writes:

> I entered academic geography in an era when the belief in uniqueness of place supposedly put the discipline 'outside of theory'. This exceptionalist claim became a matter of fierce debate in the 1960s and I, for one, have spent much of my academic life subsequently seeking to refute that proposition.
>
> (Harvey: 1996a: 110)

This doesn't mean that Harvey is uninterested in particular places – his early work on the Kent hop industry, and later works on Baltimore and Paris, contradict such a contention. The point, though, is to understand and use that particularity for theoretical ends.

Harvey implies that the kind of theory he undertakes as his later self is different from his former self (this is the upshot of 'Revolutionary and counter-revolutionary theory' paper). But there is also leakage and slippage. Impulses in Harvey theory mark I slide over into Harvey theory mark II. While Harvey rids himself of some of the characteristics of natural scientific theorizing – its mathematical nature, or its concern with rigorous verification procedures – other elements from it reappear, and are not completely erased by his new approach. He offers something in between deduction and dialectics.

For example, he still wants to uphold clarity and rigour as theoretical goals. He says as a Marxist, 'ambiguity . . . is no basis for science' (1984a: 8), and 'I am overtly rather than subliminally concerned with rigorous theory building' (1985a: xiv). But how can these ends be squared with either his 'bat-like' vocabulary where ambiguity is part of the very constitution of concepts, or his revolutionary theory based upon an unrealized desire rather than a deductive logic of the present? Or again, he says, 'The intellectual task of geography . . . is the construction of a common language, of common frames of reference and theoretical understandings, within which conflicting rights and claims can be properly represented' (Harvey 1984a: 8). As a statement, this could have come out of *Explanation* rather than his 'historical materialist manifesto' (Harvey 1984a) where it is actually from. For it is an assertion of commensurability and against which Kuhn was reacting. But surely the dialectic is about the incommensurable, the clash of opposites that drive change, and which are not resolvable into 'common frames of reference'? Or yet again, Harvey (1987b: 376) says that his Marxism 'does not entail abandoning universal statements and observations'. Universals, though, by their very definition are outside of history and geography, timeless and placeless. That is why positivism pays them so much attention; they offer Archimedean assurance. However, Harvey's dialectical materialism, and the knowledge it produces, incorporates a varied and varying geography and history, forming part of the dialectic's very dynamic. It is not universal truths on the one hand; and geography and history on the other. They are thoroughly mixed up, as Harvey affirms in this section's epigraph. So, why avow universals?

In each of these cases, it is as if Harvey is speaking from both sides of his mouth, both as a Marxist and as a positivist. These are only a few examples, but they indicate points of tension, sites where inscriptions of an older Harvey lay cheek-by-jowl with the newer Harvey. My interpretation of such tensions is contextual; they are stretched taut by a life lived. Intellectual productions are not the precipitate of a purified rationality, but are infused by a muddied existence. Harvey can't vanquish his past or his geography (nor, I'm sure, would he want to). Yet, they leave their marks and crossings, creating disjunctions and continuities.

Wittgenstein led the most spartan of lives once he left his parents' palatial home in Vienna. His rooms at Trinity College, Cambridge, were furnished with only a mattress and a deck chair. He also eschewed the good life outside. After a friend in Ireland had gone to immense trouble in preparing for him an elaborate meal following an all-night journey, Wittgenstein berated his host, and said from now on they were to have only 'porridge for breakfast, vegetables from the garden for lunch, and a boiled egg in the evening' (quoted in Shapin 1998b: 22). In spite of Wittgenstein's attempt to live the life of an ascetic, to carry out 'the duty of genius' (Monk 1990) unencumbered by the wider context in which he lived, that context, as Janik and Toulmin as well as Monk demonstrate, kept crashing down on him. It explains in part the breaks and continuity found in his various works; why they don't cohere into a seamless rational statement. Harvey has never pretended to live an ascetic life. Rather, as he makes clear, he lusts for life's texture, particularly geographical texture, whether in large North American cities, or in the rural areas in a developing country, or in his native Kent (a 'central obsession', Harvey 2002b: 156). I have argued in this chapter that Harvey's own life texture, his 'backyard', is caught up in his more general theorizing about knowledge, creating a palimpsest, which is not smooth, and where past writing sometimes shows through in present writing, creating dislocation and surprise, but which for all of that is no less powerful or compelling.

Acknowledgements

The chapter was improved immeasurably by comments from Keith Bassett, Noel Castree, Derek Gregory, Ron Johnston and Eric Sheppard. I thank them all. The charge of the editors was to write a critical chapter. I found that task enormously difficult given the influence of David Harvey on my own thought and critical sensibility, which began when I was a first-year undergraduate. In this sense, the editorial charge seemed almost a betrayal. My chapter is a tribute rather than a critique, taking the form of an intellectual biography embodied and placed.

Notes

1 In the examiner's report on Wittgenstein's dissertation, Moore wrote: 'It is my personal opinion that Mr Wittgenstein's thesis is a work of genius; but, be that as it may, it is certainly well up to the standard required for the Cambridge degree of Doctor of Philosophy' (quoted in Monk 1990: 272).
2 Wittgenstein boxed ears of students who were unable to learn especially algebra, and on one occasion pulled so hard on one girl's hair that clumps of it fell out (Monk 1990: 196).
3 Wittgenstein later said about the *Tractatus*, it 'was like a clock which doesn't tell the right time' (from 'Wittgenstein Miscellany' accessible at http://www.flashq.org/wiggy2.htm.

4 In an e-mail, Harvey (26 August 2003) said tongue-in-cheek that he had a 'boat-to-Baltimore' experience. The jukebox on the vessel that brought him to America got stuck on the Rolling Stones' song, 'I can't get no satisfaction'. So, according to Harvey, he disembarked at New York a committed Marxist. Even as a joke, the contrast with Brian Berry's experience on the same transatlantic boat trip made fourteen years earlier is marked. Berry (1993: 435) studiously read August Lösch's *Economics of Location* while on board, becoming a committed spatial scientist by the time he arrived in New York harbour.

5 Harvey's *Justice, Nature and the Geography of Difference* (1996a) and *Spaces of Hope* (2000a) continue to set out an encyclopedic, Humboldt-like vision of geography (see Eagleton's (1997) funny but sometimes pitiless review of *Justice*, and also Harvey's (1998a), spirited defence and justification). In *Spaces of Hope*, Harvey (2000a: ch. 11) discusses favourably E. O. Wilson's idea of 'consilience', the idea that knowledge is unified, and ultimately commensurate. For Harvey geography is the discipline that brings everything together, that achieves consilience, and therefore requires our commitment and passion.

6 It is unlikely that Sauer would have approved of Harvey's reinscription. Sauer wrote in a letter to Campbell Pennington the year *Models in Geography* appeared: 'I am saddened by model builders and system builders and piddlers with formulas for imaginary universals' (letter to Campbell Pennington, 4 February 1967, quoted in Martin 1987: xv). Harvey says now that he is attracted to Sauer's work because of its 'anti-imperialism', and his sympathy for 'indigenous peoples as opposed to the colonisers.' As he put it in an e-mail, 'I would now more clearly see [Sauer] as a kind of patrician Burkean anti-imperialist' (Harvey, e-mail to author, 9 June 2004).

7 (26 May 2004) Tony Wrigley says that he was 'quite unconscious' and 'greatly surprised' that 'David Harvey should have been interested in and influenced by my work in the late 1950s and early 1960s'. Wrigley goes on to say, 'I was and remain interested primarily in a range of questions related to the occurrence of the industrial revolution in England, and became interested in the possibility of exploring the interactions between demographic and economic variables in the centuries preceding the conventional dating of the industrial revolutions. This, too, was a quantitative revolution of a sort . . . but both in substantive matters and in matters of technique is stands apart from the developments which have taken place in geography. Perhaps it was this very fact which David Harvey found interesting all those years ago.'

8 In the Preface to *Explanation* Harvey (1969a: v) talks about 'technical blemishes' in his quantitative work, 'the most celebrated published example being a regression equation estimated the wrong way around – I did not realise that if X was regressed on Y it yielded a different result from Y regressed on X'. He also says attending a National Science Foundation spatial statistics conference at Evanston in 1964 was 'traumatic' (1969a: viii).

9 For example, Richard Dennis (1987: 311) complains that with respect to data Harvey's essay on Paris in *Consciousness and the Urban Experience* (1985a) 'operates on the academic equivalent of secondary and tertiary circuits of capital, trading and speculating on the labours of others'.

10 Taped interview with the author in 2002.

11 The political disenchantment with positivism may have come before *Explanation* was even published. In a letter to the author (8 June 2004), Keith Bassett who went to Bristol in the late 1960s following an MA at Penn State, remembers going around to Harvey's Bristol flat and seeing 'the floor . . . strewn with final drafts of various chapters of *Explanation*. He already seemed to be losing interest, particularly with the final chapters on systems.' That said, Bassett 'can't remember any overt Marxist utterances [by Harvey] in this period'.

3

David Harvey and Marxism

Alex Callinicos

Any historical appreciation of the development of Marxist theory at the end of the twentieth century would award David Harvey one of the first places. He has not been alone in the English-speaking world, which has for the first time become a leading centre of Marxist intellectual innovation over the past generation.[1] Like him, Terry Eagleton and Fredric Jameson have demonstrated an unwavering political and intellectual commitment to Marxism that they have pursued in defiance of changing academic fashions but also with a creative imagination and an openness that have helped them to produce work of the first quality. All three have also written influential interpretations of postmodernism that sought in different ways to fulfil Jameson's celebrated injunction always to historicize.

So Harvey is not without peers. What then are the distinctive features of his own formidable body of work? Four stand out. First, Harvey's Marxism is characterized by the establishment of a direct relationship with the central work of the entire tradition, Marx's *Capital*. He is after all the author of two major contributions to Marxist political economy, *The Limits to Capital* (1982a) and *The Condition of Postmodernity* (1989b), the first offering an ambitious reconstruction of Marx's entire theory of capitalist development, the second both applying and developing this conceptual structure by relating the experience of increased 'time-space compression' that he argues is constitutive of postmodern culture to the emergence of new forms of flexible capital accumulation. But one remarkable aspect of this theoretical project has been the sustained engagement that it has involved with the categorial framework of *Capital* itself.

Harvey has on a number of occasions stressed the impact that *Capital* had on him when he first confronted it as a member of a reading group in

Baltimore in 1971 – an experience that he has repeated annually as a teacher (Harvey 2000a: ch. 1 and Harvey 2001a: 8). As Harvey notes, his first *Capital* reading group was a product of the great radicalization that swept through the advanced capitalist world at the end of the 1960s, and thus was part of a much broader international experience. Following the example of the famous course that Louis Althusser ran at the Ecole Normale Supérieure in 1964–5 whose product was the collective work *Lire le Capital*, tens of thousands of youthful revolutionaries responded to Althusser's injunction: 'Some day it is essential to read *Capital* to the letter' (Althusser and Balibar 1969: 13). (I well remember the *Capital* reading group in which I participated at Oxford in 1972, a year after Harvey.) The effort to understand *Capital*, not as an exercise in erudition, but as a means of understanding capital*ism* the better to struggle against it was a common denominator among the various, still largely nationally differentiated Marxisms that emerged in the 1960s and 1970s – for example, the 'capital-logic' school in West Germany and *operaismo* in Italy.

Harvey begins *The Limits to Capital* with an allusion to this first encounter with *Capital*: 'Everyone who studies Marx, it is said, feels compelled to write about the experience. I offer this work in partial proof of such a proposition' (1982a: xiii). Yet in no way is the reading he offers of *Capital* a contribution to a particular school of Marxist thought: *The Limits to Capital* largely avoids the intense contemporary debates among Marxist philosophers over the extent to which *Capital* is structured conceptually by Hegel's dialectic and even largely sidesteps the more directly pertinent controversy among economists over the coherence and relevance of the labour theory of value.[2] For all that, the book is not an uncritical presentation of Marx's concepts: quite the opposite. Harvey does not labour the ambiguity of his book's title, but he nevertheless makes it clear that the progress of Marxist economic theory depends on subjecting the concepts of *Capital* to critical scrutiny as part of a process of reconstruction and restatement whose result – even if it may represent '[t]he conception towards which Marx appears to be moving' (Harvey 1985b: 42) – goes beyond and often corrects his explicit conceptualizations.

Harvey's highly individual approach is revealed in his treatment of one of the most controversial topics in Marxist political economy, Marx's theory of the tendency of the rate of profit to fall. On the one hand, Harvey criticizes Marx for not, in his exposition of the theory in part 3 of *Capital*, volume 3, integrating the results of his analysis of the process of capitalist circulation in volume 2, and in particular for not taking into account the impact of different turnover times of capital on the determination of the general rate of profit (Harvey 1982: 177–89).[3] But, on the other hand,

Harvey treats the falling rate of profit theory as only Marx's 'first-cut' statement of his theory of crisis, which portrays the self-seeking behaviour of individual capitals as generating a systemic tendency towards overaccumulation. Much of what is most original in *The Limits to Capital* consists in Harvey's analysis of how capital simultaneously seeks to offset this tendency and succeeds actually in intensifying it through the displacement of surplus capital onto the credit system, where financial markets threaten to extend themselves dangerously beyond a monetary base ultimately rooted in the process of production (the 'second-cut' of the theory of crisis) and through the search for a 'spatial fix', where surplus capital is ploughed into investments in specific geographical locations that initially offer super-profits but, over time, immobilize capital in concentrations vulnerable to further technological change (the 'third-cut') (Harvey 1982: 326, 425).[4]

This opening out of Marx's analysis in *Capital* is closely connected to the second distinctive feature of Harvey's Marxism, which is, of course, the integration of the spatial dimension: 'Historical materialism has to be upgraded . . . to historical-geographical materialism' (Harvey 1985a: xiv). But it is important to see that, even though Harvey's particular development of Marxism is inseparable from his own prior intellectual formation as a geographer, his upgrading of historical materialism does not consist in a simple addition of independently formed concepts intended to specify social spatiality. Rather than pursue such an external and potentially eclectic enterprise, he forges an analysis of the uneven geographical development of capitalism *immanently*, through a close reading of Marx's discourse, teasing out its implications, following up its hints, and exposing its limitations. Harvey was not the only leading Anglophone Marxist theorist to discern the presence of geography in the interstices of historical materialism. Expounding a very different version of Marxism from Harvey's, G. A. Cohen suggested that 'we may come to see the entire productive plant of a sophisticated economy as a humanly imposed geography' (Cohen 1978: 97). But this observation, concluding what Alan Carling (1986: 30) calls 'a brilliant fleeting paragraph', is not followed up by Cohen or any other analytical Marxist (Carling 1986: 30 n. 14).[5]

It was Harvey who developed what were at best intimations in Marx into a full-scale research programme – one indeed on which Anthony Giddens, for example, while criticizing Marxism for its alleged failure to thematize the role of space in the constitution of society, nevertheless drew (Giddens 1981: 140–50).[6] Harvey takes up the famous suggestion in the *Grundrisse* that 'while capital must on the one side strive to tear down every spatial barrier to intercourse, i.e. exchange, and conquer the whole earth for its market, it strives on the other side to annihilate this space with time' (Marx

1973a: 539) and integrates it with the theme of the turnover of capital central to his critique of Marx's crisis theory. The annihilation of space by time is driven, Harvey argues, by the search for technological changes that, by reducing the 'socially necessary' turnover time of capital, increase the rate of profit, even though the resulting geographical configurations of fixed capital are threatened with devaluation as new innovations transform the spatial organization of production and circulation.[7] Reducing turnover time is also one of the main impulses behind the partial and incomplete transition to 'flexible accumulation' central to Harvey's interpretation of postmodernism: new productive techniques such as just-in-time inventory systems sought to cut turnover times and thereby to end the crisis of over-accumulation into which the previous Fordist regime descended in the late 1960s and early 1970s (Harvey 1989b: Part II).

But if Harvey arrives at 'historical-geographical materialism' through an immanent critique that develops rather than abandons Marx's concepts, this does not imply that his own discourse is a closed one. On the contrary, the very depth of his engagement with Marx seems to have helped give Harvey the confidence to enter into dialogues with other intellectual traditions. More specifically, the third distinctive feature of his Marxism is its readiness to explore sympathetically preoccupations and themes often held to be distinctive to postmodernism. Here there is a significant difference between Harvey and other Marxist participants in the debate over postmodernity. Some, for example the present author, were unremittingly hostile to the entire postmodernist bandwagon; others, notably Jameson and Eagleton, while influenced philosophically by theorists associated (over their own protests) with postmodernism – respectively Deleuze and Derrida – nevertheless were primarily interested in the entire phenomenon as a symptom of larger historical processes, in Jameson's case the epochal transition from monopoly to multinational capitalism.[8]

Harvey, by contrast, addresses specific themes that are often associated with postmodernism – consider, for example, the discussions of the body in some of his recent writings (Harvey 2000a: Part 2). Of course, when pursuing such questions, he does so as a Marxist, but in articulating what is involved in 'historical-geographical materialism' he engages with an immense variety of different traditions. His treatment of Heidegger, for example, focuses on Heidegger's thematization of the situatedness of Being and on his critique of, in effect, time-space compression in modern capitalism while never losing sight of how this critique led to a decision in favour of National Socialism (Harvey 1989b: 207–10).[9] One impulse behind this willingness to pursue open-ended dialogues with other intellectual traditions is a broadly dialectical conception of nature, understood as a totality of internally related processes of transformation, in which one can trace many influences, Marxist and non-Marxist, from Bertell Ollman to A. N. Whitehead. A non-positivistic naturalism that is sensitive to the different ideological constructions put on the idea of nature but refuses to lapse into anti-scientism is an important affinity between Harvey's thought and that of another leading British Marxist figure, Raymond Williams (Harvey 1996a: Parts I and II).[10]

Harvey is indebted to Williams for the concept of 'militant particularism', which he uses to refer to the embeddedness of social movements and struggles in a particular time and place that provide them with their context and meaning but can damagingly limit their political and economic horizons. '*Theoretical practice*', he argues, 'must be constructed as a continuous dialectic between the militant particularism of lived lives and a struggle to achieve sufficient critical distance and detachment to formulate global ambitions'.[11] This conclusion emerges from Harvey's reflections on a campaign to save the Rover car plant at Cowley in Oxford that he supported at the end of the 1980s. Here we encounter the fourth distinctive feature of his Marxism – a concern with political activism.

Perry Anderson famously contrasted classical Marxism, by which he meant the Marxism of the first three Internationals – outside the academy, preoccupied with political economy and revolutionary strategy, rooted in mass working-class organizations – with the Western Marxism that emerged in Continental Europe after the Second World War – located within the university, focused on philosophy and ideology, divorced from political practice (Anderson 1976). Whatever its other differences from its Continental precursors, contemporary Anglophone Marxism has also been largely confined to the academy. To take once again the cases of Eagleton and Jameson, whatever role political activism may have played in their past, their present influence derives largely from the contributions they have made to debates on cultural theory in the English-speaking university world.[12] Harvey is a participant in this same world, but from a significantly different perspective. For one thing, his theorizations, however philosophically ambitious, are empirically anchored: some of his finest writing has been historical – for example, the great essay on Paris under the Second Empire (Harvey 1985a: ch. 3).[13] For another, from his early forays into radical scholarship in the 1970s to contemporary reflections on struggles such as Chiapas and Seattle, Harvey's thought is marked by a preoccupation with understanding and helping to articulate the demands of movements for social justice. It is in this context that we must see, for example, his interest in using the language of universal rights in order to widen the horizons of 'militant particularisms' whose dynamic is effectively anti-capitalist.[14]

This example immediately registers the distance that still remains between Harvey's thought and classical Marxism, which tended (quite mistakenly) to dismiss talk of rights and indeed all normative discourse as a mere cloak for class interests. Other differences quickly come to mind. For instance, the great figures of the revolutionary socialist tradition – for example, Marx, Engels, Lenin, Luxemburg, Trotsky, Gramsci – all saw a political party as the organizational form in which the mediation between theory and practice necessarily occurs (however differently they conceived such a party). Harvey, by contrast, is an intellectual based in the academy, participating in and reflecting on social movements that develop outside it and that usually lack, as the phrase 'militant particularism' implies, the comprehensive programme possession of which is surely one defining characteristic of a party. This difference is perhaps connected to another, more subtle one. The idea of, say, classical Marxism as a *tradition* implies some more or less continuous effort to carry on a body of thought that both draws on its central ideas but seeks to develop them by engaging with problems that earlier versions of the tradition had either ignored or not needed to confront. The very rich body of writing associated with the Marxist theory of imperialism is a case of this kind of development of a tradition – a collective effort by various writers (among others Hilferding, Luxemburg, Bauer, Kautsky, Lenin, Bukharin, Grossman) who sought, in ways that sometimes clashed with and sometimes supported each other's efforts, to extend the analysis of *Capital* to grasp the main features of what they generally agreed to be a new phase of capitalist development.[15] Harvey is, of course, familiar with this work: indeed *The Limits to Capital* concludes with a discussion of inter-imperialist rivalry and war that resonates strongly with Lenin's and Bukharin's version of the classical theory of imperialism (Harvey 1989b: 439–45).

But there has in general been very little sense of Marxism as a tradition (or indeed a cluster of partly overlapping, partly conflicting traditions) in his writing: the obverse of his intense involvement with Marx's economic texts is a relative inattention to the work of subsequent Marxists, and certainly to the Marxisms of the Second and Third Internationals.

In this respect, Harvey's recent *The New Imperialism* represents a certain shift. Though its theoretical parameters (the book is in part a dialogue with Giovanni Arrighi) and political focus (situating the grand strategy of Washington's neoconservatives) are contemporary, Harvey here reoccupies the terrain of the classics. His conceptualization of imperialism as a contradictory fusion of what he calls (following Arrighi) the capitalist and the territorial logics of power recalls Bukharin's analysis of the integration of inter-state and economic competition in the epoch of finance capital, while

Harvey explicitly invokes Luxemburg in his reinterpretation of primitive accumulation as 'accumulation by dispossession', not a long-surpassed originary stage of capitalist development but a continuing process expressed today in the relentless commodification of the world in accordance with the demands of the Washington Consensus – all this against the backdrop of the crisis of overaccumulation first analysed in *The Limits to Capital*.[16] Nevertheless, if amid the glare of the global state of emergency imposed by the Bush administration Harvey seems to have been drawn into a closer dialogue with classical Marxism, he continues, calmly but firmly, to develop his own distinctive take on Marx's intellectual heritage. His detachment from the particularity of Marxist debate may have helped him to see things differently and address other traditions with his characteristic combination of generosity and rigour. As this suggests, the dialectic that he evokes between militant particularism and critical and global perspectives is one that occurs within Marxism itself. We are indebted to David Harvey for helping us to pursue this dialectic in the changed world of the twenty-first century.

Notes

1 The growing significance of Anglophone Marxism is registered in a recent French survey: see Bidet and Kouvelakis 2001.

2 See, on the latter debate, Harvey 1982a: 35–8, and Steedman et al. 1979.

3 Gérard Duménil seems to have been the first systematically to develop this criticism: see especially Duménil 1978: 283–97. Harvey cites Duménil (1982a: 185 n. 13).

4 Harvey has stressed more recently: 'It is . . . wrong to see these three cuts as *sequential*. They should be understood as *simultaneous* aspects to crisis formation and resolution within the organic unity of capitalism,' (1999a [1882a]: xxii).

5 Harvey himself is hostile to analytical Marxism: see, for example, Harvey 1999a: p. xxi.

6 For a broader assessment of this text, see Callinicos 1985.

7 See, for example, Harvey 1985b: ch. 2.

8 See Perry Anderson's (1998) discussion of Marxist interpretations of postmodernism.

9 See also, for a much more extended discussion of Heidegger along with many other theorists of space and time, Harvey 1996a: Part III.

10 Compare Williams 1980: Part 3.

11 Harvey 1996a: 44 and see generally ch. 1; a slightly different version of this essay is published in Harvey 2001a.

12 Eagleton (2001: ch. 4) has written wittily about his time in one far-left group (also in Oxford, and with a dramatis personae that must have overlapped with that of the campaign to save Rover in which Harvey later became involved).
13 A revised and extended version of this essay has recently appeared as Harvey 2003a: Part II.
14 See, for example, Harvey 2000a: chs. 5 and 12 and 2001a: ch.1.
15 For further thoughts on this example, see Callinicos 2001 and 2002.
16 Harvey 2003b, esp. chs. 2 and 4. Compare Arrighi 1994.

4

Dialectical Materialism: Stranger than Friction

Marcus Doel

Theoretical innovation so often comes out of the collision between different lines of force. In a friction of this kind, one should never altogether give up one's starting point – ideas will only catch fire if the original elements are not completely absorbed in the new ones.

Harvey 2001a: 9

Solid Rock

By our theories you shall know us.

Harvey 1969a: 486

David Harvey is a Marxist, a geographer, and a writer of Marxist geography. He has sought to recover what most others have failed to grasp: 'the subtly nuanced "geographical lore" omnipresent in Marx's and Engels's texts' (Harvey 1982b: 191). For reasons that are not entirely apparent, Harvey suggests that this omnipresent geography is 'buried in Marx's and Engels's texts' (Harvey 1982b: 191). Following in the wake of those such as Lenin, Rudolf Hilferding and Rosa Luxemburg he has devoted himself to two principal tasks. First, he has sought to excavate this 'buried omnipresence'. Second, he has not been content to participate in an archaeological dig that would yield artefacts of merely historical interest. To the contrary, Harvey has endeavoured to unearth buried treasure, ingeniously supplementing it where necessary with what one might call 'authentic fakes' (e.g. 'accumulation through dispossession'). He has banked upon the fact that Marx's geography will continue to have value, currency and utility: that it will remain an asset (cf. Duncan and Wilson 1987). This wager and expectation have profound implications for the critique of capitalism. Everything hinges on 'value'. Value is made manifest in a variety of incommensurate forms (use-values, exchange-values, surplus-values, labour-values, etc.), but value 'itself' – 'arguably the most controversial' of Marx's concepts according to Mohun (in Bottomore 1983: 507) – can only ever be given. Mohun cites the famous passage in Marx's (1975 [1881]) *Notes on Adolph Wagner*: 'I do not proceed on the basis of "concepts", hence also not from the "value-concept" . . . What I proceed from is the simplest social form in which the product of labour in contemporary society manifests itself, and this is a "commodity".' In the beginning (of Marx's *Capital*, for example), something must be taken as given: in this case, it is the commodity-form of value. However, one wonders what *else* might be given other than 'value'. More importantly, one wonders what *obligation* the recipient has taken on in accepting the 'gift' of 'value', and what will have to be *given back* in return (cf. Spivak 1985; Derrida 1992; Lyotard 1993, 1998). Worryingly, one of the first things to be returned to 'value' is 'sensuous human activity' (i.e. heterogeneous material practice), which becomes 'labour', 'labour-power', 'socially useful labour' and the very embodiment of the 'self-expansion of value', all of which comes to be inflected by the shaky distinction between 'productive' and 'unproductive' labour (which is primarily used to account for the production of 'value' in the labour theory of value), and the even shakier distinction between 'surplus-labour' and 'surplus-value' (the latter of which is supposed to define the specificity of capitalism as distinct from other modes of production).

Harvey, like Marx, takes the value-form as given. Everything that figures in their respective accounts – and especially in the settling of accounts with capitalism – is, quite literally, given 'on account'. 'If anyone objects to the abstractions as inhuman and degrading', warns Harvey (1987b: 372), 'it is to capitalism rather than to Marx that complaints should be addressed.' And in so far as 'value' is given, there is always already a 'surplus' of value. It is a given that can never be accounted for. Little wonder that a 'surplus' of value and the concept of 'surplus-value' should become pivotal to Marxist geography (cf. Harvey 1973a, 2003c).

With one hand, then, Harvey reads the omnipresent but buried geography *in* Marx's and Engels's nineteenth-century texts. With the other hand, he reads geography *into* their texts. Now, it is not my intention here either to pursue the enigmatic phrase 'buried omnipresence' (which has all of the hallmarks of a structuralist formulation, despite Harvey's (1987b) protestations to the contrary) or to assess the value of Marx's and Engels's geography today. My interest lies in what Harvey has unearthed: 'the "solid rock" of historical-geographical materialism" (Harvey 1996a: 8). One should not underestimate the significance of this 'solid rock' for Harvey. It secures his footing while guaranteeing him a purchase on the world. The candid introductions to *Justice, Nature and the Geography of Difference*

(1996a) and *Spaces of Hope* (2000a) make it crystal clear that he is absolutely committed to 'foundationalism' and 'meta-theory'.[1] This is why his version of historical-geographical materialism needs to be solid. It founds critique (that is to say, it provides an institution, a security, and above all leverage), and it endures across space and time (that is to say, its purchase transcends context). For one cannot apply *force*, critical or otherwise, without a secure foundation; and one cannot *apply* force, critical or otherwise, without an ability to reach. Hence his recourse to the parable of the Pentecostal preacher.

> The preacher who opened the ceremonies that evening did so with the following invocation: 'Through these four days', he said, 'we have come to understand the foundational beliefs that keep us firmly on the rock'. . . . I myself agree that all foundational beliefs should be scrutinized and questioned. But what troubled me was the thought that when a political group armed with strong and unambiguous foundational beliefs confronts a bunch of doubting Thomases whose only foundational belief is skepticism towards all foundational beliefs, then it is easy to predict who will win.
>
> (Harvey 1996a: 2)

The force of this passage comes not only from pointing out the performative contradiction of the 'radical' sceptic's position (a foundation without foundation), but also from pointing out that one needs a 'solid rock' to counter enemy forces.[2] So, 'the task of critical analysis is not, surely, to prove the impossibility of foundational beliefs (or truths), but to find a more plausible and adequate basis for the foundational beliefs that make interpretation and political action meaningful, creative, and possible' (Harvey 1996a: 2). Accordingly, Harvey insists on standing firm against the flood of anti-foundationalism. '[W]hile I accept the general argument that process, flux, and flow should be given a certain ontological priority in understanding the world, I also want to insist that this is precisely the reason why we should pay so much more careful attention to . . . the "permanences" that surround us and which we also construct to help solidify and give meaning to our lives' (1996a: 7–8).

'Solid rock' is vital not only because it enables Harvey to account for and to come to terms with capitalism, but also because it allows him to exert force. From the outset, Harvey's encounter with Marxism has been articulated through force. Hear what he has to say about 'Theory in Geography' in *Social Justice and the City* (1973a: 150–2):

1 Each discipline locates problems and solutions through a study of real conditions mediated through a theoretical framework . . .

2 There are three kinds of theory:

(*i*) *Status quo theory* – a theory which is grounded in the reality it seeks to portray and which accurately represents the phenomena with which it deals at a particular moment in time . . .

(*ii*) *Counter-revolutionary theory* – a theory which may or may not *appear* grounded in the reality it seeks to portray, but which obscures, be-clouds and generally obfuscates . . .

(*iii*) *Revolutionary theory* – a theory which is firmly grounded in the reality it seeks to represent, the individual propositions of which are ascribed a contingent truth status . . . A revolutionary theory is dialectically formulated and it can encompass conflict and contradiction within itself. A revolutionary theory offers real choices for future moments in the social process by identifying immanent choices in an existing situation. The implementation of these choices serves to validate the theory and to provide the grounds for the formulation of new theory. A revolutionary theory consequently holds out the prospect for creating truth rather than finding it.

3 Individual propositions and, indeed, whole theoretical structures are not necessarily in themselves in any one of the above categories . . .

4 A theoretical formulation can, as circumstances change and depending upon its application, move or be moved from one category to another. This suggests two dangers that must be avoided:

(*i*) *Counter-revolutionary cooptation* . . .

(*ii*) *Counter-revolutionary stagnation* . . .

But there are also two important revolutionary tasks:

(*iii*) *Revolutionary negation* . . .

(*iv*) *Revolutionary reformulation* . . .

5 These tasks can be pursued and these dangers can be avoided only if the counter-revolutionary posture of the organized pursuit of knowledge (and in particular disciplinary division) is recognized and reality is confronted directly.

In these five propositions we can discern the animating force of Harvey's entire problematic. He insists on the necessity of being *firmly grounded* – rooted, embedded, constrained – in a *conflicted reality* that one should confront *directly*.[3] While status quo and counter-revolutionary theories either fail to appreciate or actively obscure the conflicted nature of reality, only revolutionary theory endeavours to overcome that conflicted state through a critical intervention and displacement.[4] The imperative for Harvey is not to find the truth about a conflicted state of reality. Rather, it is to find a way of gaining a purchase on the conflicted state of reality in order to manipulate its forces for the better. 'The philosophers have only *interpreted* the world, in various ways', laments Marx (1946 [1845]: 65) in his eleventh thesis on Ludwig Feuerbach; 'the point, however, is to change it'.[5] This sentiment is repeatedly echoed by Harvey. In *Social Justice and the City* he insists that 'When theory becomes practice through use then and only then is it really verified' (Harvey 1973a: 12). In *The Condition of Postmodernity* he avers that 'The proof of this conceptual apparatus lies in the using' (1989b: 10). It should now be clear why Harvey insists upon the *force* of theory, why he articulates this force on the basis of *solid* foundations, and why he privileges the *use-value* of theory (its usefulness in the struggle for social justice) over its exchange-value (its correspondence with 'the real'). Historical-geographical materialism is much more than a mere *re*-presentation of the world (a 'window' on the world, a 'mirror' for the world, an 'illumination' of the world, etc.). It is essentially performative and transformative: 'a set of generative and transformative principles, embedded in continuous processes, which, by virtue of internalized heterogeneity and contradiction, reveals the possibility to create all kinds of new but always transient states of things' (Harvey 1996a: 67).

If Harvey's texts appear sure-footed, it is above all because he invests in solidity. This is his fundamental calculation.[6] While one might wonder about the political (and libidinal) economy of this calculation and investment – especially with regard to the using and abusing of intellectual labour – one might also wonder about the political economy of solidity. Two questions spring to mind. First, can the dialectical articulation of historical-geographical materialism provide a solid and secure foundation for radical thought and action? Second, does the articulation of force require a solid ground? I want to suggest that the answer to both questions is a resounding no. In this chapter I want to bring the 'solid rock' of historical-geographical materialism to account. In particular, I wonder whether it can ensure the kind of sure-footed and self-assured theoretical practice that Harvey has come to depend upon. One wonders, for example, how he alighted upon the 'solid rock' of historical-geographical materialism in the first place. 'I regard myself primarily as a *scientist* seeking a comprehensive understanding of the world in which we live', says Harvey (2001a: 68). 'I have turned to the Marxian categories because they are the only ones I have so far come across which allow me to make sense of events.' Or again: 'The shift from one approach [Liberal] to the other [Marxist] wasn't premeditated – I stumbled on it' (Harvey 2001a: 7).

From the outset it is worth bearing in mind that Harvey 'came across' and 'stumbled on' the 'solid rock' of historical-geographical materialism. Needless to say, as he stumbled a lot of baggage fell away (compare *Explanation in Geography* and *The Limits to Capital*, for example). What interests me, however, is neither the baggage that fell away (liberal formulations and the conceits of bourgeois thought), nor the baggage that he clung to (such as 'the setting up and observation of decent intellectual standards for rational argument' (Harvey 1969a: vii), nor the new baggage that he subsequently picked up (Marxist formulations and a class-specific revolutionary thought), but how he identified and evaluated this piece of 'solid rock'. Harvey no doubt came across and stumbled upon all manner of things, so what is it that prompted him to find *value* – of all things! – in this particular chunk of 'solid rock'? Furthermore, how does his own economic calculation square with the support and leverage that the 'solid rock' of historical-geographical materialism is meant to lend to the critique of political economy? Harvey has already given us the semblance of an answer. In stumbling upon the 'solid rock' of historical-geographical materialism he would appear to have stumbled upon a use-value (it *makes the most* sense) and an exchange-value (*thus far*). This is a calculated evaluation with built-in obsolescence. Were Harvey to stumble upon something that *makes even more* sense, the 'solid rock' of historical-geographical materialism would be laid off. Meanwhile, the 'solid rock' of historical-geographical materialism is taken up as an expendable means of production; as an apparatus for ceaselessly regenerating meaning and value; as intellectual labour-power, whose 'specific' use-value is to make sense: 'accumulation for accumulation's sake, production for production's sake' (Marx, *Capital*, vol. 1, quoted in Harvey 1982a: 29). For when all is said and done, Harvey expects the world to *make sense*, just as Marx expects labour-power to *make value*. Harvey banks on this. He capitalizes on this. He speculates on this.[7] Accordingly, it is important for us to understand the weird form of 'value' that Harvey wagers upon, which he credits to Marx, who in turn drew it from capitalism.

The Enigma of Value

> Marx considers the commodity as a material embodiment of *use value, exchange value* and *value* . . . These are the concepts that are absolutely fundamental to everything that follows. They are the pivot upon which the whole analysis of capitalism turns.
>
>   Harvey 1982a: 1

Marx attempted to avoid naturalizing value – and especially 'use-value' – by situating it within definite social conditions that find a certain 'value in use'. What is useful in one context may or may not be useful in another. Nevertheless, the entire critique of political economy pivots on the leverage provided by use-value as an undivided concept. For with the advent of exchange-value (the principle of substitution, transposition, and therefore referral, deferral and dispersal), use-value is divided *from* itself and turned *against* itself. With the coming of capitalism, 'value in use' yields to 'value in exchange'. (Such is the shift from C–C to M–C–M.) Capitalists must obviously produce useful things (otherwise these would go unsold), but they do not produce them because they are useful. Instead, things are produced in order to be exchanged. Such is the perverted use-value specific to commodities. 'In order that his labour may re-appear in a commodity', says Marx (1954 [1886]: 173), 'he must, before all things, expend it on something useful, on something capable of satisfying a want of some sort. Hence, what the capitalist sets the labourer to produce, is a particular use-value.' However, 'In the form of society we are about to consider,' observes Marx (1954 [1886]: 44), use-values 'are the material depositories of exchange-value'. In short, use-value aids and abets exchange-value. Far from being dialectically opposed, they are thoroughly complicit in the circulation and accumulation of capital. Hereinafter, usefulness is wronged by the alienation, reification and fetishism of commodities. Given this wrong, one can understand the clamour for restitution and recompense. However, usefulness turned against itself long before the 'advent' of exchange-value. It has always divided, apportioned and dispersed itself on the basis of an ineluctable calculation (cf. Spivak 1985, 1995). 'Since any use-value is marked by [the] possibility of being used *by the other* or being used *another time*, this alterity or iterability projects it *a priori* onto the market of equivalences' (Derrida 1994: 162). Accordingly, the use-value of critical theory, in so far as it is figured as a 'value in use', is promised to exchange-value and thrown into the circulation of capital. Spivak (1995: 65) objects to this Derridean (1994) formulation on the grounds that it fails 'to honor the difference between commercial and industrial capital' (i.e. the difference between the *circulation* of value in the sphere of exchange and the *creation* of value in the sphere of production). When Marx attends to the creation of value, he effectively deconstructs the distinction between use-value and exchange-value. Since labour-power can create more than it needs, 'Marx makes the extraordinary suggestion that Capital consumes the use-value of labour-power' (Spivak 1985: 79). Marx tells us that 'Capital is formed because capital uses the *use-value* of labor-power . . . which is to produce more value than it needs', and he demonstrates that through the expropriation of the super-adequacy of labour-power, 'surplus-value is the birth of capital'. Labour creates use-value *and* value. Consequently, 'Derrida seems to be beating the wrong Marx and reinventing the wheel when he points out that exchange . . . is implicit in use' (Spivak 1995: 74–5).

If the distinction between 'use-value' and 'exchange-value' does not hold, what about 'value' itself? Marx considers the value of linen. 'It is not possible to express the value of linen in linen. 20 yards of linen = 20 yards of linen is no expression of value', insists Marx (1954 [1886]: 55). 'On the contrary, such an equation merely says that 20 yards of linen are nothing else than 20 yards of linen, a definite quantity of the use-value linen. The value of the linen can therefore be expressed only relatively – *i.e.* in some other commodity.' Accordingly, Marx focuses on the relationship between things, such as linen and coats: specifically, the equation '20 yards of linen are worth 1 coat'. Through this equation, a use-value (some linen) becomes an exchange-value (worth 1 coat). Crucially, the linen is not converted by labour into another use-value. It does not become a coat. Instead, the linen remains linen, but it nevertheless becomes – quite literally – *the equivalent of* a coat. It ceases to be some potentially useful linen and becomes instead a signifier, an equivalent, a currency, which may or may not be generalizable into a recognized standard of value, like gold, sterling or the Big Mac. This is why Baudrillard (1975, 1981) insists on the homology of commodities and signs: exchange-value is to use-value as signifier is to signified, each of which eclipses – or if you prefer, occults – the supposed reality of the referent: the twofold character of labour (abstract and concrete) and the twofold character of sense (meaning and intention). Formulaically, '*the logic of the commodity and of political economy is at the heart of the sign*' since 'signs can function as exchange-value (the discourse of communication) and as use-value (rational decoding and distinctive social use)'; while '*the structure of the sign is at the very heart of the commodity form* [since] the commodity can take on, immediately, the effect of signification' (Baudrillard 1981: 146). Hence Baudrillard's fascination with a form of value that surpasses value, use-value, exchange-value and surplus-value: *sign-value* (aka sign-exchange-value), and its antagonist relationship to symbolic exchange.

How does Marx account for the equation 20 yards of linen (A) are worth 1 coat (B)?

The whole mystery of the form of value lies hidden in this elementary form . . . The linen expresses its value in the coat; the coat serves as the material in which that value is expressed. The former plays an active, the latter a passive, part. The value of the linen is represented as relative value, or appears in relative form. The coat officiates as equivalent, or appears in equivalent form. The relative form and the equivalent form are two intimately connected, mutually dependent and inseparable elements of the expression of value; but, at the same time, are mutually exclusive, antagonistic extremes – *i.e.* poles of the same expression.

(Marx 1954 [1887]: 55)

Since the value relation (A is worth B) can be approached from two directions (from A and from B), it needs to be expressed in two forms that are mutually exclusive: one mediated (the relative form, where A is valued *in* B); one unmediated (the equivalent form, where B *is* the measure of value). This asymmetrical duplicity appears obvious when B is 'money' and A is a 'commodity'. All commodities have a formal equivalency (A = B = C = D, etc.), but only money *is* the equivalent. Of course, the apparent self-evidence of the value of money derives from a profound misrecognition. Here as elsewhere, since no irrelative position exists, 'the identity function is a nonstarter' (Arthur 1979: 80; cf. Olsson 1991, 2000 on the ambivalence of equivalence, i.e. on the misidentification of identity and non-identity: e.g. A = B). Given that A = B must be squared with the fact that A *is not* B, Marx ventures on a quest to discover the *true identity* of an *apparent nonidentity*, and finds it in the substance of labour imparted into and valorized through commodities (socially useful labour, in the form of socially necessary labour time). Hence the importance of the 'transformation problem' (the problem of determining money prices on the basis of labour values). It is a problem without an adequate solution, and one that Sraffa (1960) famously tried to side-step by adopting a structuralist, rather than a labour, theory of value (cf. Arthur 2002; Mandel and Freeman 1984). Harvey (1982a) makes a spirited attempt to conjure away both the so-called transformation problem and its structuralist alternative by insisting on the dialectical relationship between labour values and money prices, since only a causal relationship requires one to engage in a unidirectional transformation. Indeed, value is neither *reflexive* (the value of A cannot be expressed in A), nor *symmetrical* (the relative and equivalent forms of value are mutually exclusive), nor *transitive* ('specific' equivalents can only be exchanged via the 'universal' equivalent; only money functions as if it were nothing but value) (Arthur 1979). Consequently, it is not so much the logic of the labour theory of value that is flawed, says Harvey, as the illogicality of treating a dialectical relationship as if it were simply a causal relationship. While this is true, it fails to appreciate that the ambivalence of equivalence goes all the way down, and cannot be resolved by an appeal to the substance of labour.

Having made linen (A) active-expressive and the coat (B) passive-expressed, Marx continues:

> By means, therefore, of the value-relation expressed in our equation ['20 yards of linen are worth 1 coat'], the bodily form of commodity B becomes the value-form of commodity A, or the body of commodity B acts as a mirror to the value of commodity A. By putting itself in relation with commodity B, as value *in propriâ personâ*, as the matter of which

human labour is made up, the commodity A converts the value in use, B, into the substance in which to express its, A's, own value. The value of A, thus expressed in the use-value of B, has taken the form of relative value.

(Marx 1954 [1887]: 59)

On this point Marx is crystal clear: 'values in use' take themselves to market. The critical distinction, then, is not between the *use-value* of linen and the *exchange-value* of linen, but between *linen* and a *use* for linen. The latter is always already given over to equivalence, substitution and calculation. For as Marx points out from the start, use-value is, precisely, *value* in use.

This destabilization of use-value would perhaps be a minor irritant if it were not for the fact that Marx insists on its leverage against extant political economy. 'Even in the analysis of the commodity, I do not stop at the double mode in which it is represented [use-value and exchange-value], but go straight on to the fact that in this double being of the commodity is represented the two-fold character of the labour whose product it is: the *useful* labour . . . and the abstract labour' (Marx 1883, quoted in Althusser and Balibar 1969: 79).[8] Furthermore, the concept of 'surplus-value', upon which the entire critique of political economy depends, is shaken to the core by this destabilization of use-value in its opposition to exchange-value. For Marx insists that 'surplus-value itself is deduced from a "specific" use-value of labour-power which belongs exclusively to it' (Marx 1883, quoted in Althusser and Balibar 1969: 79).[9] It would be interesting to pursue the untold consequences of the decomposition of use-value across Harvey's texts. Given the constraints under which I am writing, however, I will hold back from this temptation since my principal concern is the treatment of 'surplus-value'. By way of foreclosure suffice to say that 'Every time the meaning of a discussion depends on the fundamental value of the word *useful* . . . it is possible to affirm that the debate is necessarily warped and that the fundamental question is eluded' (Bataille 1985: 116). As the alibi of exchange-value, use-value has always been a distraction from the vital issue: the fate of surplus-value.

Inside the Outside

My concern is . . . with trying to rebuild Marxian meta-theory in such a way as to incorporate an understanding of spatio-temporality . . . within its frame.

Harvey 1996a: 9

To get at Harvey's 'materialism' it will be necessary to inquire into the 'economy' as well as the 'solidity' of his writing: not only his writing *on* political economy, but the political economy *of* his writing, which he never fails to capitalize upon (in every sense of this term). To put it bluntly, I worry that the political economy of his writing is complicit with the political economy that he ostensibly critiques. In other words, rather than fashioning a representation of the political economy of capitalism that would enable him to gain a critical purchase on it in order to effect a revolutionary displacement (another echo of Marx's eleventh thesis, although it is striking how often Harvey characterizes his work as a 'window' on a moving world[10]), the economy of the writing echoes, affirms and conserves what it ostensibly wants to displace. I worry for the fate of Harvey's corpus because it takes the violence and ruination wrought by capital (which is to say, the violence and ruination wrought by a certain kind of writing; for capital is, as Harvey never tires of telling us, not a 'thing', but 'value in motion', 'self-expanding value': value referred and deferred, value displaced, value disseminated – from the living to the dead) into itself.

I have already mentioned that the 'solid rock' of historical-geographical materialism is meant to provide critical leverage for a rearticulation of the 'opposing' forces that organize the conflicted state of reality. As a materialist, Harvey refuses to fall back on that which is held in reserve. Everything is to be situated – embedded – in an appropriate historical and geographical context.

> The 'solid rock' of historical-geographical materialism is here used to say that dialectical argumentation cannot be understood as outside of the concrete material conditions of the world in which we find ourselves; and those concrete conditions are often so set in literal concrete (at least in relation to the time and space of human action) that we must perforce acknowledge their permanence, significance, and power.
>
> (Harvey 1996a: 8)

In other words, the 'solid rock' must be *immanent* to the situation. 'In practice man must prove the truth, that is, the reality and power, the insidedness [*Diesseitigkeit*] of his thinking' (Marx 1946 [1845]: 63). Hence Harvey's refusal to be seduced by the mirage of an external support for critique. He prefers 'the site of "immanence", of the "down here" which Marx himself opposed as "*diesseits*" (down-here) to transcendence, the beyond of classical philosophies' (Althusser and Balibar 1969: 127), and he favours the '*ascent*' from non-observable concepts, such as value and surplus-value, to the '*descent*' from the 'concrete abstractions' observed in everyday life, such as money and profit.

> Bourgeois social science ... attempts to construct a view of the world from outside, to discover some fixed points (categories or concepts) on the basis of which an 'objective' understanding of the world may be fashioned. The bourgeois social scientist typically seeks to leave the world by way of an act of abstraction in order to understand it. The Marxist, by way of contrast, always seeks to construct an understanding of society from within rather than imagining some point without.
>
> (Harvey 2001a: 89)

Since at any 'moment' everything is related to everything else, the 'inside' of Harvey's historical-geographical materialism permits of no outside. Everything is given. If we are to observe the world, then a viewing position can only come from *within* the world. If we are to change the world, then leverage can only come from *within* the world. Fortunately,

> The Marxist finds a whole bundle of levers for social change within the contradictory processes of social life and seeks to construct an understanding of the world by pushing hard upon the levers ... [T]he bourgeois academic will have to cease to be bourgeois and come to the other side of the barricades if he is really to understand what the view from inside, the view from the standpoint of labor, is all about.
>
> (Harvey 2001a: 89)

In short, the levers *of* the system must be used *against* the system. This is why it is necessary for the system to be conflicted and wracked by tension: in motion, agitation and contradiction. 'Capitalism ... constitutes a permanently revolutionary force, sweeping away all older ways of life, unleashing untold powers to expand the productivity of social labor. But it also contains within itself the seeds of its own negation, seeds which grow and ultimately crack open the very foundations in which they are rooted. Crises are inherent in capitalism' (Harvey 2001a: 310). Without such an inner dynamic, the system could no longer be turned (for either revolutionary or bourgeois ends). One can already sense the insistence of Harvey's historical, geographical and dialectical materialism. Right here, right now, the whole of existence is in a state of dynamic tension, and this build up of conflicted forces is what compels us towards something other: the absolute nihilism of capital (we fear) or the 'supersession' of antagonism (we hope). We can only depend on the *forces of the inside* playing a double game of repetition and reinscription, of reproduction and transformation and of conservation and supersession. For Harvey, like Marx and Engels before him, the primary double agents are the proletarians, who 'have a world to win' and 'nothing to lose but their chains' (Marx and Engels 1986 [1848]: 70).

This is what Harvey's corpus tells us. First, there are only forces of the inside – and *nothing but* forces of the inside. The outside is always relative to the inside. It is the outside of the inside. It is therefore always already enveloped, internalized and accounted for by the inside. Indeed, 'Marx was deeply suspicious of any idea of a "surplus" or a "residual" *outside of* the overall flow of determination within social processes' (Harvey 1996a: 106). Second, these interior forces are made up of double agents who function only in so far as they break down. Everything has two faces (at least). That is to say, everything is two-faced, duplicitous and contradictory. 'Because of the contradictions, there are innumerable leverage points *within* the system that can be seized upon by dissident groups of individuals to try to redirect social change down this or that path. There are always weak links' (Harvey 1996a: 106). Third, while some of these double agents are living (capitalists, workers, peasants, landlords, the reserve army, etc.), most of them are dead (an immense accumulation of capital; an immense accumulation of commodities; an immense accumulation of wealth; an immense accumulation of use-values, exchange-values and sign-values, etc.). Finally, in so far as the agency of double agents is always duplicitous, their work contributes to both the conservation and the transformation of the system. 'Capital is therefore always promoting "internal revolutions" within the accumulation process – revolutions which are forced through by crises' (Harvey 2001a: 83).

'Marxian theory is pre-eminently a theory of crisis. Marxian theory sees historical movement as founded in a deep and pervasive struggle between competing and opposing forces which are anything but harmonious with each other (except by accident!)' (Harvey 2001a: 74).[11] For example, one thinks of the antagonism between capital and labour over the extraction and distribution of surplus-value; the fettering of the forces of production by the social relations of production; the concentration and centralization of capital; and the tendency of the rate of profit to fall which precipitates crises of overaccumulation. Indeed, 'The theory of overaccumulation–devaluation reveals the height of insanity, the intense destructive power, implicit in the capitalist mode of production . . . the bourgeoisie turns out to be "the most violently destructive ruling class in history"' (Harvey 2001a: 309, quoting Berman 1982: 100). Hence the 'impulsion within capitalism to create a world market' to absorb – up to a point – this accursed mass of overaccumulated (i.e. underemployed) capital (Harvey 2001a: 302). Needless to say, it remains a moot point whether or not such antagonistic and crisis-prone 'tendencies [work] with iron necessity towards inevitable results' (Marx 1954 [1887]: 19).

One of the defining features of Harvey's work is the emphasis he places on the 'overaccumulation' of capital rather than on its 'uneven development'/'uneven exchange'. This is important because while the latter can be sustained (at least in principle) and perhaps even corrected (by state intervention and urban planning, for example), the former cannot. Over-accumulation is quite simply catastrophic for capital. Harvey's account of the crisis-prone historical geography of capitalism is based on his theory of overaccumulation–devaluation, which in turn depends upon the 'law' of the 'tendency' for the rate of profit to fall (see especially Harvey 1982a: chs. 4§IV and 6§III). Since capital accumulation inevitably increases the amount of constant capital (machinery, materials, energy, etc.) relative to variable capital (labour-power), the rate of profit will almost certainly fall. The relative shift in production from labour-intensity to capital-intensity means that surplus-value has to be shared across an ever-growing mass of capital. Hence the fact that the rate of profit must fall. In addition, capital-ists have placed much greater emphasis on labour-saving initiatives than on capital-saving initiatives, while class struggle has helped to moderate the rate of exploitation, both of which exacerbate the tendency for the rate of profit to fall. Given this argument, Harvey is unequivocal: crises are caused by an overaccumulation of capital, even though their effect is to make both capital and labour unprofitable. It is a 'capital surplus problem' (Harvey 2003b: 89). Through the self-expansion of value in motion, capital under-mines itself from within. Consequently, economic crises are inevitable in the long run, although their occurrence will depend on the specific articu-lation of this tendency with other social, economic or political tendencies that might counteract or exacerbate it (e.g. the different turnover times of various kinds of capital and their entrainment through a plethora of finan-cial instruments). Harvey concludes that, at best, balanced accumulation is highly unlikely. Indeed, everything we know about the circulation of capital suggests that it is extremely unbalanced. Be that as it may, the tendency for the rate of profit to fall as a result of the rising organic and value composi-tions of capital is thoroughly contested within Marxian political economy. For even if the *mass* of constant capital rises relative to the *mass* of variable capital, it does not necessarily follow that the *value* of that recomposition, and therefore the rate of profit, will change adversely once productivity changes (which tend to raise surplus-value and reduce the value of con-stant capital) have been taken into account (Sweezy 1968; Bottomore 1983; Howard and King 1985; Catephores 1989). In short, Harvey's determined account rests on undecidable ground (see Harvey 1982a: 188). The rate of profit *may* fall, but whether it *tends* to fall is another matter entirely.

Nevertheless, from the point of view of historical-geographical mat-erialism it suffices for reality to exist in a conflicted state for *something* to snap. One of the key contradictions that Harvey has pursued in his texts is the way in which the circulation of capital lays down a built environment of fixed capital in its own image that comes to act as a fetter on future capital accumulation. This precipitates 'periodic crises within the capitalist production system. These crises serve to "rationalize" the system' (Harvey 2001a: 80). 'Can civil society be saved from its internal contradictions (and ultimate dissolution) by an *inner* transformation. . .?' he asks. 'Or does salvation lie in a "spatial fix" – an *outer* transformation through imperialism, colonialism and geographical expansion?' (Harvey 2001a: 288). 'Hegel's "inner dialectic" undergoes successive representations in Marx's text. And at each point the question of a spatial resolution to capitalism's contradictions can legitimately be posed anew' (Harvey 2001a: 299).

Harvey has engaged in a sustained dialectical interrogation of the necessity and the impossibility of concluding an effective 'spatio-temporal fix' to the innate contradictions of the circulation and accumulation of capital. 'The inner dialectic of civil society is perpetually assuaged and reproduced through constant resort to the spatial fix', says Harvey (2001a: 302). In this way, 'the social relations which propel capitalism's inner dialectic are merely recreated on a wider geographical scale. There is, under such circumstances, no long-run "spatial fix" to capitalism's internal contradictions' (Harvey 2001a: 307). Consequently, 'The only effective resolution to . . . crises [of over-accumulation], in the absence of a spatial fix, is the *devaluation* of capital' (Harvey 2001a: 300). Little wonder, then, that 'the search for a spatial fix is converted into inter-imperialist rivalries over who is to bear the brunt of devaluation' (Harvey 2001a: 310). While acknowledging the power of this analysis, and appreciating that 'the intriguing configurations of internal and external contradiction . . . force the argument to spin onwards and outwards' (Harvey 1982a: 446), I wonder whether Harvey's own discourse is attempting to institute a 'spatial fix' to the inner contradictions of the critique of political economy, most obviously by recourse to the 'solid rock' of historical-geographical materialism, and 'permanences' that can effectively challenge 'the particular set of permanences that capitalism has tightly fashioned out of otherwise open, fluid, and dynamic social processes' (Harvey 1996a: 108).

The notion of crises rationalizing an irrational system echoes Engels's dialectical riposte to Hegel's proposition 'All that is real is rational; and all that is rational is real.'

[T]he Hegelian proposition turns into its opposite through Hegelian dialectics itself: All that is real in the sphere of human history becomes irrational in the process of time, is therefore irrational by its very destination, is tainted beforehand with irrationality, and everything which is rational in the minds of men is destined to become real, however much it may contradict existing apparent reality. In accordance with all the rules of the Hegelian method of thought, the proposition of the rationality of everything which is real resolves into the other proposition: All that exists deserves to perish.

(Engels 1946 [1888]: 13)

What really matters, then, is not the fact that capitalism vacillates wildly between two forms of rationalization (fixes and crises), but the fact that capitalism is essentially irrational and is therefore destined to perish. However it manifests itself, capitalism is always the *tendency* towards overaccumulation, a tendency that expresses itself in the oscillation between temporary 'spatio-temporal fixes' and periodic crises of overaccumulation-devaluation. In keeping with this structuralist disposition, Harvey (2003c: 1) announces at the outset of *The New Imperialism* that he 'seek[s] to uncover some of the deeper transformations occurring beneath all the surface turbulence and volatility'. Yet in straining to see beneath the surface of events, I have the distinct impression that Harvey fails to register their passing (cf. Harvey 1987b; Virilio 1991; Smith and Doel 2001). It is almost as if he sees only the *tendency* towards overaccumulation (the 'inside' as an irrational kernel), its *manifestation* in spatio-temporal fixes and crises of overaccumulation–devaluation (the 'outside' of the inside as a force of displacement, deferral and destruction), and the *eternal return* of 'primitive' or 'original' accumulation (an 'other' outside that sustains capital qua capital), which he dubs 'accumulation by dispossession' (Harvey 2003b).[12] By pursuing 'this 'inside–outside' dialectic' (Harvey 2003c: 141), historical-geographical materialism fails to confront reality directly. Rather than encounter events head on, they slip past – always at a remove, like vanishing mediators. The discourse is rendered in the relative, rather than the equivalent, form of value. When everything must be recognized, evaluated and accounted for, there is little scope for estrangement, otherness and alterity. One is left with the impression that for all of its openness and attentiveness, historical-geographical materialism will never be caught off guard by surprise.

Stirring Still

[F]or this is what I hold and what in turn holds me in its grip, the aleatory strategy of someone who admits that he does not know where he is going.

Derrida 1983: 50

Materialism does much more than refer us to the specificity of a context, and insist that any critique must be embedded within such a context. Crucially, without recourse to a set of values, ideals and forces held in reserve (*à la* idealism), the reality to which the materialist refers must exist in a conflicted state in order for the materialist to launch a critical intervention. Conversely, if it were not for the fact that reality exists in a conflicted state, the materialist would be unable to gain a critical purchase on reality. For the materialist, a world reconciled with itself would mark the end of all critique. Such is the dream of an end to historical geography, where historical geography is understood as the historical geography of class struggle over the production and expropriation of surplus-labour and surplus-value. From the point of view of materialism, then, everything depends on how one is to understand the conflicted nature of reality. For his part, Harvey (2000a: 15) has adopted 'a relational conception of dialectics embodied in the approach that I have come to call "historical-geographical materialism"'. The relational conception is important because it draws attention to the fact that there is always a gap within that which presents itself as fully given. Unlike atomistic conceptions of materialism, in which self-sufficient things enter into contingent relations with one another (in the manner of an assembly or an aggregation), the relational conception of materialism reveals how relations enter into things. 'Any "thing" can be decomposed into a collection of other "things" . . . *ad infinitum* . . . [T]here are no irreducible building blocks of "things" for any theoretical reconstruction of how the world works', notes Harvey (1996a: 51). Consequently, 'the only way we can understand the qualitative and quantitative attributes of "things" is by understanding the processes and relations they internalize' (Harvey 1996a: 52). So, far from being self-contained, everything depends upon its relationship with something other; and therefore finds itself in the place ostensibly reserved for the other. 'Within a relational dialectics one is always internalized and implicated in the other' (Harvey 2000a: 16). It is not sufficient, then, to acknowledge that every thing is relational; that every thing exists only on the basis of the relations it enters into, and that a rearticulation of its relations necessarily transforms the form and function of every thing (e.g. work within capitalism is not at all the same thing as work within another mode of production). One must also appreciate that this relational conception carries everything elsewhere. The relation between *Yin* and *Yang* within the Taoist erotics provides a perfect example: 'for in the one is always the kernel of the other, and the expansion of this kernel in the one leads it to become the other' (Lyotard 1993: 204). So, the water that would threaten to extinguish the fire, once agitated and excited, becomes boiling water, which is already fire. Similarly, within political economy, 'capital is defined as a process – as value "in motion" undergoing a continuous expansion through the production of surplus value' (Harvey 1982a: 83); and in so far as capital is 'in motion', it must pass through what is ostensibly other: labour, use-value, consumption, etc. '[P]roduction and consumption' (Harvey 1982a: 80).

Since the relational conception puts everything out of kilter, one can already sense the potential for a dissipation of things. Harvey blocks this dissipation in two ways: through the imposition of a holding formation – specifically a 'frame' or a 'totality' – which is more or less structuralist in its configuration,[13] and through the adoption of a dialectical conception of relations. First and foremost, he holds to a 'conception of the totality as inner-relatedness' (Harvey 1973a: 307). 'Marxian theory is holistic and works with a particular sense of how the parts relate to the totality', suggests Harvey (2001a: 75). 'The totality is regarded neither as an aggregate of elements nor as something that has meaning independent of its parts', but as a 'totality of internally related parts' each of which can be conceived of as 'an expandable relation such that each one in its fullness can represent the totality'. Accordingly, 'a particular object of enquiry must necessarily internalize a relation to the totality of which it is a part. The focus of the enquiry is, then, on the *relations* of the epistemological object to the totality' (Harvey 2001a: 75). In addition, structures mediate the relationship between the parts and the totality. 'A structure must be defined . . . as a system of internal relations which is in the process of being structured through the operation of its own transformation rules' (Harvey 1973a: 290). 'Structures may be regarded as separate and differentiable entities when no transformation exists whereby one may be derived from another' (Harvey 1973a: 291).

In and of itself, however, the fact that relations are structured within a totality does not square with the need for there to be a conflicted state of reality. This is where the dialectical articulation of a structured totality comes into play: provided that the dialectic is understood in a Marxian rather than an Hegelian way (Althusser 1979; Althusser and Balibar 1969; Arthur 2002).[14] 'The dialectical aspect of Marxist thought focuses upon contradiction . . . contradictions . . . internalized within particular objects or events' (Harvey 2001a: 76). Indeed, Harvey (2001a: 308) reminds us that Marx's 'supreme concern . . . was to unravel the nature of capitalism's *inner* dialectic'. As a materialist it is important for the dynamism to be immanent to the situation. So, 'Dialectical materialism is . . . a *method* that seeks to identify the transformation rules through which society is restructured' (Harvey 1973: 290). These transformation rules derive from the conflicted nature of reality. It is the fact that the relational configuration of parts within a structured totality is conflicted that forces the totality to transform. Crucially, the dialectic conceives of the relation as a contradiction, such that the conflicted forces within a contradiction always push towards a resolution or supersession.[15]

> The dialectic ... proposes a process of understanding which allows the inter-penetration of opposites, incorporates contradictions and paradoxes, and points to the processes of resolution ... The dialectical method allows us to invert analyses if necessary, to regard solutions as problems, to regard questions as solutions.
>
> (Harvey 1973a: 130)

Consequently, 'The evolution of society as a totality must ... be interpreted as the result of contradictions established both within and between structures' (Harvey 1973a: 293). In addition, 'we are obliged to distinguish between contradictions *within* a structure and contradictions *between* structures' (Harvey 1973a: 291).

Contradictions necessitate displacement and transformation. Consider, for example, *n* 'moments' within a structured totality of contradictory relations. Harvey (1996a: 80) begins by telling us that 'Each moment is constituted as an *internal relation* of the others' and that 'Errors arise when examination of one "moment" is held sufficient to understand the totality of the social process.' Then, he argues that 'Internal relations are shaped through an activity of *translation* from one moment to another' (1996a: 80). However,

> A gap always exists between the different moments so that slippage, ambiguity and unintended consequences inevitably occur ... So although each moment internalizes forces from all of the others, the internalization is always a translation or metamorphosis of those effects rather than an exact replica or perfect mimesis.
>
> (1996a: 80)

> Finally, I have so far construed the relations between 'moments' as flows, open processes that pass unhindered from one moment to all others. But flows often crystallize into 'things', 'elements', and isolable 'domains' or 'systems' which assume a relative permanence ... within the social process. Reifications of free-flowing processes are always occurring to create actual 'permanences' in the social and material world around us.
>
> (1996a: 81)

Taken together, then, the dialectical conception of historical-geographical materialism secures its critical power from a host of contradictions that are structured within a totality. 'The Marxian emphasis upon relations and contradictions within a totality yields, when properly executed, a unity of analysis and synthesis' (Harvey 2001a: 77). Specifically, 'The oppositions implanted within the abstract conceptual apparatus are used to spin out new lines of argument. We reach out dialectically . . . Pursuing an argument in this way allows us to follow how antagonisms get resolved under capitalism and how each contradiction gets internalized a-fresh in new realms' (Harvey 1989a: 11). For 'One of the viruses (*sic*) of a dialectical/ relational approach is that it opens up all sorts of possibilities that might otherwise appear foreclosed' (Harvey 1996a: 12).

Everything that unfolds from the dialectical conception of historical-geographical materialism derives from an understanding of the conflicted state of reality in terms of a set of contradictions structured within a totality. This conflicted state must be decidable.

> What differentiates Marx from bourgeois political economy (both before and since) is the emphasis he puts upon the *necessity* for departures from equilibrium and the crucial role of crises in restoring that equilibrium. The antagonisms embedded within the capitalist mode of production are such that the system is constantly being forced away from an equilibrium state. In the normal course of events, Marx insists, a balance can be achieved only by accident.
>
> (Harvey 1982a: 82–3)

From a deconstructive point of view, one could question the coherence of the relations, the structures, the totality, the contradictions and the solidity of the 'solid rock' of historical-geographical materialism.[16] By way of departure, however, I simply want to question the *dynamism* of the dialectical conception of historical-geographical materialism. As we have seen, this dynamism derives from the articulation of relations as contradictions within a structured totality. What I have not yet emphasized, however, is that the critique of political economy alights upon an excess that cannot be contained within the existing order of things, although it can be entirely accounted for within the existing order of things. The contradictory nature of this excess is what drives the structured totality towards the crisis of slippage, displacement and transformation. Within the critique of political economy and historical-geographical materialism inaugurated by Marx and refined by Harvey, this excess goes by the name of 'surplus-value' (i.e. the value-form of surplus-labour extracted and appropriated by capital). 'Surplus value is that part of the total value of production which is left over after constant capital (which includes the means of production, raw materials and instruments of labour) and variable capital (labour power) have been accounted for' (Harvey 1973a: 224). How can one explain the

> presence of a surplus of value in a homeostatically [i.e. tautologically] regulated system[?] How can a system obtain, at the end of a cycle, more than it consumed during the production process? Basically, the answer to this question has always been of the type: *the system is not isolated*, it deducts or receives energetic supplements *outside* itself, which it trans-forms, integrates into its circuits, and which still allow it thereafter to retain its specificity. The physiocrats call this exteriority nature, Marx calls it labour force, many Marxists or Keynesians call it the third world or unequal exchange. But in any case the concept of a *borderline* must be introduced, putting the tautological system in contact with an external reserve of energies which can be drawn on.
>
> (Lyotard 1993: 153–4)[17]

Both the critique of political economy and historical-geographical material-ism capitalize on the production of surplus-value and the crisis tenden-cies of surplus-value. Consequently, the critique *of* political economy can be reflexively applied to the *critique* of political economy. Through the circulation of capital, value differentiates itself from itself by throwing off surplus-value. This process of differentiation is both agonistic, pitching those who produce surplus-value against those who accumulate surplus-value, and crisis-prone, in so far as there is a tendency for there to be an overaccumulation of capital relative to the opportunities to employ it profit-ably. However, at the heart of this process of differentiation is neither value nor surplus-value, but labour: 'Labour is the substance, and the immanent measure of value, *but has itself no value*' (Marx, quoted in Harvey 1982a: 23). When all is said and done, then, I worry that the critique of politi-cal economy and historical-geographical materialism will perpetually run aground not only because its entire universe is deconstructable (Baudrillard 1975, 1981; Derrida 1994; Lyotard 1993, 1998), but simply because it con-tinues to bank on meaning and value.

At the outset of *The Limits to Capital*, Harvey (1982a: 1) tells us that 'a long voyage of discovery . . . led Marx to a fundamental conclusion: to unlock the secrets of the commodity is to unravel the intricate secrets of capitalism itself'.[18] Let me end by countering this historical-geographical materialism with a glimpse of an altogether different way of working with matter: Bataille's 'base materialism'.

> Most materialists, despite wanting to eliminate all spiritual entities, ended up describing an order of things whose hierarchical relations mark it out

as specifically idealist. They have situated dead matter at the summit of a
conventional hierarchy of diverse types of facts, without realizing that in
this way they have submitted to an obsession with an *ideal* form of matter,
with a form which approaches closer than any other to that which matter
should be.

(Bataille 1929, 'Matérialism', quoted in Bois and Krauss 1997: 29)

Whatever is given must be returned. So, if Marx was right to take 'value' *as
given*, then it is destined to be *given back* (Baudrillard 1996). The challenge
that faces political economists and historical-geographical materialists is to
let value, and especially surplus-value, go: without resentment and without
nostalgia. It is not that value (in all of its manifestations) is fated to return
to its rightful owner and proper place (living labour). Rather, value is destined to dissipate. My closing thought, then, is simply: Don't panic. The
dissipation of value should be an occasion for considerable laughter.

Notes

1 Indeed, Harvey (1989b: 355) cautions that 'Meta-theory is not a statement of
  total truth but an attempt *to come to terms with* the historical and geographical truths that characterize capitalism both in general as well as in its present
  phase' (emphasis added). This is a striking turn of phrase. Marxist meta-theory
  wishes 'to come to terms with' capitalism: conclude an agreement and become
  reconciled.
2 One wonders about the necessity of a 'solid rock' to counter enemy forces, especially given the tendency for forces to turn against themselves, or to be turned
  against themselves, and the availability of an enormous repertoire of guerrilla
  tactics.
3 Although Harvey has always sought to tackle problems head-on and to confront
  reality directly, I will argue that this has been done with a certain duplicity,
  particularly with respect to surplus-value. A related issue beyond the scope of
  this chapter is the relationship between critique understood as a force of opposition, and therefore production (*à la* Harvey), and critique understood as a
  force of ex-position, and therefore seduction (*à la* Baudrillard) (Baudrillard
  1990; Doel 1999; Smith and Doel 2001).
4 This critical intervention within and displacement of a conflicted situation puts
  Marxism in accord with the deconstructive operation of reversal and reinscription (Derrida 1981; Ryan 1982; Doel 1999).
5 The eleventh thesis is neither as unique nor as radical as many twentieth-century commentators would have us believe. 'A closer look at Marx's
  condemnation/appeal would have simply revealed Marx's project as a belated
  restatement of the routine Enlightenment understanding of philosophy and its
  tasks' (Bauman 1987: 100).

6 'The principles of dialectical enquiry . . . *should* generate a perpetual state of motion in our concepts and thoughts. But the negative side of this flexibility and openness is that it appears to have little chance of producing anything except a vast panoply of insecure and shifting concepts and findings . . . The purpose of multiple and relational approaches to phenomena is . . . to identify a restricted number of very general underlying processes which simultaneously *unify and differentiate* the phenomena we see in the world around us . . . In this sense, dialectics does seek a path towards a certain kind of ontological security, or reductionism – not a reductionism to "things" but to an understanding of common generative processes and relations' (Harvey 1996a: 58).

7 Refreshingly, Baudrillard (1975, 1981, 1994, 1996) advances the opposite hypothesis: that the world shirks sense, and in so doing it is fated to remain enigmatic.

8 The late arrival of labour onto the scene of value may come as a surprise, although it is certainly not intended to act as a denouement. Rubin (1973: 62) cautions that it is not so much that 'labor is hidden behind, or contained in, value: value = "materialized" labor. It is more accurate to express the theory of value inversely: in the commodity-capitalist economy, production-work relations among people necessarily acquire the form of the value of things, and can appear only in this material form; social labor can only be expressed in value.' In other words, 'value' is not an objective property found in things (e.g. a specific quantity or quality of human labour) but a social form (i.e. human relations expressed through things). Value is a form, not a content. 'It is in the "materiality" of content that form consumes its abstraction and reproduces itself as form' (Baudrillard 1981: 145).

9 In formulating her objections to Derrida (1994), Spivak (1995) fails to question the supposed 'specificity' and 'exclusivity' which is attached to the use-value of labour-power.

10 'By moving from window to window and carefully recording what we see, we come closer and closer to understanding capitalist society and all of its inherent contradictions' (Harvey 1982a: 2). 'I hang my interpretation of the "urban" on the twin themes of *accumulation* and *class struggle*. . . . different windows from which to view the totality of capitalist activity' (Harvey 2001a: 79).

11 Although Harvey often alludes to a conjuncture of *conflicting tendencies* (i.e. contingent and intertwined), he tends to fall back on an articulation of *dominant tendencies* and *countervailing forces* (i.e. necessity and constraint) (e.g. Harvey 2003b).

12 The phrase 'accumulation by dispossession' follows the logic of the gift, *à la* Mauss and Bataille: an asymmetrical structure of antagonistic reciprocity serves to extort escalating returns. 'The umbilical cord that ties together accumulation by dispossession and expanded reproduction is that given by finance capital and the institutions of credit, backed, as ever, by state powers' (Harvey 2003c: 152).

13 For more on different conceptions of totality, see Althusser and Balibar (1979).

14 According to Harvey (2001a: 285), Marx 'merely sought . . . to turn Hegel's dialectic "right side up" and give it a material base'. However, Althusser and Balibar (1979: 86) remind us that 'the "reconversion" of this dialectic, which

has to be put "back on to its feet" if it is at last to walk on the *terra firma* of materialism', did not leave the dialectic intact (cf. Marx's turning of the commodity – a wooden table – right-side up).

15 The dialectic conceives of difference (i.e. conflicted force; non-identity) as *contradiction*, thereby opening it up *in advance* to the possibility of a resolution. One cannot decide between contradictory positions because both turn out to be inadequate and malformed when they are allowed to stand alone – motionlessly – as thesis and antithesis, a position and its contrary. In striving for a resolution of contradiction – and recall that to resolve, from the Latin *resolvere resolut*, is to unfasten again and to release back into circulation – the dialectic is not static, but dynamic. For the dialectician, then, the momentary resolution of a contradiction will on reflection beget further contradictions and higher resolutions *ad infinitum*. In retrospect, there is always some 'excess' – some 'surplus' – that has not been properly taken into account. The drive to integrate all excess – to permit of no outside – is what disturbs.

16 Since the terms of a relation are ex-appropriated by an Other, '*One cannot assume a position* on the twisted, shock-ridden, electrified labyrinthine band. One's got to get this into one's head' (Lyotard 1993: 11). For example, the origin of political economy always already ex-appropriates itself: 'the producer, who, as owner of his own conditions of labour, employs the labour to enrich himself, instead of the capitalist' (Marx, *Capital*, quoted in Harvey 2001a: 306). However, although ownership, labour and enrichment are taken as given, the critique of political economy reserves its wrath for that which illicitly takes from what is given: parasitic forms, exemplified by capital. Hence the oxymoronic phrase 'accumulation through dispossession'. Surpluses are subtracted. They are 'reserved for growth', as Bataille (1988) would say – just as the critique of political economy is 'reserved' for capital.

17 Althusser and Balibar (1979: 6) put it like this: what was taken as a solution by political economists (*The value of labour is equal to the value of the subsistence goods necessary for the maintenance and reproduction of labour*) is posed as a problem by Marx ('*The value of* labour *is equal to the value of the subsistence goods necessary for the maintenance and reproduction of* labour'). Marx's solution to this problem (*The value of* labour(-power) *is equal to the value of the subsistence goods necessary for the maintenance and reproduction of* labour(-power)) took him on to a new terrain which gave him critical purchase on the conflicted nature of reality: the unruly excess of 'surplus-value' (as distinct from 'surplus-labour'), the magnitude of which is the difference between the 'value' of labour imparted by labour-power into commodities and the 'value' of labour returned to labour-power via the purchasing-power of wages. As the term 'surplus-value' suggests, capital constitutes itself on the basis of the extraction and retention of a portion of labour that is not returned to its source: labour-power. In short, the value of work exceeds the value of wages (and herein lies another explanation for crises in capitalism: underconsumption owing to a lack of aggregate demand). 'Less money pretends to be more time; hence the exchange of nonequivalents' (Spivak 1995: 77). Accordingly, capitalism is essentially the expanded reproduction of alienation and exploitation in the specific form of surplus-value.

18 Strictly speaking, Marx (1954 [1886]: 43) opens *Capital* with 'an immense accumulation of commodities', although the analysis immediately settles upon – 'must' settle upon, says Marx – a *single* commodity: the 'unit' of this immense accumulation. Unsurprisingly, however, the analysis of this 'unit' perpetually returns Marx to the world of commodities, not least because value, as we have seen, is always elsewhere: value is relative, manifold and set in motion. It will be left to Baudrillard (1998) to return to the starting point which Marx neglected – 'profusion' – and to draw out the consequences of this displacement for the critique of political economy.

5

Differences that Matter

Melissa Wright

As a dedicated socialist and dialectical theoretician, David Harvey consistently approaches the notion of social difference with the aim of achieving solidarity. And in classical Marxist tradition, the social differences at the core of his concern are the class divisions deriving from and contributing directly to the processes behind capital's relentless quest for accumulation. His corresponding vision of solidarity therefore is that of class solidarity, which in its most mature evolution as socialism erodes class divisions along with the many other social differences so vital to the organization of capital.

Harvey's focus on class as the difference that matters under capitalism does not shift throughout three decades of prolific scholarship. Yet with the 1989 publication of *The Condition of Postmodernity* (CPM) a fault-line emerges that distinguishes his pre-1989 publications from those coming after that benchmark year. From the publication of 1973, *Social Justice and the City*, to his simultaneous 1985 publications, *Consciousness and the Urban Experience* and *The Urbanization of Capital*, Harvey focuses on the 'twin themes of accumulation and class struggle' (Abu-Lughod 1988: 412). His aim is to develop a Marxist approach within geography and urban studies and to enrich Marxist political economy by incorporating space into the dialectical analysis of historical materialism (Kearns 1984: 411). Harvey embraces these objectives as a defender of Marx's applicability to contemporary urban and economic phenomena, but he does not in these pre-1989 publications justify his choice of class, over other social differences, as a socially, economically and politically significant difference. Such justification is unnecessary given the debates, namely Marxist urban and geographical studies, within which he situates his pre-1989 work. While he finds a need to defend Marxist analysis against those who criticize it as overly abstract, ideological, idealistic, deterministic and obsolete in global market contexts, he does not need to explain his emphasis on class (see Gutenschwager 1976). Within such literatures, the significance of class as a marker of power and social differentials continues to be regarded as largely self-evident.

By the time Harvey published *The Condition of Postmodernity* in 1989, Marxism was under serious attack not only from state governments, from Asia to the Americas, that sought to destroy any Marxist politics but also from poststructuralist and feminist scholars who challenged the primordial status of class as the premier category of difference and the relevance of materialist analysis for understanding power (see Eagleton 1995). While Harvey had already established himself as a formidable Marxist critic of state-sponsored neoliberalism, *The Condition of Postmodernity* represents his first response to the poststructuralist and postmodernist turn in social theory and in the arts. The provocative language throughout the book exposes his desire for direct debate with theorists who emphasize the discursive over the material and with those who emphasize the complexities of identity, rather than capitalist social structures, as their point of analysis. In *CPM*, he challenges, and sometimes even defies, such theorists (many found within poststructuralist and feminist circles) to strategize effectively over a response to the obvious miseries created by capitalism, particularly within the virulently anti-labour contexts of the Reagan–Thatcher regimes that transformed global capital–labour relations in the 1980s. Anything short of this, he asserts, is not only politically distracting but theoretically and socially irresponsible.

By expanding his targets of critique beyond capitalism's apologists and scholars who do not consider the spatial dimensions of capitalist processes to include poststructuralist and identity-politics scholars, Harvey suddenly finds himself defending Marxism's position within the political and theoretical terrain of 'the left'. Gone are the days when his assumption of class's obvious social significance, and clear relevance above other categories of difference, proceeds unchallenged. Instead, he confronts critics who accuse him, among other doctrinaire Marxists, of being sexist, ethnocentric and elitist. He must explain his use of 'metanarratives' for telling the big story of capital and, in effect, ignoring the exclusionary effects of his own language and point of view. Within such exchanges, Harvey is up against critics who argue that Marxism represents the status quo of a traditional and conservative leftist politics, organized around some old-fashioned exclusions.

Harvey responds to such critiques in his subsequent publications with an expansion of his theoretical interests to include the meaning of difference itself. In his post-1989 publications, he orients his vision of political challenges against capitalism around a vindication of class as a marker of significant social difference, among other possibilities, and as a material relation of power within a complex discursive field. While he continues to explore the 'twin themes of accumulation and class struggle', his frame for doing so shifts to examine this dynamic within 'the dialectic of commonality and difference' (1989b: 93). This shift reveals that Harvey no longer takes for granted the obvious relevance of a class experience that provides a common ground of action and solidarity. Rather, he intends to demonstrate how, despite the multiple processes of differentiation that cut across the experience of identity, class solidarity continues to represent an important strategic goal, and not a bygone conclusion, for social justice movements. Such a goal requires that he forego his former allegiance to a self-sufficient Marxist materialist analysis and attend to the discursive practices through which social differences, across multiple possibilities, take shape.

In the process, Harvey comes to engage seriously with his critics, particularly those in the poststructuralist and feminist circles who question materialism and the relevance of Marxist analysis more generally for social justice and for theories regarding political agency. And his initial dismissive stance towards such critics, as detailed in *CPM*, gives way, in subsequent publications, to an effort to reveal how Marxism provides useful theoretical tools for scholars and activists who explore social difference as a means for strategizing around social justice from different epistemological standpoints, including those of poststructuralism, environmentalism and identity politics. In fact, throughout the latter half of his oeuvre, Harvey draws significantly from poststructuralist and feminist scholarship to theorize strategies for creating social solidarity across social differences while still reinforcing Enlightenment beliefs in rational action, transparent communication and collective consciousness. In this way, Harvey remains true to his commitment to journey towards the 'grand art of synthesis' (as quoted in Corbridge 1998), as the principal route to theorizing and envisioning socialist possibilities, even as he shifts his style of argumentation and theoretical benchmarks to explain his emphasis on class, his materialist conception of difference within multiple discursive arrangements, and the importance of exploring capitalism among other possible choices for analysis. Consequently, the capitalist abstractions that characterize his pre-1989 publications yield to considerations of specific problems and processes raised not by doctrinaire Marxism but by theorists and activists who approach the interrogation of difference, rather than the assumption of class solidarity, as a starting point for justice.

I organize my discussion in this chapter around how Harvey justifies class as a difference that matters in his engagement to his critics in the wake of *The Condition*, through the response to *Justice, Nature, and the Geography of Difference (JNGD)* and *The Spaces of Hope*, and into the writing of *The New Imperialism*. I focus on these publications and their surrounding debates because they provide the basic framework through which Harvey expands his own approach to class analysis and strategies for social justice away from a self-sufficient Marxist materialism. They also demonstrate why Harvey intensifies his fight against those who dismiss Marxism outright and who diminish the significance of class for the organization of power, politics and resistance in the contemporary era of neoliberal regimes.

In the following, I begin with a brief discussion of the evolution of the concept of, and terminology for, social difference as a result of the poststructuralist interventions in social theory, associated with both Jacques Derrida and Michel Foucault. I then turn attention to Harvey's engagements with these interventions both in his publications and in the critical response to his work.

Definitions and Differences

The concept of 'social difference' both as phrasing and as a category for intellectual inquiry owes much to Jacques Derrida's mid-1960s coinage of 'deconstruction', in reference to Heidegger's 'destruction' of metaphysics (Derrida 1991 [1983]). With deconstruction, Derrida took direct aim at structural linguistics and at 'structuralism' as a mode of intellectual critique. Derrida argued that if language, as Saussure explained, is constructed through binary pairs of difference, then, as Derrida observes, language is based upon the 'sameness of difference'. (1991 [1982]: 45). Therefore, within each apparently self-contained series of oppositional significations are contained the traces of innumerable other pairs of difference, so that the meaning of any single pair exceeds the language that signifies it. His term *'différance'*, which spawned the fascination with 'difference' as a category of analysis, is a play on language (from the French *différence*) that refers to the eternal work of difference in language, such that the origins of any single concept are never discernible. Therefore, not only is the idea that we can grasp meaning through language a fiction, albeit a necessary one, but so also is the idea that we can know (conceptualize) or represent original meaning through scientific inquiry. In the 1970s, Derrida's critique of structuralism and the practice of deconstruction acquired the moniker of 'poststructuralism', a word, Derrida writes, 'unknown in France until its return from the United States' (1991 [1983]: 272).

Related to this critique of language is Michel Foucault's dismantling of the subject as a self-knowing and autonomous actor (see Foucault 1977, 1980). By, in effect, deconstructing the meaning of subjectivity, Foucault seeks to illustrate how human reality is constantly being produced through numerous signifying activities, whose origins can never be located through historical, philosophical or anything resembling 'scientific' inquiry. Instead, the subject materializes as a knowable, observable and intelligible entity only in contrast to the subject who is unknowable, unobservable and unintelligible, or the subject whose possibility of existence is foreclosed (Butler 1993). This contrast between the possible and impossible subjects also takes shape through the repetition of differences that exceed this binary configuration. The positive subject, who takes shape only in relation to an antithetical and negated one, is never fully explained in the simple terms of this binary because the origin of the binary is not contained within the contrasted pairs. There is no single point of origin for any social existence because each oppositional pair contains the multitudes of oppositions that constitute its parts. Following this logic, the subject is never fully knowable because the contrast with its unknowable pair is never self-contained. Therefore, the subject does not exist as a transparent entity whose meaning can be fully grasped or assumed. And the corresponding concepts of consciousness, experience and agency are equally impossible to determine since the subject is not grounded in a particular field of knowledge. As such, poststructuralism – and its central category of 'difference' – challenges the notion that history is made by conscious subjects who can fully know their own intentions, make them transparent to others and act upon them truly. Under such theorizations, Marx's call for workers of the world to unite appears as a dream-wish. For to assume that different workers share an experience of self based on a common experience of work is to assume that there exists not just a knowable subject but also a knowable category of experience that is common across different subjects. Such assumptions are impossible under poststructuralism.

Feminist scholars have used the poststructuralist critique of metaphysics to question the universal subject, who exercises universal reason, at the core of Marx's conception of historical agency. By exposing how this subject materializes around the exclusion of the feminine subject from the public and productive domains, these scholars have demonstrated that Marx's vision of the proletarian reproduces a conservative notion of agency and politics based on some traditional sexual divisions. This critique extends further into an interrogation of the material body that girds Marx's analysis of exploitation. By dismantling the human body as a site of grounded material reality, these scholars have shown that exploitation has its roots in the production of the embodied subject – in its very materialization as an intelligible entity. Therefore, a politics against exploitation must attend not merely to the machinery of commodity production, but to the discourses that construct the human body as an exploitable site in the first instance. And, within this perspective, Marxist assumptions of the universal subject armed with universal reason represent one set of discourses that contribute to the ongoing production of the feminine subject as lacking both the reason and the agency to exist in history (see Scott 1988). Consequently, Marxism, itself, represents a mode of exploitation that must be addressed.

Often substituted for the term 'poststructuralism' is that of 'postmodernism', a movement based in the arts and developed as a theory of social critique in 1970s western Europe. Postmodernism's meaning is murkier than poststructuralism's, although the two are often conflated and interchanged in common usage. With Jean-François Lyotard's 1984 publication of *The Postmodern Condition*, postmodernism came to be associated with a critique of knowledge and of the 'metanarratives' used across the arts and the sciences to explain and represent human reality. The postmodern 'turn' in art and architecture elevates anarchy over hierarchy, play over purpose, chance over design, performance over product, absence over presence, surface over depth, signifier over signified (Best and Kellner 1991). Within this literature, claims to social order, constancy and steadfast reality are merely contributions to the constant interplay of representational forces that intersect in the social continuum. They are no more or less real than any other set of claims.

One of the primary targets of the postmodernist critique is Marxism, with its signature claims to historical development, to transcendent consciousness, to assertions of true versus false consciousness, to coherent historical subjects, and to the origins and meaning of history. The postmodern critique of such 'big stories' for organizing information, analyses and visions for political change has set up Marxism in many ways as the standard for understanding what postmodernism is not (see Eagleton 1995). Postmodernism rejects the narratives of a coherent social order and the coherent subjects who, according to typical Marxist analysis, are required to change it. Instead, postmodernists argue that there is no a priori and directly accessible material reality that grounds any particular social order. Their emphasis is on the realm of representation as the arena wherein the material takes shape through multiple interpretations, each constructing a different version of reality. Therefore, Marxist claims that capitalism represents the material underpinnings to social reality constitute merely one set of interpretations among many others that contribute to the ongoing creation of the ever-elusive reality.

Another important domain of intellectual thought also associated with the debates regarding 'social difference' is the catch-all known as 'identity politics'. The epistemological roots of identity politics are numerous, intricate and beyond my ability to treat fairly. Yet, by and large, identity politics derives from civil rights movements and politics, notably within the 1960s–1970s United States, whose mantra 'the personal is political' swept the academic and political landscape in the West. In contrast to poststructuralism and postmodernism, identity politics' proponents hold firm to the notion of a social subject who, although perhaps fragmented, can act as a political agent for social change and who can exercise legal rights. A common thread found across identity politics is the idea that some identities have been marginalized in relation to others, and that a politicization of consciousness is necessary to subvert this power dynamic (hooks 1990).

Identity politics has been the driving force behind the creation of numerous civic movements in Western states with the aim, via constitutional redress, of reversing historical injustices levied on people owing to their racial, gendered, sexual, ethnic, physical, among others, identities. Identity political movements have also addressed the injustices of racism, sexism and ethnocentrism within the academy and within the construction of knowledge more generally. These movements have forced universities to establish such identity-based academic programmes as women's studies, Latino studies, African American studies and sexuality studies, in order to correct discrimination in curriculum and in employment practices.

The advocates of identity politics occupy an ambiguous position regarding the debates between Marxists and poststructuralists over political agency. On the one hand, many theorists and activists within the identity politics movement argue against the poststructuralists'/postmodernists' claim that a politics based on identity and on a political subject is epistemologically uncertain. On the other, identity politics' proponents have also criticized Marxists, generally, for constituting an exclusive academic and political club that has continually ignored the significance of gender, race, ethnicity and other 'non-capitalist' categories within the reproduction of economic and social hierarchies. For instance, socialist feminists, who combine class and gender identity politics, have shown how the assumptions of naturalized sex difference underpin the division of production and reproduction and of the public and private spheres within Marx's analysis; these scholars have demonstrated how Marx's conception of class re-creates the violences of sexism. A fundamental question they raise is how, without addressing the sexism within Marxist scholarship and among Marxist scholars, can socialism be fair?

By the mid-1980s, the confluence of the poststructuralist, postmodernist and identity politics critiques converged into a powerful challenge to Marxism not from its usual conservative detractors but from within the domain of leftist politics and scholarship. Marx's historical materialism, based on an acceptance of capitalism and its class divisions as the defining features of modern life, the teleology of capitalist development, and the belief in a transcendent consciousness, in a potentially unified proletariat, in a steadfast division separating labour from capital and in a common vision of socialist possibilities, was, by the late 1980s, declared 'obsolete'. The official demise of the Soviet Union in 1989 seemed only to provide further nails for the coffin that was quickly interring Marxian thought. Socialism, by numerous accounts, had 'failed'. Universal norms of truth and objectivity shattered against the ferocity of particularized interpretations of 'the real' that destabilized any foundational experience of sameness, not only with other people, but within the self. The conscious, revolutionary, transcendent hero of Marxian hopes appeared to disintegrate under multiple discursive forces into a fragmented subject, lacking internal coherence and incapable of seeking solidarity with others. Nietzsche's 'god is dead' acquired, by the late 1980s, a secular companion with 'the subject is dead'. And along with it, Marx's significance as an inspirational thinker was quickly being relegated to the shadowy corners along with other 'modernist' icons.

Harvey situates his 1989 book *The Condition of Postmodernity* within these political and intellectual debates in order to take on this new challenge to Marxism and to the socialist visions of coherent political action against capitalism. In a later reflection on this decision, which reoriented the trajectory of his publications after 1989, he writes: 'Insofar as [poststructuralism, post-modernism, identity politics] . . . were viscerally opposed to Marxism – and I submit that a lot of them were – they were devastating for conceptions of class politics . . . [they were] a frontal assault on class analysis and Marxian thinking' (1998a: 727).

The Difference a Book Makes

In *The Condition of Postmodernity* Harvey effectively attempts to frame postmodernism and its cousin of poststructuralism, as an intellectual and arts movement fashioned, primarily, by the historical-geographical developments of capitalism (1989b:). By presenting postmodernism and poststructuralism in this light, he sets up a two-pronged argument.[1] One prong aims to demonstrate the impossibility of understanding these theories without understanding the dynamic linking modern arts and culture to modern

capitalism. The other prong challenges postmodernists and poststructuralists to respond to the latest round of capitalist accumulation, which he dubs
'flexible accumulation'.

In the first part of the book, he sets out his argument that postmodernism
actually represents a continuation of the modern project of internal critique
and reformulation. He writes:

> I also conclude that there is much more continuity than difference between
> the broad history of modernism and the movement called postmodernism.
> It seems more sensible to me to see the latter as a particular kind of crisis
> within the former, one that emphasizes the fragmentary, the ephemeral,
> and the chaotic side of Baudelaire's formulation (that side which Marx
> so admirably dissects as integral to the capitalist mode of production)
> while expressing a deep skepticism as to any particular prescriptions as
> to how the eternal and immutable should be conceived of, represented, or
> expressed.
>
> (1989b: 116)

As a scholar who embraces modern thought, he lauds the 'positive influence'
of postmodernism for critiquing metanarrative and for 'acknowledging the
multiple forms of otherness as they emerge from differences in subjectivity,
gender and sexuality, race and class' (quoting Hyssens 1984: 50; 1989b:
113). Yet, he warns, there is a danger within this critique when its positive
criticism turns into a 'rage' against any project that seeks 'human eman-
cipation through mobilization of the powers of technology, science and
reason' (1989b: 41). And this rage, he argues, has resulted in a crisis 'of
Enlightenment thought', that represents 'the moral crisis of our times'
(ibid.), stemming from the silence of postmodernism against the mounting
power of global capital and the equally mounting insecurity, vulnerability
and misery of the working classes.

He organizes the second half of the book around his thesis that all of the
postmodernist attention to 'creative destruction' and 'difference' needs to
be balanced with some attention to creative visions for solidified responses
to capitalism. Towards that end, he combines regulation theory with his
version of a spatialized historical materialism to demonstrate how Marxist
analytical tools are required to understand the latest round of capitalist
production which he calls 'flexible accumulation'. While he admits that
doctrinaire Marxism could use some tweaking, for him it still provides
the basic concepts, with roots in the Enlightenment notions of equality,
freedom and universal reason, necessary for exposing the exploitation at
capitalism's core and for imagining viable alternatives for organizing social
power and production. Thinking about difference is important, Harvey

admits, but only if it helps us achieve class solidarity against the relentless march of capital.

So with *The Condition of Postmodernity*, Harvey provocatively dismisses the political possibilities of postmodernism. He does so most directly through a proliferation of rhetorical questions, such as: 'Does [postmodernism/poststructuralism]. . . have a revolutionary potential by virtue of its opposition to all forms of metanarratives (including Marxism, Freudianism, and all forms of Enlightenment reason) and its close attention to "other worlds" and to "other voices" that have far too long been silenced (women, gays, blacks, colonized people with their own histories)? Or is it simply the commercialization and domestication of modernism, and a reduction of the latter's already tarnished aspirations to a *laissez-faire*, "anything goes" market eclecticism?' (1989b: 42). And, by the way, ' if, as the postmodernists insist, we cannot aspire to any unified representation of the world, or picture it as a totality full of connections and differentiations rather than as perpetually shifting fragments, then how can we possibly aspire to act coherently with respect to the world?' (1989b: 52). Frequently, either implicitly or explicitly, Harvey provides his own response to these questions, such as the following reply to the previous one: 'The simple postmodernist answer is that since coherent representation and action are either repressive or illusionary (and therefore doomed to be self-dissolving and self-defeating), we should not even try to engage in some global project' (1989: 52). Postmodernism, in other words, may be an interesting 'intellectual fashion' (1989b: 7), but Marxism engages with the real problems at hand.

The wide-ranging and critical response to this book had a tremendous effect on the direction of Harvey's work in the subsequent decade and catapulted him beyond the disciplinary boundaries of geography to the status of 'social theorist'. On the one hand, his fusion of Marxian analysis of value and uneven development with Regulation Theory, which led to his coinage of 'flexible accumulation', gained wide acclaim across disciplines. The impressive scope of the book across the humanities and social sciences also demonstrated Harvey's facility with theoretical debates and analytical synthesis beyond disciplinary boundaries. On the other hand, Harvey's outright dismissal of the political possibilities within postmodern and poststructuralist theories and his assumption that class was *the difference that mattered* provoked the ire of some of those he had hoped to convince: scholars who worked on social justice, many of whom used Marxism, and who paid close attention to the intersections of class, with race, gender, sexuality, ethnicity and the other categories of social distinction.

Two of the most powerful critiques came from the geographer Doreen

Massey and the cultural critic Rosalyn Deutsche who, in a 1991 *Society and Space* issue, took Harvey to task for his lack of engagement with feminist research, for his reduction of social difference to class, and for an arrogant trivialization of non-Marxist conceptualizations of power, politics and agency (Deutsche 1991; Massey 1991). Deutsche criticized Harvey for discussing all social differences, with the exception of class, as if they were 'illusions' obscuring the real material relationships embedded within capitalism; and for failing to consider seriously the poststructuralist and feminist critiques of Marxism. She accused Harvey of extending a long Marxist tradition of marginalizing any theories that prioritize social categories besides class, and of theorists who do not fit the Marxian mold, and in the process of committing the very crime for which he excoriates the postmodern/poststructuralist camp: failing to attend to the productive effects of his own discourse. One of these effects is to reproduce the dismissal of theorists, many of them feminists, who use poststructuralism to open up debates over politics and agency beyond the traditional Marxist vision of a universal and masculine subject. Moreover, Deutsche argues, he creates a straw-(wo)man out of these many other theorists, many of whose principal concern is social justice, in order to demonstrate the superiority of his own ideas. If Marxism is significant for the postmodernists/poststructuralists as a negative placeholder, then, following Deutsche's critique, feminism and poststructuralism, among other theories deemed to distract from the realities of class processes, occupy the same significance for his analysis in *CPM*.

Massey cleverly plays off Harvey's argument regarding flexible accumulation as the latest round of capitalism to argue that his analysis represents the latest round of sexism, or what she calls 'flexible sexism'. She writes, 'Harvey's modernism is constructed (or perhaps I should say unreconstructed) around an assumed universal whose particular characteristics are not even recognised. Women, for instance, do not figure in the development of the argument, and neither does the possibility of feminist readings on the issues under consideration' (1991: 40). Instead, Harvey, she argues, continues the long tradition of Marxist blindness to feminist contributions by failing to see how feminist debates around postmodernism/poststructuralism could contribute to and enrich his own analysis. Moreover, she criticizes his 'universals' (the class relations he finds to be widereaching) to be, in fact, 'particulars' that reflect his assumption of a universal white, male, heterosexual as principal agent of historical change. The critique, in effect, is that Harvey's vision of solidarity comes about only through a very familiar politics of difference: sexist Marxism.[2]

In the essay 'Postmodern morality plays' (PMP), written largely in reaction to the critiques published by Massey (1991) and Deutsche (1991), Harvey (1992b) simultaneously defends his commitment to class analysis while admitting that his failure to acknowledge his debts to feminist theory limited his argument. The result is that, for the first time in his oeuvre, Harvey engages seriously with feminism in order to demonstrate his 'common cause' with some feminist and poststructuralist approaches that analyse discursive production within the material field of capitalism. Towards this end, he makes much use of Donna Haraway, who, he writes, 'recognizes the dilemma: it is not *difference* which matters, but *significant* difference' (1990: 304). And the following quote from her famous 'A manifesto against cyborgs', makes a first of what become frequent appearances throughout his following publications:

> In the consciousness of our failures, we risk lapsing into boundless difference and giving up on the confusing task of making partial, real connection. Some differences are playful, some are poles of world historical systems of domination. Epistemology is about knowing the difference.
>
> (1990: 202–3, in Harvey 1992b: 304)

These words, written in response to the debates tearing at the heart of feminist scholarship and research during the 1980s, were part of Haraway's (among numerous feminists') efforts to reform feminist work without giving up its hard-won political strength through civil rights politics. The stakes were not unlike those firing Harvey's insistence that we must support working-class politics or otherwise risk forfeiting the gains made by labour unions throughout western Europe and the Americas after years of violent struggle.

This quote reveals a shift in Harvey's approach both to the concept of difference and to his engagement with feminist and poststructuralist scholarship. While, through the publication of *The Condition of Postmodernity*, Harvey insists upon a Marxist self-sufficiency and situates postmodernism/poststructuralism within that framework, in PMP he expresses some 'consciousness of [his] failures' in making some of the connections that are so vital to his project of forming solidarity across fields of differences. This admission becomes more explicit in the 1996 *Justice, Nature and the Geography of Difference* as he embarks upon the project of demonstrating the compatibility of his Marxist approach with those feminist and poststructuralist thinkers who endeavour to make connections between discourses of difference and the material manifestations of power. In fact, he comes to rely quite heavily on Donna Haraway to articulate the significance of social difference and the connections he finds in feminist theorizations of the embodied subject with global capitalist flows. He regularly depends on Iris Marion Young's vision of alliances born out of the recognition of social differences, and he turns to metaphors provided by Adrienne Rich, Nancy Fraser and Julia Kristeva to make his central points. His negotiation of language delves into the conceptual depths behind his visions of solidarity as he moves away from a belief in an 'organic' solidarity, which emanates from some predetermined collective consciousness. Instead, he resorts to Young's argument of 'strategic alliances' by subjects who can and do make choices based on similar objectives, rather than experienced identities. This political ideal of strategic alliances balances the Enlightenment subject, so central to doctrinaire Marxism, who can act according to informed choices while rejecting the exclusions embedded within the assumption of a universal subject who exercises universal reason.

Significant Differences

JNGD opens with an almost wistful nostalgia for the days before the 'hypercritical currents of thought' muddied the political and theoretical waters. Yet, from the outset, Harvey frames this text around a reckoning with theories of difference rather than his previous dismissal. He introduces the book with a pivotal moment in this reckoning process when, in 1994, he found himself caught between a globalization conference, riddled with complex poststructuralist debates, and a Pentecostal revival, refreshingly clear and, for anyone not in the religious right, horrifyingly consolidated. Within such a contrast between the fundamentalist Pentecostals and the anti-fundamentalist theorists, Harvey finds himself musing over the dilemma that shapes this book: if he forfeits the fundamentalist positions of Marxism, he risks eroding its political force, but if he refuses to do so, he risks losing theoretical credibility. He describes this dilemma in these words:

> I wondered what on earth would happen if I started to talk about foundational beliefs in the globalization conference. The deconstructionists would go to work with icy precision, the relativists would callously sneer, the critical theorists would rub their hands and say 'this simply will not do' and the postmodernists would exclaim 'what a dinosaur!' And I myself agree that all foundational beliefs should be scrutinized and questioned. But what troubled me was the thought that when a political group armed with strong and unambiguous foundational beliefs confronts a bunch of doubting Thomases whose only foundational belief is skepticism towards all foundational beliefs, then it is rather easy to predict who will

win. Which led me to the following reflection: the task of critical analysis is not, surely, to prove the impossibility of foundational beliefs (or truth), but to find a more plausible and adequate basis for the foundational beliefs that make interpretation and political action meaningful, creative, and possible (1996a: 2).

While he is unwilling to surrender his commitment to socialism, he does recognize that such a possibility will emerge only through ongoing negotiations across multiple terrains of difference. Towards this end, Harvey chooses some key poststructuralist and feminist interlocutors to demonstrate how Marxism, combined with some of these other theoretical currents, can provide important tools for working towards a more inclusive vision of social justice. So he sets up *JNGD* around a theoretical consideration of such a negotiation between Marxist theories of solidarity and various strands of theory concerning difference. Therefore in a manner consistent with his previous publications, he approaches the topic dialectically and, in good Marxian fashion, constantly seeks the synthesis.

One of the key dialectics around which he organizes the book is that between what he calls, using Raymond Williams, 'militant particularism' contrasted against the 'universal' dimension of global capitalism. Militant particularism is a phrase for capturing the 'way in which personal and particular choices made under given conditions are the very essence of historical-geographical change' (1996a: 28). These conditions do not form an indelible part of someone's identity, but rather the systematic processes that constitute the context in which identity is formed. This emphasis is crucial for Harvey as it de-emphasizes the importance of anyone's particular identity and centres attention squarely on the social arena where the significance of identity is determined. His use of Williams indicates a refusal to allow questions of identity to displace questions of political, economic and social power; or to phrase it another way, he refuses to allow theories of agency to displace those of structure. His logic is analogous to the Marxist scholar W. E. B. DuBois, who, writing in an earlier era, also struggled with the dynamic linking individual identity to systems of racism and capitalist oppression. 'The black man', he wrote in The *Negro Problem*, is simply 'a person who must ride "Jim Crow" in Georgia.'[3] As such, to understand 'black' (or any racial) identity, we must begin with racism and its integration with class. For DuBois, an individual's particular experience or viewpoint of identity is not the starting point.

Harvey leads us down a similar logical path when, during his discussion of militant particularism, he asks:

Can the political and social identities forged under an oppressive industrial order of a certain sort operating in a certain place survive the collapse
or radical transformation of that order? The immediate answer I shall
proffer is 'no' . . . If that is so, then perpetuation of those political identities and loyalties requires perpetuation of the oppressive conditions that
gave rise to them.

(1996a: 40)

Therefore, loyalties to particularized identities are misplaced if the experience of those identities is one of oppression. Instead, we must interrogate
our particular experience of oppression, turn it into militant politics, based
not upon oppressed identities but instead upon a politics of liberation from
systematic exploitation. This assertion restates Harvey's central claim that
an identity politics that begins with social difference cannot be the starting
point for political change; otherwise it will be the ending point.

To steer us away from such a path, Harvey expands Williams's notion of
militant particularism with a theorization of place to shift the debate over
social difference away from one of identifying difference to one of locating difference in relation to similarity. The trick, he explains, is to consider
the 'problems of political identity depending upon the spatial range across
which political thought and action is construed as possible'. Such a consideration means that instead of asking 'who is or is not similar to me', we
ask 'who is or is not in the same position as I?' It is a question that asks:
'Where is the locus of agency?' This question, of course, resonates deeply
with feminist standpoint theory, in addition to other social theorists who
use spatial metaphors to address the age-old question of how do coherent
social politics emerges out of the aspirations and experiences of unique
individuals. But, says Harvey, metaphors based on bad geography do not
delve adequately into the complexities of such a matter. We risk, he writes,
believing that the metaphors of 'margins' and 'voices from the outside' refer
to some ontological location found truly outside of the forces of power they
are used to criticize. This risk poses several dangers, he says, one of which
is to 'slide into acceptance of a postmodern world of fragmentation and
unresolvable difference, to become a mere point of convergence of everything there is as if openness is by definition radical'. (1996a: 104). The key,
he urges, is to construct alliances across the scales of local (particular) and
global (universal) processes.

Crucial to Harvey's argument here is his claim that class identity is not
a militant particularity but one that, given the globality of capital, bridges
the local and global. The difference between class politics, as he sees them,
and other identity politics is that the former seeks to dissolve its identity as
a means to achieving an improved social order. The point of such politics is

not to codify this identity but instead to destroy it. As such, socialism, says Harvey, as a movement 'about the negation of the material conditions of its own political identity' offers a way out of the conundrum created by identity politics that constantly highlights social differences over the means for creating solidarity (1996a: 41). According to his analysis, no other identity politics movement, including feminism, environmentalism, ethnic movements and so on, offer such possibilities.

He makes this argument clear in his elaboration of the body as a most particularized site of identity that is caught in the continuum of global capitalist flows. Towards this end, he draws from feminist interrogations of the body as a socially constructed, rather than natural, site of subjectivity in order to connect poststructuralist theories of subjectivity with Marxist theories of capital accumulation. In this way he combines, as he puts it, 'body-talk' with 'globalization-talk', to illustrate how the discursive production of subjectivity, across diverse schemata of difference, contributes to the material reproduction of capitalism at the global level. His goal is to show how poststructuralist and feminist deconstructions of the body 'as a measure of all things' (1996a: 279) is compatible with a Marxist critique of capitalist accumulation.

For instance, in *JNGD* he extensively quotes Elizabeth Grosz's work *Volatile Bodies* (1993), whose aim, using her words, is 'to explore the constitutive and mutually defining relations between corporeality and the metropolis' (1993: 277). Harvey then concludes, 'This, again, is an unexceptionable version of Marx's argument on the dialectics of social and environmental change' because '[t]he human body is a battleground within which and around which the forces of production of spatio-temporality are perpetually at play' (1996a: 279). Therefore, the individual experience of the body is not in and of itself a measure of social difference; it is both productive of and a product of that experience borne in relation to social processes that generate differences and syntheses across a social field consisting of many bodies (and their correlated identities). Harvey squarely presents this argument in 'The body as an accumulation strategy', an article written simultaneously to portions of *JNGD* (Harvey 1998d). In this piece, Harvey makes good use of Donna Haraway's formulation that the body 'represents an accumulation strategy in the deepest sense' (Haraway and Harvey 1995: 512) (a statement she makes while in conversation with Harvey)[4] as a way to demonstrate that, as such, the body represents the most localized site of global capitalist accumulation and the struggles inherent to it.

Having combined feminist poststructuralism with Marxism to explore the body as a nexus of local-global capitalist processes, Harvey then turns to his core concern: how do we craft a militant politics based on particular experiences of differentiated identities that also challenges the effects of global capitalism that reach into every corner of the globe? His answer is quite simple. You have to choose which differences are the ones that matter in the grand scheme of things. Again, Harvey runs with Haraway's formulation of epistemology being about 'knowing the difference', to claim that 'it is not *difference* that matters, but *significant* difference' (1996a: 358). Essentially, he says that we must establish the terms of significance in the making of 'strategic alliances', of the sort imagined by Iris Young, if we are to achieve any workable vision of social justice. Harvey quotes Young to say, 'Our conception of social justice "requires not the melting away of differences", but institutions that promote reproduction of and respect for group differences without oppression.' With such an argument, Harvey abandons any notion of an organic solidarity emanating from class experience. Rather, the critique of geographical-historical materealism mapped out in *JNGD* requires a solidarity that acknowledges differences while it simultaneously co-ordinates action around agreed norms and visions.

In the end, after combining 'body talk' with 'globalization talk', Harvey reaches conclusions that many of his poststructuralist and feminist interlocutors have rejected outright. He deftly uses what he needs of the poststructuralist feminist interrogation of the embodied subject and of discursive production to prove the significance of class difference and capitalist processes in the field of experience, even though many of the theorists he uses to make this argument refuse to identify any specific difference as primordial or significant (see Haraway 1990; Butler 1993).

Yet, he is not willing to accept fully the implications of an analysis that privileges the body as a site of resistance or that dismantles the concept of conscious and embodied agency. As one critic of *JNGD* astutely writes: 'Harvey demonstrates his anxiety about the dissolution of bodily boundaries that Haraway's manifesto intentionally, perversely celebrates' (Reineke 1997: 369). Harvey's commitment to socialism means that he is committed to the concept of a coherent historical subject whose embodiment provides a basic experience within recognizable social structures. And as such he reduces, as this same critic notes, 'these nuances of embodiment to the singular perspective of monetary flow, which leads to a privileging of class as the defining difference' (Reinecke 1997: 369).

Even those theorists such as Haraway and Young who make frequent appearances in Harvey's explorations of difference refuse to specify a specific difference as significant while both recognize the need for strategizing around significant differences. Harvey is not willing to let the argument stand as they do around a general call for negotiation over differences, whatever they may be, as a common ground of action. Nor is he willing to dilute his argument that capitalist processes generate shared experiences understood at the level of an identifiable subject. Therefore, he insists that despite all of the differences we encounter, and even as we cannot and should not ignore their diversity, we need to figure out how in this capitalist world to navigate this tricky social terrain in order to strategize over a particular difference that, in his view, matters most: class. And, unlike in his pre-1989 work where he does not justify his choice of class, he does so here on the basis of his claim that, within capitalism, it is simply not rational to ignore class for a politics organized around social justice.

Harvey, thus, unapologetically concludes with an Enlightenment (and decidedly non-poststructuralist) faith in the ability of people to find common cause around class politics. While in *JNGD* he seeks dialogue with some of the theorists he had formerly dismissed in *CPM*, he still uses their work for his instrumental ends: to prove the prominence of capitalist processes and the social divisions intrinsic to them in contemporary times. Even as he forfeits his previously held belief that class solidarity derives directly from the shared experiences of the working classes and requires instead a strategic decision to organize around this difference in particular, he does not dilute his resolve that the social difference that matters most in his map of the world is the difference of class. He therefore uses poststructuralist and feminist theorizations to demonstrate the relevance of his Marxism that examines the constant production of social difference but also to make a case for making a determination that class, above other social differences, is not a militant particularity. It is a social difference that, he argues, crosses the scale from the particular to the universal.

Make of It What You Will

Within the critical response to *JNGD*, Harvey's allegiance to socialism and to a prioritizing of class difference, as indicative of a universal condition under capitalism, comes under powerful attack, even from some of those allied with his overall objective (Corbridge 1998; Hartsock 1998a; Young 1998). Iris Young, for instance, writes, 'The suggestion that feminism or environmentalism is more particularist than a working-class movement seems odd. Women are everywhere, at least, as universal a category of workers' (1998: 38). Hartsock lauds his use of dialectics while criticizing his analysis of margins to ignore how some people are marginalized and find themselves in identities that do not always suit them but which they cannot instantly discard, like old clothing. Others criticize his instrumentalist use of poststructuralism to reach his unproven conclusion that class is *the significant difference* (Braun 1998: 715). And numerous others point to the disjointed and 'craggy' nature of this book, whose own metanarrative zigzags across disciplines and rhetorical styles (Eagleton 1997; McDowell 1998a). While ranging across a number of perspectives and disciplines, these reviews strongly critique Harvey's insistence that class always matters in this capitalist world and, as such, should be given theoretical and political priority among other, more particular differences.

Harvey summarizes his response to his many critics in the article 'The Humboldt connection' (1998a). 'To begin with', he writes,

> my basic argument is that difference is as much about geography (locali-
> ties, ecologies, spatialities, places, etc) as it is about race, class, gender,
> ethnicity, religion and the like. This angle on the production of difference
> gets lamentably covered over in much of the conventional literature even
> though it is not hard to excavate its significance. The implication is that
> the understanding of difference in much of the humanities and the social
> sciences needs to be complemented in important ways by a strong appre-
> ciation of uneven geographical development. The humanities do not have
> a monopolized lock upon the definition of what is or is not significant dif-
> ference, and part of my purpose was to challenge their prevailing wisdom
> on that topic with some traditional geographic commonsense.
>
> (1998a: 728)

These words segue directly into the introduction of his subsequent book, *Spaces of Hope* (Harvey 2000a), which reads somewhat like a clarifica- tion of his main points in *JNGD* that had been bantered about in scores of critical reviews. Admitting that *JNGD* was his 'least coherent' book, Harvey explains how his effort to combine (poststructuralist, feminist, post- modernist, Lacanian) 'body-talk' with (Marxian, modernist, structuralist) 'globalization-talk' may have led to scattered theoretical formulations. Yet, his goal was to 'explore the political and intellectual consequences of making such a connection' for getting at the 'tricky question of the relation between "particularity" and "universality" in the construction of know- ledge' and political practice (2000a: 15).

Holding firm to the notion of 'militant particularity', Harvey paral- lels Williams' *Resources of Hope* with his own *Spaces of Hope* in order to juxtapose the pessimism he identifies as postmodernist/poststructuralist defeatism with an 'optimism of the intellect' whose goal is to illustrate pos- sible alliances over impossible ones. He writes:

> What is now striking is the dominance of an almost fairy-tale like belief,
> held on all sides alike, that once upon a time there was structuralism,

modernism, industrialism, Marxism or what have you and now there is poststructuralism, postmodernism, postindustrialism, post-Marxism, post-colonialism, and so forth . . . my point here is . . . to point to damage that the fairy-tale reading of the difference between the 'then' and the 'now' is doing to our abilities to confront the changes occurring around us. Cutting ourselves off from Marx is to cut off our investigative noses to satisfy the superficial face of contemporary intellectual fashion.

(2000a: 12)

In his conclusion to the book, Harvey provides his own fairy-tale based on a dream he had of a utopia called, 'Edilia'. This utopia is a post-revolutionary world led by *The Mothers of Those Yet to be Born . . .* in alliance with the scientists, intellectuals, spiritual thinkers, and artists who had liberated themselves from their deadening political and ideological subservience to class power and to military-theocratic authority' (2000a: 263). In this utopian world, where numerous individual differences (gender, race, regional . . .) exist as positive attributes of social collectivity, class has disappeared. Harvey has imagined a world where he can finally admit the insignificance of capitalism. This peculiar denouement to *Spaces of Hope* follows from chapters that spell out some of his familiar, core concerns, all organized around a geographical-historical materialism which recognizes how 'the universality of a class struggle originates with the particularity of the person'. Harvey's Edilia, his dream, carries the clear message: even in his subconscious, his vision of difference always accompanies one of solidarity. And as his subtitle to the chapter suggests, he does not wish to justify his dream for socialism but instead leaves his readers to 'Make of it what you will'.

Given that Harvey is one of the most prolific scholars of the contemporary era and that he continues to publish widely on the dialectic of difference and synthesis, it would be unwise to attempt here a conclusion of his work on the topic. In a recent book, *The New Imperialism*, he continues to challenge his readers to contemplate socialist possibilities within an increasingly hostile landscape. Notably absent from these publications, particularly the original lectures contained within the latter, is the defence of Marxism against theories of difference that has marked his work in the wake of *The Condition of Postmodernity*. Instead, he shifts his focus to contemplate the political possibilities presented by neo-Marxist scholars, particularly by Hardt and Negri in their widely acclaimed *Empire* (2000) who call for a decentralized vision of political alliances that corresponds to a decentralized vision of imperialism.

Harvey's decision not to engage with theories of difference, as articulated by feminist and postmodernist/poststructuralist thinkers, allows him to avoid the abstract negotiations over the dialectical configurations of sameness and difference and their meaning for agency. Instead, he situates his work more firmly within the contemporary Marxist debates, which emphasize the need for incorporating diverse notions of agency and politics without foregoing an analysis of a consolidated power organized around capitalist and imperialist interests. Yet, while Harvey embraces this call for a 'more inclusionary politics', that recognizes social difference as a central organizational strategy, he cautions: 'The danger lurks that . . . the exclusionary politics of the local will dominate the need to build an alternative globalization at a variety of geographical scales' (2003b: 177).

The urgency in his writing derives from his conclusion that the current wars in Iraq and Afghanistan reflect a new round of capitalist accumulation, via what he calls the politics of dispossession. And Harvey orients his argument around a pointed call to academics to seek strategies for forming alliances, internationally and across fields of difference, that will confront the powers driving the wars. So even as he agrees with Hardt and Negri that lessons for such alliances are to be learned from the many different anti-globalization or alternative globalization movements around the world, he urges that we envision such alliances, despite their diversity, around a commonly understood vision of capitalist exploitation and imperialism. He writes:

> Ways must be found to acknowledge the significance of multiple identifications (based on class, gender, locality, culture, etc.) that exist within populations, the traces of history and tradition that arise from the ways in which they made themselves in response to capitalist incursions, as they see themselves as social beings with distinctive and often contradictory qualities and aspirations . . . Some way must be found, both theoretically and politically, to move beyond the amorphous concept of 'the multitude' without falling into the trap of 'my community, locality, or social group right or wrong'. Above all, the connectivity between struggles within expanded reproduction and against accumulation by dispossession must be assiduously cultivated.
>
> (2003b: 179)

How such connections are to be accomplished remains unclear, and here Harvey is susceptible to some of his own critiques of Hardt and Negri regarding the amorphous conceptualization of alliances. He never lays out the path towards forming those ever important links, and we are left wondering how on earth people from around the world can make the leaps between the lived experiences of struggle that unfold in highly particular ways and the recognition, at some level of abstraction, that common issues bind these experiences in some important ways. That such leaps are necessary, few in leftist or progressive politics would disagree, but how to achieve them across fields and scales of differences remains the ongoing challenge for scholars and activists.

One is also left wondering why in *The New Imperialism*, after so much discussion in previous publications, Harvey does not include feminist and poststructuralist/postmodernist theories of differences in his appeal for making connections across them. His decision not to do so affords him a measure of simplicity that he longed for both in *Justice, Nature and the Geography of Difference* and in *Spaces of Hope*. This simplicity lies in the dual assumption that differences can be recognized as such and then that, through negotiation or agreement or some other enlightenment appeal to reason, these differences can be put aside for strategic purposes. The obvious necessity behind such manoeuvres, according to Harvey, is sufficient enough to motivate them. This position does not find easy supported among core poststructuralist/postmodernist and feminist scholars who have solidly argued that the goal of *moving beyond difference* as a means to achieving solidarity is misplaced. For as many such scholars have argued, this emphasis distracts attention from the many ways that difference itself can often provide the focal point for action.

Harvey does not settle this debate in his expansive oeuvre. He engages with it and then decides for his own strategic purposes to leave it aside. Whether this decision represents a failure in his analysis or whether it takes him closer to his goal of envisioning consolidated responses to capitalism remains to be seen. Certainly, we have not yet heard his final word on this matter as he continues the long, hard journey towards imagining a politics of synthesis in a world rife with difference.

Notes

1 Harvey does not always distinguish between postmodernism and poststructuralism in his work, and he often uses the former as a catch-all that includes the latter.
2 This feminist critique of the sexist and/or masculinist assumptions within traditional Marxism derives from numerous scholars who work across disciplines. See, for instance, Massey 1984; Hartsock 1987; Scott 1988; Christopherson 1989; Barrett 1991; Gibson-Graham 1996.
3 This quote and my understanding of DuBois's intention with it come from Fields 2001: 54.
4 'Nature, politics and possibilities: a debate and discussion with David Harvey and Donna Haraway' see 1995d.

6

David Harvey on Cities

Sharon Zukin

Many years ago, when I began to teach courses in urban sociology, I discovered David Harvey's *Social Justice and the City*. In the pages of this book, Harvey traced his painstaking way from a liberal to a 'revolutionary' view of the spatial organization of social inequality, locating its source in capitalism's political economy and placing the city at the centre of capitalists' – especially property owners' – constant drive to improve their moral, political and economic position relative to other social groups. I, being innocent of a geographical education but attracted to the critical tradition in sociology, felt the sting of immediate enlightenment. Sociology in the United States had a rich tradition of urban ethnography, and in the late 1960s and early 1970s sociologists, particularly in France and England, carried out critical investigations of the roles of the state, industrialists and real estate developers in urban redevelopment. But Harvey's work – which unlike sociology was discursive, though he dislikes the term, rather than empirical, and redolent with references to classical economic theories – shed a clear light on urban problems of the day that mainstream sociologists circled warily around or utterly ignored: ghettos, the enrichment of suburbs and impoverishment of cities, and redevelopment that 'merely move[s] the poverty around' (Harvey 1973a: 143). 'There is good reason to believe', Harvey wrote, 'that the market mechanism is the culprit in a sordid drama.'

This reduction of urban problems to the persistence of markets is alien to sociologists. 'It isn't sociology, it's urban economics', an older sociologist whom I esteemed for his critical acuity said when I described Harvey's work as a part of the 'new' urban sociology. Or 'if you're interested in space', as another sociologist kindly said, 'you should talk to geographers'.

But Harvey evoked another sociological tradition – that of Marx on the perpetuation of inequality and Engels on the ability of a ruling group to camouflage poverty behind a glittering façade of urban improvements – and used space to stand the Chicago School of urban sociologists on its head. By questioning the spatial centrality at the core of the famous concentric zone diagram of Chicago's historical development, he traced the roots of urban inequality to the scarcity and consequent value of well-situated land. Harvey was not interested in describing how people live in cities, or even – despite a half-hearted attempt in the first chapter of *Social Justice and the City* – in deciphering the social and cultural symbolism of either spaces or buildings. He did, however, focus on the self-interest involved in controlling urban territory. This led him to set aside the fine-grained study of neighbourhoods and communities that sociologists tend to do, for assertions of 'central business district imperialism', 'suburban exploitation of the central city', and the advantages of neighbourhoods not for collective social action but for segmenting ethnic, religious and social class cohesion and minimizing both contact and conflict among opposing groups (Harvey 1973: 78, 81). Harvey was not to find his forte in documenting the rich community life of urban ghettos or analysing the checkered successes of accumulating social capital in urban slums. Instead, his approach relied on a selective reading of urban economists, planners, political scientists and sociologists who point to clear winners and losers in the urban realm. Winners live in central districts of collective symbolic value or leafy suburbs with green trees and clean air. And losers live in slums.

No wonder Harvey's work can be intensely irritating to sociologists. His entire oeuvre is founded upon this zero-sum situation – with little concern for contingencies, since his methodology comes from Marx's *Capital* and a geographer's professional commitment to space. He also turns a blind eye, or deaf ear, towards aesthetics. Unlike most urbanists whom I know, he does not claim to be enchanted by the visual and overall sensual qualities that make cities distinctive and real. Unlike such materialist historians as Fernand Braudel, he risks masking the uniqueness of cities by emphasizing their structural conformity with general strategies of increasing economic value. Cities, Harvey teaches us, are built for the circulation of capital – whether that capital is human (the workforce), commodity (goods and information) or abstract finance (credit for buying property and creating new construction). In this view, the Cross-Bronx Expressway is just an updated version of the Boulevard Haussmann; the dystopia of Baltimore's Harborplace or New York's World Trade Center at its commanding height is countered by the remembered utopia of the Paris Commune and the even briefer utopian public space of Union Square Park after 9/11.

Yet this unregenerate Marxist structuralism isn't wrong. Harvey's grasp of the dynamics of urban growth and decline offers a surer guide to current events than a more partial, more circumspect and less reductionist view. Although the specific facts are different, a random reading of the newspaper confirms the general points he made about cities thirty years ago: the mayor of New York City has 'unveiled an ambitious plan . . . to reduce the number of homeless people in the city by two-thirds over the next five years, proposing to build thousands of units of new housing'; the new Time Warner Center has hung a giant banner advertising Samsung Electronics, whose store is a tenant in the indoor mall, over their huge glass front wall, and tried to prevent a newspaper photographer from taking a picture of the building from the public sidewalk; the private Regional Plan Association, a civic group that has long advocated building cross-metropolitan transit lines and office towers on the West Side of Manhattan, has taken a formal stand opposing the mayor's plan to build an expensive stadium there for a professional football team; and, despite extraordinarily low crime rates, a rash of bizarre incidents of 'brazen violence' has alarmed tourists and residents alike (*New York Times*, 24 June 2004). After electoral changes and endless reforms, the city is still bedevilled by inadequate provision for basic human needs, a private sector that, despite internal conflicts, implodes into and takes over the public sphere, and an uncontrollable violence that expresses the basic insecurity of modern urban life. This is indeed consistent with David Harvey's (1985a: 1) vision of the city – the result of 'an underlying process that precludes liberation from the more repressive aspects of class-domination and all of the urban pathology and restless incoherence that goes with it'.

Although Harvey has incorporated new elements over the years, his vision remains remarkably consistent. Efforts to integrate gender, culture and environmentalism into the analysis have not changed his persistent emphasis on the power of capital to make, and remake, urban space. Yet the seasoning of Harvey's approach suggests a wider appreciation of politics and culture and opens the door to a more metaphorical examination of urban imaginaries than he himself may accomplish. David Harvey's work begins, and ends, with cities as expressions of capital, passing through ever more cultural tropes of speculation, entrepreneurialism and the body politic. If 'capital' suggests the power of investors and employers to remake the physical environment and social relations of cities, 'speculation' connotes both social relations and habits of thought that, reflecting capital, spill over from the public to the private realm. 'Entrepreneurialism' is the resulting culture of cities and residents alike, as they take risks in order to survive. The 'body politic' is the imagined form the city assumes in both our collective actions and individual dreams; it represents idealism as well as opportunism, art as well as life.

Cities of Capital

Late twentieth-century Marxists characteristically struggled to define the determining power of capital *vis-à-vis* supposedly autonomous factors – culture, politics and gender – in creating social life. Cities appeared to be one of those social creations that tease the limits of autonomy, for, since they are entirely constructed by human action, they both reflect underlying social structures and shape them in unpredictable ways. Moreover, in contrast to rural life, cities create a tangible aura of difference – a way of life that emphasizes hazard, strangeness and free choice: a mental paradigm that seduces as well as abandons. Influenced by Henri Lefebvre, sociologists and geographers of the 'new' urban sociology tended to resolve the balance by making an analytic distinction between the economically determined organization of urban space and a culturally freer urbanism that serves as a form of collective self-expression. Although Manuel Castells (1976), working in Paris, boldly declared there was no 'urban' world outside of modern capitalism, David Harvey (1973a: 307), writing in Baltimore, more cautiously separated 'the city as a built form' – shaped mainly by the profit motive and the needs of production – from 'urbanism as a way of life'.

Harvey (1973a: 306) took Lefebvfre's point that urbanism is 'rather like science'. Both become more differentiated over time, to counter the increasing standardization of global systems of production, and both can either help or hinder the dominant organization of production. Like science, urbanism develops its own ideologies, discursive images, and, we may add, power players. It develops its own cognitive models that represent these power players' interests, but also develops different models – which may take the form of subcultures, alternative policies or utopias – out of more democratic or even spontaneous practices. Like other critical urbanists, Harvey acknowledged the contrast between the repressive potential of 'effective space' and the liberating potential of 'created space'. Yet even created space – as well as the activity of creating space – often seems to be outside of 'our individual or collective control [and] fashioned by forces alien to us' (Harvey 1973a: 310). The crucial point is that the major axes of repression and liberation coexist in cities, for this is where the core of modern economies lies.

Like sociologists, who have not fully escaped from defining cities according to the common-sense phenomenology of size, density and heterogeneity,

Harvey's earliest formulation (1973a: 224–40) defines the city in a fairly static way, as the geographically concentrated location of a social surplus. But he ties the development of cities in general to the broad historical shift from economies based on reciprocity to those based on redistribution. The growth of cities depends on the development of market as well as state mechanisms for moving people and goods, and when different modes of redistribution become routinized in social activity, so they also become set in place. All redistributive systems give rise to institutionalized hierarchies that carve their own moral geography and geographical order. As researchers thought at the time, each form of economic integration – with its own powerful elites or ruling class – would create its own distinctive urban forms and iconic built environment. 'It is no accident', Harvey (1973a: 32) writes with apologies for using such 'crude examples', 'that church and chapel spires dream over Oxford (a town created in the age of church power), whereas, in the age of monopoly capitalism, it is the Chrysler building and the Chase-Manhattan Bank building which brood over Manhattan Island'.

Though this is not so poetic as the literary critic John Berger's (1985: 67) depiction – 'Within the history of capitalism, Manhattan is the island reserved for those who are damned because they have hoped excessively' – it does compel us to visualize cities as landscapes of power. Without the need to carry out case studies and verify hypotheses, we immediately understand location to be a social question. Indeed, all urban questions are axiomatically social questions, founded in conflicts over power rather than – as other paradigms would say – in efforts to restore balance, improve efficiency, or sort out 'natural' ecological niches from the movement of people and activities. It is true that the original Chicago School in the early 1900s understood something of the political-economic nature of these movements, for what is the concentric zone theory but a picture of valorization and devalorization of land according to locational decisions made by social and economic elites? They also understood how problematic it is to carve a single 'moral order' out of the urban population's social and ethnic diversity. But, as Harvey (1973a: 131; 2001a: 68–89) writes, they weren't directly concerned with the conflicts – especially the economic conflicts – that shape social solidarities. By contrast, seeing a city as a landscape of power poses the question not only of where, but also of why distinctive urban communities are formed. Informal racial segregation, unequal access to mortgages, ability and desire to move industries and high-class residences out of cities to greenfield sites: these factors, that were so obvious by the 1970s, were already reshaping American cities at the time of the early Chicago School (see Rae 2003). Yet, for years, mainstream studies failed to pull them into the structural dynamic of urban growth and decline.

Harvey's early essays refer in passing to levers of social power like zoning, racial redlining and ethnic subcultures. But he himself was more interested in the instrumentality of economic power over labour and land. Following Lefebvre, he wrote that capitalists continually shift their investments from one circuit of capital to another – from one industrial sector to another, from industry to finance, from finance to real estate, and back again – to make higher profits. Though this doesn't exactly show how different areas of cities rise and fall, it does explain the ebb and flow of the growth dynamic and points to disinvestment as an inevitable process of capitalist economies that was only beginning to be discussed at the time. My own interest was piqued by the suggestion that the built environment of cities could be forced to become obsolete. While Harvey thought of this in terms of material obsolescence, his reference to the planned obsolescence of consumer products like cars, which was also beginning to be the subject of widespread criticism (e.g. Rothschild 1973), could also be applied to the *cultural* obsolescence of individual buildings, types of buildings and urban districts. What we were beginning to understand about the politics of slum clearance – the ostensible purpose of state-financed urban renewal from the 1940s through the early 1970s – underscored the manipulations of property owners, mayors, legislators and public-sector bureaucrats, who condemned huge swaths of the city's built environment as 'blighted' or obsolete, in order to wrest profit and glory from wholesale demolition and new construction (see Caro 1974). By the same token, the high stakes surrounding redevelopment of the urban centre reflected the opportunity to charge monopoly rent on a unique commodity – whether that commodity was land well served by transportation networks, historic architecture, or some other manifestation of a highly valued and labelled *terroir* (Harvey 1973a: 176–94; 2001a: 394–411). These observations led directly to Neil Smith's (1979) theory that shifts in housing investment follow a 'rent gap' and to my own research (Zukin 1982) on the manipulated obsolescence of manufacturing lofts in order to convert them to artists' and middle-class housing (but also see Topalov 1973). Even before we read Lefebvre, we learned from Harvey that the production of space, buildings and districts is a *social* as well as a material process – not only in terms of a sociological event, such as like-minded people deciding to live together, but even more so in terms of economic and political self-interest.

Harvey's historical examination of mid-nineteenth-century Paris (1985a) painted these processes on a larger, even an epic, canvas. The movement of capital from one circuit to another paid for the building of transportation infrastructure, especially railways, from which financiers, manufacturers, consumers and the city itself all drew benefits (1985a: 70–3). The 'rental sorting of land to uses' (1985a: 93) was part of a huge property boom manipulated by both bankers and the state, in which one competitive banking dynasty, the Pereires, acted in concert with the infamous prefect of Paris under Louis Napoleon's rule, Baron Haussmann (Harvey 1985a: 79). Not only did preferential access to credit fuel speculation, leading to a doubling of property values through the 1850s and 1860s, it also shaped new patterns of industrial location and social class segregation (1985a: 92–6). Industries and workers were pushed out of the centre by state-sponsored demolition, new construction and higher rents – a clear foreshadowing of twentieth-century urban renewal. By the time Harvey wrote about Paris, moreover, in the early 1980s, cities in the United States and Britain were reeling from the effects of industrial relocation to low-wage areas and gentrification. These processes were also presaged by socio-spatial changes managed by Haussmann before 1870: 'the *"embourgeoisement"* (or "gentrification", as we might now call it) of much of the Parisian housing market', and 'the deindustrialization of the city center' (1985a: 94, 103).

Studying the deliberate strategies that were used to rebuild Paris as an imperial city ripped the last shred of innocence from viewing our contemporary processes of urban change. Overcrowding and homelessness were clearly related to reducing the amount of affordable housing near the city centre. The long daily journey from home to work reflected the conquest, or reconquest, of the centre for high-status and non-productive uses, mainly state offices, monuments and banks. Inability to find jobs near traditional working-class neighbourhoods – what we began to call the 'job–skills mismatch' in the 1980s – was not only rooted in large, polluting factories' move to the suburbs, but also in the higher rents charged for property in the centre, rents that only banks, luxury goods boutiques and affluent households could afford. The redevelopment of Paris, in short, showed the strong arm of the state supporting rising land values through new transportation infrastructure, industrial relocation and gentrification. Both state and market shaped the modern city for capital accumulation and circulation.

But capitalist modernization opens contradictory paths of urban development. On the one hand, the dominant social group in Paris – the republican bourgeoisie – opened space to further its economic and political interests; on the other, this group limited the use of space to affluent consumers like themselves who could pay for the amusements (cafés, theatres) and commodities (in the display windows of department stores) that now adorned the modern city (1985a: 204–5). Everyone else was condemned to play the role of a spectator. Most Parisians took pride, no doubt, in these visible displays of modernity, but they were unable to buy their way in. Yet the public profusion of private, class-based representations also fuelled discontent.

High prices and political corruption stirred old grievances, while a bitter sense of dispossession and a creative use of all kinds of grassroots organizations eventually mobilized the population to active revolt. Modern cities give rise to dreams, as Walter Benjamin (1999) wrote. Though Harvey doesn't make these dreams explicit, he connects the experience of cities, as Benjamin does, to both the negative charge of the commodity fetish and the positive charge of urban social movements – alternatives that are made possible by new wide streets and boulevards, new means of communication and newly mobile men and women (also see Fritzsche 1996).

Reading Walter Benjamin (1973) and Marshall Berman (1982) on mid-nineteenth-century Paris, Harvey is compelled to wonder how it felt to live in the city at that time. On this point, he follows the others and turns to literature. The poems of Baudelaire, and novels by Flaubert and Zola, portray the loneliness of the crowd, the alienation of the *flaneur* in face of the fast pace of change, and the sense of betrayal, on the part of democrats who had taken to the barricades in 1848, by political authorities. Like Baudelaire and his contemporaries, Harvey is fascinated by the simultaneous swirling images of wealth and poverty, technological progress and social conservatism and alienation and association. Like Berman, his own contemporary, he is struck by the affluent classes' casual disregard of the poor in their midst. All of this connects the city to broad themes of modernity, leading to a dual emphasis on both the political economy of the rapacious capitalist 'growth machine' (Molotch 1976) and the tenacious culture of community of the urban working class. These topics were, to be sure, in the air, for, along with the translation of Benjamin's essays on Paris into English and Berman's eloquent defence of neighbourhood in the face of state-sponsored highway construction, they entered mainstream urban sociology in the United States shortly after Harvey published the essay 'Paris, 1850–1870' (in Harvey 1985a: 63–220), with John Logan and Harvey Molotch's (1986) examination of the continuing struggle between use-value (in the socio-spatial form of community) and exchange-value (in the spatial transformations of growth-mongering entrepreneurs).

Unlike these books, however, much of Harvey's essay on Paris works over data on changing industrial structure, working-class wages, division of labour in the household, divisions within the working class, and the very foundations of social history – nutrition, education and social and moral control. He uses archival research as well as new French labour history, especially Alain Cottereau's (1980) edition of a commentary on working class life *avant la commune*, written by a former worker who rose to the rank of distinguished manufacturer, which made a stir in Paris in the early 1980s. If I have a complaint about Harvey's essay, it is that there is too much material for such a short work to hold. The use of social history, moreover, raises methodological questions: How much should we know about social class formation to understand a city? To what degree does the sense of community reflect social class, and to what degree is it fostered by geographical territory? Are urban social movements – as fragmented by skill, wage and spatial divisions as Harvey shows they are, and as entranced as men and women are by spectacular shopping, entertainment and mega-events – necessarily revolutionary? But Harvey's goal is to create a detailed, in-depth panorama of a city at the crux of 'capitalist modernity' (1985a: 108). This essay is intended to be not only a study of a city on the edge, but a companion to Engels's book on the working class in Manchester in 1844, and an explanation of the conditions that produced a remarkable utopia – the Paris Commune of 1870–71 – 'a singular, unique, and dramatic event, perhaps the most extraordinary of its kind in capitalist urban history' (1985a: 218). If the essay on Paris is a slightly less orthodox Marxist product than the work that immediately preceded it, it is none the less also guided by a revolutionary eschatology.

Speculation

Harvey accepts Georg Simmel's classic formulation: the modern urban mentality, or consciousness, is permanently adjusted to flux. But in a companion piece to 'Paris, 1850–1870', he (1985a: 1–35) insists on framing the sociologist's concern with the urban dweller's mental attitude by the social power of money. What Simmel described as the metropolis's jarring effect of a constant flow of passers-by, activities and things, Harvey (1985a: 29) depicts as 'the sensation of disruption and incoherence' reflecting the fragmentation of land ownership, community, and spatial and temporal harmony – all caused by the money economy. Cities intensify the money economy by refracting its social power through many different markets – primarily, for housing, land and labour, but also for capital itself. Though the financial institutions that invested in the rebuilding of nineteenth-century Paris democratized money, by making different scales of investment available to Parisians on different income levels, they also popularized financial speculation and increased debt. The quintessential response to these stimuli was not only, as Simmel famously termed it, a 'jaded' attitude; it was the attitude of the speculator.

When Harvey later expanded his essay into a book-length treatment of Paris, he used Daumier's prints, as well as novels by Balzac and Zola, to illustrate the prevalence of speculation in all walks of urban life throughout the nineteenth century (2003a: 33–5, 39, 51, 55). The speculative schemes of property developers, who would tear the city apart and rebuild it in their image, find parallels in the dreams of young men who migrate to Paris from the provinces in search of careers and wealth and the ambitions of young women who want to join the world of fashion and celebrity. Both men and women learn to choose their clothing as a speculative investment, for Parisians judge other people by appearances. Both also try to attach themselves to patrons, friends and lovers for the social advantages they can offer, giving a more speculative cast to urban relationships than ever before. The modern city makes upward social mobility possible – at the price of betrayal of old solidarities and vertiginous reversals of fortune: 'the rapid shifts that occur as individuals participate in the high-stakes pursuit of money, sex, and power' (2003a: 39).

There is a remarkable synergy between urban redevelopment, urban consciousness and the expansion of financial credit (1985a: 76ff; 2003a: 117ff). Even in the nineteenth century, the Bourse – the stock market – dominated individuals' dreams of making a fortune as well as the fortunes of the city itself. Both 'Paris, 1850–1870' (1985a) and the later *Paris, Capital of Modernity* (2003a) reproduce Chargot's dramatic lithograph of 1875 which portrays the Bourse as a vampire preying on Parisians' souls, buttressed, in the book, by passages from Zola's *La curée* and *L'argent* (1985a: 81; 2003a: 118, 122). Speculation is both the lifeblood of the city and the mechanism that drains it of vitality, the instigator of greed that turns men and women into vampires and plunges them into debt. As Harvey realizes, this acerbic view presents a stunning analogy with indictments of the effects of financial speculation on cities in our time, beginning with the 'masters of the universe' described in Tom Wolfe's novel *Bonfire of the Vanities* in the 1980s and the dot-com boom and bust of the 1990s, and becoming more ominous with the broad dependence on speculative stock market investments through the 2000s to fund mortgages, pensions and consumer debt.

Excavating the social dynamics of speculation in nineteenth-century Paris brings up two motifs of structural change that have shadowed urban fortunes in recent years: first, the annihilation of space by time and second, creative destruction (1985a: 25–9). Just as newly built roadways and railways in the nineteenth century sped commuters and commodities from one end of the city to another, so the development of air delivery systems, fax machines and eventually the World Wide Web enabled the swift movement of plans and inventory, and soon enough, jobs, from corporate headquarters and design centres in one region of the world to factories in another (1989b: 293). As Harvey points out, both motifs of violent structural change date back to the preindustrial era. Annihilating space *and* time was first mentioned metaphorically by Alexander Pope, then picked up by

Goethe, and instrumentally revised by observers of the railway journey, including Karl Marx, in the 1840s (1985a: 15; 2003a: 48). The term creative destruction, which also originated in an eighteenth-century metaphor, was revived in a pseudonymous Parisian guidebook of 1867 (1985a: 178). By the time Harvey applied these ideas to urban redevelopment, they were less metaphor than actual strategies of shifting capital investment from high-wage to low-wage regions of the world and from less profitable to more profitable sectors. Tragically for cities, the shifts that are envisioned as a 'spatial fix', as Harvey termed it, are not permanently fixed in space. Extensive investment in urban infrastructure of any sort only represents a temporary solution to capitalists' search for higher profits.

When Harvey published the first version of his essay on Paris, it was already clear that the industrial cities of the West were becoming obsolete as sites of capital accumulation. From New York to Glasgow, the biggest, most commercial cities were eliminating all traces of manufacturing, from steel plants and loft buildings to cargo docks and working-class housing, and attempting to refashion themselves into consumption spaces, tourist destinations and command centres of the global financial economy (1985a: 269–71). Smaller cities like Liverpool or Baltimore, with a more significant working-class base, had fewer options. Indeed, they often wound up using their depleted resources to subsidize wealthy corporations either to delay closing production facilities or to locate new jobs in town. Places that had undergone roughly the same sort of industrial development in an earlier era now confronted intense inter-urban competition for new investment and employment without being able to offer any special, let alone monopoly, advantages. Under these conditions, urban populations didn't rebel, especially if they had speculated on the future of their community by buying homes; they 'tend[ed] to rally to the cause of any dominant class alliance that seem[ed] to offer even temporary or partial relief from the threat of devaluation' (1985a: 270–1). Yet, like many other observers at the time, including Michael Moore, whose movie *Roger and Me* (1989) provided a caustic view of General Motors' role in forcing Flint, Michigan, into mass unemployment and a wave of bankruptcies, David Harvey predicted that continued job loss, corporate subsidies and fiscal crisis of local government would lead to disaster, including 'explosions of uncontrollable frustration on the part of a swelling urban under-class' (1985a: 271).

But the decline of old industrial cities was neither definitive nor universal. As the highly relevant oxymoron implies, creative destruction eliminates less productive investments while sowing the seeds of new forms of economic growth. Shorn of Schumpeter's romanticism of the intrepid entrepreneur, creative destruction asserts that capitalist investors of one sort or another will continually develop new strategies of accumulation to overcome the failures of the old regime. If cities are truly spaces of capital, they will rise – in some form – again. Yet whether the investors were bankers betting on the expansion of global financial markets, computer nerds tinkering in a garage or underemployed artists renovating manufacturing lofts for studio space, the creative destruction that began during the 1970s gave rise to what looked, at first, like a drastically different world. Robotic production and electronic communication sped the pace of change and seemed to make entire social communities and geographical spaces obsolete. Governments broke the social contract between capital and labour that had supported decades of industrial peace and productivity, provided good wages for the securely employed and defended Keynesian mass consumption. The cultural paradigm of modernity, based on progress, planning and a belief that basic social security could be guaranteed, was shaken by new expressions – as well as fears – of fragmentation. In a word, social philosophers, artists and writers believed the world had entered a new age of postmodernity.

Yet David Harvey (1989b) wasn't so sure about this. Many of the new features of global capitalism looked familiar. Deregulation of financial markets enhanced the power of finance capital. Just-in-time deliveries and outsourced jobs renewed the annihilation of space by time. Shifts of manufacturing to many low-wage countries while financial firms concentrated in a few global capitals suggested a complicated reorganization of the framework of capital accumulation: a simultaneous spatial decentralization of production and an organizational centralization of power. Borrowing the language of the social regulation school of French economists, Harvey (1989b: 121–2) suggested that capitalism remained the same mode of production that we had known for years but with a different mode of regulation – and a different way of signifying social consciousness.

Most important for cities, shifts of investment and compression of space and time allowed frustration to vent through grandiose projects of urban revitalization. In New York, London and other financial capitals of the global economy, money poured into new skyscraper construction, often to supplement and expand the historic financial centre. High-rise, mixed-use projects glorified individual urban speculators like New York real estate developer Donald Trump and the Toronto firm Olympia and York, as well as collective speculators in the new transnational order, mainly major financial corporations and investment banks. The 'signature' designs of celebrated new architects put their mark on the cities' skylines and differentiated one product of property speculation from another. Yet, though cities began to look different, especially in the expensive central districts where land values were high, the compression of space and time shaped a portfolio of visual images that was quickly applied all over the world. Just as in manufacturing, product differentiation and image valorization in cities established a new dialectic of specialization and standardization that only sharpened inter-urban competition.

So Harvey traces the origins of the 'postmodern turn' to the competitive dynamics of capitalist markets. But unlike modernism at its mid-twentieth-century peak, the great new projects of postmodern urban redevelopment originated in, and served, the private sector. Property developers glamour-ized the volatility of capital by erecting new objects of attraction on the ruins of the past; they mirrored the shallowness of economic recovery by offering reflective surfaces of glass and marble and, eventually, of new materials like titanium. Elected officials and community groups worked with urban designers to incorporate eclectic references to local history, paying tribute – at least in visual terms – to popular, as well as populist, local identities. But Harvey connected the sea change from Fordism to flex-ible accumulation in global production systems with the volatility of image production in urban industries like fashion, media and finance (1989b: 285–7). He associated the ephemeral spectacular events that city govern-ments sponsor, from celebrations of winning sports teams to the more recent 'cow parades', with the pressure for quick turnover time (1989b: 157). With all this image management, the glittering postmodern city is 'a façade, a stage set, a fragment' (1989b: 95) that is intended to obscure the real city and its social problems.

If postmodern architecture creates a fictive city (1989b: 97), it is a suit-able realm for financial, or fictitious, capital in the Marxist sense. And there were many elements of 'fantasy cities' (Hannigan 1998) in new urban projects. Shopping centres, or festival marketplaces, which often replaced a working waterfront, offered clean, guarded, private places amid the down-town's chaotic patchwork of dangerous or declining public spaces; they were as open to consumers as they were closed to producers. Like Faneuil Hall in Boston, many of them played on visual themes of local history while selling souvenirs made in China (Zukin 1991: 50–1). The production of these spaces dramatized an image of place in the face of a drastic decom-position of local labour markets and bases of social solidarity – partly to restore a sense of civic pride that had been shattered by urban uprisings in the 1960s and ground into dust by factory shutdowns in the 1970s and 1980s (1989b: 89), and partly to invoke a comparative advantage over other cities in the effort to attract new investors, tourists and affluent resi-dents (1989b: 92, 295).

Baltimore, which Harvey knows so well, offered him a rare opportu-nity to write a case study of how these strategies create a new landscape of power (1989b: 88–91; 2001a: 128–57). Without a doubt, the city was shaken to its roots by riots in the late 1960s and in 1970, testifying to a deep discontent in the large African American population and among alienated white youths as well. The modernist city centre, completed in the 1960s, had shown the determination of local business leaders not 'to abandon the symbolic and political center . . . to an underclass of impoverished blacks and marginalized whites' (2001a: 132–3). Yet, as in other American cities like Philadelphia and Hartford, new downtown office buildings did not foment a wave of new business activity. Deals to build office space typically leveraged public subsidies against private funds, and, to the degree that these buildings made a profit, that money went into the pockets of speculative private-sector developers. Though subsidies in the form of lower tax assessments continued to drain the city's treasury for years, suburban residents who commuted into Baltimore in the morning and left the city at night held most new downtown jobs – especially at the higher levels.

During the early 1970s, community groups joined with bankers, lawyers, downtown developers and well-intentioned social elites to resurrect a sense of pride in the city. They created a major public event – a fair – that would take place in the city's streets and 'build on neighborhood traditions' (2001a: 136). In its first three years, the fair attracted increasing crowds, who showed they 'could be attracted downtown' and have a good time 'without having a riot' (2001a: 137). The fair's apparent success deepened interest in public celebrations as both a form and a symbol of urban renewal, and, when it was moved from the new financial centre to a section of the defunct working waterfront, it set the stage for the commercial redevelopment of Inner Harbor into the festival-themed Harborplace. Though Harvey notes the election of a strong, new mayor in 1971, in the context of the shutdown of the city's steel plants and port and disappearing federal subsidies, I think it is also important that Harborplace was supported by the real estate developer James Rouse, who was well known for both his promotion of urban marketplaces in Boston and New York and his commitment to urbanism. At any rate, private development only followed the steady drumbeat of publicly supported ethnic festivals and special events that the city government had started, and it was buttressed by public investment in a new science centre, aquarium, convention centre and marina. Hotels, restaurants and shops soon followed, built mainly for the tourist trade. Meanwhile, the new interest in the city centre spilled over into some adjacent neighbourhoods with historic housing stock, prompting reinvestment by gentrifiers. All of this created the supposedly postmodern and postindustrial scenario that has become so familiar from Baltimore to Bilbao: a formerly industrial city is reimagined as a centre of cultural consumption.

Yet, as Harvey (2001a: 141–56) reminds us, Baltimore's triumph is not complete. Many projects have not been realized, and most of the old industrial sites have not been transformed by new activities. A lot of the new construction has been plagued by corruption; funded in part by municipal subsidies, it hasn't returned a profit to the city. The highly visible concentration of stores and restaurants in Harborplace hides the low quality of shopping and lack of entertainment in other areas of the city, especially in the poorer neighbourhoods. Moreover, though 'banks and financial institutions dominate the downtown skyline' (2001a: 147), Baltimore is not a headquarters city. Still dependent on decisions made in global capitals, the city has not found a sure way to survive. New landscapes of power – like the view from Baltimore's Federal Hill – are intriguing, but deceptive.

Entrepreneurial Cities

It is not so clear that Harvey is correct in the economic determinism that finds 'an architecture of spectacle . . . essential to a project of this sort' (1989b: 91). But postmodern architecture clearly plays a large part in magnifying, or even creating, an image that a city is up to date, that it can cast off the impediments to growth – or to capital accumulation – that gradually built up in the past, and that it is prepared to take an entrepreneurial role in supporting new growth strategies. In very visible ways, postmodernism supplied a conceptual toolkit (Swidler 2001) for producing a different kind of urban space; it emerged at a specific moment as a space of representation (Lefebvre 1991 [1974]) for a new wave of financial speculation. During the 1970s and 1980s, sloughing off the modernist designs that had become stereotypical of public housing and government offices implied breaking free of bureaucracy and state regulation, as well as entertaining a more playful view of cities themselves. Even when private corporations did most of the building and municipal governments lacked money and vision to plan, design emerged as a city's marketing tool and the key to a city's distinction. Postmodern design aestheticized a city's industrial past – while making it clear that the urban working class was obsolete.

For David Harvey (1989b: 77), reading Pierre Bourdieu's work *Distinction* (1984) suggested the enormous usefulness of the built environment as collective symbolic capital. At a time when cities seemed to have lost their uniqueness, the built environment – historic, eclectic, capable of inducing aesthetic pleasure – could assert itself as both a tangible form of place-based identity and a tradable symbol of value. Architecture, especially the highly visible and reproduced kind we now call 'iconic' architecture, could become a city's trademark or brand. Still conscious after all these years of the value of monopoly rent, Harvey believes (2001a: 405) that a city's distinctive architecture represents the sort of symbolic capital that would provide significant financial returns. In contrast to Bourdieu, Harvey connects symbolic capital to places rather than to social groups. And in contrast to some researchers' singular focus on tourism, he thinks that the symbolic capital of the built environment attracts general flows of financial capital. Objectively, 'diminishing spatial barriers give capitalists the power to exploit . . . small differences in . . . labor supplies, resources, infrastructures, and the like'. Subjectively, 'as spatial barriers diminish so we become much more sensitized to what the world's spaces contain' (Harvey 1989b: 294). Of course valorization of the built environment also depends on the hyping of design by the media, beginning with architectural journals and expanding through television, travel guides and general magazines. Architecture is not only the symbol of capitalism, as Fredric Jameson (1984) notes; it is the capital of a media-based symbolic economy (Zukin 1991: 260; 1995: 1–11).

The rise of the symbolic economy, based on finance, information, fashion and other rapidly shifting forms of advantage, has pushed men and women to become entrepreneurial in the broadest sense. Many of the jobs in these industries are part-time or temporary, contingent on a project's success in pleasing clients, workers' self-investment and a firm's market success. Culturally, both individuals and groups aim to capture the temporary benefits of priority (the 'next new thing') and location (the 'unique' thing). For cities as well as individuals, this entrepreneurial behaviour is fuelled by economic pressure. Increasing privatization of public resources and diminishing federal (or central) government funds make it necessary to gather financial support by any means. But entrepreneurialism doesn't reduce the pressure. Both cities and nations aggressively pursue capital investment, which only intensifies competition. And the entrepreneurialism of workers and communities borders on masochism – with givebacks of wage increases and benefits, elimination of public goods, voting for local alliances that won't contest the abandonment of the 'managerial' central state (Harvey 1993c). Typically, as in Baltimore, the collective entrepreneur is a public–private partnership, which leverages public and private funds to the benefit of the private sector. What distinguishes this *modus operandi* of the local state from earlier policy orientations is the willingness to absorb financial risk without really believing in guaranteed returns (Harvey 2001a: 353).

Yet local officials continue to make the argument that cities must speculate or die. Harvey (2001a: 363, 406–7) is one of relatively few critics of entrepreneurial projects like Barcelona's hosting the 1992 Olympics, for he believes that such speculation may be too expensive for cities to bear.

Leveraged public–private financing for athletes' housing, sports stadiums and recreational facilities may produce new urban infrastructure – but for whose ultimate use, generating what kind of financial profit, and under which aesthetic regime? Moreover, the benefits of such grand projects may be narrowly concentrated in just a few areas of the city (Harvey 2001a: 353). These remain urgent questions in light of the competition among cities to host the 2012 Olympics and other mega-events, to build more sports stadiums and convention centres, and to support modern art museums and 'creative clusters' of cultural industries.

I do not mean to downplay Harvey's continued optimism about revolutionary alternatives. He (2001a: 410) finds much to hope for in the alliance between cultural movements and opposition to capitalist models of globalization. But in an age when cultural careers so often bring superstar rewards, it is tempting to dance to the tune of the entrepreneurial piper. Cities, like artists, don't appear to benefit from clinging to a dowdy image and an outmoded style.

The Body Politic

David Harvey was a fortuitous choice to write a keynote essay for the recent edited volume on *Wounded Cities* (2003e), for the city as a body politic is a theme that has run through his work since he began to look at images of women representing liberty in the French Revolution (1985a: 191–7; 2003a: 59–89). Or perhaps even earlier: since he began to think of cities as self-managing bodies of organized complexity, as Jane Jacobs's (1961: 430–4) describes them, but without either Jacobs' romantic idealism about community or her lack of faith in state regulation.

The iconography of cities varies with the immediate political circumstances. Like a nation, a city may be portrayed as a nurturing mother, a hungry whore or a youthful, aggressive warrior. Harvey reminds us that these symbols represent collective ideals, which in turn reflect ideological choices of rules and norms. Not coincidentally, the illustration he chose for the cover of *The Condition of Postmodernity* (1989b) shows one of the best-known feminine representations of justice – the Statue of Liberty – jumping out of the Chrysler Building amid the architectural ruins of hierarchical civilizations: the Pyramids, the Sphinx, the Empire State Building and a postmodern skyscraper. Icons can break free from convention, Harvey implies, or they can uphold it. Though artists help us to visualize these options, the choice is ours.

If we choose rules that rely on the state to restrain capitalist markets, we have the chance to build a more democratic, more egalitarian city. But if we go along with the choices that are made for us by speculative property developers, growth-mongering public agencies and entrepreneurial public–private groups, we risk creating a monster, like the vampire of the Bourse who preys on Parisians in that mid-nineteenth-century print. It is important to remember, despite the extreme degrees of competition that we face, that we have a choice. None the less it is painful to acknowledge, in these days of property 'bubbles' and general jubilation about the rising value of property investments, that the institution of 'land rent' places cities in a difficult situation (Harvey 2003e: 37). At least in the United States, too many men and women believe that prosperity, as well as controlling crime, requires raising rents – at the price of evictions, personal bankruptcies and homogenizing the city's fruitful mix of social, ethnic and functional diversity.

Harvey uses the building of the World Trade Center in New York as a key to the city's malleable body politic. Conceived and run by a powerful public agency with no electoral mandate, the Twin Towers represented the will of public and private entrepreneurs to subvert the city's many democratic traditions. The buildings embodied the pre-eminence of finance capital in the city's economic composition, the arrogance of a business establishment that did most of its business electronically and overseas, and the casual disregard of the mayor, Rudolph Giuliani, for the city's poor and its ethnic minorities: 'The Towers were not, therefore, neutral or innocent spaces in the global or even local scheme of things' (Harvey 2002c: 59). But after the Twin Towers were destroyed by a terrorist attack in 2001, Harvey (2003e: 39) discovered 'a different kind of body politic, latent and submerged'. Commercial television broadcasts were replaced by non-stop discussion of the attack and its victims (2002c: 61). Men and women 'rallied around ideals of community, togetherness, solidarity and altruism', often expressed in gatherings in public spaces like Union Square Park (Sorkin and Zukin 2002; Harvey 2003e: 39;). 'An abrasive and divisive mayor was transformed into a ministering angel of the streets . . . Government, which had been castigated for the preceding 20 years as all bad, except when it reduced taxes and crime, was suddenly looked to as a source of comfort and good' (Harvey 2003e: 39). Despite obvious differences, this sounds remarkably like Harvey's view of the Paris Commune. Personally, however, as someone who has lived in New York for years, I don't know why he was so surprised.

Perhaps Harvey wants the body politic to suggest a softer, more variable vision of the city than reading *Capital* implies. As a trope, it opens the door to political and cultural as well as economic analysis. Whether the 'body' is the image of a woman, the steel girders of a building or the collective legacy of policy choices, it surely guides the future as much as it speaks to past conflicts over power. That the body politic in our time is bloated by the 'supersize' fast food of rising stock and property values and addicted to the bromides of dishonest politicians makes it all the more difficult to conceive of a democratic path of change. But it is always easier to criticize landscapes of power than to think of ways to transcend and reshape them. If any analyst can goad us to hope we can change cities, it must be David Harvey. The consistency of his critique, as well as his unswerving devotion to 'life space' over the space of capital, forces us to think continually about changing the rules.

7

David Harvey and Dialectical Space-time

Eric Sheppard

Space remains the final frontier for geographers, and David Harvey is no exception. Since geographers turned in the 1960s to seek a theoretical basis for the discipline, a persistent question has been what distinctive theoretical issues emerge from geographical scholarship. Other distinctive features of Geography are invoked at times, such as its synthetic treatment of nature–society relations or its concern for maps (Rediscovering Geography Committee 1997). Yet the question of whether, and how, space matters in understanding society and nature, remains central to the identity of the discipline.

Questions of space also have been central to Harvey's writing throughout, making any assessment of this aspect of his scholarship daunting. Fortunately, six books, each marking a key moment in the evolution of his ideas and including extensive discussions of space and time, can be taken as texts for this exegesis: *Explanation in Geography* (henceforth *EG*), *Social Justice and the City* (*SJC*), *The Limits to Capital* (*TLC*), *The Condition of Postmodernity* (*CPM*), *Justice, Nature and the Geography of Difference* (*JNGD*) and *Spaces of Hope* (*SH*) (Harvey 1969a; 1973a; 1982a; 1989b; 1996a; 2000a). Together, these contain or reiterate much of his theorization of space-time, offering a resoundingly affirmative answer to the question of whether space matters.

Much has been made of a division between the 'young' and the 'mature' Harvey, marked by the shift around 1973, coinciding with his migration from Bristol to Baltimore (Barnes, this volume), from a logical empiricist to a Marxist philosophical foundation. I argue that there is more continuity than change in his thinking on space and time: a concern for both space and time; a constructionist and relational reading of space-time; attention to how space-time is experienced, perceived and imagined; and a close grounding in classical western philosophy. I also review the impact of his scholarship on space. While this has been broadly influential beyond the discipline, shaping an increased interest in spatiality across the critical human sciences, other geographers seem less impressed: 'oddly, I do not get many invitations from geography departments any more' (Harvey 1998a: 725). This asymmetric positionality, I suggest, reflects both how disciplinary politics intersect with his citation strategy, as well as the emergence of post-Marxian philosophical influences in critical social theory.

Finally, I assess Harvey's conceptualization of space under capitalism: an abiding concern and anchor for his political economic writings since 1982. While sharing his relational dialectical approach to space and time, I will argue that in certain respects he fails to press home the dialectical tensions that he advocates. I suggest that careful attention to the spatiality of capitalism reveals problems in Harvey's tendency, in a pinch, to privilege Marx's law of value, and in his argument that time-space compression is marginalizing the importance of relative location. This opens possibilities to transcend the schism that has emerged between Harvey and his post-structural critics.

Genealogy

Logical empiricism

In *Explanation in Geography* (1969a), the discipline's canonical explication of logical empiricism, Harvey stressed three spatial themes: grounding conceptions of space and time in humans' experiences of the world, abandoning absolutist conceptions of space, and developing a formal analytic language of space. In his analysis, human conceptions of space and time depend not only on individual experience, but also on imagination and culturally derived representations of space. Based on these considerations, he argues that geographers must rebuff absolutist conceptions of space and time, i.e. the idea that these are externally fixed. He follows other proponents of 'spatial science' in rejecting the idea that space is a container, as in the classical geography of Kant, Hettner, Humboldt and Hartshorne; as well as Newton's position that space and time constitute an exogenous co-ordinate grid, 'independent of all matter' (1969a: 207). He favours a relative conception, in which space is a 'positional quality in the world' (1969a: 195), and pursues its distinct implications for geometry as the analytical language of space. Euclidean geometry cannot capture the complexity and variety of human conceptions of space and time, because of its reliance on a Cartesian grid of orthogonal space and time co-ordinates, but there are many alternative non-Euclidean geometries. A key challenge, he argues, is developing transformations between the different geometries implied by distinct experiences and conceptions of space.

Logical empiricist spatial science has faced widespread criticism from social and cultural theorists for its methodological individualism and spatial fetishism, but these problems never plagued Harvey's logical empiricism. In *EG*, and the philosophically cognate early chapters of *Social Justice and the City*, he stresses how spatial concepts are shaped by social processes ('Cultural change often involves a change in spatial concepts', 1969a: 194). He utilizes Cassirer to articulate a tripartite division of experience as organic (shaped by biology), perceptual (individual and cultural) and symbolic (in our imagination) (Harvey 1973a). Distance is not a Newtonian metric, but 'can only be measured in terms of process and activity' (1969a: 210). He notes (with Einstein) that 'Activities and objects themselves define the field of influence' (1969a: 209), and introduces Leibniz's relational conception of space as 'only a system of relations' (196). In *SJC*, he stresses how social processes shape space, but also how architects and planners seek spatial forms that shape social behaviour. By stressing that social processes and spatial form are mutually interrelated he foreshadows what subsequently became known as a social constructionist conception of space, an enduring trope of geographic theory since the mid-1980s (cf. Gregory and Urry 1985). He also presages radical geographers' later critiques of spatial fetishism in economic geography, noting that location theorists neglect how their preoccupation with exogenous, unbounded and homogeneous space determines their 'specification of equilibrium' (1973a: 48).

Marxist political economy

The latter half of *SJC* begins to explicate a Marxist approach to space, using Marx's theory of land rent to explore the relationship between Marxism and conceptions of space. He notes that monopoly rent draws on an absolute or container conception, because monopoly ownership implies absolute control over space. Differential and absolute rent are associated with relative space, because they depend on socio-spatial relationships linking different spheres of economic activity. Relational space can be used to understand the general determination of rental value: 'rent is determined relationally over all spheres of production in all locations, with future expectations also incorporated . . . the value of any one parcel of land "contains" the values of all other parcels . . . as well as the expectations of future parcels' (1973a: 186). In short, 'urban space is not absolute, or relative, or relational, but all three' (1973a: 184).

In this view, relative space, the relative distance between places, should be distinguished from Leibnitz's relational space, which is a single measure of 'the system of relations' connecting it to all other places. Interestingly, spatial science also had formally distinguished these, without exploring the philosophical implications, describing relative location in terms of a matrix of distances and relational location in terms of geographic potential (Sheppard 1979). As Harvey notes, in a relational approach to space 'there is an important sense in which a point in space "contains" all other points (this is the case in the analysis of demographic or retail potential, for example . . .)' (1973a: 168).

He turns to Henri Lefebvre for a Marxist theorization of the social construction of space, highlighting Lefebvre's arguments that created space replaces effective space as the overriding principle of geographical organization (1973a: 309), and his two-circuit model (circuits of investment in production and the built environment) that places the production of space at the centre of capitalist dynamics. Yet Harvey remains sceptical of Lefebvre's broader claims (subsequently taken up by Ed Soja 1989, 2000) that spatial formation (i.e. urbanism) now dominates the economic process (industrial society): 'The hypothesis can at this point not yet be substantiated' (1973a: 311).

The Limits to Capital contains Harvey's most sustained and coherent economic analysis of space and time under capitalism (Harvey 1982a). He organizes his analysis around three 'cuts' at a theory of crisis, beginning with conventional Marxist crisis theory, and progressively complicating it by paying attention to time and space. His 'first cut' emphasizes how cyclical dynamics of overaccumulation and devalorization are endemic to capitalism. In this account, capitalists' profits are gained by paying workers less than the (labour) value they contribute to production. In addition, capitalists reduce their labour force, as they seek to out-compete one another by introducing labour-saving technologies that enhance productivity. This accelerates accumulation, as more output is brought to market, but working families have less money to purchase those commodities. Sooner or later this tendency to overaccumulation results in a realization crisis (output remains unsold, meaning that investments are not recouped as profits). As Marx put it, operation of the law of value tends to reduce the (value) rate of profit, resulting in economic restructuring: firms close, and machinery and equipment are abandoned.[1] Such devalorization of fixed capital eventually writes off enough of the previous overaccumulation for production to initiate a new cycle of boom and bust.

Harvey's second cut at crisis theory examines the degree to which a temporal fix can be found that can smooth out disruptions to accumulation due to the time that production takes (adding a third circuit, of finance capital, to Lefebvre's two-circuit model, Harvey 1978a). Large-scale production requires raising large sums of money, to pay for extensive fixed capital equipment that may not make a profit for years. Finance and credit are essential institutions for assembling the necessary resources for large purchases, and for managing the variable and sometimes long time lags between investment and payoffs. Finance markets ease capital flows from less to more profitable areas of the economy, smoothing out cycles of over-accumulation and devaluation. Fictitious capital (e.g. derivatives) further augments investors' options and flexibility. In all these ways, the financial credit system promises a temporal fix to capitalism's crises. Yet Harvey argues that this is a false promise. By easing the flow of capital, finance markets accelerate accumulation and technical change, and the speed at which old equipment becomes obsolete. Old buildings and machinery become a barrier to accumulation, as new technologies emerge to replace them before their economic value has been amortized. Fictitious capital, whose value is rooted solely in investors' confidence, is subject to dramatic speculative booms and busts. Cycles of boom and bust are only temporarily displaced, because temporal fixes ease the operation of the law of value (and thereby 'first-cut' crises).

The possibility that crises can be managed through spatial fixes is the subject of Harvey's third cut. He identifies four kinds of spatial fix. First, the land market helps reconfigure the built environment and make it more flexible, by directing investments in land to 'highest and best' (i.e. differential rent maximizing) uses. Land markets thus mediate space in the same way that finance markets mediate time. Second, the geographical separation between places of production, where capital is invested, and places of consumption, where profits on those investments are generated, creates uncertainty and slows capital accumulation: Such spatial barriers to profit realization can be mitigated by developing communications technologies to accelerate the movement of commodities and capital. Third, the global diffusion of capitalism mitigates accumulation problems at home by creating new markets for investment abroad. Fourth, territorial governance structures emerge to facilitate local capital accumulation; a theme subsequently examined by research on regulation and regime theory, industrial districts and local entrepreneurialism. Once again, Harvey argues that any kind of spatial fix is at best a temporary ameliorative. Mechanisms smoothing capital flows across space, accelerating the mobility and diffusion of capitalism, and underwriting territorial accumulation strategies, only promote capital accumulation and competition – allowing the law of value to operate more freely. Once again, the economy returns to the boom and bust dynamics of the first-cut theory of crisis.

Harvey's spatialization of Marx in *The Limits to Capital* stresses how space is produced by, but also shapes, capitalism (cf. Soja 1980). As noted above, capitalism creates built environments and transportation and communications infrastructures to facilitate capital accumulation. Yet Harvey also shows how space and place have an active influence over profit rates, and thereby capitalist dynamics. For example, whereas Ricardo and von Thünen conceptualize rents as a drain on profits and capital accumulation, in Marx's theory rents may enhance and thereby shape profit-making. More broadly, the productivity of the spaces produced by capitalism is provisional: built environments and communications systems that are ideal for one phase of capitalism may become lead weights, slowing down capital accumulation in a later era. As a result, capital accumulation lurches from one location to another, in cycles of what he dubs geographical uneven development, or spatial economic restructuring. In short, paralleling arguments by first-generation location theorists that space matters (Harvey 1999a [1982a]: xxvi), the emergent spatial organization of capitalism shapes its economic trajectory.

Dialectical elaborations

While *TLC* offered a foundational argument about capitalist spatial dynamics, Harvey was not content to leave it here. He has offered four major elaborations, examining: non-economic aspects of space and time; the changing importance of place, space and scale under contemporary globalization; a dialectical account of relational space/time; and alternative geographical imaginations.

Non-Economic Aspects

Three issues are at the centre of his analysis of non-economic aspects: perceptions and experience, aesthetics and nature.[2] He turns to Lefebvre, equating experiences, perceptions and imaginations of space, respectively, with Lefebvre's concepts of spatial practices, representations of space and spatial representations (1986b: 220–1). Yet this is not convincing. There is confusion, because Lefebvre offers a different classification, equating spatial practice with perception, representations of space with conceptions of space and spatial representation (or representational space) with both experienced ('lived') and imagined spaces (Lefebvre 1991 [1974]: 38–40).[3] Furthermore, Harvey himself does not seem convinced. While drawing closely on Lefebvre in theorizing circuits of capital accumulation and the switching of capital between them, Harvey makes very little use of his somewhat confusing (at least in English) distinction between spatial representations and representations of space (unlike such other Marxist spatial theorists as Neil Smith and Ed Soja; see also Gregory 1993).[4] Paralleling a different line of Lefebvre, he has turned to the body, interrogating how '[t]he production of space-time is inextricably connected with production of the body' (1996a: 276). The spatial dynamics of capitalism play a central role here, but constructions of space and time also reflect the forms of space and time that humans encounter in daily struggles for material survival, as well as being culturally embedded in 'language, belief systems, and the like' (1996a: 211).

Harvey turned to aesthetics, in part as a potential resource for alternative geographical imaginations. He argues that aesthetic theory is dialectically opposed to social theory: social theory prioritizes time and change, whereas aesthetic theory spatializes time – seeking to convey immutable truths amidst the maelstrom of flux (1989b: 205). He endorses Heidegger's distinction between space and place. Space is continually reshaped under capitalism and is the realm of change and Becoming, whereas place is about Being and aesthetics – acclaimed by Heidegger as 'the locale of the truth of Being' (1996a: 299). Harvey argues that place-based aesthetics prioritizes spatiality. 'Being is suffused with spatial memories and transcends Becoming . . . And if . . . time is always memorialized . . . as memories of experienced places and spaces, then . . . time [must give way to] space, as the fundamental material of social expression' (1989b: 218). This view of aesthetics, as spatializing time and creating immutable truths, raises a series of questions, however. I cannot address these adequately here, but it is hard to conceive of music, for example, in these terms.[5]

Harvey sees place-based aesthetic sensibilities as playing an important geopolitical role, because aesthetic judgment is a powerful motivator of place-based social action, and can articulate alternative geographical imaginations. This aestheticization of politics must be taken seriously as a non-economic aspect of geo-politics under capitalism. Yet, while it may lead to positive alternatives, empowering marginalized communities (Escobar 2001), Harvey worries about the conservative parochialism of place-based imaginations. From regional separatist movements, to the national socialism that fascinated Heidegger, to current attempts to globalize American conservative values, 'The aesthetization of geopolitics . . . poses deep problems for doctrines of untrammeled social progress . . . sparking geographical conflicts between different spaces in the world economy' (1989b:). In Harvey's view, Heidegger panders to militant particularism because he 'rejects any sense of moral responsibility beyond the [local] world of immediate experience' (1996a: 314).

Globalization, Place, Space, Scale and Value

Such concerns articulate with Harvey's analysis of the changing importance of place, space and scale under contemporary globalization processes. He argues that the commodification of space-time, time-space compression, and the ability of mobile capital to command space, together condemn place-based social movements, of any kind, to fighting a rearguard action against capitalism that is particularistic and always in danger of being compromised by the dissolving power of money. Harvey narrates how time and space became commodified under capitalism (see also Harvey 1985a: ch. 1): the emergence of clock time, and of chronometers to measure it ever more precisely; and the cataloging and privatization of space and resources through cadastral and topographic mapping. He argues that this commodification leads to time-space compression, as a distinctive contemporary feature of globalized capitalism (*CPM*). This, in turn, is a consequence of what Marx analyses as a tendential 'annihilation of space by time' (Harvey 1985a): 'die Vernichtung des Raums durch die Zeit, d.h. die Zeit, die Bewegung von einem Ort zum anderen kostet, auf ein Minimum zu reduzieren' (Marx 1983 [1857–8], 445).[6]

Summarizing the economic logic, the second spatial fix of *TLC* (above) entails eliminating any spatial transactions costs associated with transportation and communications, in order to minimize temporal barriers to the turnover of capital. Harvey argues that globalization has dramatically reduced such costs, catalysing space-time compression. This has made relative location within the global economy less vital to capital accumulation, making place characteristics more important. As communications costs fall, relative to other costs, it matters less whether one location is more accessible than another. Thus the location for a new computer assembly facility, for example, is chosen not on the basis of access to markets or inputs (i.e. relative location), but because of differences in local conditions, e.g. labour costs and skills, taxes, or the regulatory environment. Such local differences among places are not given, but are (re)produced through uneven capital investment, the geographical division of labour, spatial segregation of reproduction activities and the rise of spatially ordered (often segregated) social distinctions. They have come to matter more as relative location matters less (*JNGD*), catalysing a politics of place in which cities and regions compete intensively against one another to offer attractive local conditions to geographically mobile capital. Under this kind of local entre-preneurialism, increasingly pitting locations around the globe in direct competition with one another, place-based cross-class alliances become more important relative to class struggle – illustrating how space compli-cates standard Marxian principles (Harvey 1989c; Leitner 1990).

With relative location no longer regarded as crucial, Harvey turns in *Spaces of Hope* to conceptualize uneven development in terms of scale. Drawing explicitly from the geographic literature that theorized the produc-tion of scale during the 1990s (Delaney and Leitner 1997; Marston 2000), he distances himself from earlier formulations of uneven development that, like other Marxian theories of dependency and underdevelopment, theorize how core locations exploit peripheral ones. Instead, 'The general conception . . . entails a fusion of changing scales and the production of geographical difference' (2000a: 79), as capital leapfrogs to any location with emergent local differences that promise greater profitability. A 'glocal' corporation uses its global capabilities to cherry-pick localities where its facilities must be located: picking places worldwide with the right local con-ditions for each part of the production process, and brow-beating localities into offering more favourable conditions for capital. As the world shrinks, beggar-thy-rival competition between places intensifies and working condi-tions deteriorate everywhere.

Harvey insists that such redefinitions of time and space are political: con-stantly struggled over, even though they often operate with 'the full force of objective facts' (1996a: 211). He argues, in essence, that capital commands space, whereas workers struggle to control place. Whereas the dynam-ics of capitalism progressively speed up and shrink the world, as turnover time accelerates and spatial barriers break down, proletarian classes strug-gle against these processes by contesting the working day and seeking to dominate place. Although capital is always somewhat dependent on place, through its sunk investments in the built environment and the local work-force, nevertheless its greater geographical mobility gives it an advantage in struggles over space and place. Thus, notwithstanding the persistence of local activism, capital's command over space eventually trumps workers' command over the politics of place. Time-space compression reinforces the inequality of this struggle, as immobile places compete for the attentions of ever more mobile capital by improving the 'business climate' to attract investment.

Finally, Harvey argues that commodification and time-space compres-sion have catalysed the emergence of money as the dominant way of valuing space-time. He argues that space-time and valuation are always intimately related: 'the circulation of information and the construction of discourses about things . . . then and there, as here and now, becomes . . . vital . . . in the construction of space-time relations [and] the constitution of the value, however fetishized, of both people and things' (1996a: 221). Indeed (as argued for rent in *SJC*), 'value is a socially constructed spatio-temporal relation' (1996a: 287). Under capitalism, money becomes the value-form that both shapes and is shaped by commodified space-time. This implies that when place-based movements seek an alternative geographical imaginary, they seek to rethink simultaneously value, time and money. But they face 'a seemingly immovable paradox . . . [M]ovements have to confront the question of value . . . as well as the necessary organization of space and time appropriate to their own reproduction. In so doing, they necessarily open themselves to the dissolving power of money' (1996a: 238).

Dialectical Space-Time

Harvey offers a full-fledged dialectical grounding for the relational conception of space and, to a lesser extent time, in *JNGD*. Lacking precedents among other dialecticians, he turns to Leibniz and Whitehead, since both philosophers offer an account of space that is consistent with the relational dialectics favoured by Harvey since *TLC*. For Leibniz, space and time are 'nothing apart from the things "in" them', and 'owe their existence to the ordering relations among things'.(Rescher 1979: 84, quoted in 1996a: 251). For Whitehead, space is only the expression of the interaction of bodies in that space. Leibniz's religious idealism and Whitehead's empiricist tendencies make neither an ideal interlocutor, but Harvey takes key ideas from their thought into his dialectical account. First is the inseparability of time and space. Second is Whitehead's idea of 'permanences', which Harvey sees as equivalent to dialectical accounts of how seemingly fixed objects coalesce out of a world of constantly shifting relations. These are applied to analyse space and place: 'what goes on in place cannot be understood outside of the space relations which support that place, anymore than the space relations can be understood independently of what goes on in particular places' (1996a: 316). Under capitalism, places are erected as permanences within the flux of capital circulation: internally heterogeneous, dialectical and dynamic configurations (cf. Massey 1991b).

The third key idea is the possibility of multiple spatialities, in two senses. First, differently situated agents develop distinct spatial and temporal perspectives, or spatio-temporalities, on the same 'universe'. This allows for situated knowledge, while raising the question of how different spatio-temporalities can be brought into conversation with one another. Leibniz refers to such potential common ground between situated understandings of the world as 'compossible worlds', whereas Whitehead refers to it as 'cogredience' – how 'multiple processes flow together to construct a single consistent, coherent, though multi-faceted time-space system' (1996a: 260). Second is Leibnizs' idea of 'possible worlds': the possibility of imagining very different worlds from the capitalist one we inhabit. Both are central to Harvey's recent concern with how to realize alternatives to the commodified space-time imaginary associated with capitalism.

Alternative Geographical Imaginations

The theme of alternative geographical imaginations has become increasingly central to Harvey's writing, culminating with the set of essays in *Spaces of Hope* (Harvey 2000a). Picking up on the idea of alternative possible worlds, and in counterpoint to his own frequent pessimism about broad-scale social change, he engages in more prospective, hopeful, thinking about space. At the core of this is an analysis of the space-time assumptions underlying utopian thought, identifying a problematic tendency to treat space and time separately (a problem with his analysis of aesthetics and geographical imaginations in *CPM*, see above, although he does not take up this opportunity for reflexive critique). He argues that utopias of spatial form, envisaging an ideal world, suffer from an unrealistic belief in the possibilities of isolation and a fixed final utopian state, and an unwillingness to recognize the authoritarian nature of the social engineering entailed in creating such utopias from scratch. By contrast, he argues, conceptualizations of utopia as a temporal process fail to recognize that such processes must be grounded in real places and institutions, whose inevitable fixities necessarily shape and limit the utopian dynamic. Instead, he proposes a 'utopian dialectics', articulating the dimensions of space and time that are separated in utopias of spatial form and utopias of process. He sees this as a way of anchoring utopian thinking in the concrete possibilities of current geographies, while confronting problems of authority and closure. Harvey feels that dialectics can bring utopian thinking down to earth, making it harder to dismiss utopian thinking as unrealistic and a distraction from political mobilization for change. 'The task is to pull together a spatiotemporal . . . dialectical utopianism – that is rooted in our present possibilities as it points towards different trajectories' (2000a 196).

He is not optimistic, however, about present possibilities. For alternative geographical imaginations to challenge the 'master-narratives' of a capitalist world (1996a: 286), where money links space-time together into a conflicted yet coherent system, it is necessary to overcome local militant particularisms. His argument that capitalism plays places (and their particular place-bound aesthetic politics) off against one another through its mastery of space motivates his scepticism of the current emphasis on difference in critical social theory. In his view, success in building a global alternative to capitalism requires finding cogredience among manifold particularist worlds.

> Uncovering cartographic affinities and unities within a world of highly expressive difference appears more and more as the key problematic of the times . . . The relational conception of space allows for diversity in the social construction of space-time while insisting that different processes may relate and that, therefore, the space-time orderings and cartographies of resistance they produce are in some way or other also inter-related.
>
> (1996a: 290)

Marx provides the vision for this. Whereas Heidegger stresses the power of immediate experience, and thus place, Marx goes beyond this to construct a conception of species being that makes collective action possible.

Characteristically, Harvey argues that space/place and universal/particular are not dualisms, but dialectically related oppositions that have always run through modernity (*CPM*). 'Our future places are for us to make. But we cannot do this without struggling in place, space and environment in multiple ways . . . A renewed capacity to reread the production of historical-geographical difference is a crucial preliminary step towards emancipating the possibilities for future place construction' (1996a: 326). Practically, he suggests that this means abandoning the Leninist strategy of a vanguard party, because this does not take into account how uneven geographical development complicates the social identities that political movements take as foundational. Since identities, agendas and imaginations are shaped by geographical as well as social location, progressive movements must transcend traditional labour issues, and learn to operate simultaneously, often in contradictory ways, at multiple geographical scales (2000a).

Implications

David Harvey's trajectory of research conceptualizing space thus contains four enduring themes that transcend his philosophical shift from logical empiricism to Marxism. First, he insists that space is relationally constructed, as part and parcel of societal and bio-physical processes. While replacing a relative with a more sophisticated relational and dialectical conception, the spirit of his philosophy of space has not changed. Harvey thus anticipated 1980s arguments that space is a social construct rather than a Cartesian grid (Soja 1980; Peet 1981; Smith 1981; Gregory and Urry 1985; Sheppard 1990).

Second, Harvey has sought to treat time together with space. At times he limits himself to examining parallels between the two, in the structure of *EG* but also in accounts of how capitalism reshapes space and time (*CPM*). More significant are his attempts to replace this dualism with space-time, dating back to *EG* and central to *JNGD*. This sets him apart from the vast majority of theorists of space in the human sciences, who separate time from space (but see Massey 1999b; May and Thrift 2001). At the heart of *JNGD* is the most explicitly dialectical analysis of space-time, society and nature to date, of which Harvey (1998a) is justifiably proud.

Third, Harvey argues that experience and culture need careful attention when conceptualizing space. His theorization of this shifts from an individualist focus in *EG*, albeit recognizing that 'culture' also shapes experience, to a relational dialectic of the body and social structure in *SH*. By comparison with other Marxist theorists of space, he pays little attention to Lefebvre's trilogy of spatial practices, representations of space and spatial representations. Challenging the methodological individualism of rational choice and what he sees as parallel problems in poststructural work on the body, he adopts a relational account in which apparently objective and highly differentiated personal spaces are produced at the intersection of the body with society, particularly with its political economy.[7] He also pays attention to how geographical imaginations – of planners, architects, capitalists and activists – shape space. However, he insists on 'wiring' representation and imagination, on the one hand, to the spatial dynamics of capitalism on the other (Gregory 1995: 411).

Finally, Harvey calibrates his arguments with respect to canonical Western philosophy. Leibniz's anti-Newtonian philosophy of space remains key, with Heidegger emerging as counterpoint. Kant, Hempel, Cassirer, Foucault and Whitehead are just some of a long supporting cast. By contrast, he has paid scant attention to geographers writing on space, with the signal exception of his own protégés.

Harvey's theorization of space-time has been enormously influential, shaping thinking on space across the human sciences. It is this, as much as his work on capitalism, that has garnered such a broad following. Yet a curious asymmetry has emerged. As his reputation as a theorist of space has strengthened beyond Geography, his contributions as a social theorist have undergone increased scrutiny within the discipline. Some of this may be due to resentment at his reluctance to draw explicitly on the broad body of socio-spatial theory in Geography, in stark contrast to the frequency with which other geographers cite him. This makes his work more accessible to an interdisciplinary audience, who thereby are not required to familiarize themselves with the geographic literature in order to read Harvey, and arguably stimulates broader interest in Geography. But it creates tensions closer to home. Some of this is little more than the personal jealousies and thin skins that plague us all. But in other ways, in unconsciously reproducing the impression that this is all there is to geographic work on space, Harvey has a real effect on which theoretical work on space is, or is not, taken up.

To take a recent example, in turning attention to scale in *SH*, he does recognize that geographers have pioneered theorization of the production of scale, but in focusing on the lineage of Smith, Swyngedouw and Herod he leaves out a variety of interesting work that focuses less on the spatial dynamics of capitalism, and more on how politics, discourse and gender shape scale (cf. Delaney and Leitner 1997; Kelly 1999; Marston 2000). Distinctive feminist theorizations of space, which have examined *inter alia* the possibilities of paradoxical space, a global sense of place, non-capitalist spaces and topographies, are also left to one side (cf. Deutsche 1991; Rose 1993; Massey 1994; Gibson-Graham 1996; Katz 2001).

The mounting critical assessments of Harvey from within the geographic literature (cf. Saunders and Williams 1986; Katz 1998; McDowell 1998b; Jones 1999) rarely tackle his theorization of space. Differences on this do exist, of course, as alluded to above. Even within geographical political economy, Andrew Sayer (2000) has a distinct take on space, one that is not explicitly dialectical and is more sceptical that space can be theorized (Castree 2002: 205). Nevertheless, there has been no sustained critique of Harvey's dialectical space-time. Instead, he (with Sayer) takes much criticism for concentrating on commodity production, class and dialectics, while failing to give difference and actor-networks their due. He has also been attacked for a lack of attention to the insights of feminism. Again, some of this boils down to the everyday rivalries of academia, where attacks on prominent opinion-makers can kick-start a career (a strategy not unknown to Harvey 1972c), compounded by his own occasional intemperance when responding to critics. Yet there are issues of substance.

Harvey's theory of space under capitalism is central to his position on such questions as the economy, nature and difference. To recall, Harvey's analysis in *TLC* is that spatio-temporal 'fixes' to the contradictory dynamics of capitalism cannot trump the law of value. The dialectics of space-time are thus inextricable from those of capitalism as identified by Marx. As

I have tried to indicate above, Harvey's scepticism of the effectiveness of identity politics and environmental and other non-class social movements is rooted in this analysis. His analysis can be questioned, however, even within Marxist economic geography, with the implication that differences between Harvey and his social theoretic critics may be more bridgeable than they seem.

Assessment

Harvey's theory of space under capitalism remains rooted in the argument that spatial and temporal fixes cannot divert capitalism from the contradictions expressed in Marx's law of value (*TLC*). This argument, developed more than two decades ago, is not fundamentally revised in subsequent work. For example, the value of space and nature is an enduring theme in *JNGD*, where he notes that value is itself spatial: a product of the relational and commodified space-time of capitalism. As noted above, this point first was made in *SJC*, presaging a full elaboration of how it works under capitalism in *TLC*. *JNGD* does not include a clearly articulated theory of value, but the argument echoes *TLC*: discursive and material spatial interactions, always associated with how space gains meaning, gradually have been collapsed into exchange-value under capitalism. Given this, it seems appropriate to return to *TLC* in order to assess Harvey's dialectical account of space-time under capitalism.[8]

At the centre of *TLC* is the law of value (1999a: 142).[9] He then associates with this an economy-wide warranted rate of accumulation (determined by the average rate of surplus value in the economy) that, if maintained, enables all profits (net of luxury consumption) to be reinvested in capital accumulation, allowing the economy to reproduce itself *ad infinitum* through expanded reproduction (1999a: 159–60). Yet Harvey follows Marx in rejecting Say's Law. Say's Law states that supply creates its own demand, thereby providing a mechanism for maintaining such a dynamic equilibrium in classical political economy. Instead, capitalists' strategies for enhancing their profits tend to have the unintended consequence of reducing profitability for the overall economy (the falling rate of profit thesis), inducing the cycles of overaccumulation and devalorization of his first-cut crisis theory. In short, under the law of value the dynamic equilibrium given by the warranted rate of accumulation is unstable (1999: 176). Spatio-temporal fixes can overcome time and space co-ordination problems, but they promote competition and thereby eventually reinforce the law of value and economic instability.

A second implication of the law of value is that accumulation dynamics become the driving force of the economy. Harvey rejects even class struggle as playing any determining role (1999a: 55–6), although interestingly he accepts it as a determinant of the equilibrium share of rents (1999a: 362). A number of analysts have reacted to this position by dubbing Harvey a 'capital logic' Marxist, i.e. one who argues that the logic of capital accumulation is the driving force of capitalism.

Harvey finds, then, that dialectical space-time does not compel us to question Marx's central claims about value, accumulation, crisis and class struggle. Yet his analysis is not based on a close analysis of how capitalist space-time both is produced by the evolving transportation and communications sectors and infrastructure, developed to overcome space-time co-ordination problems, and also reciprocally affects accumulation dynamics. An analysis detailing these interrelationships confirms many aspects of Harvey's analysis (Sheppard and Barnes 1990), including the unstable nature of capitalism, value as a spatial relation, the constitutive role of space and time, the unintended consequences capitalists create for themselves, and the ways that place alliances complicate class conflict. The geography of value and exchange-value is indeed an expression of the relational space of capitalism – extending even to the formalism intuited in *SJC* that relational space, geographic potential and the geography of value are equivalent (Sheppard 1987). Other aspects of Harvey's analysis turn out to be problematic, however.

First, Harvey's reliance on the law of value forces him to make labour-value foundational to his analysis. His initial dictum (1982a: 4), that exchange-value and labour-value are 'relational categories, and neither . . . can be treated as a[n] immutable building block', does not apply at critical points in his analysis, where labour-value becomes a sufficient and independent determinant of capitalist dynamics. In our analysis, by contrast, the two indeed exist in a dialectical relation with one another: Neither labor-value nor exchange-value can be taken as foundational in analysing the capitalist space-economy. Second, the warranted accumulation rate is not an exogenous reference point, with respect to which overaccumulation and devalorization can be tracked. The warranted accumulation rate shifts with technological change, with spatial restructuring and, crucially, with the social forces shaping real wage rates – forces that are not economically determined.

Third, there do exist conditions under which Say's Law holds, and future demand matches current supply. For any given warranted rate of accumulation, a social division of labour can be constructed that allows output to match future demand, making unlimited extended accumulation possible (cf. *Capital*, vol. 2).[10] This means that overaccumulation is not inevitable, even though the best-laid plans of capitalists indeed lead oft astray. This growth path is unstable, as Harvey notes, but not simply for the reason he gives: overaccumulation driven by the law of value. Any technological change, geographical restructuring or successful move by organized labour or capitalists to enhance their share of the surplus can undermine this balance between future demand and current supply. This implies, for example, that social and political struggles, played out in space and time, can have substantial independent influence over capitalist dynamics.

Detailed consideration of the constitutive role of space thus leads to a much more complex narrative of capitalist crisis, in which labour values, the law of value and the warranted rate of accumulation each play a less determinant role than Harvey argues, at key points, in *TLC*. Capitalism is an unstable and crisis-prone system. The spatiality of capitalism only compounds these complexities and contradictions: capitalists' initiatives have all kinds of unintended consequences; capitalist dynamics depend on class struggles; and class identities are profoundly complicated by space. The instabilities described by Harvey's discussion of the law of value are vital to understanding capitalism, but we cannot conclude that they are any more fundamental than class, or even space. In short, Harvey's argument that space matters can be taken further than he acknowledges. Space forces us to rethink not only the dynamics of capitalism, but also the role of Marx's fundamental fulcrum: value theory. Barnes (1996) has indeed taken this as his starting point for articulating the cultural turn in economic geography.[11]

Harvey's thesis of time-space compression is important, since it provides him with a potential riposte to this critique. Time-space compression implies that relative location is becoming less important than place-to-place differences, with the implication that the differential geography of communication, on which the above critique is based, is of diminishing significance. Time-space compression also seems essential to Marx's theoretical abstraction from concrete labours to abstract labour, and thereby labour value. By contrast, under persistent and noteworthy differences in relative location labour values generally vary across space, making abstraction to a generalized labour value impossible (Sheppard and Barnes 1990; Webber 1996). This profoundly complicates the plausibility that common class interests, let alone identity, can transcend spatial difference.

We should be wary of accepting time-space compression at face value, however. While few would dispute that the world is getting smaller and faster in absolute terms, it does not follow that relative location no longer matters, or, equivalently, that place and scale are sufficient metaphors to capture the spatiality of contemporary capitalism. To précis a more extensive argument

(Sheppard 2002), there is much evidence to suggest that such absolute changes disguise persistent relative differences. Just as an absolute increase in real wages for all members of society may well coexist with increased relative inequalities between rich and poor, so an absolute decrease in costs of communication across space may be accompanied by persistent differences in relative accessibility, or positionality, within the global economy. Consider, for example, how global telecommunications networks still bypass large parts of the global South, much as steamship, railroad, telegraph and road systems have done since the beginning of colonialism. Even the United States' vast telecommunications infrastructure has, if anything, increased differences in relative location between cities, and between rich and poor within cities. As Homi Bhabha (1992: 88) has quipped: 'The global perspective in 1492 as in 1992 is the purview of power. The Globe shrinks for those who own it; for the displaced or the dispossessed, the migrant or refugee, no distance is more awesome than the few feet across borders or frontiers.'

Globalization has profoundly altered the topography of relative location, when expressed on a conventional map. It increasingly resembles worm-holes, rhizomes, networks, fractals and folds. Distant places are connected seamlessly into a global elite space scattered across the globe, connected by air travel, the Internet and shared interests, identities and consumption norms. The global South may reside right next door, in the midst of unhealthy social and bio-physical environments, but disconnected from jobs, meaningful entertainment and social networks. When the global South impinges too closely on the daily lives of elites, defensive architectures are erected to control access: ranging from CCTV and gated communities to three-strikes-and-you're-out laws and global anti-terrorism measures.[12]

Harvey is certainly well aware of such processes, but has not parsed out their implications for his theory of space under capitalism. Indeed, he has paid limited attention to the global South, beyond the geographic boundaries of the advanced capitalist nations. Even in *The New Imperialism* Harvey (2003b) pays little attention to concrete developments in the Middle East or other parts of the postcolonial world. His idea of accumulation by dispossession describes well the continuities between old-style colonialism and contemporary empire, but its spatiality is not unpacked. In my view, his recent stress that place and scale dominate uneven geographical development (*SH*) needs to be qualified. Such container-like perspectives on space, as bounded territories albeit nested within larger ones, run the danger (noted, *inter alia*, by Massey 1991b) of neglecting the ongoing influence of connectivity across space. Notwithstanding its fluidity and shifting concrete geographies, connectivity still (re)produces stark inequalities in geographic (as well as socio-cultural) positionality that undermine conditions of possibility for the majority of the world's population.

Bridging Difference?

This assessment is offered as an internal critique from a shared intellectual framework. It contrasts with existing external critiques: poststructural accounts of Harvey's inability to take social theory's cultural turn properly on board. I suggest, however, that this internal critique provides some foundation for throwing a rope across the chasm between Harvey and his external critics – a chasm currently policed with equal vehemence on both sides. To sketch how this may be possible, I consider the work of Gibson-Graham (1996). Gibson-Graham, like Harvey, is centrally concerned with class and seeks to theorize space.[13] She also shares Harvey's hope for optimism: 'we are interested in promoting an anti-pessimism of the intellect, as a condition for the reinvigoration of the will' (Gibson-Graham 1996: 237). 'The inability to find "an optimism of the intellect" has now become one of the most serious barriers to progressive politics' (2000a: 17). Yet Gibson-Graham has been influential among poststructural geographic and economic analysts, and is looked at askance by Harvey. Although Gibson-Graham and Harvey share a vision, they offer very different analyses of how to realize it.

Gibson-Graham (1996, 2003) argues that there are many overlooked non-capitalist spaces within contemporary capitalism, the recognition of which provides critical theorists with a fulcrum from which to imagine and develop real alternatives.[14] They begin with the household, but extend their analysis to cover any economic activities that are not based on commodity production. Drawing on poststructural feminism, they seek to break down dualisms through which such spaces are seen as marginal and secondary to capitalism. In their view, consciousness of and local participation in such practices provides the 'micropolitics' necessary to imagining alternatives and unthinking capitalism. The differences between and within such communities of local practice should not be sublimated to a common project, but must be respected and built on. '[W]hen expressed and heard, these multiple . . . perspectives help everyone produce a more objective and comprehensive account of the issues that face them' (Young 1998: 41).

By contrast, Harvey argues that alternative place-based practices are always in danger of being overwhelmed by capitalists' command over commodified space-time, and the dissolving power of money. The centrality of value to his analysis implies that non-commodified aspects of the abstraction of space under capitalism (cf. Hayden 1982; Poovey 1995), and non-monetary economic activities such as those in the household, are accorded little autonomy. Instead of invoking alternative local practices, he seeks to motivate alternative imaginations through theoretical critique. Making good on local imaginations, he argues, requires overcoming local particularism, jumping scale and identifying and building a common identity, presumably based on shared interests.

If theorizing relational space under capitalism means that labour value cannot be accorded the privileged position it occupies in Harvey's analysis, then the duality separating Gibson-Graham and Harvey begins to dissipate. Those following Harvey are pushed to make more room for other aspects of difference than class and space, and for other spatio-temporal registers of value than those of money. This creates more space for recognizing alternative practices. Those following Gibson-Graham are pushed to make a realistic assessment of the difficulties posed by global capital's command over commodified space-time, in order that local initiatives foster sustainable alternatives that can underwrite optimism. Of course, it is also necessary to engage in an ethic of knowledge production that gives different viewpoints equal voice and opportunity to engage critically with one another (Longino 2002). The relentless pace of knowledge production and the premium accorded to reputation and productivity in contemporary academia militate against pursuing such radical democracy even inside the Ivory Tower, from which we preach its values for society as a whole. Nevertheless, a theory of space under capitalism with ontological room for Harvey and his critics is one place to start.

Acknowledgements

I wish to thank, without implicating, Trevor Barnes, Noel Castree, Derek Gregory and Erica Schoenberger for comments on an earlier draft.

Notes

1 According to the law of value, under full capitalist competition the rate of profit (in labour-value terms) will be equalized across the economy, as investment flows from less to more profitable opportunities.
2 I do not discuss nature here. See Braun (this volume).
3 See also Soja (1996).
4 It is important to note that there is no single Marxist theorization of space, although the contours of this terrain have not been fully analysed. Harvey

draws closely on Marx's theorizations in *Capital* and *Grundrisse*, but other theorists have distinct takes.

5 I am grateful to Derek Gregory for this example.

6 The annihilation of space through time, i.e. reducing to a minimum the time it costs for movement from one place to another (author's translation).

7 Lefebvre also discusses the body at length, but with less concern with how it directly articulates with economic processes.

8 This draws on a more detailed discussion in Sheppard (2004).

9 See note 1 above.

10 This 'socially necessary' division of labour is not determined by labour values (contra Rubin 1973)

11 While I would not travel as far along this path as Barnes, I agree that this critique of value theory creates conditions of possibility for his analysis.

12 I do not use global South/North here to describe distinct world regions, but to indicate what Esteva and Prakash term the 'one-third' and 'two-thirds' worlds that occupy broadly different positionalities within the global economy (Esteva and Prakash 1992; Mohanty 2003; Sheppard and Nagar 2004).

13 I agree with Harvey that space is a source of difference, which his critics by and large are not willing to recognize (Harvey 1998a; 1999e). Gibson-Graham do not make this error.

14 This discussion is more suggestive than analytic, since Gibson-Graham's treatment of space is cursory.

8

Spatial Fixes, Temporal Fixes and Spatio-Temporal Fixes

Bob Jessop

It is especially productive to probe major thinkers on issues central to their work and widely regarded as their strong points. Accordingly, my contribution reviews Harvey's concern with the spatialities and temporalities of capitalism and capitalist social formations. Harvey is famous for stressing the importance of spatiality for an adequate historical materialism. If one phrase symbolizes this, it is surely 'spatial fix'. He has also shown how capitalism rests on a political economy of time and has explored the dynamics of time-space compression in both modern and postmodern societies. More recently, he has introduced the term 'spatio-temporal fix' to decipher the dynamics of capitalist imperialism and its grounding in the interaction between capitalist and territorial logics of power. These interests are reflected in his successive but overlapping accounts of three interrelated fixes: spatial, temporal and spatio-temporal. Each works in its own way to defer and/or displace capitalism's inherent crisis-tendencies but does so only by subsequently intensifying these tendencies and their effects. My chapter affirms Harvey's key contributions on these themes but also suggests that they have significant ontological, epistemological, methodological and substantive limitations. It also proposes a potentially more productive reading of the spatio-temporal fix that is none the less consistent with and, indeed, inspired by his approach.

Harvey on Methodology, Dialectics and Internal Relations

Harvey's work on spatial fixes is obviously rooted in his long-standing interest in land-use patterns and locational dynamics, spatial forms, spatial justice and urbanism, and his later sustained engagement with Marx's method and theory and with capitalist dynamics (2001a: 8–10; Merrifield 2003). But it is also informed by a deeper ontological and methodological project, namely, 'to reconstruct theory with space (and the "relation to nature") clearly integrated within it as foundational elements' (1996a: 9). This project corresponds in part to his desire to overcome the privileging, in conventional dialectics, of time over space (1996b: 4; cf. 1989b: 207, 273). Thus Harvey suggests that an '[e]scape from the teleologies of Hegel and Marx can . . . most readily be achieved by appeal to the particularities of spatiality (network, levels, connections)' (1996a: 109). A further, and later, justification suggests that, whereas neoclassical economics collapses when it confronts spatial issues, these are foundational for Marx's critique of political economy.[1] This holds both for the general ontological importance Marx attaches to place and space in social life and for the substantive importance of possible (dis)connections between qualitatively different forms of labour performed in different places and times and their integration as abstract labour into the circuit of capital. Finally, whatever his intellectual motivations, Harvey's interest in space and place also reflects his view of political practice, inspired by Raymond Williams, namely, 'militant particularism' rooted in local mobilization but linked to wider social movements (1996a, 2000a, 2001a).

Whereas his training as a geographer, his inquiries on cities and his intellectual and political projects all motivate Harvey's spatial interests, his interest in temporal fixes owes more to his knowledge of Marx's critique of political economy and his own growing recognition of the tendential autonomization of financial capital. Thus his key contributions on the spatio-temporality of accumulation are rooted in Marx's dialectical method as developed in the 1857 'Introduction', the *Grundrisse* (1973a) and *Capital* (1970). Harvey deploys this method to respecify and elaborate key economic categories and crisis mechanisms and to reveal their inherently spatio-temporal qualities. His broader contributions to historical-geographical materialism are further rooted in a broader understanding of the dialectic, the ontology of internal relations, and the cogredience and compossibility of social relations with different spatio-temporalities (Harvey 1973a: 285–301; 1982a: 1–2; 1996a: 286). This dual approach, indebted to Marxian political economy and the theory of internal relations, shapes his analysis of all three fixes.

Harvey remarks that 'Marx chose never to write out any principles of dialectics . . . The only way to understand his method is by following his practice' (1996a: 48; cf. 1973a: 286). On this basis, Harvey incisively summarizes Marx's overall method. This involves a movement from abstract to concrete, i.e. the increasing concretization of a given phenomenon (e.g.

commodities in general versus the real wage). It also involves a movement from simple to complex, i.e. introducing further dimensions of a given phenomenon (e.g. capital in general versus competition between states to control new markets on behalf of their respective national capitals). Hence concepts are never introduced just once but are continually developed, expanded and refined. Indeed, 'since we cannot possibly have that understanding at the outset, we are forced to use the concepts without knowing precisely what they mean' (1982a: 1–2). Harvey's 'first-cut' theory of crisis, based on the tendency of the rate of profit to fall, is relatively abstract-simple, for example referring mainly to capital in general. The second- and third-cut theories become more concrete and complex. In this context, Harvey's key contribution to the *concretization* of Marxist analysis concerns his exploration of 'socially necessary turnover time'; and, regarding *complexification*, it concerns his work on finance capital and the inherent spatiality of capital accumulation. Yet theories never reach completion. The coherence and explanatory power of concepts and arguments are therefore always relative to a given stage in the spiral movement from abstract-simple to concrete-complex. Thus we should not criticize a theoretical approach just because that movement is incomplete – a point relevant to Harvey's work too. But we may properly critique it in so far as later productive development is blocked by the way in which earlier concepts are presented.

Harvey describes his own approach as 'a dialectical, historical-geographical and materialist theory . . . [that] deals with totalities, particularities, motion, and fixity in a certain way, hold[ing] out the prospect of embracing many other forms of theorizing within its frame, sometimes with only minimal loss to the integrity of the original' (1996a: 9). Likewise, disavowing any interest in developing a theory of the capitalist state, he describes his task as:

> to construct a general theory of space-relations and geographical development under capitalism that can, among other things, explain the significance and evolution of state functions (local, regional, national, and supranational), uneven geographical development, interregional inequalities, imperialism, the progress and forms of urbanisation and the like. Only in this way can we understand how territorial configurations and class alliances are shaped and reshaped, how territories lose or gain in economic, political, and military power, the external limits on internal state autonomy (including the transition to socialism), or how state power, once constituted, can itself become a barrier to the unencumbered accumulation of capital, or a strategic centre from which class struggle or interimperialist struggles can be waged.
>
> (2001a: 326–7)

Both quotations illustrate Harvey's recognition of the limits of a purely value-theoretical analysis and the need to explore the totality of internal relations in capitalist societies. But what do such relations involve?

Harvey's response offers various propositions that stress, *inter alia*, the primacy of processes and relations over things and structures; the importance of internal contradictions; the importance of external boundaries as well as internal relations; the multiplicity of spaces, times and space-times; the mutual constitution of parts and wholes; the reversibility of cause and effect within a relational analysis; the grounding of transformative processes in heterogeneity and contradictions; and the universality of change in all systems. These principles also apply to dialectical inquiry itself, which, he writes, is a reflexive, self-potentiating process and must explore possible worlds as well as actually existing worlds (1996a: 49–56).[2]

While there is little harm in using an ontology of internal relations heuristically in the process of discovery, dangers arise if it becomes an all-purpose method of presenting research results at the expense of detailed concern with specific causal mechanisms and dynamics in specific domains. Harvey avoids this risk in his analysis of the value-theoretical dimensions of his critique of capitalism. Thus, although he claims that *Capital* adopts a dialectical approach based on internal relations, he also gives a more specific account of Marx's method. He suggests that Marx builds more and more specific versions of his argument to establish the highly differentiated, internally contradictory nature of capital accumulation; and that Marx uses these increasingly specific versions as explanatory devices without ever completing the analysis (1996a: 62–7). The same spirit imbues Harvey's remark that *Limits to Capital*,

> seeks to integrate the financial (temporal) and geographical (call it global and spatial) aspects to accumulation within the framework of Marx's overall argument. It attempts to do so in a holistic rather than segmented way. It provides a systematic link between the basic underlying theory . . . and the expression of those forces on the ground as mediated through uneven geographical developments and financial operations.
>
> (1999a [1982a]: xix)

In these respects Harvey's approach is remarkably similar to recent critical realist readings of Marx (see, for example, Brown et al. 2001). But when he moves to the extra-economic aspects of the capital relation, Harvey has tended to revert to a more general ontology of internal relations that lacks the same focus on the specific causal mechanisms, pursued at increasingly concrete-complex levels of analysis, that connect the circuits of capital to the wider social formation.

Harvey on Spatial Fixes

Harvey's 'trademark' notion of 'spatial fix' is loose and heterogeneous. It is a general term that refers to many different forms of spatial reorganization and geographical expansion that serve to manage, at least for some time, crisis-tendencies inherent in accumulation. Harvey first discussed 'spatial fixes' at length in an essay on Hegel, von Thünen and Marx (2001a). Curiously for one whose studies are generally seen as firmly grounded in Marx's work and who later stresses the latter's spatial foundations, Harvey's essay argues that Marx cast his critique of capitalism in an 'aspatial mould' and also separated the economic (market-mediated, profit-oriented) and political (territorially grounded, power-oriented) aspects of accumulation (2001a: 308). Harvey is not claiming here that Marx ignored space or the organic connection between economics and politics – only that he did not consider it theoretically appropriate or relevant politically to highlight them. Thus he writes:

> Marx, though supremely aware of the underlying unity of political and economic affairs as well as of the global dynamics of capitalism, excluded specific consideration of the spatial fix on the grounds that integrating questions of foreign trade, of geographical expansion, and the like, into the theory, merely complicated matters without necessarily adding anything new. Again and again he seeks, as in the chapter on 'Colonization', to close the door to a possibility which Hegel left open . . . Marx had little incentive to go beyond depicting the spatial fix as anything other than the violent projection of the contradictions of capitalism onto the world stage. His supreme concern, and contribution in *Capital*, was to unravel the nature of capitalism's *inner* dialectic.
>
> (2001a: 308; cf. 2000a: 28–30)

Hence Marx's theory of accumulation was 'spelled out, for the most part, in purely temporal terms'[3] and neglected the '*outer* transformations of the capital relation'. It was later Marxists (e.g. Bukharin, Lenin, Luxemburg) who reconnected the economic and political in exploring the historical geography of capitalist imperialism (1981a: 308–9). Harvey follows this later tradition, of course, having long emphasized the propensity of capitalism to lead to violence and war (2001a: 309–10; 1982a: 438–45; 2003d: 64, 80–1). More recently, he has emphasized the distinction, the intertwining and the potential contradictions between the now familiar *globalizing logic* of mobile individual capitals operating in continuous space and time and the – less well specified and grounded – *territorializing logic* of states oriented to imagined collective interests defined in terms of residence within relatively fixed boundaries (2003b: 27–32; see also below). These two logics are most closely articulated (although still contradictory) in the strategies pursued by the current US hegemon because its global economic expansion impels a corresponding expansion of military power as well as political and 'soft' ideological capacities to support and protect its economic interests (2003b: 34–6).

Harvey develops two analytically distinct but overlapping perspectives on spatial fixes, each with its own internal complexities. These perspectives correspond to two different types of fix: a more literal fix in the sense of the durable fixation of capital in place in physical form; and a more metaphorical 'fix' in the sense of an improvised, temporary solution, based on spatial reorganization and/or spatial strategies, to specific crisis-tendencies in capitalism.[4] Harvey sometimes implies that these also correspond to two types of capitalist transformation: *inner* and *outer*. This latter terminology derives from Hegel but Harvey does not define it clearly or consistently. Below I will relate these terms respectively to (a) the internal transformation of capitalism within a given territorial space or economic region marked by a certain structural coherence and (b) its transformation through the export of surplus capital or labour beyond the boundaries of the space or region in which it was generated. Although studies of imperialism often treat this space as a national space, there is no reason to privilege this scale. Thus Harvey also argues that structural coherence is a key feature of regional spaces (see below).

The role of spatial fixes in internal transformation is linked to capital's expanded reproduction. Harvey stresses the general need for long-term investment in fixed, immobile capital to facilitate the mobility of other capitals and explores how such investments affect locational dynamics. He starts from 'the interface between transport and communication possibilities on the one hand and locational decisions on the other' (2001a: 328). This reflects Marx's claim that the productive forces of capitalism include the capacity to overcome spatial barriers through investment and innovation in transport and communication (2001a: 328). This connects to expanded reproduction in so far as capital's growth imperative leads to market expansion and hence to the need to intensify transport and communication links within and/or beyond a given region (Marx 1970: 351–64; 1973a: 524ff). Such responses reduce the turnover time of industrial capital and accelerate the circulation of commercial and financial capital. Besides the normal role of infrastructural facilities in *annihilating space by time* and expanding the market, Harvey also addresses their role in *buying time through fixed investments* in general conditions of production. He notes especially how crisis-tendencies can be overcome in the short to medium term through investments that absorb *current* surplus capital and increase its *future* productivity and profitability. This involves both senses of 'fix'. For not only are these typically long-term investments, they also provide a potential escape from crisis via market expansion. This enables *ex post* validation of these investments as productive forces are upgraded, relative surplus-value is increased, or effective demand grows. Harvey also describes this second, 'escape' moment of the internal spatial fix as a temporal displacement (and, occasionally, as a temporal fix) because it involves long-lived physical and social infrastructures (in transport and communications networks, and education and research, for example) that take many years to return their value to circulation through the productive activity they support (1989b: 182–3; 2003d: 63).[5]

Harvey argues that these attempts to resolve capital's contradictions through internal transformation reflect the inherent tension between the 'fixity' and 'mobility' of capital at any given moment and over time. This tension is evident within fixed capital itself (e.g. the mutual presupposition of fixed airports and mobile aircraft), circulating capital (raw materials, semi-finished goods, finished products versus liquid money capital), and the relation between fixed and circulating capital (e.g. commercial centres and commodity flows). It also unfolds over time. For 'capital has to build a fixed space (or "landscape") necessary for its own functioning at a certain point in its history only to have to destroy that space (and devalue much of the capital invested therein) at a later point in order to make way for a new "spatial fix" (openings for fresh accumulation in new spaces and territories)' (2001e: 25; cf. 1996b: 6). Successive rounds of spatial fix are facilitated, of course, by innovation in physical and social infrastructure; but their particular form varies according to whether capital is seeking a spatial fix to overcome overproduction (new markets), to reduce surplus population, to access new materials, to deal with localized overaccumulation (new investment opportunities), etc. (1982a, 2003d). Moreover, fixing capital and labour in the production and maintenance of infrastructure (whether this is undertaken by the state and/or private capital) works only in so far as the remaining capital 'circulates down spatial paths and over a time-span consistent with the geographical pattern and duration of such commitments' (1985c/2001a: 332). Overall this means there is 'no long-run "spatial fix" to capitalism's internal contradictions' (1981a/2001a: 307).

This argument enables Harvey to link Marx's historical and Lenin's geographical accounts of accumulation (1981a/2001a: 332–3). For it is the role of spatial fixes in the *outer* transformation of capital that Marx allegedly neglected in his 'aspatial' analysis.[6] Harvey suggests that this external fix does have a positive, albeit temporary, role in resolving the tendential overaccumulation of capital and labour-power. Overaccumulation occurs when capital and labour can no longer be reinvested at the average rate of profit (or, worse, any profit) in their originating territory/space. This threatens 'the *devaluation* of capital, as money (through inflation), as commodities (through gluts on the market and falling prices), as productive capacity (through idle or under-utilized plant and equipment, physical infrastructures and the like, culminating in bankruptcy), and the devaluation of labour power (through falling real standards of living of the laborer)' (1981a/2001a: 300). The export of surplus money capital, surplus commodities and/or surplus labour-power outside the space(s) where they originate enables capital to avoid, at least for a period, the threat of devaluation. So the necessity of a 'spatial fix' derives from 'capitalism's insatiable drive to resolve its inner crisis tendencies by geographical expansion and geographical restructuring' (2001e: 24).

A spatial fix can only be temporary. For the search to escape the contradictions and crisis-tendencies of capitalism through profitable reinvestment of surplus capital elsewhere typically spreads these contradictions and crisis-tendencies and thereby subsequently intensifies them. This holds for all four modes of externalizing contradictions: (a) developing external markets elsewhere in the capitalist world in response to underconsumption; (b) trading with non-capitalist societies to widen markets; (c) exporting surplus capital to establish new production facilities; and (d) expanding the proletariat by separating peasants, artisans, the self-employed and even some capitalists from control over their respective means of production. Each solution creates its own distinctive problems in balancing the mobility of capital and labour at home and abroad and this generates in turn chronic instability in regional and spatial configurations, from the local level through to the imperialist chain and the world market (1981a/2001a: 304–6; 2001e; 2003b; 2003d)

The Temporal Fix

It is important to distinguish words from concepts. Thus, although Harvey seldom uses the *phrase* 'temporal fix', its *concept* is implicit in his second-cut theory of capitalist crisis and his recurrent reflections on the temporal displacement of crisis. The absence of the phrase may stem from Harvey's dismissal, in his early work, of the importance of time. He argued that:

> viewed abstractly, space ... possesses more complex and particularistic properties than time. It is possible to reverse field and move in many

different directions in space whereas time simply passes and is irreversible. The metric for space is also less easily standardized. Time or cost of movement over space do not necessarily match each other and both yield different metrics to simple physical distance. Compared with this, the chronometer and the calendar are wondrously simple. Geographical space is always the realm of the concrete and the particular. Is it possible to construct a theory of the concrete and the particular in the context of the universal and abstract determinations of Marx's theory of capitalist accumulation? This is the fundamental question to be resolved.

(2001a: 327)

This statement considers only the metrology of time. It seems to imply that time was more complex before chronometers and calendars were invented. If so, the complexity and heterogeneity of modern space-time (or spatio-temporality) would arise from the *particularistic spatial* overdetermination of an essentially *universal time*. Yet this fits ill with Harvey's subsequent recognition that time measurement and command over time are sources of social power (1989b: 226, 252) and with the many particular concrete-complex temporalities that Harvey reveals in later studies (e.g. 1982a, 1989b). These discuss differential turnover times, the spatio-temporality of international currency markets versus long-term projects of environmental transformation, the role of credit in managing uneven development, and the resulting problems for capitalism, if crisis is to be avoided, in 'establish[ing] mechanisms of "cogredience" or "compossibility" between such radically different processes' (1996a: 286). He has also written on the heterogeneity of natural time, environmental time, the everyday routines of the individual lifeworld, the rationalized time of monetized relations, and the more general social construction and contestation of times and temporalities (1989b, 1996a, 2002). Moreover, although Harvey once stressed the need to bring space in to compensate for the primacy of time in the dialectic, he later declared that:

Marx was not necessarily wrong to prioritize time over space. The aim and objective of those engaged in the circulation of capital must be, after all, to command surplus labour *time* and convert it into profit within the *socially-necessary turnover time*. From the standpoint of the circulation of capital therefore, space appears in the first instance as a mere inconvenience, a barrier to be overcome.

(1985c/2001a: 327)

This rediscovery of time and temporality as key moments in accumulation is extensively elaborated in *Limits*. Indeed, one of its major contributions is the concept of socially necessary turnover time and its central role alongside socially necessary labour time. This corresponds to Marx's grounding of capital accumulation in the 'economy of time' and his highly original development of temporal categories to explore its dynamics (Grossman 1977; Postone 1993). This said, when moving beyond questions of socially necessary labour time, Harvey tended in *Limits* and elsewhere to equate the temporal with the financial and credit aspects of accumulation, the geographical with its global and spatial aspects (1999a [1982a]: xix). This explains his interest in how credit and finance can provide a temporal solution to capital's crisis-tendencies. It may also explain the temporal aspect in his analysis of spatial fixes based on investments with a long gestation and turnover time. As for the 'temporal fix' proper, Harvey's 'second cut' at crisis theory reveals how the credit system can secure a short-term, provisional, contradictory and eventually crisis-magnifying 'temporal fix' for accumulation. This occurs through the articulation of uneven development and differential turnover times, the stock market and securitization, the pseudo-validation of long-term investment through private and/or state credit creation and, linked to the outer transformation of capitalism, the export of money capital, commodities or labour-power to compensate for their lack elsewhere (1982a; 2003b: 98–9; 2003d;). Yet, 'resort to the credit system simultaneously makes territories vulnerable to flows of speculative and fictitious capitals that can both stimulate and undermine capitalist development and even, as in recent years, be used to impose savage devaluations upon vulnerable territories' (2003d: 67).

There is another sense in which it is important to distinguish words from concepts in Harvey's analysis of 'temporal fixes'. For his recent interest in primitive accumulation and his renaming it as 'accumulation by dispossession' suggests a new approach to the search for temporal fixes for a crisis-ridden capitalism; and a new basis for periodization in terms of the primacy of this kind of temporal fix in the latest stage of capitalist imperialism as well as the primacy of financial over industrial capital (cf. 2002a, 2003b, 2003d). The most evident temporal aspects of this particular fix are seen where resources are expropriated once and for all from a 'commons' that has been built up over many years and/or where the rate of economic exploitation of a given resource exceeds its natural rate of renewal or the absorptive capacity of the environment (cf. Stahel 1999; Brennan 2000). Analogous processes can be found in the privatization of public utilities, collective consumption, or the expropriation of occupational or public pensions and other funded future welfare entitlements for immediate profit. Although Harvey mentions such private capitalist-initiated and/or state-sponsored forms of dispossession, he does not consider them under the rubric of temporal fix. Yet this could be a fruitful line of investigation.

On Spatio-Temporal Fixes

Many of Harvey's interests come together in his recent work on the new imperialism. This introduces the notion of 'spatio-temporal fix' to explore the forms and periodization of capitalist imperialism and to explain the overall logic of its latest, neoconservative phase. However, although Harvey has written explicitly about spatio-temporal fixes only recently, he has long emphasized the importance, complexity and heterogeneity of the spatio-temporalities of contemporary capitalism (1996a: 234–47), the dynamics of time-space distantiation and, especially, albeit initially in a rather mechanistic fashion, of time-space compression (1989b), and the 'ultimate unity and multiplicity of space-times' (1996a: 218).[7] All of this requires, claims Harvey, that we 'identify the modes of translation and transformation from one spatio-temporality to another, paying particular attention to the mediating role of things' (1996a: 233).[8]

Writing on the 'new imperialism', Harvey notes that spatio-temporal fix is 'a metaphor for solutions to capitalist crises through temporal deferment and geographical expansion' and involves many different ways to absorb existing capital and labour surpluses' (2003d: 65; cf. 2003b: 115). The basic idea, he claims, is simple enough:

> Overaccumulation within a given territorial system means a condition of surpluses of labour (rising unemployment) and surpluses of capital (registered as a glut of commodities on the market that cannot be disposed of without a loss, as idle productive capacity, and/or as surpluses of money capital lacking outlets for productive and profitable investment). Such surpluses may be absorbed by (a) temporal displacement through investment in long-term capital projects or social expenditures (such as education and research) that defer the re-entry of current excess capital values into circulation well into the future, (b) spatial displacements through opening up new markets, new production capacities and new resource, social and labour possibilities elsewhere, or (c) some combination of (a) and (b). The combination of (a) and (b) is particularly important when we focus on fixed capital of an independent kind embedded in the built environment.
>
> (2003d: 64; cf. 2003b: 109)

This passage combines themes from Harvey's earlier work on temporal and spatial fixes. It does not introduce a distinctive third type of fix that involves more than the sum of its two parts (see, for example, 2003b: 121–4). The new element in this new work is its focus on the long-run periodization of spatio-temporal fixes and their current dynamics as each group of recipients of exported capital is forced in turn to export capital to another set.

Thus Harvey now examines international spatio-temporal fixes, provides a threefold periodization of imperialism, highlights the changing structure and dynamics of American capitalism, and explores the USA's hegemonic role in orchestrating the succession of the last two stages of US hegemony – from what some term postwar 'embedded liberalism' based on the primacy of productive capital to an open imperialism based on the primacy of neoliberal financial capital and characterized by rounds of primitive accumulation through dispossession and a general propensity to war (2003b: 46, 124). And, as in his earlier work, he concludes that 'such geographical expansions, reorganizations and reconstructions often threaten . . . the values fixed in place but not yet realized. Vast quantities of capital fixed in place act as a drag upon the search for a spatial fix elsewhere' (2003d: 66; cf. 2003b: 100).

Spatio-Temporal Fix, Regional Structured Coherence and the National Scale

Just as Harvey does not use the *phrase* 'temporal fix' but none the less introduces the *concept* in his second-cut theory of crisis, his earlier work develops an implicit concept of spatio-temporal fix that is more than the sum of spatial and temporal fixes. This is clearest in his use of the concept of 'structured coherence' adopted by Philippe Aydalot (1976). He introduces this notion as follows:

> There are processes at work . . . that define *regional spaces* within which production and consumption, supply and demand (for commodities and labour power), production and realization, class struggle and accumulation, culture and lifestyle, hang together as some kind of structured coherence within a totality of productive forces and social relations.
> (1985c/2001a: 329; cf. 2003b: 101–3)

Harvey suggests four possible bases for such bounded regional spaces: first, the space in which capital can circulate without the cost and time of movement coming to exceed the potential for profit tied to a given socially necessary turnover time; second, the space within which labour power can be substituted on a daily basis – the commuter range defined by cost and time of daily labour movement; third, the formal territory towards which local, regional or national states orient their economic and extra-economic policies to produce coherence and cohesion; and, fourth, the informal territory invested with meaning and identity by local or regional cultures (2001a: 328–9). He adds that such structured coherence provides the basis for defensive regional class alliances, loosely bounded within a territory and usually (though not exclusively or uniquely) organized through the state. These alliances emerge to defend regional values and coherence and to promote them too through the provision of new economic and extra-economic conditions favourable to further accumulation (2001a: 333). None the less, for reasons rooted in underlying crisis-tendencies, in the increasing porosity of boundaries as new spatial fixes are sought, in the continued logic of capitalist restructuring, and in the potentially explosive nature of class and factional divisions, regional class alliances are bound to be unstable (2001a: 329–30, 336–9). Harvey concludes that '[t]he persistence of any kind of structured regional coherence, in the face of such powerful forces, appears surprising' (2001a: 330; cf. 1989a: 147, 150–2).

Harvey has since elaborated the state's key role in shaping structured coherence and regional alliances. He attributes this to its distinctive concern with territory and territorial integrity, its capacity to impose relatively firm boundaries on otherwise porous and unstable geographical edges, its wide range of fisco-financial and regulatory powers, and its authority to shape regional class alliances through various mechanisms of government and governance. The state thereby actively promotes and sustains the structured regional coherence that emerges from capitalist dynamics and gives it a political as well as economic character (2001a: 334; 2003b: 105–6). But this capacity is also closely linked to the rise, consolidation and strategic capacities of regional ruling-class alliances (1989a, 2003b: 105). This implies that structured coherence results as much from political and cultural processes as from an economic dynamic – a point made explicit in *The New Imperialism* (2003b: 102–3).

While this account focuses on the regional scale, elsewhere Harvey examines the national scale and the national state. He argues that the state, like capital, is a social relation and emerges historically to control a society split into irreconcilable class antagonisms. He then develops a form-determined theory of the capitalist type of state, derives its distinctive functions in and for capitalism, emphasizes the contradictions and limitations of liberal bourgeois democracy, and explains the ruling class's preference for governing – as far as possible – through hegemony (see 1976a). These ideas reappear in *Limits* but are supplemented by Harvey's recognition that institutions vital to capitalist reproduction (such as the central bank) are separated from those concerned with reproducing the labourer and labour power; and that state institutions must attain a certain unity if society as a whole is to be reproduced. This raises questions about the displacement of class struggle from the point of production to the political and ideological class struggle to control the state apparatus and its policies (1982a: 449)

In this context Harvey prioritizes the national rather than the regional scale. The same priority appears later, when he writes that 'the political power to act, decide upon socio-ecological projects and to regulate their unintended consequences has also to be defined at a certain scale (and in the contemporary world the nation states mostly carved out over the last hundred years maintain a privileged position even though they make no necessary politico-ideological sense)' (1996a: 204). It is unclear, however, why the national scale is so important. For, as Harvey himself notes, 'if . . . there are no basic units to which everything can be reduced, then the choice of scale at which to examine processes becomes both crucial and problematic. The difficulty is compounded by the fact that the temporal and spatial scales at which human beings operate have also been changing . . . there is an instability in the definition of scale which arises out of practices of capital accumulation, commodity exchange, and the like' (1996a: 203). In noting this problem, Harvey invites us to consider other approaches to spatio-temporal fixes.

The Capitalist and Territorial Logics of Power

While Harvey's *The New Imperialism* involves an incremental extension of his work on spatial, temporal and spatio-temporal fixes and reaffirms his arguments about the structured coherence of regions (and regionality), it also tries to develop a novel theory of capitalist imperialism based on the interweaving of the familiar capitalist logic of power and the 'territorial logic of power'. In contrast to the systematic movement from abstract-simple to concrete-complex in his analysis of the capitalist logic of accumulation, however, his analysis of territorial logic switches between generic transhistorical and particular conjunctural statements. Thus Harvey presents only a few simple *ad hoc* generalizations about the territorialization of political power and the general politics of states and empires. In so far as he identifies any distinctive features of this territorial logic outside the framework of the capitalist state, they concern the self-interest of state managers and politicians, particular styles of nation-building and governance, specific condensations of the balance of forces in political class struggle, rivalry over strategic geo-political resources (such as oil), or a Mackinder-esque struggle for control of the Eurasian heartland (2003b: 19–20, 23–5, 27, 42, 44, 85, 124, 183–9, 198, 209). In practice he focuses on the overdetermined territorial logic (and strategies) of capitalist states in their inner (domestic) and outer (inter-state) dimensions and, indeed, takes such states for granted when analysing the capitalist logic of power (2003b:

93). And, while he does refer in passing to the path-dependent effects of the historical development of states in capitalist societies (2003b: 91–2, 183–4), Harvey nowhere addresses the problematic relationship between these political trajectories and states' capacities to function as a normal capitalist state. Instead he moves directly to specific statements about the relative importance of the historically specific capitalist and the generic territorial logics of power in particular periods, stages or phases of capitalist imperialism. This means that his account of territorial logic is already overdetermined by the logic of capital rather than unfolded in pure geopolitical terms before it is articulated with that logic.

The basic steps in Harvey's argument can be reconstructed as follows:

1 'Power' (an undefined primitive term in this analysis) can be accumulated through a territorial and/or a capitalist logic. These logics are variously described as distinct, intersecting, intertwined, correlated, interdependent, internally related, dialectically related, primary or secondary in relation to each other, complementary, mutually constraining, mutually frustrating, contradictory, antagonistic, or even mutually reinforcing with potentially catastrophic results (2003b: 27, 29ff, 33, 89, 103–4, 140, 183–4, 204).

2 Whereas the state is based in the first instance on the territorial logic of political, diplomatic and military power oriented to fixed territorial boundaries; capitalism is based in the first instance on the spatial logic of [economic] power that flows across and through continuous space and time.

3 Each logic generates contradictions that must be contained by the other. This results in a spiral movement as contradictions are displaced from one logic to the other in a continuing process of mutual adjustment and reaction. This is reflected in different forms and dynamics of uneven geographical development, geo-political struggles and imperialist politics.

4 Imperialism refers to inter-state relations and acquires a distinctively capitalist form once the logic of capital accumulation dominates economic organization. For Harvey, capitalist imperialism can be understood by 'invoking a double dialectic of, first, the territorial and capitalist logics of power and, secondly, the inner and outer relations of the capitalist state' (2003b: 183–4).

5 There are different forms of capitalist imperialism depending on the relative primacy of the capitalist or territorial logics of power in the dialectical

fusion of the strategic politics of control over territory and the molecular processes of capital accumulation in space and time (2003b: 26). It is false to assume that 'political-economic processes are guided by the strategies of state and empire and that states and empires always operate out of capitalistic motivations' (2003b: 29). Instead there are potential tensions, disjunctions, contradictions or even antagonisms between these logics. If the territorial logic blocks the logic of capital, there is a risk of economic crisis; if capitalist logic undermines territorial logic, there is a risk of political crisis (2003b: 140).

A more detailed presentation of the analytically distinct but contrasting logics of power is presented in Table 8.1 (see next page), which systematizes as far as possible the diverse and scattered remarks presented in *The New Imperialism*.

Harvey alludes to these contrasting logics in his largely 'thickly descriptive' – but often confusingly dense – division of capitalist imperialism into three periods, argues that a disjunction between these logics between the two World Wars led to the economic and political catastrophes that unfolded in this period, explores them more fully in his analysis of the contrasting logics of neoliberal and neoconservative imperialism, and exploits them most in his account of the internal contradictions of this latest phase of American imperialism as a global project (respectively, 2003b: 42–74, 140–1, 69, 204–5ff). He also suggests that these logics can be seen in strategic terms, as elements in imperialist and sub-imperialist strategies, as elements in sub- and counter-hegemonic state strategies to resist imperialism, and as tactical elements in regional and/or middle- and working-class resistance to predatory capital (2003b: 82–3, 185–6, 188–9, 202). Of particular interest here are his remarks on American efforts to weaken the EU *both* as a potential hegemonic bloc oriented to a capitalist logic *and* as a potential 'Fortress Europe' oriented to a territorial logic of power through the use of NATO as a distinct apparatus for the exercise of military (territorial) power that remains under US control (2003b: 82–3).

Overall, then, Harvey's recent attempt to integrate the territorial logic of power into his analyses of capitalism remains underdeveloped and largely pre-theoretical. The asymmetrical conceptual development of the two logics leads him to privilege the capitalist logic of power in both his theoretical and his empirical analyses. Indeed he explicitly states that capitalist imperialism is typically associated with the primacy of this capitalist logic but does not explain why this is the case. He therefore prioritizes the long-term logic of capital – with attempts by state managers, subaltern fractions of capital and/or subordinate classes to promote a relatively autonomous

Table 8.1 The capitalist and territorial logics of power

	Capitalist logic of power	Territorial logic of power
Key actors	Mobile, potentially short-lived private capitals operate in open, spatially dynamic field of accumulation.	Territorially bounded, durable states on different scales operate to defend/expand territorial borders.
Main logic	Geo-economics of capital flows, emergent spatial monopolies and production of new economic scales have inevitable political effects (e.g. regional nodes of economic power as base for dominant classes that seek to engage in regional and imperialist expansion). Regional interests can capture territorial state.	Geo-politics of territorial strategies of states and empires to accumulate control over territories have inevitable economic effects (e.g. growth of military–industrial complex, access to resources, protectionism during crises, promoting free trade). Primacy of political interests can lead to 'failed' or 'rogue' states.
Core feature	Economic power flows in networked, molecular fashion across continuous space and time. Cross-territorial integration results from monopolistic spatial strategies. Flows and spatio-temporal fixes ignore borders.	Politico-military power defends and expands segmented territorial control in order to advance state's own interests. It involves strategic decisions and claims at state level and is tied to territorial borders.
Role of space/ territory in main logic	Capitalist logic exploits uneven geographical conditions, 'asymmetries' rooted in spatial exchange relations, but also overflows territorial boundaries. Molecular processes overflow regional and national boundaries and states must try to manage molecular flows.	Territorial logic is oriented to increased wealth and welfare of one territory at expense of others. It can involve sub-national states, regional blocs, etc.; may lead to rise of territorially based global hegemon. A risk of imperial overreach if territorial logic pushed to its limits.

Secondary logic	Capitalist logic is best advanced through territorial states that secure key external conditions of circuit of capital. Capitalist states orient their policies to economic, legal, political and social needs of profit-oriented, market-mediated capitalism. Latter also requires institution-building capacity of state (especially that of territorial hegemon). State territorial actions also open new fields of investment for private capital.	Politico-military power depends on an economy that generates wealth and resources, strong tax base, military strength. So state governs its economy to maximize money, productive capacity and military might. It uses coercion, diplomacy and politics to promote economic interests that also serve the state's territorial interests. A territorial hegemon manages capital logic to sustain its power.
Inter-dependencies	States support primacy of capitalist logic in interests of private business at home and abroad. Failure to do so weakens their own wealth and power and can culminate in 'failed' states.	States steer regional dynamics in their own political interests. They try to capture molecular processes of capital accumulation in space and time within their own borders.
Mode of steering	Economic logic is private, diffuse, molecular, hard to control ex ante.	Political logic is public, open to pluralistic debate and goal-oriented.
Crisis	This is solved by new spatio-temporal fixes tied to capitalist logic of surplus. This involves more complex articulations of fixity and motion, reinforcing the spatial logic of accumulation and the key role of capital mobility (i.e. switching) in absorbing crisis.	This is solved by inter-regional and inter-state clashes – economic and military confrontations contribute to localized and regional devaluation and destruction of capital. Continued territorial expansion can culminate in imperial overreach.
Imperialism	(Neo-)liberal imperialism is based on free trade – with state power used to impose (or resist) conditions of free trade, including adoption of intellectual property rights.	Neoconservative imperialism aims to consolidate hierarchical world political order to secure outlets for US surplus capital and to advance accumulation by dispossession.

territorial logic, whether offensively or defensively, leading variously to 'failed' or 'rogue' states, potential economic catastrophes within imperial or sub-imperial blocs, or economic marginalization. This contradicts Harvey's own aspiration that 'concrete analyses of actual situations . . . keep the two sides of this dialectic simultaneously in motion and not to lapse into either a solely political or a predominantly economic mode of argumentation' (2003b: 30). Perhaps this aspiration could have been realized if he had combined his value-theoretical interest in spatial, temporal and spatio-temporal fixes with a more concrete-complex state-theoretical interest in the 'territorial fixes' that might enable the territorial logic of power to constrain the tendential ecological dominance of the logic of capital by restricting the scope of its operation within definite boundaries and so limiting the full realization of the capitalist world market (Jessop 2002: 24–8).

An Alternative Approach

Harvey's approach to capitalist temporality and spatiality can be criticized on three grounds. First, while noting that they operate at the same time, for many years he treated temporal and spatial fixes as distinct or else combined them in an additive rather than interactive manner. This is especially clear in *Limits* and involves more than the order of presentation. For the two fixes are presented as resolving different crisis-tendencies. And, while spatial fixes are said to displace and defer the contradictions produced by temporal fixes, the latter seem to have no role in displacing or deferring the contradictions of spatial fixes.[9] It would have been better to analyse the spatio-temporal complexities of both fixes. For the credit mechanism is inextricably spatial as well as temporal because it is linked to spatially specific circuits rooted in the tension between national money and international currency. Further, as Harvey notes, the distinction between fixed and circulating capital involves temporal as well as functional issues. The mutual implication of spatiality and temporality in these fixes is much clearer in his more recent work.

Second, Harvey's account of spatial fixes in expanded reproduction focuses on just one of capital's interrelated economic contradictions. This concerns productive capital's alternating 'modes of being' as concrete stock of time- and place-specific assets in the course of valorization and as abstract value in motion (notably as realized profits available for reinvestment).[10] Although Harvey refers to temporal problems regarding both modes of being, the solution he identifies is spatial. It involves, as we have seen, a dialectic of fixity and mobility in the circuit of capital. Localized geographical landscapes of long-term infrastructural investments (of place relations, territorial organization and interlinked places) are produced only to be destroyed later and then rebuilt to accommodate a new dynamic of accumulation (1996b: 6). This underplays the importance of other economic contradictions, each of which has its own spatio-temporal aspects and associated dilemmas (Jessop 2002: 19–22). These are more significant in Harvey's account of the role of spatial fixes in crisis-management and crisis-displacement as capital is switched from one place, space or sector to another. A coherent spatio-temporal fix must reflect all aspects of capital's spatio-temporal contradictions in regard both to 'normal' periods of expanded reproduction and to more or less prolonged moments of crisis.

Third, Harvey's analysis of temporal and spatial fixes is primarily value-theoretical. There is little explicit concern with the explanatory limitations of economic categories and, despite his emphasis on 'internal relations', the extra-economic dimensions of the capital relation generally enter only in his more expansive and historically specific analyses (e.g. on successive spatial and/or temporal fixes in Paris) and/or in a relatively *ad hoc* manner. Thus the clearest examples of Harvey's interest in the articulation of the economic and extra-economic occur in his analyses of structured coherence (especially in the context of urbanism), the state's form and functions and imperialism. Like Marx, he emphasizes that capital's economic laws are historically specific and mediated through class struggles; that the state is crucial in securing conditions for capital accumulation; and that the development of class consciousness and class action is deeply problematic. But Marx also considered the capitalist mode of production to be political as well as economic (Krätke 1998a). This can be seen in Marx's planned 'Weiterentwicklung der Theorie' (1977 [1847]), which promised a critique of the political economy of the state that would focus on 'taxes as the essence of the state, economically expressed'; and from his intention that *Capital* should include a book on the state. Economic laws are definitely not un- or apolitical, then, but always profoundly political (cf. Théret 1992).

This is not surprising. For one cannot adequately determine the elementary categories of the capitalist mode of production – commodity, money, exchange, wage, capital – without including the distinctive forms of modern politics and the capitalist type of state. In particular, the basic economic forms of the state (taxes, the national money, state credit, state spending, etc.) are also juridio-political forms; the state has a constitutive role in capital's economic forms and organizing the circuits of capital, including production as well as credit (cf. Harvey 1982a: 281–2, 306–12, 321); and the state's own economic activities are conducted under the primacy of the political, i.e. the importance of maintaining social cohesion in a class-divided society (Poulantzas 1979). This introduces an inescapable political dimension into the historical materialist critique of capitalism. This holds not only for individual states, of course, but also for the inter-state system (Rosenberg 1994). In short, 'politics' is an immanent necessity for every capitalist economy, without which the latter could not appear as a 'closed' and self-reproducing system (Krätke 1998b: 153). Moreover, according to *Limits*, once the frontiers for 'normal' primitive accumulation were closed in the late nineteenth century, inter-state wars became a new form of primitive accumulation and the ultimate means of devaluation when 'normal', market-mediated and profit-oriented competition became ineffective (1982a: 445).[11]

To understand the political character of the capital relation as an articulation of the economic and the extra-economic, we must ask why market forces alone cannot reproduce capitalism. The answer lies in three aspects of the indeterminate but antagonistic nature of capitalism. First, there is capital's inherent incapacity to reproduce itself wholly through the value form in a self-expanding logic of commodification. This is linked to the fictitious nature of land, money and, above all, labour-power as commodities and the dependence of accumulation on various non-commodity forms of social relations. Second, more concretely, these problems are reinforced by the structural contradictions and strategic dilemmas inherent in the capital relation and their changing articulation and forms of appearance. And, third, conflicts occur over the regularization and/or governance of these contradictions and dilemmas through a variable mix of temporal fixes, spatial fixes, spatio-temporal fixes and institutionalized compromises that help to stabilize, albeit provisionally, the circuit of capital and wider social formation (Jessop 2002).

In short, there is no single best way to regularize accumulation in the long term. Instead, various second-best solutions emerge as different accumulation regimes, modes of regulation and associated compromises get institutionalized. These compensate partially for the incompleteness of the pure capital relation and give it a specific dynamic through the linkage between its economic and extra-economic elements. This permits an alternative reading of spatio-temporal fixes. A spatio-temporal fix resolves, partially and provisionally at best, the contradictions and dilemmas inherent in capitalism by establishing spatial and temporal boundaries within which a relatively durable pattern of 'structured coherence' can be secured and by shifting certain costs of securing this coherence beyond these spatial and temporal boundaries. This sort of spatio-temporal fix displaces and defers contradictions both within a given economic space and/or political territory and beyond it. It also involves an internal as well as an external differentiation of winners and losers from a particular fix, linked to the uneven social and spatial distribution of benefits from a given fix and to its associated uneven development. An adequate account of such spatio-temporal fixes must consider their extra-economic as well as their value-theoretical dimensions. Without the former the analysis of spatio-temporal fixes would degenerate into a reified and largely economistic analysis of the logic of capital; without the latter, it would degenerate into a 'soft' economic and political sociology. Harvey gives us many useful concepts to resist the latter temptations – witness his value-theoretical insights into time-space compression and flexible accumulation in an emerging post-Fordism (1989b: 121–97 and *passim*). But he has not explored capitalism's extra-economic dimensions at the same high levels of abstraction and to the same extent as its economic dimensions nor shown convincingly how they belong to the essential 'internal relations' of capitalist societies. Some contributors to the regulation approach, with which Harvey coquetted briefly in *The Condition of Postmodernity*, have attempted these tasks – albeit often at the cost of abandoning value-theoretical issues and with sometimes disappointing overall results, which may explain why Harvey did not take this flirtation further. In short, compared to developing the more stratified and asymmetrical ontologies found in critical realist readings of Marx (cf. Brown et al. 2001; see also Sayer 1995), there are serious limitations to what is often a banal and tautological emphasis on internal relations and/or a focus on general institutional linkages. Nor has Harvey addressed the forms of spatio-temporal fix in different stages or forms of accumulation or their links to institutionalized class compromise or modes of regulation. For, while he gives examples of spatial and temporal fixes from different stages of capitalism, he does not see different scales or temporal horizons as being more or less important in particular periods or forms of capitalism.

This does not exclude future integration of these issues into Harvey's work. Indeed, he has already hinted at elements of this wider and deeper understanding of spatio-temporal fixes. Thus he discusses the importance of the specific 'time-space frameworks' in which accumulation occurs (1982a: 236). He notes that the 'third-cut' crisis theory assumes the co-existence of relatively closed, self-contained regions and more open spaces beyond their borders that offer opportunities for crisis-management or displacement and can be turned, within limits, into their 'appendages' (1982a: 427). And, introducing the reprint of *Limits*, he notes:

> Crises have no existence outside the matrix of spatio-temporalities that capitalism itself creates. Crises are as much about reconfiguring the

spatio-temporal form of class relations (through all manner of stressful adjustments) as about the internal class contradictions of capitalism specified in some absolute and immutable space and time.

(1999a: xiv)

Relevant spatial factors in these matrices include place-based social relations, the built environment, land markets, the rural-urban division of labour, urban hierarchies, locational policies, the territorialization of political power and attempts to manage uneven geographical development. Harvey also refers to temporal aspects, such as fixed capital and consumpton funds, the rhythms of everyday life (including the domestic sphere, individual and collective consumption), social reproduction and the dynamics of class struggle. The resulting time-space frameworks (or, in my terms, spatio-temporal fixes) are inevitably political as well as economic and have a key role in displacing, deferring and defusing crisis-tendencies and contradictions. They are also strategically selective, i.e. some classes, class fractions, social categories or other social forces located within these spatio-temporal boundaries are marginalized, excluded or subject to coercion. Beyond these boundaries the course of accumulation is more chaotic and anarchic, lacks structured coherence, and proves more disruptive and exploitative as particular capitals (or their states) seek to transform external spaces into useful appendages. The overall course of accumulation depends on the complementarity (or not) of different solutions within the world market and the extent to which the resulting uneven geographical (and temporal) developments provoke increasing opposition and resistance (1982a: 427).

Conclusions

This chapter has explored Harvey's arguments on time and space, temporal and spatial fixes, spatio-temporal fixes and structured coherence. These are integral to his rich elaboration of Marx's method and its application to accumulation and they play a key role in his brilliant analyses of: (1) the money form and its various contradictions; (2) the credit form, the temporal fix of accumulation and financial crises; (3) the partial, temporary spatial fixes of accumulation as capital seeks to resolve crises through geographical expansion, uneven geographical development and switching into new investments; and (4) the linkages among crisis-tendencies, the conflicts between capital in general and individual capitals, the class struggle and competition. None the less his work on these issues is limited by a one-sided, value-theoretical analysis of the capital relation to the frequent neglect of its extra-economic dimensions. Moreover, where it does go beyond a purely value-theoretical analysis, his work is strongly influenced by a general Marxian ontology of internal relations and a strong commitment to the capitalist nature of social formations considered as totalities. This means that Harvey has no *systematic* conception of a 'constitutive outside' of capital as a social relation (with all the problems that this poses for securing the extra-economic as well as economic conditions necessary to capital's expanded reproduction) or of modes of societalization that might challenge the dominance of self-valorization in contemporary social formations. *The New Imperialism* does contain one half-ironic reference to constitutive outsides (2003b: 141) and also provides some pre-theoretical comments on the territorial logic of power as an alternative mode of societalization. But Harvey does not develop these comments systematically. I suggest that an alternative account of spatio-temporal fixes and the introduction of arguments about the tendential ecological dominance of the logic of capital can help redress his one-sided emphasis on the value-theoretical analysis of capitalism, his neglect of the inherent incompleteness of capitalist social formations and alternative modes of societalization, and his failure to theorize why the logic of capital none the less tends to prevail in certain historical conditions. However, as careful readers will have noted, my preferred account of spatio-temporal fix extends and amplifies Harvey's account and is, I would argue, consistent with its general line of development to date.

Notes

1 I owe this argument to Derek Gregory, personal communication, 26 November 2003. He and Noel Castree provided other excellent comments too. The usual disclaimers apply.
2 *Social Justice and the City* includes a less developed but broadly similar account of internal relations (1973a: 287–96).
3 It is unclear whether this claim should be read teleologically and/or financially, i.e. as concerning the inevitable future of capitalism and/or describing the role of credit in providing a temporal fix for accumulation.
4 Although Harvey first identifies this double meaning in exploring the new imperialism (2003b: 115; 2003d: 65–6), it is implicit in his 1981 discussion of the spatial fix inspired by Hegel, von Thünen and Marx and several later works.
5 This indicates either confusion in the notion of 'spatial fix' or the inherent spatio-temporality of all resolutions of capital's crisis-tendencies.
6 Given Marx's many references to space, place and scale in the *Grundrisse* and *Capital*, this is the only reading that makes sense of this criticism.

7 In *The New Imperialism*, Harvey even claims that, 'beginning more than twenty years ago, I proposed a theory of a "spatial fix" (more accurately a spatio-temporal fix) to the crisis-prone inner contradictions of capital accumulation' (2003b: 87). This claim to a long-standing interest in spatio-temporal fixes is double-edged because it minimizes the novelty of his subsequent theoretical arguments.

8 Marx writes that 'capital is not a thing, but a social relation between persons, established by the instrumentality of things' (1964: 717).

9 This is implied in the movement from the first- to the second-cut theory of crisis.

10 Given the continuing, spiral development of Marxist analysis, this is not problematic in itself: non-value aspects of spatial fixes could be integrated later.

11 Harvey now writes that primitive accumulation, renamed 'accumulation by dispossession', is a permanent but fluctuating feature of capitalism (2003b, 2003d).

9

Globalization and Primitive Accumulation: The Contributions of David Harvey's Dialectical Marxism

Nancy Hartsock

Marxism has been declared dead from a variety of perspectives. Certainly the neoliberals were happy to see it fall along with the Berlin wall, the Soviet Union and all of its hopes and failures. Postmodernists of all stripes warmly greeted the end of grand narratives pronounced by Lyotard. And even some Marxists themselves said farewell to Marxism. As Ronald Aronson put it, the project itself, as a 'celebration of human power', could not be sustained. Also, 'Feminism destroyed Marxism.' Not alone, he states, yet, given the influence of socialist feminism, Marxism became 'one narrative among others' (Aronson 1995: 124–39). Yet, Marxism remains far from dead, and indeed in some of its most classical forms has a great deal to contribute to understanding capitalism in the twenty-first century. I say this despite the fact that I am one of the feminists Aronson cites who supposedly contributed to the destruction of Marxist theory by demonstrating that it was not the total theory which could unproblematically subsume the oppression of women and others. I continue to have the problems with Marx's theories which I articulated some twenty years ago, among them that: (1) class understood centrally as a relation among men is the only division that counts; (2) the analysis is fundamentally masculinist in that workers' wives and their labour are presumed and left unanalysed; (3) homosocial birth images mark the analysis in important ways; (4) women come and go in the analysis and are profoundly absent from his account of the extraction of surplus value – the heart of his analysis (Hartsock 1984: 145–52).

Still I continue to identify myself as a Marxist as well as a feminist, and refuse to reject Marxism as simply another form of masculinist or economistic theorizing. I still find some versions of Marxism to be fundamental to understanding contemporary global capitalism. I recently taught *The German Ideology* and was once again struck by Marx's and Engels's stress on the importance of the globalization of capital – which they saw as already existing in the middle of the nineteenth century.

I have found David Harvey's work very helpful in understanding the contemporary world of global capitalist domination. I was interested to read in their prospectus for this book, that the editors noted that what made Harvey's work distinctive was that it advocated a very 'classical' kind of Marxism. They also referred to his work as 'unreconstructed'. And they suggested that Harvey succeeded in showing 'the continued explanatory power of an undiluted version' of historical-geographical materialism. Many might find it a bit odd, therefore, to find him also grouped with Fredric Jameson as 'perhaps' a postmodern Marxist theorist (Burbach 1998).[1] It may seem hard to square these two readings of Harvey, but in fact they are both right. He does in fact follow Marx's own writings quite closely, but also reads and understands Marx dialectically. It is this latter quality which can allow him to be read at once as 'classical' in the sense of returning to Marx's own texts and as a postmodern thinker.[2]

As Harvey describes his own work, he chose to see Marxism as a critique of 'actually existing capitalism' which was 'rampant' in the USA, and thus believed that the USA should be the appropriate focus of his attention (Harvey 2000d). I have learned and continue to learn a great deal from David Harvey's focus on capitalism and most centrally on the processes of the accumulation of capital. His discussion of the significance of *The Limits to Capital* in his intellectual life is important. This was, he states, an effort really to understand Marx but also to discuss 'the temporality of fixed-capital formation, and how that relates to money flows and finance capital, and the spatial dimensions of these' (2000d).

Indeed, I see his focus on the accumulation of capital as a fundamental, central and ongoing theme of his work. His emphasis on the accumulation of capital expanded in *The Condition of Postmodernity* where he laid out four different tasks which required 'integration (with all kinds of open possibilities for transformation) into the understanding of capitalist dynamics' (Harvey 1992b: 305; 1989b: 355). These tasks included the recognition of issues of difference as theoretically fundamental, a recognition that representations are important rather than peripheral, a conviction that space and time should be better understood, and finally an insistence that a 'meta-theoretical approach' could accommodate an understanding of differences, 'provided that we understood the full potentialities and perpetual open-endedness of dialectical argumentation' (1992b: 305). In short, one could read this formulation as an effort to include the many dimensions of being. But Harvey does insist that 'Anyone who in these times fails to situate themselves inside of the capitalist relations of domination is . . . simply fooling themselves'. (1992b: 305). Thus, at its root, Harvey's project is the analysis of capitalist relations of domination – but an analysis open to the inclusion of other forms of domination. Despite his efforts to accommodate difference, which go further than many other Marxists, he does remain committed to the Marxist project of accounting for class domination.

At the same time I read his work as motivated by two texts which have been very important to my own work – both theoretical and political. The first is the eleventh thesis on Feuerbach, 'the philosophers only interpret the world in various ways, the point is to change it' (Marx and Engels 1976: 3). The second is Engels's graveside eulogy for Marx. Engels stated that Marx had 'discovered the special law of motion governing the present day capitalist mode of production and the bourgeois society that this mode of production has created'. But more important is the fact that he continues by noting that 'this was not even half the man . . . for Marx was before all else a revolutionist' (Engels 1978: 681–2). Thus, he stresses the importance of Marx's political legacy, his role as a revolutionary committed to change the world for the benefit of the working class. Harvey too emphasizes the 'pressing need to understand both the possibilities and the potential sources of truly transformative and revolutionary changes in social life' (Harvey 1992b: 30)

Harvey has always been an activist as well as a scholar. When I first met him, we were both teaching at Johns Hopkins University in Baltimore, and he was working with activists in South Baltimore. His activism has continued – in Baltimore, in England, and now, I am sure, in New York. The struggle for justice is, then, also an important aspect of Harvey's theoretical commitments. He notes that Marx understood ideas of justice as simply versions of redistribution, but argued that there were indeed other ideas of justice involved in Marxist theory (Harvey 2000d). In this, as well as in his dialectical reading of Marx, I regard him as a kindred spirit and a continuing inspiration.

It is important that Harvey reads Marx not as a theoretical authority to be followed but as a theorist who provides invitations; he focuses on the possibilities that Marxism opens for both theory and practice. Therefore, here I propose to read Harvey himself as providing an invitation to think about important contemporary issues which come to a head under the overused and ill-defined term, globalization. In doing so, it is important to say something about how Harvey approaches the topic of dialectics in general and the concept of moment in particular as he theorizes the contemporary

moment of informational or globalized capitalism, because it is his understanding and use of Marxist dialectics which I believe accounts for the
perceptions of his work as both 'classical' *and* 'postmodern'. And it is just
this dialectical understanding that is essential to any understanding of the
variety of forces and processes which come together in the contemporary
moment defined by the term 'globalization'.

My own work has in recent years paralleled some of Harvey's, as I have
begun to look at the global accumulation of capital to retheorize these processes as a new moment of primitive accumulation. I want to take Harvey's
work and his ongoing focus on the accumulation of capital as an invitation
to invoke my contention that the globalization of capital should be reun-
derstood as a moment of primitive accumulation which is very significantly
marked by gender, that is, a moment which has very different consequences
for men and women and which opens different possibilities for both economic and political participation by women and men. Briefly, what I mean
(what has been meant) by primitive accumulation comes from Marx's
account of it as the series of processes by which capital became concentrated in fewer and fewer hands in western Europe between roughly the
fifteenth and the eighteenth centuries. These were violent, though often
legal, processes of dispossession, removal of people from the countryside,
forced labour, theft and sometimes murder. The emblematic practices
included the Atlantic slave trade, the Enclosures in England, Ireland and
Scotland, the extraction of gold and silver from the Americas and the
destruction of the indigenous populations in these places. As Harvey does
in *The New Imperialism*, I see some different mechanisms but similar processes at work in contemporary global capitalism.

However, I will argue that these processes contain important gender
dimensions. First, contemporary processes of capital accumulation are not
gender neutral but are built importantly on the backs of women – in terms
of the exploitation of women, harm done to women, but also in possibilities
opened to women. Second, it is important that women, historically, have
been more theoretically alert to many of these processes. Third, the gender
and indeed 'feminized' dimensions of contemporary capital accumulation
may, as Harvey himself very interestingly notes, allow for the development
of different agents of political transformation (Harvey 2000a: 46). Unfortunately he does not follow up on this idea and his inattention to gender
leads him to miss one of the central features of the processes now driving
the global accumulation of capital.

Feminist Critiques versus Feminist Critiques

The hasty reader might view my argument as yet another feminist trashing of Harvey's work. However, I endorse only a few of the criticisms made by authors such as Deutsche (1991), Massey (1991) and Morris (1992). As a group they both fail to understand Harvey's project and also present a partial and one-sided image (not account) of feminist positions. Harvey's project is a dialectical historical-geographical materialism which focuses on the processes which constitute and shape the accumulation of capital. But his focus on political economy is not a simple one, devoid of issues of gender, race, class, sexuality and, for his critics, the infamous 'etc.'. My current project is very similar to his, but I emphasize more than he has that accumulation carries marks of gender, race and nationality as well as class.

Let me describe three errors made most clearly by Deutsche (and to a lesser degree by Massey and Morris). As a group, these critiques engage in several moves which are contrary to my purpose here. First, they misunderstand the dialectical epistemology which underlies Harvey's historical-geographical materialism. Second, they dismiss Harvey's project of a focus on accumulation of capital as economistic and monistic and thus abandon the terrain of political economy. Third, they unify feminist perspectives under the banner of postmodernism and thus dismiss and ignore a wide range of feminist positions. Two slippages are involved in these moves: first, Harvey's Marxism is translated into a form of positivism, and second, feminist theory is reduced to a variant of postmodernist thought. I want to differentiate my views from theirs in order to lay out more clearly Harvey's project and also to locate my own feminist critique not in work on images and representations or on the terrain of postmodern theories but as one centred at the core of his own project – understanding the accumulation of capital. I should state that I found his critique of postmodernism to be both wonderfully written and essentially correct.

Deutsche states that Harvey wants to 'unify' all social relations and political practices 'by locating their origins in a single foundation' (1991: 6). Moreover, 'the subject of Harvey's discourse generates the illusion that he stands outside, not in the world. His identity then owed nothing either to his real situation or to the objects he studies' (1991: 7). Massey echoes this point, as does Morris (Massey 1991: 46; Morris 1992: 274–5) Deutsche (1991: 9) goes on to suggest that Harvey sees his approach as 'disinterested, because it has been determined solely by objective considerations of social justice and explanatory adequacy' and suggests that Harvey might see knowledge as neutral (1991: 10). Since she lists a concern with justice as a part of Harvey's efforts at analysis, it is difficult to understand how she can see his work as positivist.

Deutsche translates/rewrites Harvey as a positivist who assumes an 'ultimate visibility and knowability of an autonomous reality' (1991: 10). She goes on to characterize him as an 'unfragmented, sovereign, unsituated' subject who understands an 'objective reality' which exists solely for him, and tellingly states that the 'objective theorist is a masculine, not universal subject'. She asks quite rightly, 'Whose subjectivities are the casualties of epistemologies that produce total beings?' (1991: 12). She is right that it is masculine subjectivities who are threatened (Hartsock 1987, Hartsock 1989). Massey takes a similar position and concludes that Harvey takes a view that is 'white, male, heterosexist, Western: and one in which the male is not recognized as gendered' (1991: 43). I am familiar with the God-trick of seeing everything from nowhere but this is not the Marxism I or Harvey know. These claims/charges turn a dialectical understanding into a positivist one, and therefore I must spend some time in describing the dialectical epistemology/ontology which underlies Harvey's work. Harvey's response to their arguments very effectively locates his work as a form of situated knowledge (1992b: 302). This is the subject of the next section of this chapter.

Second, these critics object to Harvey's focus on the accumulation of capital and see it as a form of economistic reductionism. I think it is useful here to quote in full a paragraph from *The Condition of Postmodernity*. One of the areas of theoretical development which Harvey lauds is:

> The treatment of difference and 'otherness' not as something to be added onto more fundamental Marxist categories (like class and productive forces), but as something that should be omni-present from the very beginning in any attempt to grasp the dialectics of social change. The importance of recuperating such aspects of social organization as race, gender, religion, within the overall frame of historical materialist enquiry (with its emphasis upon the power of money and capital circulation) and class politics (with its emphasis upon the unity of the emancipatory struggle) cannot be overestimated.
>
> (1989b: 355)

Deutsche quotes only the second sentence of this paragraph in her critique and is then more easily able to characterize Harvey's argument as one of 'class only' politics. While I would not go as far as her and the others, there is a sense in which Harvey may not appreciate the profoundly revolutionary character of feminist, anti-racist and lesbian/gay/bisexual/transsexual work.[3]

Yet one emerges from reading their critiques with the sense that they see no connection between the accumulation of capital and issues of gender or feminist critique. Thus Deutsche objects that Harvey wants to look at a single foundation for understanding both social relations and political practices and asserts that economic relations are the origins of contemporary social conditions (Deutsche 1991: 6, 13). Massey makes a similar point when she argues that Harvey's lack of recognition of the feminist literature leads to a conclusion that 'the only enemy is capitalism' (Massey 1991: 31). Morris argues that Harvey is engaged in a form of 'class fundamentalism'. and is involved in 'economic determinism' (Morris 1992: 256–7), and objects that political economy is not 'the queen of the disciplines' (1992: 273). But in putting forward these arguments they have both limited the field of political economy to masculine actors, thinkers and concerns and then abandoned it as an area of study central to feminist theory. As I will argue, both the field of political economy and the accumulation of capital have definite gender and race components as well as class ones.

Third, these arguments support an integration/equation of feminist theory and postmodernism which leaves major segments of feminist theory off the map. Thus, Morris responds to Harvey's suggestion that 'if there is a meta-theory [available] . . . why not deploy it' by stating with certainty that it is 'a feminist claim that there is no such meta-theory' (Morris 1992: 258). Instead 'feminist and psychoanalytic critique' claims that meta-theory is simply a 'fantasy projected by a subject who imagines that his own discursive position can be external' to historical 'truths' (Morris 1992: 274–5). And Harvey is accused of searching for unity when fragmentation is the reality (Deutsche 1991: 29). Certainly not all feminist theorists would agree with this dismissal of meta-theory or with the claim that the only alternative to accepting postmodernist claims about fragmentation, complexity and unknowability require a retreat to positivism and the view from nowhere. The first corrective to these rewritings/translations of Harvey's work that I propose here is an examination of his understanding of dialectics.

Dialectical Thinking

One of David Harvey's most important contributions to contemporary discussions of Marxist theory is his insistence that the world is composed not of 'things' but of 'processes'. In addition, things do not 'exist outside of or prior to the processes, flows, and relations that create, sustain, or undermine them' (Harvey 1996a: 49).[4] But there is more to dialectics than this. While Marx developed and used a dialectical method, he never wrote a companion to Hegel's logic. So one must look at the substantive work and explore the method and epistemology contained within it. A few scholars have taken on this project. Ollman's *Dialectical Investigations* (Ollman 1993) is perhaps the most systematic. Harvey, however, presents a very succinct and important account (1996a: 46–68). He argues that Marx foregrounds the importance of thinking in terms of processes and remembering that every historical form is constituted by its fluid movement. Rather than thinking about things in motion, Marx urges us to think instead about a series of processes which sometimes crystallize into 'permanences' which are of course never really permanent. In addition, he makes very clear the ways in which human possibilities as well as 'permanences' such as institutions and structures are socially constructed, but not just as we choose.

Harvey develops the concept of moment as a particularly useful way of gaining purchase on a world which must be understood as a series of processes in motion. How to abstract, how to develop concepts which can recognize the embeddedness of processes in a totality, concepts which can recognize the complexity involved, are important issues. Marx constructed categories of analysis for particular purposes, to isolate elements of the social structure without removing them from the structure as a whole. The concept of moment is most provocatively (and evocatively) illustrated in a famous passage from Marx's *Grundrisse*, one to which Harvey refers and which is worth quoting at length here.

> The conclusion we reach is not that production, distribution, exchange and consumption are identical, but they all form members of a totality, distinctions within a unity ... A definite production thus determines a definite consumption, distribution and exchange as well as *definite relations between these different moments*. Admittedly, however, *in its one-sided form*, production is itself determined by the other moments. For example if the market, i.e. the sphere of exchange, expands, then production grows in quantity and the divisions between its different branches become deeper. A change in distribution changes production, e.g. concentration of capital, different distribution of the population between town and country, etc. Finally, the needs of consumption determine production. Mutual interaction takes place between the different moments. This is the case with every organic whole.
>
> (Marx 1973b: 99–100 italics in original)

This statement provides a lot of information about what Marx means by moment – some of which Harvey takes up and some of which I would like to flesh out. The most fundamental point is to understand power relations – in Marx's case, power relations centred on the development of capitalism and the commodification of ever greater areas of human existence. But the point of understanding power relations is to change them. And to this end, Marx's categories (and Harvey's) move and flow, enacting the fluidity that many contemporary postmodernist theorists find attractive. (It is perhaps for this reason that some have been able to characterize him as 'perhaps' a postmodern Marxist.) Thus to take the idea of moments seriously is to notice that capital can be seen as existing in several different moments when different features of capital become central to the analysis. For example, at different points, capital is described as 'raw materials, instruments of labor, and means of subsistence of all kinds *which are utilized* to produce new raw materials, new instruments of labor, and new means of subsistence', as 'accumulated labor', as 'living labor serving accumulated labor', as 'a bourgeois production relation', 'a social relation of production', as 'an independent social power'. (Marx and Engels 1976: 176, 207, 208). Capital is all these things at various moments and for various analytical purposes. Thus, when Marx wanted to call attention to the specifics of the production process, he was likely to refer to capital as raw materials and instruments of labour. But when he wanted to point to the power of capital to structure society as a whole he was more likely to refer to capital as an independent social power.[5]

The concept of moment, as Harvey points out, reminds us that social processes must be understood as flows in which a 'thing' that dialectical analysis has dissolved into flows of processes can assume at one point and from one perspective the form of money, and can at other points and from other perspectives take the form of an independent social power. Harvey suggests that moments are linked to but not bounded by time or space in any simple way: they are instead conceptual tools which can help to address complex and overdetermined social relations. Perhaps another term that would capture the meaning would be the term 'nodal points'.

I would like to think of moments as translucent filters through which one can view the totality of social relations. The filter will determine which features of social life will come to the foreground, and which will recede. The filter can be changed as one moves analytically among different moments. And then different aspects of social relations will be revealed. Second, one must pay attention to historical processes to understand how each moment plays a role in determining others. For Marx, production creates a particular kind of consumer who then requires certain products. One might think as well about the ways in which relations of gender domination produce persons who are comfortable with and even demand the continuation of these relations. Despite the sense of a still picture that the term 'moment' suggests, the link with time pushes analyses to explore both the past and the future possibilities the moment contains. Third, the concept of moment, with the added claim that the processes that we ordinarily call 'things' are better understood not only as moments but as moments which profoundly structure each other, reminds us of the interconnections among social relations. Thinking in terms of moments can allow the theorist to take account of discontinuities and incommensurabilities without losing sight of the presence of a social system within which these features are embedded. Thus, incommensurability and differentiation need not be recast as incomprehensibility. The concept of 'moment', then, can be analytically very useful in both separating out the social relations the theorist wants to concentrate on while at the same time reminding us that these social relations are in fact connected with and defined by other social relations and with their own pasts and future possibilities.

A New Moment of Primitive Accumulation

The moment I want to address here is the present moment, one that David Harvey has recently characterized as a moment of accumulation by dispossession. In *The New Imperialism* Harvey takes the position, supported by the work of Arendt and Luxemburg, that the process of primitive accumulation that Marx described in volume 1 of *Capital* did not end but remains,

> powerfully present within capitalism's historical geography up until now. Displacement of peasant populations and the formation of a landless proletariat has accelerated in countries such as Mexico and India in the last three decades; many formerly common property resources, such as water, have been privatized (often at World Bank insistence) and brought within the capitalist logic of accumulation; alternative (indigenous and even, in the case of the United States petty commodity) forms of production and consumption have been suppressed. Nationalized industries have been privatized; family farming has been taken over by agribusiness; and slavery has not disappeared (particularly in the sex trade).
>
> (Harvey 2003b: 145–6)

Harvey argues there are a number of 'wholly new mechanisms of accumulation by dispossession'. First, he argues, the credit system that Lenin, Hilferding and Luxemburg studied at the beginning of the twentieth century has become a far more important means of accumulation through corporate fraud, raiding of pension funds, speculation by hedge funds, etc. Second, Harvey cites many new ways in which the global commons are being enclosed in both the advanced countries and the global South: among them,

1 the development of intellectual property rights, especially patenting of genetic material, and seeds that are then used against the very populations who developed those materials;
2 the depletion of the global environmental commons (land, air and water) that now require capital-intensive agriculture;
3 the corporatization of previously public assets such as universities, water and public utilities;
4 the rolling back of regulatory frameworks so that 'common property rights' to a state pension, to welfare, to national health care are under attack.

(Harvey 2003b: 147–8)

I agree with Harvey in general, as well as the several other theorists who have argued that primitive accumulation has been an ongoing feature of capitalism rather than simply a precapitalist phenomenon. Yet Harvey's project is different from mine. He is interested in what he terms 'accumulation by dispossession' because it might help solve the theoretical and practical problem of the overaccumulation of capital. I am agnostic on the question of overaccumulation versus underconsumption. Instead, my focus is on the gender dynamics of accumulation. In addition, Harvey points out that primitive accumulation or accumulation by dispossession is not extrinsic to capital as theorists such as Luxemburg have argued, but intrinsic. I believe that the gender dimensions of these processes make it both intrinsic and extrinsic.

My argument about primitive accumulation, then, is both parallel to Harvey's and different from his. First, I argue that primitive accumulation is not gender neutral but involves important differential treatment of women and men. Second, I see these processes as both internal to the accumulation of capital (as does Harvey) and external, since women worldwide exist to a certain extent outside the capitalist market. Women are involved in social reproduction to a greater extent than men. But third, I think his conclusion about political action is correct: accumulation by expanded reproduction is dialectically intertwined with new social movements' stress on accumulation by dispossession. And so it may be that accumulation by dispossession is the 'fulcrum of what class struggle is and should be construed to be about' (Harvey 2003b: 176–8). This would fundamentally change understanding of what class struggle is so that it would become indistinguisable from those of new social movements; it would firmly shift the focus away from any even remotely economistic understanding – something I would applaud.

However, I think that Harvey misses several important points about the contemporary moment of globalization. First, what is going on at present is remarkably similar in basic pattern if not in exact empirical form (in the nature of the processes themselves, rather than the mechanisms used) to what went on from the fifteenth to the eighteenth centuries in western Europe: the global poor, now located more substantially in the global South are being systematically deprived of their ability to provide subsistence for themselves and being forced to seek work in factories and to find other employment possibilities in major cities around the world. The term, 'primitive accumulation' is still apt because it marks the coercion and violence involved, whether it takes legal form or not. Moreover, the term calls ironic attention to the savagery with which the forces of civilization conquered the savage and barbarian peoples of the world. Thus, while Harvey and I agree on much of the substance, my focus is more on the recapitulation of the processes by which capital is able to become concentrated in fewer and fewer hands, and his more on the new mechanisms by which a variety of tools for dispossession feeds the accumulation of capital.

Second, Harvey has missed the gender dimensions of what is happening in this moment of capitalist accumulation. He is of course not alone in this matter, and in defence pays more attention to gender than many theorists who have addressed contemporary global capitalism. It is very striking that neither Hardt and Negri's monumental book *Empire*, nor Samir Amin's less ambitious *Capitalism in the Age of Globalization*, contains even an index entry for 'women'. Castells, in his sweeping three volume treatment of 'informational capitalism' devotes one chapter to 'The fall of patriarchy' where he covers the status of women worldwide, and the feminist, lesbian and gay rights movements. It is noteworthy that the volume is entitled *The Power of Identity*. Issues of gender are hardly mentioned in the sections of his work on the reshaping of the global economy (Castells 1997; Hardt and Negri 2000).[6]

From the little I know as yet it is clear that what happened to women and men differed importantly during the periods of the Atlantic slave trade, and the various enclosures in England, Ireland and Scotland, during the period covered by Luxemburg's accounts of the importance of non-capitalist surroundings for capital accumulation. I want to add that in the present moment of globalization, women are being made to serve as models for the more generally feminized, 'virtual' workers demanded by contemporary globalized capitalism and flexible accumulation. That is to say, as women have been increasingly drawn into the wage-labour force worldwide, men have been increasingly forced to work under conditions which were formerly only enforced for women – conditions which include the increasing flexiblization of labour, part-time work, the absence of job ladders, etc. Thus, I want to suggest that the contemporary moment of globalization should be retheorized as a moment of primitive accumulation which is simultaneously a moment of the feminization of the labour-force wherein workers are denigrated, made powerless, invisible[7] and unreal.

Third, it is significant that there is a remarkable lineage of women theorists who have given attention to these sometimes substantially non-market processes.[8] I would like to suggest that it is perhaps women's structural position as differently and more complexly connected to the market *and* barred from it that may have allowed women theorists to notice more easily some of the links with non-market contexts in the context of capitalist reproduction and accumulation, whether or not they were interested in accounting for women's roles in the social division of labour. This has some significance for understanding contemporary globalization.

Primitive Accumulation: Then and Now

If we go back to Marx's chapter on primitive accumulation we find that he writes that 'the methods of primitive accumulation are anything but idyllic', and that 'conquest, enslavement, robbery, murder, briefly force, play the great part' (Marx 1967: 714). Primitive accumulation, is by definition, 'nothing else than the historical process of divorcing the producer from the means of production'. Marx goes on to state that 'it appears as primitive, because it forms the pre-historic state of capital and of the mode of production corresponding with it' (1967: 714–15). As Marx described the process, what was required was the expropriation of the agricultural population from the land. In Europe the expropriation of the small farmers and peasants was aided by the Reformation which took church properties and gave them to royal favorites or sold them at cheap prices to speculators who then drove out the tenants (1967: 721–2). As Marx tellingly put it,

> The discovery of gold and silver in America, the extirpation, the enslavement and entombment in mines of the aboriginal population, the beginning of the conquest and looting of the East Indies, the turning of Africa into a warren for the commercial hunting of black-skins, signalized the rosy dawn of the era of capitalist production. These idyllic proceedings are the chief moments of primitive accumulation.
>
> (1967: 751)

He goes on to say, 'The spoliation of the church's property, the fraudulent alienation of the state domains, the robbery of the common lands, the usurpation of feudal and clan property, and its transformation into modern private property under circumstances of reckless terrorism were just so many idyllic, methods of primitive accumulation' (1967: 732–3).

While Marx held that these forms of accumulation occurred prior to and were the preconditions for capitalist development, I want to argue, following Rosa Luxemburg and Maria Mies, that these forms of accumulation represent an ongoing part of capitalist accumulation itself. Harvey himself has argued that Marx's account needs supplementation. Thus, he suggests that predation and fraud continue within contemporary capitalism; the processes of proletarianization are more complex than Marx allowed for and required an appropriation of local cultures; and some of the mechanisms of primitive accumulation (e.g. credit) have become much stronger than in the past (Harvey 2003b: 144–7). Yet we both agree that 'the features of primitive accumulation that Marx mentions have remained powerfully present . . . up until now' (Harvey 2003b: 145). Harvey presents a sophisticated account of the workings of these processes, and I am largely in agreement with him. But rather than suggest that there are wholly new mechanisms at work, I want to stress, first, that the fundamentals are being reprised in remarkably similar ways, and second, that there are important gender dimensions to be examined. As Marx looked at England from the sixteenth to nineteenth centuries he saw, and documented in the pages of *Capital*, roughly seven processes which I see being repeated literally in the contemporary moment of globalization of capital, each with differential consequences for women and men. These are:

1 The expropriation of the land and the disconnection of workers from the soil, coupled with laws against the expropriated. Part of the old expropriation laws were also vagrancy laws, in some cases specifying branding on the forehead for a second offence. Now, as women are becoming 50 per cent of the world's migrants we are seeing a tightening of the world's immigration laws, higher penalties for being illegal in the global North, yet more pressure on women in some countries in the global South to emigrate in order both to support their families and to earn foreign exchange for their countries.

2 The depopulation and abandonment of some regions, as first enclosures were converted to sheepruns and then to deerparks. Some of the parallels in the USA can be seen in places such as the rural Midwest, Detroit, or places simply abandoned by capital and subjected to social exclusion, well documented by Manuel Castells and labelled as Fourth World areas. It is telling that he uses as examples both sub-Saharan Africa and South Central Los Angeles (Castells 2000: ch. 2). As these parts of the world are abandoned, it is sometimes only the women who either can migrate to earn money to send home or must take up work in informal sectors in Africa or in service sectors in Los Angeles to keep families going.[9]

3 The rise of a new religion/the Reformation in England. I am tempted to point to the rise of neoliberalism and market fundamentalism as semi-religious forces that have reshaped the lives of the vast majority of the world's population over the last thirty years. Yet others have stressed to me the importance of Christian, Islamic, Jewish and Hindu fundamentalism in shaping very different visions of the world. I believe all are important in reallocating resources in important ways. And each of these regimes has been important in depriving women of access to resources, respect and power. Whether the tools have been structural adjustment policies administered by the World Bank and the International Monetary Fund, welfare reform laws in the USA, the application of fundamentalist readings of Sharia legal systems in some Muslim countries, or the teachings of the Catholic or evangelical churches around the world, the results have been the exploitation and disempowering of women and have contributed to the creation of a new generation of female illiterates worldwide.

4 Creation of a new class of landless free laborers. Many forces are at work at present which are creating new classes of, especially, women workers. The number of women wage workers worldwide has vastly expanded since the 1980s. Moreover, the skills required by the new networked, informational economies tend to draw on women's relational skills. One can point as well to many specifics that push/pull women into the labour force: the fact that in many places women cannot own land, the pressures that lead women to migrate in search of jobs to support their children, the worldwide traffic in persons, especially women and girls, the impact of welfare reform in the USA, with its work requirement for recipients, etc.

5 Collaboration of political and economic leaders to enrich themselves at the expense of the poor. The recent US tax cuts provide an important example, with most of the benefits going to the top 1 per cent of tax payers. Or one could think about the astronomical growth in US chief executive officers' salaries since the 1980s, or even recent reports that two thirds of large US corporations paid no income taxes at all during 2004.

6 The disappearance of 'old fetters on usury' and 'enrichment of royal favourites'. The literal repetition of this aspect of primitive accumulation can be found in the increase in the debt the global South has come to owe the North. The ways in which risky loans by private banks to private businesses in poor countries came to be public debts managed under conditions of structural adjustment policies dictated by the IMF and World Bank have been succinctly described by a former officer of the Bank itself (Stiglitz

2003: ch. 8). And of course we are seeing the enrichment of 'royal favour-ites' such as Halliburton, Bechtel and others in Iraq reconstruction projects.

7 The slave trade, accompanied by the witch trials which were part of the dissolution of the previous mode of social reproduction/subsistence. Here we need to look at the new slavery – especially the increased traffic in women and children (Bales 1999). This traffic is now the number two source of profit for organized crime around the world. The sale of women and children is second only to the sale of guns and/or drugs (I believe that guns are number one at this point) as a source of profit.[10] Harvey takes from Luxemburg the idea that capitalism has a dual nature – including both peaceful reproduction and looting (Harvey 2003b: 137–8 citing Lux-emburg's *Accumulation of Capital*, np (1951)).

Women, Primitive Accumulation and Social Reproduction

I would like, however, to reformulate the central issues involved in primitive accumulation, and to suggest first that, although an ongoing process, it pro-ceeds in uneven waves that are related to the strength of capital relative to that of labour in general, but that this strength depends on many processes and factors working both together and against each other. The last thirty years have marked an important expansion of these processes on a global scale. In this most recent round of primitive accumulation (as probably in earlier rounds) I would argue that there are really four dialectically inter-related processes at work: first, the breaking of the previous social contract means that expectations about social relations generally are being renego-tiated or refought. These include employer/employee relations, what can be expected from the commons – whether from public universities, social security, rights to social welfare programs, water, etc. Second, there have been changes in religion/ideology which in the present cycle have meant the rise of neoliberalism, and fundamentalist Christianity and Catholicism in the West and Muslim and Hindu fundamentalism in other parts of the world. Third, primitive accumulation has increased inequalities which have left the poor no options but to accept the terms the rich are offering: the past thirty years of primitive accumulation have witnessed a broad increase in inequalities worldwide and the increasing impoverishment of masses of people. As Manuel Castells notes, 'The poorest 20 per cent of the world's people have seen their share of global income decline from 2.3 per cent to 1.4 per cent in the past 30 years. Meanwhile, the share of the richest 20 per cent has risen from 70 per cent to 85 per cent' (Castells 1998: 78).

Fourth, and most fundamentally, primitive accumulation involves a transformation in social reproduction. As Isabella Bakker has put it, 'Social reproduction can be defined as the social processes and human relations associated with the creation and maintenance of the communities upon which all production and exchange rest' (Bakker 2001: 6). She goes on to specify three aspects of social reproduction: biological reproduction, reproduction of the labour force, and reproduction of provisioning and caring needs. Thought of in this way, primitive accumulation is very clearly and perhaps at its very core a gendered set of processes, a moment which cannot be understood without central attention to the differential situations of women and men. I want to suggest that this may be true of capital accumulation more generally.

It is in the context of suspecting that primitive accumulation has always been a highly gendered process, but being certain that this moment of primitive accumulation is definitely built on the backs of women, that I want to focus on issues of accumulation and social reproduction. And it is in this context that women theorists can be particularly important. While Luxemburg did not focus her analyses on gender, it is significant that she did focus on issues of consumption, social reproduction and non-market social relations – areas in which women tend to be more involved.[11]

Luxemburg argues that capitalism needs new arenas of consumption, new market areas into which it can expand (1951: 345). She argues that Marx's original diagram of social reproduction included only two parties, where workers and capitalists were the sole agents of capitalist consumption. In terms of this diagram, the 'third class' –' civil servants, the liberal professions, the clergy, etc. – must, as consumers, be counted in with these two classes, and preferably with the capitalist class' (1951: 348). She argues, however, that the surplus produced by capitalist production must be sold to social strata whose own mode of production is not capitalist – non-capitalist strata or countries, and cites the expansion of the English cotton industry which supplied textiles to the peasants of Europe, India, Africa, etc. (1951: 352ff)[12] Moreover, Luxemburg is alert to the fact that even within capitalist economies, 'there is no obvious reason why means of production and consumer goods should be produced by capitalist methods alone'. And she cites the imports of corn raised by peasants to feed industrial labour as an example (1951: 357). She notes that the capitalist mode of production constitutes only a fragment of total world production, and while that is no longer true, we should still remember that a very large proportion of the world's women are still engaged in small-scale agricultural production.

Second, she adds a great deal to what Marx had to say about the industrial reserve army. In Luxemburg's view, the (male) capitalist waged

proletariat cannot provide an adequate industrial reserve army (1951: 361).
I read her as arguing that the need is too vast and the requirements too flexible and variable for this labour force to be able to supply. Instead, labour
must be recruited from 'social reservoirs outside the dominion of capital'.
As she puts it:

> only the existence of non-capitalist groups and countries can guarantee
> such a supply of additional labour power for capitalist production. Yet in
> his analysis of the industrial reserve army Marx only allows for (a) the dis-
> placement of older workers by machinery, (b) an influx of rural workers
> into the towns in consequence of the ascendancy of capitalist production
> in agriculture, (c) occasional labour that has dropped out of industry, and
> (d) finally the lowest residue of relative over-population, the paupers.
>
> (1951: 361)

Because capital requires labour power that is involved in precapitalist and
indeed noncapitalist forms of production, Luxemburg notes the peculiar
combinations of modern wage systems and primitive authority that may
arise in colonial systems.[13]

At the same time Luxemburg makes several claims which I find extraordinarily interesting in the context of contemporary global capitalism. For
example,

> [C]apitalism in its full maturity also depends in all respects on non-
> capitalist strata and social organizations existing side by side with it
> ... Since the accumulation of capital becomes impossible in all points
> without non-capitalist surroundings, we cannot gain a true picture of it
> by assuming the exclusive and absolute domination of the capitalist mode
> of production ... Yet if the countries of those branches of production are
> predominantly non-capitalist, capital will endeavour to establish domina-
> tion over these countries and societies. And in fact primitive conditions
> allow of a greater drive and of far more ruthless measures than could be
> tolerated under purely capitalist social conditions.
>
> (1951: 365)

Yet for Marx, Luxemburg notes, these processes are 'incidental' (1951:
364). Perhaps this is a bit too strong, but colonization and the extraction
of labour from areas which are not a part of the male labour–capital nexus
are not really central to Marx's project. I have problems with Luxemburg's
claim that capitalist accumulation requires consumption in non-capitalist
strata or countries, etc. Certainly at present the global South contributes
more to production than to consumption. And obviously her arguments

were not generally persuasive to other Marxist theorists. For my purposes, however, it does not matter so much whether or not capitalism requires consumption and markets in non-capitalist sectors. It certainly does require interchange with these sectors and needs the availability of labour and other resources from these sectors on a very flexible and variable basis.

Harvey, however, makes an important modification to both Marx's and Luxemburg's arguments. Thus, he insists that accumulation based on 'predation, fraud, and violence' should not be seen as outside of capitalism, and suggests that an analysis of these processes as ongoing is very much in order (Harvey 2003b: 144). He is certainly right. But the complications introduced by giving attention to women – their work and activities – requires an account of these processes as both intrinsic to and extrinsic to capital to the extent that women's lives are in some measure structurally defined as outside of capital.

Luxemburg's sensitivity to non-capitalist surroundings and contexts can potentially highlight the fact that the accumulation of capital requires actors other than simply capitalists or workers – both presumed to be men by Marx himself. That is, the accumulation of capital requires women as well as men, and the colonies of the global South as well as the metropoles of the global North, especially during the contemporary moment of primitive accumulation.

Maria Mies built on Luxemburg's analysis of the importance of non-capitalist strata for capitalist accumulation to develop an explicit analysis of the importance of women's labour. She connected the sexual division of labour and the international division of labour, and argued that these too needed to be included in an analysis of women's work under capitalism. Mies argues that contemporary capitalism needs both colonies and housewives to serve as non-market sectors for its expansion. She argues that,

> the division of labor in general, and the sexual division of labor in particular was/is not an *evolutionary* and peaceful process, based on the ever progressing development of productive forces (mainly technology) and specialization, but a violent one by which first certain categories of men, later certain peoples, were able mainly by virtue of arms and warfare to establish an exploitative relationship between themselves and women, and other peoples and classes.
>
> (Mies 1986: 74)

She goes on to argue that the predatory patriarchal division of labour, based on a structural separation and subordination of human beings, also leads to a separation between man and nature, and ties the rise of capitalism to an important ideological change, one that includes 'a cultural redefinition of Nature and those who were defined into nature by the "modern" capitalist patriarchs: Mother Earth, Women and Colonies' (1986: 75). And she suggests that the subordination of women, nature and the colonies is the underground of capitalist patriarchy, otherwise known as civilized society. Instead of being the precondition for capitalist accumulation, over the course of the last four or five centuries women, nature and colonies were 'externalized, declared to be outside civilized society, pushed down, and thus made invisible as the under-water part of an iceberg is invisible, yet constitute the base of the whole' (1986: 77).

That is, the subordination of women, nature and the colonies – processes that might have been supposed to lie outside the core processes of the reproduction and accumulation of capital instead constitute its 'base'. Mies has thus dialectically transformed the current 'moment' of primitive accumulation to one in which women, nature and the colonies are central, rather than peripheral and invisible. Thus, while Harvey attempts to incorporate these exclusions into the intrinsic logic of capitalism, I find myself agreeing with Mies that we need to recognize the dialectical relationships of social processes which are both external and intertwined with capitalism. I find hers a very powerful series of theses – one of whose virtues is that they bring into relation sets of processes which are usually seen as profoundly disparate. Moreover, Mies directs our attention to some important features of the contemporary moment of globalization – what I want to call the feminization of primitive accumulation.

In the context of the shift of relatively labour intensive work to the former colonies, and the use of women's labour in those places to produce products for export, Mies (1986: 116) herself has argued that international capital has rediscovered Third World Women and suggested several important theses to guide analysis:

1 Women, not men, are the optimal labour force for the capitalist accumulation process on a world scale.
2 Women are the optimal labour force because they are now being universally defined as 'housewives', not as 'workers'. This means their work can be bought at a much cheaper price than male labour since it is not defined as income-generating activity.
3 Moreover, by defining women 'as housewives, it is possible not only to cheapen their labor but also gain political and ideological control over them'. They remain focused on their families, and trade unions continue to ignore them.
4 'Due to this interest in women, especially women in the colonies, we do

not observe a tendency towards the generalization not of the free proletarian and the typical laborer, but of the marginalized, housewifed,
unfree laborers, most of them women.'

5 'This tendency is based on an increasing convergence of the sexual and
the international division of labor; a division between men and women
... and a division between producers (mainly in the colonies) and consumers (mainly in the rich countries or the cities).'

Thus, she concludes, the ideological offensive that treats women as housewives whose work is not valued, who are in many cases unable to own
land, etc., is a necessary precondition for the smooth functioning of global
capital: 'it makes a large part of labor that is exploited and super-exploited
for the world market invisible' (1986: 120). She is right that it is made
invisible. But I would suggest that in the moment of contemporary globalization, Mies's concept of housewifization should be reformulated as the
virtualization of workers, as the making of workers into not real workers.[14]
Virtualization can be understood as covering a series of processes which
includes housewifization, flexiblization, casualization, devalorization and
feminization, and most profoundly the denigration of labour in general. All
are processes in which the roles of women in the labour force are being generalized to all workers.

Conclusion

I have argued that Harvey's understanding of dialectics and his focus on
the accumulation of capital can be very helpful for those who want to
understand the dynamics of globalization. I have suggested that some of
the prominent feminist critiques of his work have failed to understand
what is involved in a dialectical understanding of Marxist theory and have
also failed to understand the importance of gender in the area of political
economy. But these critiques do not exhaust the field of gendered analysis
– especially when centred on Harvey's work on the accumulation of capital.

I believe it is important to understand the dynamics of this moment of
primitive accumulation or accumulation by dispossession in order to recognize some of the political possibilities for change. Thus, I have argued
that this round of primitive accumulation is not gender neutral but is built
on the backs of women. It has required their massively increased incorporation into waged labour, while at the same time denying that they are real
workers deserving of a real wage; it has generalized the work of women to
a much more feminized working class internationally, whether the workers

are women or men; it has made use of non-market or semi-market sectors as needed as sources for labour-power or (sometimes) consumers. Yet as women have been drawn into wage-labour and the capitalist market, to some extent their power within the family has increased, as have their options. While they remain at the lower levels of the working class, classified as mostly 'unskilled', they have at least to some extent escaped from the confines of the patriarchal families to which they were subjected. They have some of their own money, however little. They have in some cases a little more freedom, some possibilities that were not there before. I think it is worth thinking about Harvey's suggestion that there might be a 'strongly feminized proletarian movement (not an impossibility in our times) [which] might turn out to be a different agent of political transformation to that led almost exclusively by men' (Harvey 2000b: 46). While he does not elaborate on this point, I think it can be an important insight, especially when coupled with his comment in *The New Imperialism* that class struggle should be organized around these processes (2003b: 178).

Nancy Naples notes that the terms 'global, transnational, international, and "the" grassroots' are contested among postcolonial, Third World and international feminist scholars when analysing women's agency. Women are increasingly involved in transnational projects of resistance, but on different terms than men, often in much more locality-based movements, often in struggles that may not be recognized as 'political', or work related in any traditional sense (Naples and Desai 2002: 5). There are contradictory problems and possibilities. On the one hand women are increasingly drawn into global capitalism but on greatly unequal terms. On the other hand women are freed from some patriarchal oppressions. On the one hand women become aware of and are included in global/transnational processes. On the other their resistances are for the most part localized. To understand both the problems and the possibilities in this situation an understanding of dialectics is essential. Harvey's work can be very valuable in this project.

Acknowledgements

This chapter has been much improved by comments and guidance from Noel Castree, Rob Crawford, Michael Forman, Derek Gregory and Victoria Lawson.

Notes

1 See also Harvey's somewhat annoyed responses to the 'surprise and disbelief at how [he] seem[ed] to merge modernist and postmodernist, structuralist and poststructuralist arguments in *Justice, Nature, and the Geography of Difference*' (Harvey 2000d: 12).

2 I would like to think that my own work shares some of these characteristics. See for example my essay, 'Objectivity and revolution: the unity of observation and outrage in Marxist theory' (Hartsock 1998b); see also Hirschmann 1997)

3 For example, Harvey suggests that the fire at the Imperial Foods chicken processing plant in North Carolina could have been addressed through 'simple class politics' (1992b: 322). I think that class politics must be seen as inflected by issues of 'race' and gender as well.

4 See also Ollman's statement quoted by (Harvey 1996a: 48. 'Dialectics restructures our thinking about reality by replacing the common-sense notion of "thing" as something that *has* a history and *has* external connections to other things, with notions of "process" which contains its history and possible futures, and "relation", which contains as a part of what it is its ties with other relations' (Ollman 1993: 11).

5 As I read Marx, the separation of epistemology and ontology breaks down. Because of his emphasis on the centrality of human activity what we do and what we know are mutually constitutive. I see these issues most prominently in some of the *Economic and Philosophical Essays of 1844*.

6 I have not done the historical research (yet) to know what happened to gender relations during previous rounds of primitive accumulation, but things like laws against more than three women assembling on a street corner in revolutionary France, and the contradictory attention paid to the situation of women by the varieties of socialist theorists in France, England and the United States throughout the nineteenth century, make me believe that some important changes in the situation of women were taking place. (There is a sign in a Seattle suburb that reads 'horses prohibited on sidewalks'. What must be prohibited matters.) What is certainly clear is that the accumulation of capital during the present moment is not gender neutral, but is built importantly on the backs of women. Maria Mies, however, has made some important and suggestive connections between the subordination of nature, the subordination of women in Europe, and the ways these two processes were linked to the colonization of lands and peoples – thus the links between the persecution of witches, the rise of modern science, the slave trade and the destruction of subsistence economies in the colonies (Mies 1986; Pinchbeck: 1969 [1930]).

7 See Naomi Klein's work in *No Logo* (1999) where she cites Disney's claim that they have no employees in Haiti (ch. 10).

8 I find Harvey's use of Arendt very intriguing and plan to explore her theoretical contribution to this issue in the future. I found her work very important to a similar female theoretical lineage in debates on the concept of power in my earlier work (Hartsock 1983, 1984)

9 Castells and others have noted that in the new informational economies it is

women's relations skills that are in demand rather than men's muscular skills (see also Breugel 2000; McDowell 2000).

10   Harvey points out, citing Luxemburg, *The Accumulation of Capital* (1951), that Luxemburg sees the dual character of accumulation. One is the transaction between the capitalist and the wage-labourer which takes place where 'in form at any rate, peace, property and equality prevail' and the other is in relations between capitalism and non-capitalist modes of production where 'force, fraud, oppression and looting' are common (Harvey 2003b: 137). This is an important distinction with definite gender dimensions. Violence against women is rampant in the world.

11   I have made a similar argument about Arendt (see Hartsock 1983, 1984). Despite her admiration for ancient Greeks, her discussion of power added the dimension of natality to their more unidimensional concern with mortality – a concern I argued provided suggestive evidence that women writing about power were more able to see different dimensions than men. Neither is a feminist argument as such but both were women's arguments which were taken up later by other women making points about questions of women's roles.

12   It is my assumption that this is a male workforce, theoretically, given Marx's two class/two man model. The problem is of course when Luxemburg begins to apply realworld conditions and to argue that the reserve army of the unemployed cannot come solely from the working class of the industrialized European world.

13   This is particularly interesting in the context of Kevin Bales's book on contemporary slavery (1999) and also Naomi Klein's *No Logo* (1999) on the new forms of corporate awfulness in both the first and the third worlds.

14   See also Klein, 1999: ch. 10 on this point where she describes the jobs that are jobs only for students or other non (real) workers but which are held by people in their thirties and beyond. See also Peterson (2003), who introduced me to the term the 'virtual economy'.

10

Towards a New Earth and a New Humanity: Nature, Ontology, Politics

Bruce Braun

That man's physical and spiritual life is linked to nature means simply that nature is linked to itself, for man is a part of nature.

Karl Marx

We might just as well rename environmental ecology *machinic ecology*, because Cosmic and human praxis has only ever been a question of machines, even, dare I say it, of war machines.

Félix Guattari

Introduction

The writings of David Harvey are commonly associated with the reassertion of space in social theory. This is especially true in the humanities, which since the 1990s have found in Harvey's historical-geographical materialism a powerful means to 'situate' cultural practices within capitalism's changing geographies (see Harvey 1989b). Far less attention has been paid to Harvey's ongoing interest in nature. This association of Harvey with space is in large measure warranted; many parts of Harvey's corpus deal exclusively with the 'socio-spatial dialectic' – arguably his most important contribution to Western Marxism – while ignoring entirely the many non-human entities that are also constitutive of the worlds he seeks to understand. As such, Bruno Latour's (1993) trenchant critique of the 'modern Constitution' – that habit of thought that assumes a world divided into distinct ontological domains – applies as readily to Harvey as to any other social theorist: society is often depicted solely as 'humans among themselves', an autonomous realm that obeys its own historical dynamics, while non-humans enter the story only as fetishized commodities or fixed capital.

Such a reading, however, would miss key aspects of Harvey's thought. Consistent with his dialectical method, and the relational ontology that informs it, Harvey at times sketches his analysis of the spaces and times of capitalism on a more expansive canvas so as to incorporate the non-human within it. Indeed, when he turns explicitly to these matters, Harvey argues that the production of space cannot be thought *independently* from productions of nature.

> Since spaces, times, and places are relationally defined by *processes*, they are contingent upon the attributes of processes that simultaneously define and shape what is customarily referred to as 'environment'. . . [T]he idea that spatio-temporality can be examined independently of those processes evoked in environmental and ecological work cannot be sustained. From this perspective the traditional dichotomies to be found within the geographical tradition between spatial science and environmental issues, between systematic and regional (place-bound) geographies appear totally false precisely because space-time, place, and environment are all embedded in substantial processes whose attributes cannot be examined independently of the diverse spatio-temporalities such processes contain. The implications for the philosophy of geographical thought are immense.
>
> (1996a: 263–4)

Although later we will find reasons to question how these 'processes' are understood, the key point for Harvey is that within these integrated totalities 'no part can be construed without the other'.

This chapter explores Harvey's attempts to develop a fully fledged historical-geographical materialism that extends to, and incorporates, the non-human world. We will see that from the perspective of Western environmentalism, Harvey's project is nothing short of scandalous, for he refuses to posit nature as external to society, and, accordingly, undermines any eco-politics – of the Right or the Left – that does. All *radical* environmentalisms, he argues, must conceive of nature differently. Harvey's critique of dualist conceptions of nature – and his efforts to develop a materialist approach to the environment – will be my initial focus. In the second half of the chapter, however, I explore how these efforts have drawn Harvey into 'strange proximity' with another materialist tradition that many historical materialists, including Harvey, have approached with caution, if not outright scepticism.[1] This tradition – which I will call 'machinic ecology' – draws upon sources as diverse as Lucretius, Spinoza, Bergson, Deleuze and Serres – in order to propose a materialist understanding of nature that is decidedly *non-dialectical* and *immanentist*. As I will explain later, from this perspective it is Harvey who may not yet be materialist enough. The point of this comparison is not to dismiss Harvey's important contributions to radical environmentalism, but rather to clarify further what is at stake, analytically and politically, in how society–environment relations are conceived on the left today.

The Problem of Bourgeois Environmentalism

Let me begin with a tautology: to speak of nature is to presuppose an ontology. It requires an understanding of being, whether of the earth as a whole, or of the specific entities that compose it. This is an irreducible element of *all* socio-ecological thought, even if unstated. Moreover, it is shot through with ethical and political significance, for how we conceive of nature relates directly to our environmental practices and eco-politics.

Harvey rarely addresses ontological questions directly. Rather, he proceeds from an implicit ontology that can be summarized in a simple statement: nature exists as a dynamic unity. In other words, nature and society are not separate or opposed realms, but internal relations within a larger totality.[2] Later we will see that Harvey derived his concept of nature – and his ontology – from Marx, but it is perhaps equally as important to recognize that he developed it in the context of the massive popularity, in the 1970s and 1980s, of what Harvey's friend and collaborator Neil Smith (1984) called 'bourgeois' environmentalism.[3] From the beginning, then, Harvey's contributions to a Marxist theory of nature were as much political as they were theoretical.

Defetishizing nature

Harvey's first writings on the environment date from the 1970s, a period in which growing awareness of resource scarcity, air and water pollution, and habitat destruction contributed to a sense of ecological crisis. It is now commonplace to suggest that there were two dominant responses to the perceived crisis: one, often labelled technocratic, which imagined that environmental problems could be overcome through the application of reason, and which placed great faith in science and technology; and another, often

labelled ecocentric, which assumed that the problem was humanity's inter-
ference in nature, and thus held that the solution was not more reason, but
less humanity. For historical materialists like Harvey, neither approach was
sufficient. The former erased the social and political-economic causes of
environmental problems and justified a managerial environmentalism that
laboured in the interest of capital accumulation, while the latter made analysis of the causes of environmental change irrelevant, since humans as a
whole were to blame.

One of the most significant contributions of historical materialists was
to show that both responses took recourse to the same, flawed, understanding of nature as a realm *external* to society. For Harvey and Smith,
the notion of 'external' nature was at once conceptually incoherent and
politically problematic: conceptually incoherent because it made it next to
impossible to imagine humanity's place *within* nature; politically problematic because it translated environmental problems into either a technical
problem, or a universal and ahistorical problem, and thereby erased the
specific social and political relations that shaped environmental change.
This is perhaps most immediately evident in the ecocentric position, which
imagines nature opposed to humanity. From this perspective *any* sign of
human presence signalled the 'end' of nature, for nature could only be
truly 'natural' in the absence of people (see Cronon 1995). Not only did
this lend support to an environmentalism that privileged 'wilderness' over
the everyday socio-ecological environments of local communities (see Di
Chiro 1995), it also gave rise to what Smith (1996) called the 'fetishization' of nature – or 'nature idolatry' – whereby in the rush to 'save' nature
from humans the social content of putatively 'natural' entities was entirely
hidden from view. Harvey's (1996) provocative claim that there is nothing
'unnatural' about New York City was explicitly designed to contest this
fetishization of external nature. As too was his argument that the very
nature that environmentalists sought to save *from* humans wouldn't exist
in its present form had humans not been mixing their labour with the
land all along (see also Williams 1980). To remove humans, then, would
not 'save' nature, as many ecologists thought, it would only transform it.
Indeed, so intricately intertwined were humans and the environment that
far from preserving nature, removing humans could well be disastrous 'for
all species and forms [of life] that have become dependent upon it' (Harvey
1996: 186).

Ultimately, Harvey and Smith contest nature idolatry because it hinders
our ability to understand *how* and *why* environmental change occurs.
Smith (1996) goes so far as to suggest that the fetishization of nature results
in contradictory politics, for it enables one to advocate for the preservation

of nature in one place even as one contributes to, and extends, a set of social and economic practices that relentlessly objectify and exploit the earth elsewhere (see also Cronon 1995; Davis 1995). To do this, one need only imagine that ecology (nature) lies in one sphere, and the economy (society) in another, and thus fail to see how they are linked.

Contesting neo-Malthusianism

Is the answer to locate humanity 'within' nature? Perhaps, although this carries a different risk – that of subsuming humanity within nature and making social life subject to natural law. This danger is most acute, Smith (1984) argues, when notions of external nature are combined with notions of universal nature. If nature is posited as external, the argument goes, it becomes possible to imagine that it has its 'own' order and its 'own' immutable laws, independent of human activities and observations; if subsequently combined with notions of 'universal' nature these 'laws' can then be seen to apply to humans too, invoking a transcendental order against which humanity can do nothing.

As early as his 1974 essay 'Population, resources and the ideology of science', Harvey energetically attacked this understanding, as part of his critique of a resurgent Malthusianism in social, political and ecological thought.[4] At one level Harvey's argument was about the relation between science and ideology. Science, Harvey claimed, was not neutral; particular scientific methods led to particular conclusions. For instance, Malthus reached his conclusions about natural limits by adhering to an empiricist position – the apparent 'self-evidence' of scarcity – all the while assuming two a priori postulates: that food is necessary but limited, and that passion between the sexes is constant. Hence, what the empiricist Malthus 'saw' everywhere in the world around him – scarcity – could be understood as a 'natural law' hard-wired into the way that the world worked (universal nature), even though his presuppositions were thoroughly ideological. This had great consequences, for Malthus would go on to develop his ideas into a political-economic theory that claimed to explain – but in Harvey's view merely sanctioned – the necessity of surplus consumption by landholders and the unavoidable poverty of workers.

Harvey's critique makes clear why for Smith the conjunction of 'external' and 'universal' nature makes for such a potent brew: it naturalizes existing economic and political relations, replacing history and politics with inevitability. The solution was not to fall back into the old dichotomy but to understand nature as a 'unity' that included human labour. This placed humanity within nature, to be sure, but it did so *as one of its constituent parts*, rather than subject to its transcendental laws. On this basis Harvey could argue that nature and resources were not asocial givens, but historical outcomes. As he later explained,

> To say that scarcity resides in nature and that natural limits exist is to ignore how scarcity is socially produced and how 'limits' are a social relation *within* nature (including human society) rather than some externally imposed necessity.
>
> (1996a: 147)

By refusing the notion of universal nature, scarcity could be seen to have social causes 'peculiar to the capitalist mode of production' (Marx 1967 [1867]: 632–3); to the extent that capitalist production replaced variable capital with constant capital, a 'surplus population' was created which routinely faced scarcity and experienced want. At its core, Harvey argued, the problem of scarcity was historical and political, not natural and inevitable.

Anticipating arguments later in this chapter, we should note that in his 1974 essay Harvey went to great pains to show that Malthus was trapped within an 'Aristotelian' understanding of the world. Most readers pass over this aspect of the essay, but in so doing they miss one of the earliest – and most explicit – statements of Harvey's underlying ontological commitments. The problem with Aristotelian thought, Harvey argued, was that it imagined the world to be a realm of distinct and autonomous things, each with its own essence. It was this assumption that had led Malthus to assume an immutable nature that consisted of eternal forms with no real history, and to extend its laws to humans. Ultimately, Malthus' Aristotelian ontology, combined with his empiricism, had led him to impose 'stationary tools' upon a 'changing world' (1974d: 176). This was a crucial error for, as Harvey put it, 'elements, things, structures and systems do not exist outside of or prior to the processes, flows, and relations that create, sustain or undermine them'. Later we will see that this critique of Aristotelian ontology places Harvey's work in close proximity to the non-essentialist ontologies of a number of his contemporaries, including Deleuze, Serres, Latour and others. At present we need only note that in his 1974 essay Harvey turned to Marx to provide an alternative way of imagining the problem of nature and resources.[5] Marx's dialectical materialism, Harvey claimed, refused to understand things – 'resources', or even 'needs' – independently of the relations that constituted them. Resources had to be defined relationally, in terms of a *mode of production* or a *social formation* that continuously 'produced' them through the physical, mental and technological activities of people: 'There is, therefore, no such thing as a resource in abstract or a resource which exists as a "thing in itself'" (1974d: 168). For Harvey, what counted as a resource at any given moment, and the limits of such a resource, was something determined by the totality of the relations in which resources were materially and discursively constituted.[6]

In sum, while Malthus – and many of his interpreters – imagined a world of immutable natural laws to which humanity must submit, Harvey posited a socio-ecological world that was *actively being shaped*. This also stood as an indictment of empiricism, for 'to define elements relationally means to interpret them in a way external to direct observation' (1974: 169). One must attend to the dynamics *shaping* the world, rather than accept what 'is' as either self-evident or immutable. Harvey's later work on the environment and social justice is remarkable for its consistency with these initial ontological, epistemological and political positions. In his 1974 essay, for instance, he had already identified Leibniz and Spinoza, in addition to Hegel and Marx, as forming the basis for his 'relational' understanding of the world. Some twenty years later Harvey (1996) would return to these thinkers – this time adding Alfred Whitehead to the mix – in his most thorough working out of a 'historical-geographical materialist' understanding of society–environment relations.

Towards a non-Malthusian eco-Marxism

I will return to Harvey's ontological claims later. First, it is important to note that Harvey's historical-materialist approach has led him to distance his work from many if not most eco-Marxists (i.e. James O'Connor, Elmer Altwater, Ted Benton, John Bellamy Foster and Paul Burkett). Although it initially seems counter-intuitive, it demands emphasis, lest Harvey be saddled with contradictory views. While many eco-Marxists sought to bring about a *rapprochement* between Marxism and ecology, finding in the latter terms and concepts to modify the former, Harvey has consistently sought to *incorporate* ecology and eco-politics within the terms of an expanded historical-geographical materialism. Or, put better, when it comes to the matter of ecology we can locate within Marxism two competing strands: those who seek to extend the insights of historical materialism to questions of the environment, and thus understand 'nature' as itself an effect of historical forces (i.e. Harvey, Smith), and those who accept nature's externality and seek to 'renovate' Marxist theories of economic crises so as to take external nature (i.e. natural limits) into account.

The difference may at first seem insignificant, but if we turn to the work of Elmar Altvater (1991) we can gain an appreciation of its importance.

Like Harvey, Altvater is interested in the relation between capitalism and environmental change. But his starting point and thus his conclusions and politics are quite different. Altvater begins with the laws of thermo-dynamics. These laws in turn become the basis for an *ecological* critique of capitalism, because, as Altvater explains, the expansionary logic of capital (which requires ever more production) necessarily runs up against the limited quantity and quality of the earth's energy. The result is environ-mental degradation or eco-scarcity. Stated in this way, we might initially think that the problem is capitalism, since in the face of the earth's limited energy its expansionary logic makes it unsustainable. However, turning to the second law of thermodynamics, Altvater argues that it is not simply *capitalist* production that increases the earth's entropy, but *all* production, since the creation of use-values necessarily involves the thermodynamic transformation of matter (see also Martinez-Alier 1987). Because energy cannot be created (Altvater assumes a closed system, or 'celestrial con-straints'), all activities in nature move energy from 'higher' to 'lower' levels. It turns out, then, that for Alvater what is specific to capitalism is merely its tendency to *increase* entropy, owing to its expansionary nature. Crucially, since humans must work to live, entropy remains the 'bottom line' of *all* social formations.[7]

I have perhaps stated Altvater's position in too stark terms. There is, after all, considerable subtlety in his work. For instance, he sets out a complex understanding of the 'social fabric' of capitalism, as part of how capitalist economies are shaped and regulated, and as part of how con-tradictions – economic, social and ecological – emerge and are resolved. Accordingly, he explains that capitalism must not be seen to have an inexor-able 'inner logic'. This aligns Alvater with certain post-Marxists who seek to avoid economistic understandings of society, and with geographers such as Eric Swyngedouw, Gavin Bridge and Karen Bakker, who have sought to develop a *regulationist* approach to eco-Marxism. Yet, for all the sophisti-cation in Altvater's conceptualization of the 'social', ecology provides him with an ahistorical and apolitical bottom line: nature is external, the laws of thermodynamics are immutable – over time human actions will 'wind down' the earth's energy and resources. The problem with capitalism is not that its logic is bent on nature's destruction – for all human labour plays that role – but rather that its imperative towards growth means that it will radically foreshorten the earth's 'best before' date. To be sure, Altvater imagined the possibility of establishing economic systems that could *reduce* the rate of entropy, but ultimately these merely postponed the final day of reckoning.

It would be a mistake to paint all eco-Marxists with the same brush.

Some, like Ted Benton (1989), have argued for a more historically specific, and thus contingent, notion of 'limits', a position closer to Harvey's own. Nor should their desire to 'bring nature back in' to Marxist theory be summarily dismissed. Arguably Marx downplayed the constitutive role of non-human nature in social life (owing perhaps to his focus on *industrial* rather than *primary* production). And we would be silly to think that current economic and social practices can be sustained indefinitely. There is abundant evidence that a market economy dependent upon oil can be maintained only so long before resource scarcity, air pollution or global warming starts to exert its influence. For the eco-Marxists, the materiality of nature matters and any theory of capitalist society that ignores this is woefully incomplete. Yet, despite their desire to overcome dualism, most retain in some measure a sense of nature's externality. This may be in part because dialectics represents too crude a method to overcome dualism, retaining the terms of the binary even as it seeks to place them in relation. With the world so divided it come as little surprise that a discourse of 'limits' – and thus the ghost of Malthus – slips back into their analytical frames, for all that remains to do is conceive both sides of the dualism – society and nature – as governed by laws: in the case of society, the 'iron laws' of capitalist accumulation, and in the case of nature, the laws of classical physics. This is most immediately evident in the case of Altvater, where the ghost of Malthus is alive and well, even if now travelling under a different guise, no longer the passion of the sexes and the inelastic supply of food, but the second law of thermodynamics and the inevitable increase of entropy.

Of the eco-Marxists, Ted Benton goes the furthest towards eschewing *natural* limits, and at points Harvey's 1974 arguments parallel his:

> Marx saw the capitalist law of accumulation always pushing society to the limits of its potential social relations and to the limits of its natural resource base, continuously destroying the potential for 'the exploitation and exchange of nature and intellectual forces'. Resource limitations could be rolled back by technological change, but the tide of capitalist accumulation quickly spreads up to these new limits.
>
> (2002: 53)

To be sure, nature matters, but approaches that locate scarcity *in* nature – posited as simultaneously external and universal – must be distrusted, for, as evident in the work of Malthus, they are nothing less than 'a sad capitulation to capitalistic arguments'(Harvey 1996a: 146).

To return to an earlier point, we might say that the problem with the eco-Marxists was that they got their ontology wrong; theirs was an 'Aristotelian' ontology of fixed forms, despite their allegiance to Marxism. What was needed was a fully fledged *historical-geographical materialism* in which all things were understood in terms of their emergent properties, and in which nature was seen to be *produced* through specific material practices.[8] Without this, eco-Marxism was destined to proceed 'at a level of historical-geographical abstraction that is most un-Marxist' (Harvey 1996a: 183).

Marx and the Production of Nature

What, then, would it mean to approach the question of nature in a *Marxist* manner? After all, it is widely known that Marx's ideas of nature were far from systematic. Nevertheless, the broad outlines of a historical-materialist approach can be sketched with some confidence, with the labour process firmly at its centre (see also Schmidt 1971; Smith 1984; Castree 1995).

As Harvey and countless others have noted, Marx understood the labour process – the appropriation and transformation of non-human nature to meet human needs – to be a quasi-transcendental condition (see Harvey 1982a: 100). Marx sets this out clearly in his *Economic and Philosophic Manuscripts*:

> Nature is man's inorganic body . . . Man lives from nature, i.e. nature is his body, and he must maintain a continuing dialogue with it if he is not to die. To say that man's physical and mental life is linked to nature simply means that nature is linked to itself
>
> (Marx 1975: 328)

Humanity exists as a part of nature; people must work to live. These two statements are crucial, for, taken together, they imply that labour is not something imposed upon nature from the outside, as if an external force that destroys nature, but is itself one of nature's constituent parts. As Marx would later explain:

> [Man] opposes himself to Nature *as one of her own forces*, setting in motion arms and legs, head and hands, the natural forces of his body, in order to appropriate Nature's productions in a form adapted to his own wants. By thus acting on the external world and changing it, he at the same time changes his own nature.
>
> (Marx 1967 [1867]: 173, italics added)

Stated simply, society and nature name an *internal relation* within a larger unity.

To the extent that a separation of humanity and nature exists at any given moment, Harvey (1982a) argues, it is as an historical effect of the labour process, in which humans actively oppose themselves to non-human nature. There is no prior ontological divide, for that would be to separate humanity from nature at the outset, precisely the error of bourgeois ideologies of nature. Further, if we accept these propositions, then nature can be conceived as neither external nor asocial, but as something *socially produced*. Neil Smith readily admits that this idea sounds 'quixotic', but explains that

> What jars us so much about this idea . . . is that it defies the conventional, sacrosanct separation of nature and society, and it does so with such abandon and without shame. We are used to conceiving of nature as external to society, pristine and pre-human, or else a grand universal in which human beings are small and simple cogs.
>
> (1984: xiv)

This claim has understandably scandalized many eco-centrics, for it refuses to posit non-human nature as pristine and in need of preservation. It instead turns towards a different basis for environmental politics, one firmly focused on how future natures are to be produced, and with what consequences for humans and non-humans alike. The underlying ontological condition – that humanity must leave marks on the world – leads directly to ethical-political questions concerning our responsibility for the *future* of socio-nature, since, by definition, it is something to be determined by history and politics, rather than by necessity. In short, while bourgeois ideologies imagine an external nature prior to politics, Harvey reveals the need for a *political theory* of nature (see also Smith 1995: 45).

Clearly one of the strengths of the production of nature thesis is that it presents nature as a historical product. This suggests the possibility of an *analytics* of nature's production, to the extent that we can identify and understand the practices and forces shaping everyday environmental practices. Moreover, it suggests that it may be possible to consider how *capitalism* produces nature in new and unique ways, giving shape to specific – and highly uneven – geographies of social nature with consequences for humans and non-humans alike, from the production of GMO seeds by capitalist agribusiness to the privatization of the genetic commons facilitated by neoliberal regimes of intellectual property rights and free trade.

Despite these strengths, the production of nature thesis has not avoided criticism, much of it sharp. A common complaint is that writers like Harvey and Smith present an *economistic* and hence *reductionist* understanding of nature's production. The production of nature, critics contend, is not solely determined by the imperatives of capitalism. One must take into account the heterogenous cultural practices – from science to aesthetics

– that contribute to the production and transformation of social natures (Haraway 1997; Braun 2000). Others have found the production of nature thesis deeply anthropocentric. We can understand this in two ways. On the one hand it privileges human needs and desires; non-human nature appears to have value only in relation to social goals. Thus, Harvey risks reproducing the same *Promethean* or *instrumental* relation to non-human nature that at other points he places at the feet of capitalism and its relentless pursuit of profits. A popular response to this sort of anthropocentrism has been to argue that nature has 'intrinsic value'. Harvey (1996a) is deeply sceptical of this move, and rightly so, since it reasserts an external and essentialist understanding of nature, and fails to recognize how all valuing is inescapably a *human* valuing. There is a another sense in which the production of nature thesis is anthropocentric that is not so easily sidestepped: its tendency to place *human action* – and in particular *human labour* – at the centre of nature's dynamic history. Within Marxist approaches, natural history is often reduced to the labour process. It is only humans, often only capital, which acts: everything else is *subject to* the work of humanity. This comes perilously close to reasserting the subject–object dichotomy of the Enlightenment, where human will and ingenuity is played out on a passive earth. In short, there is little or no room in the production of nature thesis for actors that are not human. Not all Marxists accept this position. Geographers as diverse as George Henderson (1999) and Gavin Bridge (2000) have emphasized the 'instransigence' of nature (see also Castree 2003), although even these accounts tend to posit non-human agency only to the extent that the environment *resists* commodification or creates *barriers* to the circulation of capital, an approach that still places human action firmly at the centre of the drama.[9]

Finally, a number of other scholars – like Sarah Whatmore, Donna Haraway and Bruno Latour – suggest that dialectics is too crude a method for understanding the heterogenous processes that constitute the environment. For Bruno Latour (2004), for instance, any talk of 'nature' or 'society', even if 'internally related', remains pitched at too great a level of abstraction, repeating Harvey's charge against the eco-Marxists. For him, there is no 'nature in general' any more than there is a 'society' which exists as a unified totality – there are only hybrid networks composed of *specific* human and non-human actants, that are of greater or shorter length, are more or less dense, and 'hold together' for longer or shorter periods of time. If we are to be proper ecologists, he suggests, we need to forget about 'nature' and 'society' altogether – we need to be even *more* materialist than historical materialism.

These objections merit close attention. Accordingly, the remainder of the chapter compares and contrasts Harvey's historical-materialist approach to the environment with an approach that seeks to overcome these difficulties, and which has begun to garner considerable attention in the social and environmental sciences: the 'new materialisms' of writers such as Deleuze, Serres, Latour and Whatmore. I am interested less in drawing sharp contrasts than I am in attending to the 'close proximity' between the two approaches. It is notable, for instance, that Harvey's reliance on Marx, and the latter's insistence on placing human labour *within* nature, leads him to share a great deal with the non-essentialist ontologies of a writer like Deleuze. For instance both emphasize that nature (being) is historical and open-ended. This should perhaps come as little surprise, since Deleuze shares with Marx – and thus with Harvey – the strong influence of writers like Spinoza, for whom that which exists (Substance) has no transcendental cause, but is instead the effect of forces immanent to the earth. But important differences also exist, and, as we will see, these hold immense consequences for how we imagine the site and goals of eco-politics.

Machinic Ecology

Affinities between Harvey and the new materialists can be seen clearly in *The Three Ecologies*, an extended essay by Félix Guattari, a frequent collaborator with Gilles Deleuze. In it, Guattari argues that any truly revolutionary ecology must replace 'environmental ecology' with 'machinic ecology'. This is the case, Guattari explains, because 'cosmic and human praxis has only ever been a question of machines, even, dare I say it, of war machines' (2000: 66).

This is odd language for environmentalism, as jarring as Smith's production of nature thesis. It is so in part because it flies in the face of our common association of nature with balance and order. For Guattari 'machinic' refers less to actual machines or mechanical processes than to what Casarino (2002) has felicitously called the 'explosive corporeal potentiality' of the earth. To the extent that the earth is characterized by productive forces rather than immutable objects, and to the extent that it undergoes continuous codings and decodings, territorializations and deterritorializations, it is a 'chaosmos' or 'abstract machine' that is continuously attaining novel forms. Hence, to speak of cosmic (and human) praxis as war machines – practices that actively deterritorialize – is to orient thought away from the contemplation of static forms ('being') and towards understanding the forces that continuously produce or dissolve them ('becoming'), forces that are not limited to human actions alone.[10]

The proximity to Harvey's understanding of nature is striking, and as we will see, so are the differences. Before I turn to this, however, somewhat more needs to be said about the ontological presuppositions that under-write Guattari's claims and the work of related writers like Deleuze, Serres and Latour. The first thing to note is that they work within the terms of a thoroughly *materialist* and *immanent* ontological discourse, which, in the words of Michael Hardt (1993: xiii), 'refuses any deep or hidden founda-tion of being'. For these writers, 'there is nothing veiled or negative' about being, 'it is fully expressed in the world' (xiii). This doctrine of immanence – with its antipathy towards external determination – rejects the possibil-ity that there can be any *supplemental* dimension to reality that orders it, as if from the outside, a position to which I will return later. For Deleuze, drawing upon Spinoza, the earth consists of 'a common plane of imma-nence on which all bodies, all minds, and all individuals are situated' (Deleuze 1988: 122).

We can draw several conclusions from this. For one, it suggests that all things participate in being equally – there are no entities that are more or less real than any other, that have a different ontological status, or that stand above, beneath or apart from the world. All things that exist – whether organisms, economies, institutions or texts – are precarious outcomes of the play of force. It is precisely in terms of such a 'common plane of immanence' that we should understand Bruno Latour's (1993) call for an *amodern* ontology that eschews all talk of 'nature' and 'society'. For Latour, as well as Donna Haraway, these categories leave us unable to understand the lively materiality of the world and the 'monstrous' becomings that occur within it. In important respects this position resembles Smith's (1984) and Har-vey's (1982, 1996) insistence on the unity of nature, although it decisively throws their economic reductionism and their anthropocentrism into ques-tion, as well the levels of abstraction at which their discussion of nature's production are pitched. It merits comment too that Deleuze's ontology is as far removed from classical physics, with its fixed laws and immuta-ble objects, as it is from transcendentalism, with its cosmos governed by final causes (Deleuze 1990b: 176; see also Ansell-Pearson 1999; DeLanda 1999, 2002). This is not to say that there is no organization to the world and that everything happens in a chaotic manner, nor that bodies have no permanence, only that there is no *pre-existing* order that defines the earth's socio-ecological organization in advance. Whatever organization exists at any given moment must be understood as an effect of the forces and prac-tices that cause things to hold together in a particular way, even if to us the 'things' of the world appear stable and unchanging.

It is not difficult to see that Deleuze's non-essentialist ontology has consequences for the question of nature, and for eco-politics more generally. If we accept its terms, for instance, then we must also accept that nature has no essence that requires preservation, no former balance that must be recovered, and no timeless truths that await our discovery. In the words of Deleuze and Guattari:

> Natural participations or nuptials . . . [are] the true Nature spanning the kingdoms of nature. These combinations are neither genetic nor structural; they are inter-kingdoms . . . That is the only way Nature operates – against itself . . . Becoming has neither beginning nor end, departure nor arrival, origin nor destination.
>
> (Deleuze and Guattari 1987: 241–2, 293)

The earth, then, is conceived as pure virtuality:

> The earth is not at all the *opposite* of deterritorialization: This can already be seen in the mystery of the 'natal', in which the earth as ardent, eccentric, or intense focal point is outside the territory and exists only in the movement of deterritorialization. More than that, the earth, the glacial, is *deterritorialization par excellence*.
>
> (1987: 509, italics added)

Far from a ground upon which movement occurs, the earth *is movement itself*. As Patrick Hayden puts it, the earth is itself

> the force of 'deterritorialization' and 'reterritorialization', since its continuous movements of development and variation unfold new relations of materials and forces . . . In this sense, the Earth is . . . the open-ended sum of a plurality of elements in constant interaction, rather than as an absolute order of Being transcending what is constituted in nature.
>
> (1997: 191–2)

It is in terms of such a naturalism – a naturalism without essences or final causes, a naturalism in which humans are both constituted and constitutive – that Deleuze and Guattari ultimately describe their work as geo-philosophy, a 'thinking that takes place in the relationship of territory [coding] and the earth [decoding]' (1994: 85).

From the perspective of 'environmental' or 'romantic' ecology this non-essentialist ontology can only be disorienting, for what is the purpose of ecological politics if nature has neither beginning nor end? Doesn't eco-politics need a firm ground from which to proceed? This approach appears fraught with danger, yet, as Manuel DeLanda (1999) succinctly explains, a great deal may actually be gained, for whereas in the modern ontology inherited from classical physics there is no place in nature for *time* (the future is already given in the past, since physical laws are assumed to be both universal and timeless, or because Nature is taken to be both external and fixed), in the amodern, non-essentialist ontology proposed by Deleuze (and extended by Serres and Latour), time is both directional and irreversible (although not necessarily linear) since the earth is continuously 'becoming otherwise'.[11] Deleuze's ontology allows for an understanding of the earth as always *in the making*, always an effect of the forces and practices that constitute it, in ways that cannot simply be 'undone'. In other words, it presents the future as open rather than closed, and thus brings us face to face not with the essence of things, but with questions of power, ethics and politics. There is no room for nostalgia here. Indeed, the radical ecological conclusion of Deleuze's ontology is that *all* entities are, in some way, artefactual and historical. Precisely for this reason it is essential to move beyond an environmental ecology preoccupied with parsing the 'pure' from the 'impure', the 'authentic' from the 'inauthentic', or the 'natural' from the 'artificial' (see Haraway 1997). Machinic ecology recognizes, and takes responsibility for, the future of nature that is still to come.

Perhaps now we are in a position to understand the radical import and revolutionary appeal of Deleuze's non-essentialist ontology, as well as its relation to environmental ethics and politics. Cesare Casarino (2002: xviii) notes that any ontological investigation that thinks of being as becoming 'immediately grounds being in politics'. In other words, politics comes before being. Practices make nature. It is this condition that Guattari most certainly had in mind when he argued that we must adapt our environmental ethics to 'this terrifying and fascinating situation' (2000: 66). This situation calls for a politics 'focused on the destiny of humanity' (2000: 67), which, since 'humanity' is relational – constituted within this common plane of immanence – means necessarily to engage in a politics of the earth. To be faithful to the 'terrible truth' of an amodern ontology, then, would be to follow Deleuze and Guattari and face without flinching the reality that ethics and politics must be understood in terms of *force* and *affect* rather than *truth* and *essence*, that eco-politics must be about creation, even experimentation, about 'eco-art' rather than preservation. In the provocative language that Guattari employs, it must be, and always is, about 'war machines', about practices that code and decode. Ultimately, what a philosophy of immanence suggests is that eco-politics must begin 'in the middle of things', for as Casarino explains, this is the only world there is.[12]

Here we should note again the close proximity to Harvey's historical materialist approach to nature. Like Deleuze and Guattari, Harvey imagines a nature whose future is open. Or, as Neil Smith (1984: 31) pithily puts it, the production of nature thesis 'implies an historical future that is *still to be determined* by political events and forces, not technical [or ecological] necessity'.[13] And, like Deleuze and Guattari, Harvey insists that we understand 'things' in terms of the processes that constitute them. Harvey's recent fondness for the philosopher-mathematician Alfred Whitehead's discussion of the 'fallacy of misplaced concreteness' (1948: 52) is noteworthy in this respect. Whitehead understood entities not as essences but as 'events' in which 'the potentiality of one actual entity is realized in another actual entity' (1929: 28). 'Misplaced concreteness', then, refers to mistaking things as concrete entities separate from their constitutive relations, in a fashion similar to Marx's critique of commodity fetishism.[14] It should come as no surprise, then, that Harvey locates in Whitehead an understanding of nature as the 'continuous exploration of novelty' (Harvey 1996a). Nor should we be surprised to learn that there is now an emerging conversation between the 'process philosophy' of Whitehead and the 'machinic ontology' of Deleuze and Guattari (see essays in Keller and Daniell 2002; Stengers 2002). As Anne Daniell (2002) explains, this comparative scholarship, while retaining differences between the thinkers, has sought 'to counter modern, Western assumptions of a substance-based, dualistic cosmology with expressions of a more fluid, multifaceted, ever-materializing cosmology'. Finally, Harvey's (2000a) recent calls for 'utopian' thinking that shuns appeals to 'form' or 'teleology' resonate with the 'eco-art' that Guattari offers radical ecologists, or the active experimentation proposed by Deleuze and Guattari as the task for geo-philosophy.

Historical Materialism and the New Materialists: External Determination versus Immanent Causality

We have clearly moved some distance from 'bourgeois' ideologies of nature, or the neo-Malthusian echoes found in the work of many eco-Marxists. Yet, it would be a grave mistake to collapse Harvey's historical materialism into the new materialisms offered by Deleuze and his interpreters. Despite their similarities, Harvey has consistently remained deeply sceptical of the latter, and his disagreements are instructive. Ultimately, what is at stake in their competing materialisms is nothing less than how we *understand* and *intervene* in present socio-ecological conditions. Here I focus on two points of contention: whether an emphasis should be placed on fluidity or permanence; and what it means to speak of specifically *capitalist* productions of nature.

Flow and permanence

In *Justice, Nature and the Geography of Difference* (1996a), Harvey has argued that the emphasis on 'flow' in contemporary social theory is wildly exaggerated. In his words, 'the reduction of everything to fluxes and flows, and the consequent emphasis upon the transitoriness of all forms and positions has its limits' (1996a: 7). He insists that we must attend equally to the kind of *permanences* constituted within these flows, something that for Harvey has a great deal to do with the pragmatics of politics: 'if everything that is solid is always instantaneously melting into air . . . it is very hard to accomplish anything or set one's mind to do anything' (1996a: 7).

This complaint is common, and it has considerable importance for how we envision the site and goals of eco-politics. Before turning to this, though, it is essential to avoid reading Harvey's emphasis on permanences as the reassertion of an outmoded ontology that seeks comfort in fixed forms and determinate processes. As a dialectician, Harvey strives to avoid any simple return to things-in-themselves. Rather, it is possible to read this as an attempt to amplify an aspect of non-essentialist ontologies on which the volume has been turned down by writers like Deleuze and Guattari, but which arguably is more fully addressed in Bergson's notion of 'duration', Latour's insistence on the 'relative stability' of networks, or the geographer Sarah Whatmore's attention to how things 'hold together'. While each adheres to a non-essentialist ontology, the stability of particular configurations of entities and flows – the manner in which they hold together and go on to produce effects of their own – is held to have considerable consequence, and forms a key focus for analysis and politics.

For Harvey specific socio-ecological forms are historical, reflecting the processes that produce them. At the same time, they have consequences for the future. This is consistent with his work on space and spatiality during the 1980s, most evident in his magisterial *Limits to Capital*, in which he sought to understand the production, durability and consequences of spatial forms (such as built environments), even as he analysed the forces that caused their inevitable dissolution. The non-human is decidedly absent in much of that text, but a similar emphasis pervades Harvey's later work on the 'dialectics' of space, place and environment:

> There is, I believe, little point in asserting some sort of 'dissolution of all fixity and permanence' in the famous 'last instance' if, as far as we human beings are concerned, that last instance is nowhere in sight . . . Dialectical argumentation cannot be understood as outside of the concrete material conditions of the world in which we find ourselves; and those concrete conditions are often so set in literal concrete (at least in relation to the

time and space of human action) that we must perforce acknowledge their permanence, significance, and power.

(1996a: 8)

For Harvey, flows continuously 'crystallize' into things. These require constant attention, and it is Whitehead as much as Marx who provides him with the needed conceptual framework. While Whitehead's 'processual' ontology enables Harvey to avoid the 'Aristotelian' trap he criticized in earlier work, it also allows him to attend to the 'relative fixity' of things in the world:

> I have so far construed the relations between 'moments' as flows, as open processes that pass unhindered from one moment to all others. But flows often crystallize into 'things', 'elements', and isolable 'domains' or 'systems' which assume relative permanence (and sometimes even acquire limited causal powers) within the social process. Reifications of free-flowing processes are always occurring to create actual 'permanences' in the social and material world around us . . . Whitehead's doctrine of 'permanences' firms up the idea. A 'permanence' arises as a system of 'extensive connection' out of processes. Entities achieve relative stability in their bounding and their internal ordering of processes creating space, for a time.
>
> (1996a: 81, 261)

It is not enough to insist, with the geographer Marcus Doel (1999), that 'permanence is a special effect of fluidics' and leave it at that. One must attend to permanences because they *contribute something* to history; they are not simply the outcome of constitutive processes, but affect those processes.

This critique has been made in more ecological terms by Mark Hansen (2000), who takes issue with Deleuze's concept of 'creative involution' by turning against Deleuze the very biological discourse upon which he so often relied. Deleuze's concept – influenced by Bergson's notion of 'creative evolution' – referred to the continuous folding and refolding of being, and has been taken by some as the basis for a revitalized bio-philosophy that encompasses humanity within it (see Ansell-Pearson 1999). Hansen argues that Deleuze reads Bergson incorrectly, and relies on outmoded ideas from biology, such that the 'machinic becoming' that he posits is seen to operate entirely independent of the existence and agency of actually existing entities. The point of contention is less the ontological status of the 'thing' or 'organism' (which Hansen, like Deleuze and Harvey, accepts as historical), than the possibility that the 'thing' or 'organism' might be more than just an outcome of historical change.

Despite Deleuze's debts to Bergson, Hansen suggests that the two writers held somewhat different understandings of the organism. For Bergson,

Hansen argues, the organism was at once an *outcome* of creative evolution and an *obstacle* or *limit* to the open-ended actualization of being. Moreover, if we add the recent insights of biologists, the organism – as a bundle of qualities and capabilities – comes to be seen also as part of what *shapes* the future. As Hansen explains,

> What Deleuze and Guattari seek is an understanding of the complex, relational causality that underlies the emergence of organismic effects from the molecular standpoint, that is, from a perspective or on an ontological level at which the organism has no causal autonomy. Such a perspective is, quite simply, alien to the conceptual terrain of current biology and complexity theory, where the tendency of morphogenesis to favor 'natural kinds' (Goodwin, Kauffman) and the fractal multilevel nature of the 'self' (Varela) necessitate interrelation between the plane of organization and the plane of immanence, between incipient order and transversal communication . . . [This] serves perfectly to illustrate what is crucial here: emergent actuals do not limit the virtual by means of an operation of negation, but rather express a concrete differentiation that *remains in contact with the domain of intensity* (or the virtuality) from which it emerges.
>
> (2000: 18, italics added)

For Hansen, Deleuze places too much weight on the fluidity found in population ecology and in notions of sub-organismic communication. What is underplayed in Deleuze's work, he argues, is the *productivity* of the organism itself, the effects *specific to* and *enabled by* any particular assemblage, not as something that merely arrests movement, stalling for a time the inexorable movement of the earth, but as something that actively produces and directs it, thereby contributing to its future.

Although pitched in more ecological language, the parallel with Harvey is clear: completely dissolving things into their relations – placing all theoretical and philosophical emphasis on the plane of intensity – runs counter to the same biological sciences that provided such a rich source of concepts for Deleuze's non-essentialist ontology. To posit Nature – or the 'machinic assemblage' that is the earth – as a 'cosmic expressionism through which Nature ceaselessly generates differentiation by cutting across any and all boundaries' (Hansen 2000: 21), appears unwarranted.

Whether we agree with Hansen's critique – and its application to more social and political entities – rests partly on what status we grant knowledges derived from the science of biology.[15] It is also a matter of how we read Deleuze's (and Guattari's) work. Although Deleuze is often read as an anarchist, even a nihilist, his writings are not exclusively concerned with deterritorialization and chance. Even Deleuze's harshest critics recognize this. Alain Badiou (2000), for instance, notes that it is Deleuze's acolytes who are more likely to follow this nihilist line. Indeed, in Deleuze's writings can be found many concepts and cautions that anticipate a critique such as Hansen's. His concept of 'assemblage', for instance, is flexible enough to be read as a continuously evolving configuration of elements, but *also* as a configuration of entities and forces that attains a certain kind of spatio-temporal durability. In short, it combines contingency *and* organization in the same concept. Likewise, his distinction, with Guattari, between 'molar' and 'molecular' forms – and their consistent emphasis on the simultaneity of each – is meant to avoid the fetishization of flow, as is their reminder that 'arboreal knots' can be found within rhizomes. The same is true of their discussion of 'state thinking', understood as that which limits, channels and disciplines the movement of becoming. Ultimately, Deleuze and Guattari do not argue that any and all configurations of being are possible – or desirable – only that entities do not exist as natural kinds, as if outside history.[16] At any given moment the rules of combination are precise: they have to do with *this* practice, *this* connection, *this* bifurcation – which is why becoming is the domain of ethics and politics, not blind chance, and why politics must always begin 'in the middle of things'. In this light, Harvey's desire to return our attention to 'permanences' is certainly justified, but it may be motivated more by immediate political concerns – in the face of dramatic socio-ecological change, how do we understand and respond to the WTO, World Bank and trade legislation? – than by philosophical differences with writers like Deleuze and Guattari. For Harvey is equally concerned to draw attention to, even to celebrate, the 'future becoming' of the earth, to remember that the earth defines a realm of potentiality with many possible socio-ecological outcomes.

A more serious reservation, and one that has occupied Harvey for years, is that while non-essentialist ontologies render socio-ecological futures a matter of power and politics, they do not in themselves provide a guide to what these politics should be. The hard question, then, is to know what kinds of politics are needed for what kinds of present conditions.

Capitalism and the production of nature: iron laws or immanent practices?

For Harvey, the question of nature invariably turns on the question of capitalism and its future, for it is capitalism that provides the 'generative processes' through which the production of nature occurs. On this he is unequivocal:

capital circulation . . . has made the environment what it is . . . Prevailing
practices dictate profit-driven transformation of environmental conditions
and an approach to nature which treats of it as a passive set of assets to be
scientifically assessed, used and valued in commercial (money) terms.

(1996a)

This is familiar language. It echoes eco-Marxists like James O'Connor
and John Bellamy Foster, and draws heavily on the work of Neil Smith,
who claimed that the events and forces by which nature is 'produced' are
'precisely those that determine the character and structure of the capitalist mode of production' (1984: 31). Under dictate from the accumulation
process, Smith continued, 'capital stalks the earth in search of natural
resources . . . No part of the earth's surface, the atmosphere, the oceans,
the geological substratum or the biological superstratum are immune from
transformation by capital' (1996a: 49, 56).

At the heart of eco-politics, then, must lie an analysis of capitalism and
its ecological and geographical effects. Here the significance of Marx again
comes to the fore. For Harvey, Marx provides much more than an ontology
in which nature exists as a unity; his economic writings provide analytical
tools for understanding the historical transformation of socio-ecological
conditions. Thus, for Harvey (1996a) the analysis of the production of
nature necessarily begins with the value form. As we saw earlier, in Marx
the production of use-values is understood as part of the 'species-being' of
humans, who must transform nature in order to live. Exchange-value, on
the other hand, names the particular *historical form* that the production of
nature takes under capitalism. It is the latter, then, that must be the focus of
analysis, for only by understanding dynamics specific to capitalist production and exchange can we fully understand the specific spatial and temporal
character of nature's production. This extends to environmental issues a
set of ideas Harvey first set out in *Limits to Capital*, in which he argued
that the need to overcome periodic overproduction crises gave rise to specific, albeit changing, historical geographies of capitalist development (i.e.
through a 'spatial fix'). Hence, to the extent that non-human nature is part
of the conditions of production it is a relatively simple matter for Harvey to
incorporate it into a 'fully-fledged' historical-geographical materialism, for
the same 'generative processes' that underwrite uneven development can be
enrolled to explain why specific productions of nature occur in particular
places, and to understand the tangled knot of social and ecological relations that arise at these sites.

This gives Harvey's account a certain explanatory power, but at the risk
of rendering it totalizing and reductionist, for the future of socio-nature is

very quickly reduced to a movement *internal* to the temporal rhythms and spatial orderings of capitalism (see Braun 2000). Despite Harvey's commitment to an ontology of multiple flows and forces – including at least nominally the agency of non-human actors – his analytical and political positions tend towards deterministic accounts that come down to 'the iron laws within the contingencies' (2003b: 152). Indeed, on this matter Harvey at times seems at odds with himself. In *JNGD*, for instance, he insists that we must maintain a focus on the value form, for this is the form that *all* environments, cultural artefacts and social relations assume in capitalist economies (see also Castree 2002). Yet at other moments he steps back to consider the multiple ways nature can be, and is, 'valued', and gestures towards the position that other forms of value – aesthetic or mythic for instance – have real effects in the world. A value-theoretical analysis, after all, may not be able to explain on its own the difference between specific productions of nature in North America (shaped in part by its preoccupation with wilderness) and Europe (with its more pastoral aesthetic), never mind the complex 'culture–natures' found elsewhere. Nor can a value-theoretical analysis adequately grasp the heterogeneity and creativity of technoscientific practices, which today are increasingly central to our socio-ecological assemblages (see Haraway 1997). In Harvey's recent work on nineteenth-century Parisian nature (Harvey 2003a), the same tensions are again on display. While duly noting that pastoral and arcadian visions influenced the produced nature of Haussmann's Paris, his underlying story is one of capitalist development. Again, it is not entirely clear whether Harvey sees the former to be determined by the latter, or whether the articulation is more provisional and less unidirectional, as if the form that capitalism took might *itself* have changed under the force of pastoral ideologies. The strong tendency in Harvey's work is to assert the former rather than the complexity implied by the latter. No wonder, then, that Noel Castree (2002: 132) worries that in approaches like Harvey's 'it is capitalism that appears . . . to have all the moves', while Donna Haraway feels it necessary to remind her readers that 'corporealization [the material-semiotic making of bodies] . . . is not reducible to capitalization or commodification' (1997: 141).

Ultimately, Harvey's desire to find 'foundational concepts' and locate 'generative processes' sits uneasily with the generalized relationality that he proposes in the opening chapters of *JNGD*, for while the latter hints towards a heterogeneous socio-ecological field that has no prior or external determination, and no single spatio-temporality, the former imagines an underlying logic that in the final analysis drives all socio-ecological change. Some might be tempted to take this as reason to dismiss Harvey's focus on capitalism and its ecological consequences altogether, or to dispense with all reference to capitalism. A more productive response, however, may be to ask how our analysis might change if we conceived of capitalism – and capitalist productions of nature – in terms of a *materialist* and *immanent* ontology. For this we must return a final time to Harvey's 'strange proximity' to writers like Deleuze and Latour.

What might it mean, then, to locate capitalism – or the 'economy' – within the same 'plane of immanence' on which 'all bodies, all minds, and all individuals are situated' (Deleuze 1988: 122)? In contrast to Harvey, such an approach would understand capitalism – and forms of capitalist calculation – as the outcome of a set of heterogenous and often mundane practices rather than an abstract logic that stands before or above the world. This does not mean that any talk of 'logics', 'generative processes', 'capitalist imperatives', even 'capitalist spirit', must be shunned. All are still possible, but from the perspective of an immanentist ontology they come to be seen, like all other things, in performative rather than deterministic terms, as inseparable from the myriad practices that constitute their conditions of possibility. Likewise, a value-theoretical understanding of nature's production is not rejected *tout court*, it is merely shown to apply in specific situations, and not to exhaust the processes by which socio-ecologies are constituted and differentiated. A value-theoretical understanding of nature's production is valid in the general or universal sense that Harvey presumes, *only so far as such conditions that make capitalist calculation possible are extended and 'hold together' over space and time.* To imagine otherwise – to posit 'global capitalism' as an all-encompassing, ever-expanding system that engulfs all of nature and society within its logic – is to fall prey to a kind of 'capitalo-centrism' that grants capitalism far more coherence than it has (see Gibson-Graham 1996). The result may be politically disabling, since it gets in the way of recognizing capitalism as the precarious achievement that it is. In practice this is to say nothing more than that capitalism is 'local at all points' – that it exists as a coherent entity only through the linking and extending of networks which are themselves composed of specific, situated practices (for example, the mundane practices that constitute the WTO and World Bank, the linking of financial markets through electronic communication, or the negotiation of an international system of intellectual property rights).

To understand capitalism in terms of a materialist and immanent ontology, then, is to understand it as a 'skein of networks' (Latour 1993), all of which are specific and finite. Its stability has no basis apart from these networks, even if the 'permanences' that result have generative effects of their own. For Deleuze and Guattari, capitalism is an 'acentered multiplicity' that consists of finite networks of automata in which communication runs from any neighbor to any other, the stems and channels do not preexist, and all individuals are interchangeable, defined only by their *state* at a given moment – such that the local operations are coordinated and the final, global result synchronized without a central agency.

(1997: 17)

To the extent that intervention in any specific network necessarily changes the configuration of these acentred systems, 'every politics is simultaneously a *macropolitics* and a *micropolitics*' (1997: 213). This does not rule out the possibility of increasingly global forms of capitalism (or the need for organization in politics). Deleuze and Guattari are clear about this: for them capitalism constitutes an 'axiomatic' (production for exchange) that is increasingly global, but this axiomatic 'holds' only within particular socio-technical-economic networks, and is 'global' only so far as these networks are extended across space and time. In their words, 'there can only be a world-economy when the mesh of the network is sufficiently fine' (1987: 468).

This is a lengthy detour, but it bears directly on how we theorize the production of nature. One of the difficulties with Harvey's approach is that the production of nature seems to be guided by something beneath or prior to the level of practice, as if there were two realities – one reality consisting of the everyday practices and physical forces that constitute socio-ecological conditions, and a second reality that consists of the logics that determine them. To posit capitalism in such terms is to imagine a doubled ontology: on the one hand a world of practices and things, and on the other hand, a separate world of logics and spirit.

In his brilliant study of the intricate ways that hydro dams, weaponry, mosquitoes, water, oligarchs and capital came to be connected in post-Second World War Egypt, Timothy Mitchell (2002) illustrates what is at stake in these debates. Not only does he reveal the abstraction 'capitalist logic' to be dependent upon 'complex statistical information in a centralized, mini-aturized, and visual form' (2002: 9), and 'the powers of government, law, statistical production, and economic knowledge that structure the economic whole' (2000: 11), he also, by bringing in all manner of non-human actors (water, blood, mosquitoes) shows why it is so difficult to squeeze everything into a simple 'economic' – and ultimately anthropocentric – explanation about the expansionary nature of capital:

If the web of events in wartime Egypt offers a certain resistance to [abstract] explanation, part of the reason may be that it includes a variety of agencies that are not exclusively human: the anopheles mosquito, the faciparum parasite, the chemical properties of ammonium nitrate, the 75mm guns of the Sherman tank, the hydraulic force of the river . . . These do not just interact with the activities of human agents. They make possible a world that somehow seems the outcome of human rationality and programming. They shape a variety of social processes, sometimes according to human plans, but just as often not, or at least not quite. How is it, we need to ask, that forms of rationality, planning, expertise, and profit arise from this effect?

(2002: 30)

Arise from this effect, rather than drive it. To assume the latter is to attribute to capital, reason or expertise 'enchanted powers'. The calculations made by individuals, Mitchell suggests, are not intrinsic properties of the 'self'. Nor does the self merely 'personify' an abstract rationality (Capital). As Mitchell explains in the case of one Egyptian capitalist:

> The circuits that 'Abbud tried to control and transform into sources of profit involved family networks, the properties of sugar and nitrates, the labor of those harvesting cane, imperial connections, and the shortages brought by war. The production of profit, or surplus value, came about only by working within and transforming such other forces and reserves. *Thus a term like 'capitalist development' covers a series of agencies, logics, chain reactions, and contingent interactions.*
>
> (2002: 51, italics added)

That we think otherwise is the effect of a sleight of hand whereby specific events in particular places come to be situated within a 'universal framework' and, within this framework are seen merely as 'the local occurrence of something more general' in which 'one always knows in advance who the protagonists are' (2002: 28, 29).

There is nothing here that suggests that we cannot speak of capitalism when we interrogate the shaping of socio-ecological assemblages. To put it more prosaically, there is nothing in Mitchell's account to suggest that an individual, or a corporation, faced with the question of profitability in a generalized system of private property, commodity production and competitive market exchange, would not seek to reduce the costs of production, 'stalk the earth' in search of cheaper raw materials, 'externalize' the ecological costs of production, and so on. Such practices occur daily. It only means that the possibility of a specifically *capitalist* form of rationality at any given moment must be understood in terms of a web of practices that articulate into a stable network such things as property law, trading blocs, scientific laboratories, machines, legislators and bureaucrats, not to mention insects, viruses and blood. By this view capitalism is not 'a ubiquitous entity, which reaches out powerfully in all directions, but . . . a network which is stronger in some places than in others and which needs to be constantly worked at to remain coherent over time and through space' (Leyshon 1998: 435). Such networks are necessarily heterogenous and open, continuously reinforced or broken, stabilized or destabilized by the practices and actors that compose them, human and non-human alike.

Contrary to what critics of Deleuze and Guattari suggest, they are not giving up on the critique of capitalism. They are suggesting something else: if, at the dawn of the twenty-first century, capital has become an axiomatic, it is so not because it has magical powers, but because of the fine weave of practices – from the congresses of the WTO to the boardrooms of the World Bank, from intellectual property laws to labour legislation in developing countries, from the laboratories of US universities to the field mapping of genetic materials in Mexico and Costa Rica – that produce a *territory* for the 'law' of value to operate on, and where profit-oriented economic rationalities can both occur and, moreover, contribute to the 'decoding' of the social-ecological assemblage defined by these networks. To the extent that networks are constituted in such a manner, then an analysis of capitalism, its institutions and its imperatives is clearly on the table. And to the extent that these 'hold together', then Harvey is entirely correct to call attention to how the drive for profit can draw new places and new ecologies into relation, and how capitalism can 'reterritorialize' the earth. As Deleuze and Guattari (1987) argue, in so far as capital is today an axiomatic it continuously 'decodes' existing socio-ecological assemblages (and may produce new – and potentially undesirable – natures in the act of doing so). But there is nothing magical about the process; it is grounded in the mundane, everyday practices that give capitalism its ontology.

With this in mind, it becomes possible to see a paradox within Harvey's discussion of the production of nature: to the extent that he slides quickly into global abstractions, his analysis seems at odds with his avowed objective of developing a fully fledged historical-geographical materialism. He may be, as Latour (1986) argues of historical materialism in general, *inadequately materialist*, for the search for profits must be situated on the same plane as marine clocks and the keeping of log books: each is cause and effect of the other.

Stated baldly, the difference between Harvey and the new materialists is the difference between immanent causality and external determination (see Hardt 1991). Crucially, we cannot simply 'split the difference' between these, despite the obvious attraction of doing so (for an attempt see; Swyngeduow 1999). One cannot have a 'less exacting' philosophy of immanence, or a 'modified' transcendentalism. The result can only lead to contradictory statements, such as calls to 'historicize' or 'contextualize' networks and their heterogenous associations, as if there was a second history apart from the immanent practices that constitute the first one. However many dimensions the world may have, it 'never has a supplementary dimension to that which transpires upon it' (Deleuze and Guattari 1987: 266).

Conclusion: Political Natures

I began this chapter by arguing that Harvey sets out the terms of a scandalous environmentalism. For him, 'nature' names a unity; it cannot be separated from society as its own autonomous domain. It should come as no surprise, then, that Harvey sees all ecological projects as social projects, and vice versa, for to imagine one without the other would be to fall prey to the sort of dualistic thinking that stands in the way of understanding the 'becoming' of the world. Nature has neither beginning nor end: all nature is political nature.

Harvey develops this line of thought most thoroughly in *JNGD*, in which he forcibly wrenches eco-politics from a complacent middle class who imagine 'nature' in the image of national parks, wilderness reserves and the 'last great places' thought to be untouched by humans, all the while ignoring the environmental problems that most directly affect the working poor and racialized communities – air and water pollution, lead paint, inadequate housing, workplace hazards – naively displacing the very people, often indigenous groups or poor rural residents, who lived and shaped the apparently 'wild' places that they fetishize, and failing to understand the relation between their own economic practices and ecological change. This is the bread and butter of the environmental justice movement's critique of mainstream environmentalism, and informs their attempt to place race and class at the heart of eco-politics. It has also forcibly demanded of middle-class environmentalists that they reconsider the bourgeois ideologies of nature that shape their political agendas (see Di Chiro 1995). It was precisely such an inversion of bourgeois ideologies that lay behind Harvey's provocative claim that New York City is an 'ecosystem', but the larger point is that for Harvey *all* nature is urban nature, for to the extent that systems of production, exchange and consumption have become global, 'distant' natures and everyday urban environments are woven into tight webs of socio-ecological and spatial relations. This does much more than disturb the distinction between nature and society; it also radically reconfigures the terrain – and the goals – of green politics. It makes urban issues – water supply, clean air, sewage and trash, green space in the inner city, consumption and overconsumption – an issue for environmentalists as much as wilderness areas and hiking trails. But it also demands that we think about the city in terms of its spatio-temporalities, in terms of the intricate web of connections that constitute urban nature, connections that in the case of New York City's (previously public) infrastructure include the hydroelectric dams of James Bay in northern Quebec, the aqueducts and pipelines that draw water to New York from lakes and rivers in upstate New York, and the gravel pits of New Jersey which provide the raw materials for the city's streets and sidewalks (see Gandy 2002). Add in the consumption practices of the city's residents, and these political-ecological networks extend to the ends of the earth, taking in ecological and labour conditions from the coffee plantations in Brazil to the sweatshops of mainland China. Precisely for this reason, Harvey's historical-geographical materialism is well suited for a radical environmentalism, for it provides an understanding of nature as something continuously being made and remade through the situated practices of countless actors, both near and distant. The *future* of nature – or more correctly, the future of *socio-nature* – is therefore an ongoing ethical and political project.

It is precisely Harvey's commitment to open-ended futures that distances him from other eco-Marxists, whom he finds compromised by a static, Malthusian view of the earth. And, arguably, it is also what stands behind his recent turn to 'utopic' thought (2000a). To the extent that socio-nature names an open rather than a closed field, eco-politics must be oriented not towards conservation, since the world never holds still, but to the possibilities and consequences of a 'new earth' and 'new humanity' that is still to come. The latter phrases are, of course, Deleuze and Guattari's, not Harvey's, but what is striking about Harvey's recent call to 'spatial play' (which, as we now know, must necessarily involve the non-human) is that it closely parallels the 'ontological politics' of the new materialists. Guattari too wished to avoid a politics of fixed forms and determinate futures. His nature was 'machinic', his future natures all about praxis. There is nothing given in advance about the play of the world: 'anything is possible – the worst disasters or the most flexible evolutions' (2000a: 66).

All nature is political nature. Yet, are all eco-politics equally political? I have dwelt at length on the 'strange proximity' between Harvey and the new materialists in order to call attention to both the similarities and the differences in their materialist approaches to nature and the environment. For while they share a critique of the essentialist ontologies of modernist physics and environmental ecology, each leads us to imagine the site of eco-politics differently. Arguably, Harvey's recourse to 'metatheoretical' positions contrasts with the 'pragmatics' of Deleuze and Guattari. While

Deleuze and Guattari insist that we must begin 'in the middle', they do so because they refuse to presuppose what presents itself as the most urgent site of political intervention. There are, as Deleuze and Parnet (1987) put it, 'many politics' rather than 'Politics'. It is the present moment – the way that any given assemblage is composed – that *gives us* our politics: we cannot know the political terrain in advance. Harvey, on the other hand, is more likely to presuppose what sort of eco-politics is needed, precisely because he reserves a privileged place for certain abstractions – 'capital', 'logics of accumulation', 'generative processes' – which appear to have magical powers separate from the micropractices and the conjunctural moments that hold such importance for Deleuze. Hence, while it is true that for both of them 'eco-art' is the art of 'becoming', for Harvey what this art can or should be appears at times rather constrained. We must ask, then, whether the charge often levelled against Deleuze – that he makes it difficult to conceive of politics – may apply also, and perhaps even more so, to Harvey. For, while Harvey's recourse to a 'value-theoretical' analysis of the present appears to be the more 'materialist' and 'practical' approach, it runs the risk of providing the activist with little precision, and even less hope, if it produces Capitalism in monolithic terms and endows it with more power and coherence than it may actually have. The irony here is that the more modest kind of explanation put forward by Deleuze may allow for a more effective eco-politics, for it is *this* body, *this* assemblage, *this* set of practices, *these* links, that must be understood before political struggles can be properly conceived.

It is perhaps in this light that we should understand the recent struggles by eco-activists around the activities of the World Bank: to the extent that the World Bank – as a specific set of institutional and environmental practices – produces a more dense weave of practices, laws and regulations that enable capital to become a 'global axiomatic', its structure must be subjected to a politics of 'decoding'. And precisely because the micropractices of the World Bank – its reports, conventions, pacts and agreements – help create a 'global' space safe for capitalism, the distinction between a 'micro' eco-politics and a 'macro' eco-politics melts away. The future of nature – the new earth and the new humanity still to come – hangs in the balance of such spatial play.

Notes

1 My use of the phrase 'strange proximity' is meant to signal two approaches that are similar despite profound differences (see Nancy 1996). It is meant to avoid

the trap of seeing traditions of thought either as binary oppositions or as differences that can be overcome through combination. See below, pp. 203–18.

2 Harvey's arguments are not always consistent with his historical materialism. It would be difficult, for instance, to reconcile his claims about the continuous production of 'novelty' in nature, and his emphasis on 'becoming', found in *Justice, Nature and the Geography of Difference* (1996a), with his arguments for 'species being' in *Spaces of Hope* (2000a), a decidedly non-dialectical concept derived from the early Marx and that flirts with essentialism. For a critique from an otherwise sympathetic ally, see Smith (2001).

3 Harvey's work on nature and the environment displays an immense debt to Neil Smith, whose book *Uneven Development* (1984) developed a specifically *Marxist* understanding of nature (see also Smith 1996).

4 Arguably, neo-Malthusian thinking reached its apogee in Western environmental thought with pronouncements about future scarcity from the Club of Rome (Meadows et al. 1972) and Paul Ehrlich (1968).

5 Crucially, Harvey did not claim for Marx a place *outside* ideology, but instead extended his conception of ideology to encompass science.

6 Harvey's notion of 'internal relations' is already at this point taken from Ollman (1971).

7 Although he refrains from naming Altvater, Harvey is ruthless in his criticism of such approaches:

> It is one thing to argue that the second law of thermodynamics and the laws of ecological dynamics are necessary conditions within which all human societies have their being, but quite another to treat them as sufficient conditions for the understanding of human history. *To propose the latter would imply that the whole of human history is an exercise in unsustainability in violation of natural law. This is so grand an assertion as to be pointless* (1996a: 140).

8 'Against the idea that we are headed over the cliff into some abyss (collapse) or that we are about to run into a solid and immovable brick wall (limits), I think it consistent with both the better sorts of environmental thinking and Marx's dialectical materialism to construe ourselves as embedded within an on-going flow of living processes that we can individually and collectively affect through our actions' (Harvey 2000a: 218).

9 Harvey (1996a) quotes affirmatively Richard Lewontin's claims about nature as an 'active subject', but this rarely, if ever, finds its way into his accounts of the production of nature.

10 For Deleuze (1990: 172) a war machine has 'nothing to do with war but has to do with a particular way of occupying, taking up, space-time, or inventing new space-times: revolutionary movements . . . artistic movements too, are war machines'. Nevertheless, the language is clearly masculinist, for which Deleuze has encountered sharp criticism.

11 In later works Deleuze and Guattari draw upon non-equilibrium physics to found their ontological claims, and in particular, the work of Prigogine and Stengers (1984).

12 See also Latour 1998, 2004.

13 Smith's target was not only neo-Malthusians, but the pessimism of the Frankfurt School, whose members could only imagine a future in which nature – external and internal – was entirely subjugated to 'instrumental' or 'technical' reason (Schmidt 1971; Horkheimer and Adorno 1972); for a summary see Vogel 1996). As Smith rightly noted, the pessimism of the Frankfurt School was in part a consequence of their adherence to a 'bourgeois' ideology of nature, which allowed them to posit human reason (and work) as necessarily leading to the domination of 'external' nature.

14 Donna Haraway (1997) draws out the parallels between Marx's critique of 'fetishization' and Whitehead's critique of 'misplaced concreteness'.

15 It is worth noting that while Deleuze (1990) values scientific concepts for what they can 'do' rather than their reference to the world, many of his interpreters understand his use of scientific concepts as a sanction for a renewed realism that presumes that science reveals nature and its processes and thus provides the 'truth' of ontology (for a critique, see Massey 1999).

16 It is often overlooked in work on Deleuze that he routinely cautions against *too rapid* deterritorialization.

11

David Harvey: A Rock in a Hard Place

Nigel Thrift

The war is endless. The most we can hope for is an occasional pause in the conflict. Do you realise that you could be seriously under-armed?

Moorcock 2003: 229

Un monarque est-il necessairement plus intelligent que ses ministres ou ses sujets?

Tarde 1999 [1898]

L'univers est plein de rhythmes multiformes, entrecroisés à l'infini.

Tarde 1999 [1898]

Introduction

I have struggled long and hard with this chapter and it has had several false starts. To explain why requires a little bit of personal history for which I beg the reader's indulgence: this is not some awful exercise in autoethnography but an attempt to position what I will subsequently have to say.

I have grown up in a discipline – geography – in which David Harvey's work has been canonical. Indeed, David Harvey often seems to be one of the primary points of reference in many of the discipline's contemporary tales of itself: his writings have conditioned much of what has been subsequently said. One of the reasons for this is undoubtedly the success of his works in travelling outside the discipline. That, in turn, means that his work is refracted back into the discipline from all points of the globe, so to speak, thereby further validating it.

But for a long time I have tried to do something different both intellectually and politically from David Harvey, and so, for me, his work has constituted something of a problem. Should I go for obeisance, rebellion or something in between? Truth to tell, I have taken all of these positions at one time or another, a lack of position born of equal parts lack of confidence, overconfidence and a longing to be somewhere else.

In this chapter, I want to reflect on what David Harvey has wrought, keeping these brief biographical thoughts in mind. The chapter is in three parts. In the first, I will simply try to obtain some sense of the sheer breadth of Harvey's influence, using a few very simple indicators. In the second part, I will try to explain why that influence has been so great. Though the quality of Harvey's work is undoubtedly very high, I argue that there are some intriguing social and cultural factors that also need to be taken into account to explain his work's pre-eminence. Then, in the final part of the chapter, save for the briefest of conclusions, I will argue that it might be possible to construct another kind of approach to capitalism, politics and the stuff of the world more generally which no doubt draws on Harvey's work but moves to a rather less certain beat.

The Impact of David Harvey's Work

David Harvey's work has had an extraordinary influence over a sustained period of time. We can chart the course of that influence in all manner of ways. But I will fix on just three. One is mechanistically through citation indices. Citation indices do have their uses if they are not taken too seriously. The most recent study I have been able to find of social science and humanities citations shows that David Harvey had 3508 citations[1] between 1981 and 2002, of which 1920 were to *The Condition of Postmodernity* (Yeung 2002). This count was far above that of the nearest comparable luminaries in geography like Doreen Massey, of social theorists like Ulrich Beck, Michel Foucault or Bruno Latour or of well-known sociologists and anthropologists like Arjun Appadurai or Manuel Castells. Only Anthony Giddens amongst social scientists, along with economists like Michael Porter, Joseph Stiglitz and Oliver Williamson, came out higher. Another indicator of influence is the large number of non-English editions of his works that have been published. Harvey has had his work translated into Chinese, Italian, Japanese, Korean, Portuguese, Romanian, Russian, Spanish and Turkish.

But we can use other equally valid indicators too. For example, over three evenings in 2003 Harvey gave the Clarendon Lectures in Geography at Oxford University and they attracted enormous audiences: at least 500 on the first night and nearly as many on the subsequent nights, many of them young and eager for enlightenment. In other words, David Harvey has become a kind of academic brand, or even monarch, cited by his peers to register their presence in that world, mobile across linguistic borders and inspirational across generations.

The Reasons for David Harvey's Pre-eminence

Why has David Harvey's work been so magnetic for so many for so long? I take it as read that his work is good and that, given its Marxist slant, it was always likely to circulate in and amongst a large number of preformed left-wing communities around the world. But I think there are a series of other sociological and cultural reasons why it has become so iconic.

First, much of the attraction of reading David Harvey consists of the fact that he provides a point of theoretical certainty in an uncertain world. He knows what he thinks and he thinks what he knows. He is no crude materialist, of course. His excursions into Bohm and Whitehead, his work on nineteenth-century Paris (Harvey 2003a), his forays into the dynamics of 'nature', all show that Harvey understands and works with uncertainty and with a version of dialectics that emphasizes process and emergence. But, at the same time, he has not radically changed his theoretical position since the late 1970s or early 1980s. Rather, he has continually revised it. This has real attractions for many readers: they can read him as an unchanging point of certainty in a turbulent world. He brings messages down from the mountain of theory which are generally clear and almost always uncompromising. Although Harvey himself continually emphasizes the sheer hard work of critique, for many I suspect that the hard work has been done for them by his works.

Second, he also provides a certainty of critique. He knows what he likes and dislikes. He is absolutely clear what is bad – capitalism – and he is pretty clear what is needed to finish capitalism off: class politics. Thus 'the only way to resist capitalism and transform society towards socialism is through a global struggle in which global working-class formation, perhaps achieved in a step-wise fashion from local to national to global concerns, acquires sufficient power and presence to fulfil its own historical potentialities' (Harvey 2000a: 39).[2]

Third, and most simply, he is physically available. Into his seventies, he has kept up a punishing schedule of talks and appearances around the world. He reeled off his list of travels in 2003 to me in an encounter that year and it was a daunting experience: I would feel frightened for my health! Fourth, he represents a particular historical conjuncture which, still, I think has a real iconic grip: the 1960s. Harvey acts as a living representative of another age. Rather like his friend of that time, Michael Moorcock, he continues to act out a set of values and images which represent one of the high water marks of the left, and the historical associations of his presence (replete with long hair and beard) do, I suspect, foster a kind of legitimate anti-legitimacy (Watts 2001).

Fifth, and closely associated, he is a representative of a particular academic form: the US radical. Notwithstanding David's tenure of a Chair at Oxford, and the undoubted English elements of his character (cf. Harvey 2002b), I think it is fair to say that many of his political attitudes and friendships were forged in the heated community of the 1960s and 1970s US left. This was and continues to be a declarative community which often feels peripheral and beleaguered.[3] In this regard, I think it bears a quite different political-cum-cultural subjectivity from, say, the European left which, for all the setbacks of the last twenty years or so, is still much closer to power and can still – to a greater or lesser degree – call on a much more general public intellectual sphere for sustenance and standing. The result is that Harvey's work reflects a particular cultural style which contrasts with that of, for example, French *engagé* counterparts, one which gives a much greater legitimacy to political statement in academic fora precisely because such a politics has so little grip in other contexts of action. As Duell (2000: 97)[4] puts it:

> Many of the most prominent paradigms [in the United States] ... are explicitly political, and often base their legitimacy upon the notion that they represent perspectives which have traditionally been excluded ... The intellectual climate appears to be sufficiently permeated by politicization that even those scholars who have no wish to be 'political' often cannot help but see many of their everyday activities through a political prism. . .

But, that said, this form of intellectual practice also plays well in certain communities all across the world, precisely because it provides a clear political location from which action can sally forth or be justified.

Sixth, he provides a strong story. Sometimes this story may be a little too strong – or, more likely, that is the way it is interpreted by many readers. For example, I have noticed the frequency with which cultural commentators in the arts and humanities disciplines in particular draw on Harvey's work in a quite specific way: to provide the economic analysis which they can then quickly move on from. Thus, some of Harvey's work provides a nice shorthand for those who want to acknowledge the economic but do not want to make it their focus.[5] Anna Tsing's (2001: 119) reading of the situation in anthropology is instructive. She points to the way in which Harvey's *The Condition of Postmodernity* is used to establish the fact of epochal change, laying the ground for subsequent interpretations. Those familiar theoretical tags like 'flexible specialization' and 'time-space compression' become hooks on which to hang a predetermined story.

The Condition of Postmodernity is polemical. It ranges over a wide variety of scholarship to criticize postmodern aesthetics. This is not a science experiment but, rather, a book-length essay. Yet somehow Harvey's description of economic evolution comes to have the status of a fact when drawn into globalist anthropology. Harvey has the ability to read economics, a skill few anthropologists have developed. It may be that anthropologists ignore the discussion of aesthetics, thinking they know more about culture than he does, and are drawn to the accumulation strategy and associated space-time requirements because they believe that macroeconomic facts are outside their knowledge base. The result is that a selection of Harvey's terms is used to build a non-cultural and non-situated futurist framework 'beyond culture'. As Tsing (2001: 119) goes on to point out.

This poses certain immediate problems. One set of problems derives from the attempt to make this future global: as anthropologist Michael Kearney admits, Harvey's thesis is 'not dealing with globalization per se'. Indeed, Harvey has a distinct blindness to everything outside dominant Northern cultures and economies; to make his story applicable to North–South articulations is not impossible, but it is a challenge. Another set of problems seems even more intractable. If we drop Harvey's discussion of aesthetics (as Culture) but still ignore the ethnographic sources through which anthropologists identify culture, just how do we know the shape of space and time? The pared-down Harvey readings preferred by anthropologists have lost even filmic and literary representations of temporal and spatial processes; we are left with economic facts . . . Another way Harvey's work could be used is to scale back its more epochal claims to look at some limited but powerful alliances between aesthetics and economics. Harvey's claim that postmodernism and flexible accumulation have something to do with each other could be pursued by locating patterns and players more specifically.

Seventh, as the mention of *The Condition of Postmodernity* makes clear, Harvey has consciously and very successfully played to his imputed audience, in part no doubt creating it. He wanted his ideas to reach a wider audience and he has adopted strategies that would achieve this. Thus his programme of work has included pieces aimed at a popular audience and pieces that would get a high academic severity mark on any conceivable index. In adopting these strategies, Harvey has paralleled the strategies of many key public intellectuals in attempting to touch many audiences at once.

If we add these social and cultural causes together, they begin to explain why Harvey's work appeals rather more widely than its often academic nature might imply. As I think is clear, that has in many ways been a good thing. For example, Harvey was one of the figures who galvanized the practice of geography and he brought that renovated practice face-to-face with a political world which it had all but abandoned. Similarly, his work has been a touchstone for several generations of young radicals, inspiring them by providing a guide to both theory and practice. But if the reader detects a note of caution in what I have written so far, then that is correct. The very certainty which has made his work so successful is also something I would want to eschew. I thought that, in a sense, I would therefore use the latter part of this chapter to enter a mild note of dissent and to suggest a slightly different way of proceeding.

Another Way

Harvey's work is based on a number of abiding notions that together form a distinct project, a project which he has consistently defended against all comers.[6] The first notion is that there is a coherent system of relations called 'capitalism'. The second is that the main political task is the construction of the political wills/forms of association that can combat the depredations of capitalism. The third is that space is crucial to both capitalism and the task of combating it. But though these notions might seem indisputable I think it is possible to start from somewhere near the same point and yet produce a radically different account by making different assumptions about what the warp and weft of the world is. This account would differ not only in its content but also, crucially, in its style.

To illustrate this point, I want to start from Harvey's short third chapter in *Justice, Nature and the Geography of Difference*, 'The Leibnizian conceit'. It is a remarkable piece of writing: pithy, and very clear. In certain senses, the chapter is quite unlike much of Harvey's oeuvre in its spareness and lack of political statement and yet it could well be read as a key to much of his later work as it sets the stage for both dialectics and various oft-repeated attacks on political quietism. Harvey interprets Leibniz's monadology as heralding a retreat into contemplation of the internal conditions of an inner self; monads represent a kind of personalist absolutism and the commonwealth a mere aggregation of these monads. Now, I am not at all sure (to put it but mildly) that this is exactly what Leibniz meant, but putting that gripe aside for now, Harvey then uses this conception as a foil to belabour idealism and to put in its place a more open conception in which 'the notion of internal relations is situated not in a world of monadic entities (which appear as "permanences") but as continuous transformations and internalisations of different "moments" (events, things, entities) within the overall process of political-economic reproduction' (Harvey 1996a: 74).[7]

However, there are other rather more sympathetic ways of thinking about and working with monadology[8] that can still accommodate Harvey's fluid metaphysics. Perhaps the best way of illustrating this point is by reeling back in time to the end of the nineteenth and the beginning of the twentieth century and to the differences between Gabriel Tarde and the upstart Emile Durkheim. Durkheim won this particular battle hands down, of course, and it is only recently that Tarde's work has been excavated and its contemporary relevance reasserted (e.g. Millet 1970; Deleuze 1994 [1968]; Alliez 1999; Latour 2002, 2003; Toews 2003).[9] Durkheim wanted to explain the social (as a specific domain of human symbolic order) by means of the social and, in doing so, he disbarred all manner of other forms of aggregation from making their mark. The world is left half-furnished. Tarde, on the other hand, never makes this distinction. For him, the world is a set of monad-like agencies, influences and imitations which can aggregate in all manner of ways. Tarde made another innovation: he did not distinguish between large and small: 'the big, the small, the great, is not superior to the monad, it is only a simple, more standardised version of one of the monad's goals which it has reached in making part of its view shared by others' (Latour 2002: 122). Finally, Tarde was clear that no matter how much effort is expended, no social order could ever be totally regnant. It is simply a set of standardised connections that occupy some of the monads for some of the time. It is possible to enrol some aspects of monads but never to dominate them entirely: 'revolt, resistance, breakdown, conspiracy, alternative is everywhere' (Latour 2002: 124). The social is never the whole. It is always a part – and a pretty fragile one at that. As soon as its tiny networks are left behind, 'you are no longer in the social, but down in a confusing plasma composed of countless monads, a chaos, a brew, one that social scientists will do anything to avoid looking straight in the eye' (Latour 2002: 125).

Tarde's viewpoint has obvious consequences. Most particularly, it emphasizes the roiling contingency of so much of the world and its consequent inability to be tied down by the simple complexities of social theory. The world constantly overflows the boundaries that theory sets for it. But there is rather more to it than this. First, society becomes a consequence, not a cause. Second, social laws cannot be distinguished from the agents acted upon by those laws: the law and what is subject to the law are not able to be set apart. They co-exist in actor-networks. This is not some mad individualism: all that is being stated is that to understand the actor it is necessary to follow the network and to understand the network it is necessary to look for the actors. In each case, the work of tracing the work of connection substitutes for the idea of the social. Third, it follows that the work of aggregation is crucial. Instead of thinking of beings or identities, Tarde wants us to think of the work of possession, the creation of attachments and translations which, in turn, produce what we recognize as properties and degrees of avidity.

We can now return to the issues of capitalism, political will and space. For, in this kind of depiction, 'capitalism' no longer exists as a singular entity or a set of laws. Rather than an emanation from or a projection onto things such as institutions or persons, it is a constantly shifting set of translations dependent on a vast number of different but entangled actor-networks for its survival, incarnated in and emergent from those networks as they struggle to repeat themselves (Castree 2002; Thrift 2004d). Recently, Michel Callon (1998) has notoriously argued that 'capitalism does not exist', a statement that has been greeted with howls of protest by many who seem to assume that such a move will diffuse/defuse the target of their attentions. But what Callon means is that capitalism exists only as a continually updating drawing board of different actor-networks and associations between actor-networks, and that to try to name one beast may sometimes be politically convenient – even necessary – but can never encompass all that is being done. In making this move, Callon also seems to me to set the scene for a much *more* active anti-capitalist politics, one which is willing to take the prodigious nature of the world seriously. Consequently, capitalism is not a deific force issuing forth from every wordly portal[10] – and it is not therefore necessary to try to give every political activity marks out of ten for class struggle content.

Talking of politics, political will becomes a more diffused but no less active resource based on a rather different 'performative' style of politics relying on a Leibnizian method of *inventio* rather than the game of truth of *adequatio*, and working from a metaphysics of birth (Battersby 1998). This is a more open-ended politics wedded to the idea of the practice of functional disunity, of, in Corlett's (1993) phrase, 'community without unity'. That makes it more interested in aggregation than in assimilation to a single conceptual or consensual point, more able to understand that the significant can also often be absurd, much less tolerant of the political moralism that characterizes much of what passes today as radical politics, and therefore rather less willing to proclaim its own certainty. The rationale for this style of politics is only just being worked out (cf. Thrift 2004a, 2004b, 2004c) – in Europe especially[11] – but its practices already surround us. Finally, space (or, rather, time-space) becomes key. There are numerous, frequently intersecting time-spaces continually being produced by actor-networks and therefore numerous points of intervention (Thrift 2003). The production of new editions of time-space becomes a key point of political operation, making Lefebvre's by now familiar point – but taking it rather more seriously than he took it himself.

In turn, these thoughts might lead to a rather different project. It would be one which, frankly, would be more inclusive, more willing to participate in multiple conversations, more willing to form multiple alliances. So, it would no longer need to police the borders of theory and practice so rigorously because the borders would be seen no longer as a threat but as an opportunity for revitalization and renewal. It would no longer need to be quite so certain but it would not interpret this uncertainty as a sign of weakness: rather it would be seen as a sign of an immodest hope (Zournazi 2002). It would no longer need to mimic the capital-intensive, monumental styles of the mass public but would instead cleave to all manner of outside belongings (Probyn 1996), and for their own sake. It would no longer argue for a superhuman politics (which individual instances illustrate) but would recognize the sheer complexity of tapping into the longing for what Fredric Jameson (1979: 136) calls the 'underdefined something' and thereby expanding the range of thinkable democratic forms and the imagery of collective senses of social belonging (Berlant 2003). It would no longer . . . But, of course, this would no longer be David Harvey's project. Indeed, I suspect that he would view it as a pacification. On this, we can only disagree – and move on.

Conclusions

In this brief chapter, I have tried to sketch out why David Harvey has been so influential and has acted as an inspiration to so many. His has been a signal achievement. But I have also tried to begin to show how his fluid metaphysics could have become something rather more if he had not interpreted the ideas of writers like Leibniz and others as those of opponents. As it is, I find that David Harvey's convictions weigh too heavily on me: his theoretical work, at least, is a kind of juggernaut which, to me, in any case, already contains within it the expectation of acceptance.[12] But I do not want liberation to mean having to agree. And I am not at all sure that meeting force with something that too often looks like its analogue can provide a lasting answer. In the end, so I would argue, injustice and spite and wasted personhood cannot be fought with just one set of tools. All kinds of arts and sciences are required to forge oppositions and to bring new worlds about.

Acknowledgements

As usual, Derek Gregory's comments have immeasurably improved the tone and content of this paper.

Notes

1 According to a count from the Social Sciences Citation Index and the Arts and Humanities Citation Index combined (16 May 2004).
2 Harvey is here describing the political trajectory of *The Communist Manifesto* but he makes it clear that he agrees with it.
3 This may begin to explain many of Harvey's own citation habits which rarely include, for example, geographers who are not considered a part of his project, even other Marxist geographers. The geographers who are cited often seem to be his former research students. More generally, it would be possible to mount an argument that David has actually been remarkably inattentive to recent developments in Geography, reflecting, I suspect, some degree of disillusion-ment.
4 Duell is writing about literary studies but his description applies equally well across a wide variety of disciplines in the United States currently.
5 Though clearly not many of these commentators have read *The Limits of Capital*, a book which would detain them for rather longer than *The Condition of Postmodernity*.
6 Indeed, rather often, Harvey's defence has seemed to conform to the maxim that the best form of defence is offence. Harvey's arguments may be strong but taking such a Man in the High Castle stance makes it more difficult to learn from critics (for example, some feminist authors) or take in other experiences (for example, those of the global South). More generally, it makes it difficult to see the unexpected, even when that may be an important new political resource.
7 This conception is not, it should be said, as far as Harvey seems to think from that of many contemporary thinkers. Indeed, given a common ancestor in Whitehead, there are clear affinities with the work of Deleuze which Harvey has criticized.
8 I choose Tarde here but it would, no doubt, have been equally possible to choose Deleuze (cf. Deleuze 1993 [1988]) or Latour. However, since Deleuze acknowledges Tarde as 'next to Leibniz, one of the last great philosophers of Nature' it seems sensible to work with the forefather. Interestingly, Deleuze's early reading of Tarde's microsociology also prepares him for his evaluation

of Foucault's later works (see Lambert 2002) while Latour (2002) now claims Tarde as the forefather of actor-network theory.

9 This reassertion has been made possible by the reprinting of most of Tarde's work in France over the last few years, mainly by Institut Synthelabo.

10 As indeed did Marx in the writings where he did not let his gift for polemic take over.

11 Though there *are* North American exemplars, most notably writers like Jane Bennett, William Connolly and Bonnie Honig (for a recent North American review see Castronovo and Nelson 2003).

12 As an ironic aside, Harvey's latest work on imperialism (e.g. Harvey 2003b) seems to me to contain uncanny echoes, in both its diremptive style and its centred content, of the US military–industrial complex which is its main target.

12

Messing with 'the Project'

Cindi Katz

David Harvey is one of the most rigorous dialectical Marxists working today, and, as the rigours of the dialectic might suggest, that is his strength and weakness. His contributions in geography and well beyond have been singular and formidable. Harvey defined and exquisitely worked out 'an historical geographical materialism', wherein the social and political economic relations and practices of capital accumulation are spatialized. In carrying out this project, which began with *Social Justice and the City*, was most forcefully taken up in *The Limits to Capital*, and permeates the entire corpus of his scholarship in the last thirty years, Harvey has worked along and transformed two fronts. Outside of geography his writings have made it impossible to imagine capitalism or analyse capital accumulation without a geographical imagination and sensibility, while within the discipline his work – and spirit – have been pivotal to formulating a meticulous Marxist analysis of the production of space, place and nature.

These accomplishments almost inevitably invoke, draw upon and produce 'metanarratives' and totalizing theories. Despite the lack of vogue and some forceful critiques of this mode of working, Harvey has not shied away from the master narrative of Marxism as theoretically necessary and politically compelling. And for this I and many others are grateful. Someone has to lug this beast over the vast time-space of revolution's becoming, and Harvey has been tireless not only in this project, but in honing the analysis to keep up with the changing nature of capitalism's uneven developments. I am in full agreement with Harvey that Marxism offers the best means of understanding the social relations, material social practices and contradictions of capitalism, and thereby of responding to its myriad injustices. The brilliant clarity and disciplined focus of his analysis dovetail with Lukacs's 'possibility of the revolution' in their inspiration. But even if capitalism has proven adept at drawing on and generally strengthening other modes of oppression and domination that exceed it, Marxism does not have the last, and certainly not the only, word on how to confront all forms of power and dominance, even when they intersect with class exploitation. And making that claim, all too frequently, seems to have been Harvey's ambition. Of course, Harvey's writings acknowledge that Marxism has its limits, but their overall effect has been to underplay these, eschewing the messy in favor of the elegant and systematic; the totality over the partial or contingent. And while this approach has enabled him to produce a formidable and crucially important body of work – which I and many others rely upon to work out theories and ideas about the social relations and historical geographies of production and reproduction – it would be illuminating and useful if Harvey were more adventurous in the ways he worked through the Marxian methodology of theorizing *up* from the abstract to the concrete (Marx 1973a), tangling along the way with the work that people like me do with his theories. Theory construction is not a one-way street.

The notion of position is an abstraction that relies upon as it calls forth a web of social relations. Marx made clear that the position of labour in the social relations of capitalism, when consciously apprehended, afforded a privileged perspective on the nature of capitalist exploitation. Beginning, then, with the abstract social relations of position entangled in matrices of power whose moments are expressed as exploitation, oppression and dominance should, by extension, lead to an analysis that demonstrates not only the ways class is constitutive of other social relations such as race or gender but the ways it is itself concretely constituted by them. Despite rhetorical sympathies with this position, Harvey's work effectively recoils from materializing his rhetoric, sidestepping Donna Haraway's insistence that the political charge of epistemology is to discern which differences matter under particular historical-geographical conditions (Haraway 1991). He continues to argue that class offers the most effective and expansive means of redressing what he scripts as the mother of all power relations, capitalism, the sympathetic critiques of such scholars as Iris Marion Young (1998), Nancy Hartsock (1998a) and Linda McDowell (1992) notwithstanding.

If, in recent years, Harvey's notions of class formation are complicated by examining its intersections with other modes of difference, these never seem constitutive rather than modulating. In past interchanges, I suggested that this line of argument was a form of 'strategic reductionism', as he absolved himself by suggesting that the world is pretty reductionist (Katz 1998; cf. Harvey 1998a). Reductionism – strategic, mimetic or otherwise – is reductionism, and in any event capitalism is way better – and more

formidable – than that. Capital accumulation depends in part on productions of difference, not just between capital and labour, but within and
across class formations. Capitalists and their various agents have been wily
– and *expansive* – in deploying and reinforcing various forms of difference,
whether of race or nation, region or gender, industry or age. Rather than
working across these differences, the labour movement often follows suit
– if only strategically – and thus has been prey to the pitfalls of localism, its
militarism too particular to be internationalist, to connect production and
reproduction, or to organize across sectors so that workers (and would-be
workers) coming up against historic (de)formations of 'race', gender and
nation are reached by an invigorated class politics. While Harvey is lucid
and forceful on the problems of this trap when it is spatialized (cf. his position contra Teresa Hayter's on the Cowley auto workers, which brings the
politics of scale to the fore (Harvey 1995a)), he is less compelling on social
forms of localism and particularism, opting instead for a fantasy of class
politics that might embrace all difference without seriously engaging it, its
sources, and its stubborn reinforcements in everyday political-economic
life. All of which brings me to the mess, and Harvey's reluctance to engage
it in his theory-making.

Harvey is a precise dialectical thinker, and his work is magisterial in
showing how to move systematically and clearly from the abstractions of
Marxist theory to their concrete instantiations in the material world. But
in his ambition to produce a fully elaborated historical-geographical materialism of capital accumulation, he tends to exclude other realms of power
and a wealth of other concerns. Harvey's insistence on Marxian categories and his tendency to look at uneven geographical development in and
through urban processes lead him to look at certain scales (and not others),
certain practices (and not others), and particular kinds of social actors
(and not others). Granted, boundaries and definition are necessary to any
intellectual project or practical endeavour. But Harvey's project is by now
highly refined and would benefit from more open and lively engagement
with these excluded categories and the theories that animate them. When
critical scholars – among them Marxist scholars – engage Harvey's theories
and categories from other scales or with regard to other material social
practices, the theories are transformed and their motion follows an altered
trajectory. These shifts – which may strengthen, not weaken, Harvey's
class analysis – are not explicable from a stance that cleaves to the original
frame. Harvey often writes as if the analysis of difference were something
mechanical (the stupefying rote of class/ethnicity/gender/'race'/sexuality),
additive (take gender and stir) or a playful distraction in *Spaces of Hope*
he grumpily remarks that 'cultural' analysis is more 'fun' than 'the dour

world . . . of capitalism') (2000a: 5). Leaving aside the question of capitalism outside of culture – or perhaps reckoning what would be at the heart of that impossible construction – one can more clearly see that many of the serious critiques of Harvey's work are less concerned with the play or work of difference than a call for him to work differently with theory; to have his analysis intersect with other modes of thinking; to work at other scales; and to enter the dialectic from new locations that might lead to vibrant alternate 'permanences'.

Such calls to work differently with material in analyses of social relations of power recall Susan Christopherson's passionate critique of what she memorably dubbed 'the Project'. Christopherson's article, which appeared in *Antipode* in 1989, was written in angry (but unstated) response to a series of special sessions at the 1988 AAG meetings in Phoenix on reconstructing human geography. These sessions were a powerful call to remake human geography in a post-positivist, situated, culturally nuanced and for many participants, poststructuralist way. I remember the sessions vividly because I saw them as a call for the things I thought of myself as doing, albeit without the guidance of the various 'big boys' who were leading the sessions, and only a dim awareness of their existence. I had gotten my chops from feminist theory, cultural studies (via Birmingham), postcolonial theory and the Social History Workshop, all of which had leavened my Marxism for all the lonely years I spent writing my dissertation. Emerging from this solitary but pleasurable confinement, I was astonished to find all these guys calling for a geography in that image. The pleasure of seeing my work in everything they said was engulfed in the chagrin of not being there at all. My narcissism notwithstanding, the latter was no surprise – after all, I was 'a nobody' – but neither were any of the more established feminist theorists working in (or outside of) geography. Nor was there any recognition at all that feminists, among others, had pioneered working along similar lines as the poststructuralists being celebrated at those sessions. Christopherson railed against these exclusions and saw this revamping of geography as little more than a trendy power move, all the more frustrating because it could have been framed in a way that opened rather than closed down the field. If the reconstruction of human geography had simultaneously loosened up the Marxism and politicized the humanism of critical geography, its practitioners, she suggested, had by and large remained as inured to taking non-class forms of difference seriously as they were to revamping the ways theory was made and remade.

Harvey was not a proponent of this reconstruction of human geography – he'd begun that project on a different note fifteen years earlier – but he saw its 'postmodern challenge' as emblematic of larger cultural practices, which he sought to make sense of through a Marxist analysis (Harvey 1989b; cf. Dear 1988). He scripted much of what took place under the new banner as an evasion of political economy and a troubling identitarian turn away from class, and he was right in many ways. Lost in the poststructuralist twists and cultural turns was that there were grounds for common cause in Harvey's and Christopherson's responses to the reconstructionist jamboree. Had more Marxist and feminist theorists – and by extension, radical and critical theorists concerned with issues like racism, homophobia and imperialism – worked together to engage their concerns and differences, the reconstruction of human geography would have been better at taking on the intersecting power relations of capitalism, patriarchy, racism, imperialism and heteronormativity in all their unevenness across the taken-for-granted spaces of our concern.

Instead, Christopherson's article was one of the first salvos in a series of feminist critiques of the masculinism of human geography in both its muscular Marxist and pulpy postpositivist forms. These critiques most forcefully targeted Harvey's *The Condition of Postmodernity* and Edward Soja's *Postmodern Geographies*, a testimony to their ambition and importance (Harvey 1989b; Soja 1989). Most notable among these were Rosalyn Deutsche's piercing critique of Harvey, which argued that his totalizing vision required both 'a refusal of feminist theories of representation' and a disavowal of the partiality of all subject positions, and Doreen Massey's more scattershot and self-righteous critique, which addressed the authors' 'assumptions of universals' that were 'particulars' made possible by their reluctance to deal seriously with questions of difference, as well as the style and scope of their work (Deutsche 1991; Massey 1991a).

Harvey responded angrily and somewhat defensively to these critiques in *Antipode* (1992b). Apart from an annoying tendency – by no means unique to Harvey – to use feminist shields while arguing against other feminists, the response acknowledged the resonances between his critique of postmodern theory and those of feminists, and conceded the limitations of his engagement with feminist theories of difference. At the same time, while he noted that he was interested in looking at questions of difference in relation to *one of* the key systems of world-historical systems of domination, capitalism – a focus (or target) I share as well – the effect of his writing has nevertheless continued to seem as if capitalism is the *only world historical* system that matters. While he correctly insists that 'situatedness must always be related . . . to socially constructed systems of domination' (1992b: 310), he does not seriously address how these systems might work with or against one another. As a result Harvey may now produce more expansive accounts of capitalism that 'embrace' gender or 'race', but not ones that imagine the social relations of capitalism themselves constituted in indeterminate ways by those of patriarchy or racism. And so on, blah blah blah.

Frankly, I'm tired of covering these old grounds. This back and forth about the material social practices and effects of disparate relations of power has become stale and boring. And yet we are still here. David Harvey is a close friend, comrade, colleague and an important supporter of my work over many years. He has been an energetic champion of critical human geography and radical geographers of all kinds; a supporter of feminists in the field, in his departments, in his universities, in his political work; and an activist in labour campaigns, such as Baltimore's living wage campaign, that are very much about how gender and race infuse and alter class. All of this practice is not just 'relevant' to who David Harvey is as a theorist, it *makes* him who he is. For these and many other reasons I honour and deeply appreciate him as a person and have the highest regard and admiration for his work in the world. But I am also incredibly frustrated by the stubbornness of his modes of engaging other kinds of theory. In writing this I feel crummy. Something about it reminds me of how I feel when I write about things like public–private partnerships. While they are deeply problematic, these partnerships are not the 'bad guys'. Indeed, many of them do much good in the world or at least their bailiwicks of it. But in their good-doing they fashion a mode of working that is dangerous to public life and in many ways threatens the survival of the public sphere as it was known before neoliberalism. I nevertheless sometimes ask myself why I go after the relatively good guys instead of the truly bad ones? And I always answer, because the good guys could be so much better, and a small branch of my political hope resides there.

A good guy tossing a bone should not demarcate the limits of anyone's political horizon. I not only want David Harvey to turn the brilliant force of his analysis on the mutually constitutive intersections and articulations of capitalism, patriarchy, imperialism and racism; I also want him to take seriously other ways of making theory, of working with material, and of making sense of oppression, exploitation, domination and power more generally. In other words, to grapple more fully with the indeterminate and uneven effects of varying relations of power in articulation, and to recognize a shared intellectual and political project among those striving to understand and rework those relations of power. Marxism and feminism are strengthened by their incorporation of those who work in a different register. David Harvey need not do his work differently to recognize – and really engage – what can be seen at different scales of analysis or following different entry points. These moves would make his historical-geographic materialism more supple. Yet, as many have noted, Harvey tends to treat such analyses as distractions or dilutions, effectively relegating other modes of difference as elaborations or additions to class rather than integral to class formations.

If I am re-covering some old ground it is, as I suggested above, because in many ways we haven't been able to leave it thanks to the relentless masculinism of so many human geographers, among them Marxists *and* poststructuralists from whom we might expect more. But also, my task in this essay was to offer a critical assessment of David Harvey's relationship to 'the Project'. As the editors of this volume framed it in their by now yellowing letter, 'to what extent does Harvey's project depend upon various exclusions and excisions (gender, ethnicity etc)?' I am not sure that Harvey's project *depends* upon those exclusions and excisions, but it is certainly made more elegant and in some ways more forceful by them. Yet elegance and force can become brittle with age and in changing times. Moreover, they are often purchased – somewhat tautologically – through refusing the messiness of theory making. And Harvey has been remarkably steadfast in his refusal to mess up class. But messing it up – in a way that Gertrude Stein might enjoy – would strengthen rather than evacuate class. To mangle Stein, if such a thing is possible, 'race' is not class and class is not gender, but neither is gender gender without class, class class without gender, nor 'race' race without class, to say nothing of class gender race. Is that so hard?

Since the editors used Christopherson's essay as a marker, and that essay can now be seen as part of a larger critique of the unwillingness of many human geographers to engage with the methodologies and theoretical categories of feminism, and Harvey has been a central focus of these critiques and participant in these debates, I thought it would be useful to see whether and how his work changed in their wake. In preparing to write this essay, then, I went over all of Harvey's books since *Social Justice and the City*, but focused especially on his work since the early 1990s when the most concentrated and vociferous feminist critiques were launched (in response to *The Condition of Postmodernity*). Much of what I have said thus far draws from this reading. While, as noted above, Harvey dispatches the two most prominent critiques the book received, and I have no need to rehearse that response here, it is telling how little these critiques really altered his project. They may have gotten under his skin but they didn't change his constitution. Worse, the critiques (not helped by their nastiness) may even have hardened Harvey's outlook, so that his engagements with difference return him more forcefully to class. But this tendency is not so much resistance as a reluctance to dilute, mess up or seriously call into question the theoretical and practical benefits of a rigorous class analysis. And yet that would not be the effect of Harvey's more openly engaging the feminist critique of his project. Just as Sandra Harding (1986) demonstrates that exposing the structure of how a particular question is framed or the specifically positioned nature of an analysis strengthens claims to objectivity, subjecting class to a rigorous analysis of its limits would make it a stronger, more effective-to-organize-around notion of class. People might recognize themselves and all the messiness of their affiliations and antagonisms in a notion of class that doesn't encompass, but is faceted by – as it simultaneously cuts through – gender, race, sexuality, nation. It's not just that the category of class would be altered by this engagement, but the engagement itself might provoke a different way of working with theory and praxis.

In friendly provocation, then, I want to look at Harvey's stance as a refusal of certain kinds of mess: the mess of difference, the mess of scale and the mess of indeterminacy. As suggested above, while Harvey responded to his feminist critics in part by attending to differences other than class more than he had before, it remained that he regarded these different kinds of difference not as mutually constitutive with class, but as modifiers or supplements to it. Moreover, he continued to see class as the most embracing position from which to confront exploitation, while other positions were represented as sideshows if not distractions from the core problems of capitalism. His often-cited discussion of the Hamlet, North Carolina chicken factory fire is a case in point.

In *Justice, Nature and the Geography of Difference*, Harvey's first book after the critiques, he juxtaposes the devastating fire at the Imperial chicken processing plant, which killed 25 workers (half of whom were black and the majority of whom were women), with the Triangle Shirtwaist Fire of 1911, the Anita Hill/Clarence Thomas hearings, and the Rodney King beating (Harvey 1996a). Harvey suggests that the Imperial fire might have been avoided if there had been 'a simple, traditional form of class politics [which] could have protected the interests of women and minorities as well as those of white males'. Granted. His argument rests on the notion that class cuts across all of the other forms of identification and thus would have encompassed the poorly paid, non-unionized and illegally endangered workers in the broiler processing plant. I agree, but this interpretation revolves around a structural notion of class that sidesteps the history of class politics in the US and ignores questions of how differently embodied and positioned social actors are classed and class-consciousness is shaped. It is not at all clear, for instance, that the Imperial plant workers would have been open to unionization and activism around safety issues – North Carolina's 'right to work' laws notwithstanding – if approached by organizers focused on traditional shop floor issues and working with received notions of class. Class formation is not separable from racialization, nation or gender. Quite the reverse, it is squeezed through them. Ignoring the all too often racist history of the US labour movement or its refusal to address the (re)production of workers and particular class formations diminishes the possibilities for revitalizing a 'simple, traditional' working class movement in the USA.

In the discussion of the Imperial Foods fire, Harvey makes clear that cap-italists work as a class. Of course they do, and this was one of the reasons occupational safety regulations were gutted in the 1980s. He does this in an almost taunting way – they know they're a class and act like one, while 'we' are distracted by sexual harassment and racist state violence.[1] But one of the marvels of neoliberal capitalism is how deft capitalists *as a class* have been in articulating (and even masking) their class interests with the patri-archal, homophobic, racist and/or fundamentalist religious concerns of others with whom they have formed potent alliances. This potency is built in part on the recognition that class is sieved through other modes of identi-fication such as race or gender, and that the means of capital accumulation exceed the extraction of surplus value through the exploitation of labour power. It is precisely recognizing that racialization, embodiment, sexual-ity, national interests and the like make class formation what it is that has strengthened the position of capitalists in the USA and buoyed their vision of a neoliberal state, which is punitive around social welfare, exacting in the control of private bodies, and lax around health and safety regulations.

Harvey is also reluctant to engage the mess of scale, by which I mean both the multiple and active interpenetrations of geographic scales and the messy materiality of social practice at every scale. While Harvey has not partici-pated in the production of scale debates of the last twenty years, his central concern with capital accumulation tends to privilege the national and global scales at which the structuring forces of capitalism appear to operate more forcefully. Harvey is of course nothing if not an urban theorist. But he tends to see the urban scale as – again – one of and for capital accumula-tion at the same time as he renders the urban (and regional) scale legible as a labour market. Likewise, his approach to the body, which he brilliantly illuminated as an accumulation strategy but not much else (Harvey 2000a; Haraway and Harvey 1995). Harvey might have approached his analysis of the urban scale as a labour market through the material social practices of production *and* social reproduction. But almost everywhere that he might examine the material social practices and relations of social reproduction, and thereby work out the production of the urban scale in and through its mutual constitution with scales such as the home, the neighbourhood and the body, he retreats. Rather than understand the 'messy fleshy' making of the urban (and other) scales, Harvey centres his gaze upon the structural forces of capitalism that produce space and by extension scale (Marston 2000; Katz 2001b).

The forceful clarity of his analysis, purchased through the singularity of his perspective, would actually be strengthened by the kaleidoscopic view he so values in literature but recoils from in his own work. In *Paris, Capital of Modernity* Harvey (2003a) looks fondly at Balzac's treatment of the details of everyday life and acute attentiveness to the domestic environment. Part of this appreciation revolves around an acknowledgement that Balzac's nuanced attention to the comings and goings in a single room reveals and illuminates structural and other relations that among other things produced Paris as such. But nowhere does Harvey's work reflect a similar engagement with the domestic scale and its productive possibilities. The productions of space, social relations and forces of production, along with the social actors to animate them, which occur at this scale and in the realm of everyday life, remain largely occluded in Harvey's consideration.

My argument here is that this disregard stems in part from what appears to be an unwillingness to give serious attention to the material social practices associated with scales smaller than the urban, and perhaps a reluctance to risk muddying what he seems to think are purely capitalist processes. How else to understand a chapter on 'The reproduction of labor power' (in nineteenth-century France) that addresses the home only as 'housing', and never mentions patriarchal relations even as they are entangled with those of capitalism (Harvey 2003a). Instead, Harvey focuses on how the long-term reproduction of labour power was 'very much a provincial affair', illuminating how the (re)production of workers in the French countryside subsidized the nascent urban capitalism of Paris (2003a: 195). Granted. But while he can clearly resolve and imagine the mutual embeddedness of the urban and regional as the scale of the labour market, he does not analyse the simultaneous mutuality between the urban and domestic scales on precisely the same grounds; the (re)production of labour power (and much else). These material social practices at the domestic scale, which many geographers have examined – aspiring to the same kaleidoscopic ambition as Balzac if not quite achieving his delicacy – are routinely intertwined with patriarchal relations of power to subsidize the social wage, and thereby capital accumulation, in ways analogous to the rural–urban subsidy Harvey identifies (e.g. Marston 2000; Mitchell et al. 2004). This reluctance to attend to the 'historical-geographical materialism' of the household (or at the scale of the body) limits Harvey's ability to examine the production of scale as relationally as he might or as their mutually constitutive nature requires (cf., e.g. Smith 1992; Swyngedouw 1997; Howitt 1998; Marston 2000; Wright 2004; Sheppard and McMaster 2004).

Finally, although Harvey is inspirational as a dialectical thinker, he seems more comfortable with 'permanences' than with the messy entailments of indeterminacy. The 'mess of indeterminacy' crops up both in the sorts of conclusions that can be drawn from any analysis and in the mode of working with theory and material. On the first, Harvey's interest in constructing an historical-geographical materialist analysis of capitalism draws him – like Marx – to attend much more thoroughly to the structuring forces of a social formation, such as capital and the state, than to the practical engagements of the social actors who comprise it and the contradictions that riddle it everywhere. Harvey is neither a structuralist nor a structurationist – his dialectical imagination is way too lithe for that – but his desire to analyse the effects of the structuring forces and social relations of capitalism comes at the expense of attending to the acts of agency that always already and everywhere produce, contest, delimit, constrain, further or oppose these forces. The result is of course Harvey's trademark orderliness and clarity, but also a tendency more towards determination and resolution than the contingent possibilities and perils of contradiction. Both aspects of dialectical analysis are important, of course, but I can understand how one or the other might be emphasized in any analysis, and here I want simply to appreciate Harvey's close and sophisticated analyses of capitalism and the uneven geographies it spawns. This work across four decades forcefully makes clear what we who oppose capitalism and its myriad injustices are up against, even if the analyses would be enlivened by greater attention to some of capitalism's contradictions and to social practice at all scales. But sidestepping the 'mess of indeterminacy' also affects Harvey's mode of working with theory and material, and that is what I want to address here. This concern was at the core of Christopherson's argument – the 'project' is a way of working that incessantly valorizes itself – and has animated many of the subsequent critiques of Harvey's (and others') work (e.g. McDowell 1992; Katz 1996).

The arguments around the way theory is produced and deployed are old and just about as tedious as the ones around difference. And yet they continue to haunt. The imperviousness of Harvey and many many other theorists to these arguments – that the construction of theory is inextricably related to the construction of power; that experience and position come into play profoundly in the construction of all theory and only the disembodied power that comes of being 'unmarked' would allow this to be eclipsed; that to proceed from a single position with a single totalizing framework for analysing the conditions, contradictions and tendencies of everyday life will necessarily subsume all social relations and thereby efface whole 'realms of social life' and power; and that to acknowledge the partiality of any epistemological stance strengthens its claims – has itself become a trope.[2] Still, why the insistent refusal to work a different way or to at least acknowledge the value of these other ways of working? Why not risk the 'mess of indeterminacy'? What would be lost? What's now at stake for a theorist like Harvey who has produced a magnificent body of work that elegantly and thoroughly illuminates an historical geography of contemporary capitalism? His accomplishment in geography is unparalleled; why not mix it up a little? Since feminist and other epistemological arguments with Harvey (and others) have so often been met defensively or by indifference, I thought I might appeal to the self-interest at the heart of struggles over the production of knowledge.

Given the scope and influence of Harvey's project, it seems all that's at stake for him at this point is a claim to power that he must imagine obtains only from the bracing wholeness of his analysis. But by its very nature that claim has become self-undermining. If Harvey has been impervious to two decades of deep and often sympathetic epistemological critique of his project, from people working in fields as disparate as literary theory, philosophy, art history, political science, cultural studies, anthropology, sociology and of course geography, so too have become those fellow-travellers and comrades who have tried in vain to alter his way of working. Nobody is convincing anyone around here; differences may in fact be hardening in a wash of untranslatability just at the moment when making the connections between differentiated modes of exploitation and oppression in a rigorous and informed way is everyday more urgent. Refusing his synoptic but singular vision, these critics and many others might be more convinced by the power of a Marxist analysis if Harvey were more open about its limitations, its contradictions, its indeterminacy, rather than repeatedly demonstrating its all-encompassing power. On these grounds of indeterminacy, a more vigorous, supple and multiply fanged oppositional theory might be developed; invigorating Marxism (*and* feminism and other modes of oppositional praxis) for the twenty-first century by attending to the differences and intersections of capitalist and other modes of oppression and exploitation. This way of working might lead to praxis – across space, across scale, across militant particularlisms – that has a fighting chance of achieving social justice on the many grounds where capitalism, racism, imperialism, homophobia and sexism make it impossible.

David Harvey, more than anyone else in geography, has made such a prospect plausible. He has produced an incomparable body of work that not only provides a luminous and comprehensive historical-*geographical* materialism, but also brilliantly exposes and supplements 'the limits to capital'. This work, and the restless outrage that drives it has been a gift to me (and countless others), and here I want only to return the favour by encouraging David Harvey – if only for a few days – to 'become minor' or at least to venture outside 'the project'; to work in a register in which he doesn't feel at home, to write so that he breaks the limits of what is untranslatable between his theoretical framework and others, and to draw differently on his theoretical imagination so that he theorizes *up* from the abstract to the concrete. Working this way – and the struggle to do so – would strengthen his analysis, engage his critics and allies in new ways, and produce knowledge that has a good chance of altering not only theory and practice, but the historical geographies of injustice.

Acknowledgements

Thank you to Gillian Hart, Eric Lott and Sallie Marston for their encouragement, critical readings, thoughtful suggestions and much more, over way too many discussions of this piece. Thanks also to Noel Castree and Derek Gregory for their patience and the alchemy of benign neglect, cajoling, humour and flattery.

Notes

1 Harvey, of course, acknowledges the gravity of sexual harassment, racism and state violence, but he associates them with oppression rather than exploitation, and implies that exploitation has no hold on the public imagination.
2 These arguments have been developed clearly and rigorously across more than two decades of feminist scholarship, but the phrasing I have used here is most directly from the work of Sandra Harding (1986), Susan Christopherson (1989) and Linda McDowell (1992).

13

The Detour of Critical Theory

Noel Castree

Introduction

As he enters his 70th year, one might expect David Harvey's writings to peter out in exiguous fragments and glosses. Yet he continues to shout his heresies with relentless erudition, having lost none of the vigour and verve that marked his turn towards 'revolutionary theory' some three decades ago. *The New Imperialism* (2003b) is one of several recent publications that demonstrate his determination to keep the flame of Marxist scholarship alive in the current conjuncture. These writings crown a canon of commanding weight. Even the most gifted thinker would be pleased to pen one or two germinal texts in a lifetime. That Harvey has written several – including many now-classic papers and essays – speaks to his prodigious talents and immense intellectual energy. The architectural sweep and grandeur of his intellectual edifice knows few equivalents within contemporary Marxism, and certainly none within his home discipline of geography. Equally, Harvey's contribution to the field of urban studies has been paradigmatic: his writings on the city helped pioneer the search for holistic theory among analysts whose inquiries had all too often been piecemeal and fragmented.

In short, for long-standing admirers of Harvey's work what Perry Anderson (1980: 2) once said of E. P. Thompson's corpus holds true: 'The claim on our critical respect and gratitude . . . is one of formidable magnitude.' Yet within the three intellectual communities mentioned above – those that Harvey has most obviously influenced – his work has received no systematic evaluation. One more often finds scattered appropriations and evaluations of ideas contained in his various books and essays than an overall assessment of his intellectual and political project this last thirty years.[1] It is, perhaps, a sign of how overdue a synoptic appreciation of Harvey's work is that the present book be published at a time when everything that he stands for appears to many to be congenitally defective or simply passé. Here the line separating eulogy and elegy is very fine indeed. Even if Marxism – a discursive tradition to which Harvey has so richly contributed – were still dominant within left intellectual circles, any evaluation of his achievements would inevitably be tinged with a certain sadness. After all, as he enters his eighth decade, an assessment of his career must proceed in the certain knowledge that he has more days behind him than ahead of him. But the fact of Marxism's eclipse within those many disciplines where it was once the pre-eminent critical paradigm (human geography included) lends the timing of this book an added poignancy.

Harvey is above all else a Marxist – more than any other label this one cuts to the marrow of his thinking. He belongs to a cohort of highly talented scholars who made Marxism a living force in the Anglophone academic world from the early seventies onwards. Prior to the remarkable efforts of this generation, only a few Anglophone Marxists had paved the way – figures such as Thompson, Eric Hobsbawm and Raymond Williams. As they reach the end of their careers, the intellectual legacy of Marxists like Harvey is by no means secure. True, their influence lives on in the work of their former graduate students and those acolytes educated during the eighties, when Marxism was *de rigeur* for aspiring leftists in the social sciences and humanities. But today the long-term survival of the ideas that Harvey and his fellow-travellers have professed is in question. Those Leftists who passed through bachelors programmes and graduate school from the early nineties were inculcated into ways of thinking which, in the main, defined themselves as post- or non-Marxist. In Harvey's case, once the careers of his former supervisees (like Neil Smith) come to an end, my own generation of Marxist scholars – already a minority in geography, as in most of the human sciences – will be the only ones left to keep the ideas Harvey has so brilliantly expounded alive.

These comments notwithstanding, it is not my intention to post Harvey's obituary notice or read him his last rites. I do, however, want to offer some sober reflections on what he's achieved in his three decade journey from being 'a Marxist of sorts' in *Social Justice* to being what he is today: among the most feted living Marxists (and certainly the most famous living geographer) operating in an intellectual environment where his ideas are no longer at the cutting edge of leftist thinking. I here use the word 'achieve' in a very practical sense. In one of his most famous theses, Marx made much of the two-way relationship between understanding and change. Harvey's oeuvre, it seems to me, expresses its author's overwhelming desire to explain and to diagnose. But it is much less clear how this quest for understanding can translate into informed anti-capitalist struggle.

Specifically, I want to answer the following question in this chapter: in what senses, and with what consequences, has Harvey been a *critical theorist* of capitalist society this last thirty years or so? Both the italicized terms are significant. Though anyone familiar with Harvey's work would agree that it's 'critical', few have troubled to inquire into the meaning of this appellation when applied to his restatement and extension of Marx's thinking. Likewise, though the commitment to it runs like a red thread through virtually all of Harvey's publications, it is not at all obvious why *theory* should be the privileged vehicle of critique – especially when its author has made few extended comments on the matter.[2] Yet it seems to me that an understanding of what connects critique and theory is essential if we are to grasp what Harvey's years of thinking, speaking and writing as a Marxist ultimately amount to. If the point is to change the world, then what contribution to this endeavour has Harvey's prodigious theoretical output made?

I realize, of course, that in one sense this question is both unfair and unanswerable. It is unfair because the ideas of one person – however revelatory they may be – can only do so much in a world as large and complex as our own. And it is unanswerable, in the abstract at least, because only an empirical analysis of who has heard or read Harvey, and with what effects, can ultimately tell us how influential he has been. In short, the impacts of Harvey's Marxism have been (and remain) radically underdetermined by the content of his writings and many speaking engagements. Whither his ideas have travelled and with what consequences is a contingent question. However, the *content* of these ideas clearly does matter, as do the various *media* that he has chosen to propagate them in. In what follows, I thus want to take an overview of Harvey's writings as a theorist, asking what makes them substantively 'critical', while also scrutinizing his preferred vehicles for disseminating these ideas.

I begin with some comments on the 'theoretical imperative' that pervades virtually all of Harvey's writings as a Marxist, whatever his particular subject of inquiry (cities, space, culture, finance, etc.). The detour to which my title refers is a cognitive one: for Harvey has long insisted that progressive change can only result from proper understanding and, for him, such understanding is furnished by theory. His project has been to abstract from one kind of complexity – that of everyday life in a capitalist world – in order to make plain another that should, in his view, be the real object of whatever transformatory agency can be brought to bear at any given moment in history: namely, the underyling complexity of those relations, tendencies and processes that appear as something other than themselves. The following three sections examine what I see as the principal dimensions of the 'work' that Harvey's theoretical animadversions aim to do. These concern (i) the supposedly 'organic' connection – internal to theory – between explanation and evaluation of Harvey's object, capitalist society; (ii) the identification of subjects or agents who are actually or potentially capable of effecting significant societal change; and (iii) the capacity of academic discourse – Harvey's stock-in-trade – to tap into wider currents of social discontent and insurgency. I conclude, perhaps ungenerously, that Harvey's work can be found wanting in all three areas. Its critical edge, when examined closely, appears blunt. For those, like myself, who have been deeply inspired and influenced by Harvey the challenge is clear. If the embers of Marxism are to be kept aglow in the years ahead, the powerful diagnostic impulses represented by his work need strenuously to be maintained. But its normative dimensions will need particular attention if change is to follow meaningfully from analysis. After all, Marxism, in all its baroque permutations, has always suffered an imbalance between its explanatory and practical dimensions since the days of Lenin, Trotsky and Luxemburg. The lacunae in Harvey's work only serve to demonstrate how enduring this imbalance is.

Theory Matters

'By our theories you shall know us' was the stirring and, as it turned out, premonitory conclusion to David Harvey's first book (1969a: 489) – one published before the Damascene conversion recorded in the thrillingly schizophrenic pages of *Social Justice*. Personalized, it could stand as the epigram for virtually all Harvey's writings as a Marxist. Aside from one ostensibly empirical contribution (the Paris chapters of *Consciousness and the Urban Experience* (1985a) and a more philosophically inclined treatise (*Justice, Nature and the Geography of Difference* (1996)), the bulk of his publications comprise a quest to fashion a 'cognitive map' or 'encompassing vision' that can help us see the political economic logics that underpin seemingly disparate aspects of contemporary life (1989b: 2, 4). In metaphorical terms, if Harvey is a commando of the word, then theory is his most potent weapon.

As such, Harvey's Marxism is neither forbiddingly abstract nor cloyingly concrete. Typically, his theoretical elucidations are specific enough to capture those invariant processes, relations and tendencies that give capitalism its structured coherence and dynamic instability. In this he emulates the late Marx, and intentionally so: from *The Limits to Capital* through his two 'Studies in the History and Theory of Capitalist Urbanization' to *The*

Condition of Postmodernity and his recent books on imperialism and neo-liberalism, Harvey has adumbrated a classical version of Marxism. Drawing upon *Capital*, the *Grundrisse* and *Theories of Surplus Value*, he has taken Marx at his word and his work 'without too much assistance from else-where' (2000a: 82). The result is a corpus that both explicates the logic of capitalism in general while linking it to the conjunctural particulars of the postwar political economy. As those familiar with his theoretical writings know, Harvey has a knack of leavening what is essentially a general theory of the capitalist mode of production with present-day evidence, anecdote and observation. This gives his theoretical texts a grounded feel, even though he rarely subjects his conceptual claims to extensive empirical scrutiny. Rather as Marx fleshed out volume 1 of *Capital* with observations on working-class life in Victorian England, so Harvey breathes life into his conceptual com-pages through suggestive factual material and illustrative asides.

He is not, of course, the only contemporary Marxist to read Marx directly, rather than through lenses provided by the latter's many distinguished epig-ones (like Althusser). In fact, he is one of a fairly sizeable cohort of scholars who have little time for the several postclassical Marxisms that have exerted an influence in the Anglophone academy – including, most recently, analytical Marxism and the 'overdeterminist' Marxism championed by Resnick and Wolff. But among classical Marxists today Harvey's theoreti-cal contributions have, I think, been doubly distinctive. For not only has he extended Marx's political economy into topical regions few others have explored – like built environments of production, distribution and con-sumption. He has also made singular contributions to our understanding of a phenomenally wide range of issues – wider, even, than those of a poly-mathic contemporary like Fredric Jameson.

In all this, there is a consistency and seriousness in Harvey's theoreti-cal work that is profoundly impressive. His characteristic manoeuvre has been to proceed from his peerless grasp of expanded capital reproduction (laid out in *The Limits to Capital*) and from there 'deepen and sharpen [Marxian] theory so that it can reach into realms that have hitherto remained opaque' (1989a: 16). This organic extension of Marx's later writ-ings has involved many 'intuitive jumps . . . and speculative leaps' (1999a: xxii). For Harvey is far more than an accomplished imitator of his master's voice. In Dick Walker's (2004: 434) apt words, while Harvey's theorizing possesses 'a degree of fidelity to the original spirit and letter of Marx that is quite remarkable [it] is not an epiphany that rewrites the word according to Saul along the road to a New Church, but a judicious rendering and exten-sion of Marx's unfinished project'. Harvey has said much the same. 'I much prefer', he writes, 'to treat [Marx's] . . . statements as . . . suggestions and rough ideas that need to be consolidated into a more consistent theor[y] . . . that respects the spirit rather than the verbal niceties if his largely unpublished studies, notes and letters' (Harvey 2001a: ix).

Representing and intervening

Why does Harvey place such emphasis on (Marxist) theory over and above any of the other products of intellectual labour? To answer this question we need to understand his conception of knowledge in general. Since *Social Justice* Harvey has held fast to an 'activist' view of knowledge. This has a double aspect. It means first that knowledge is no mere 'reflection' of a material world that imprints itself unproblematically on the human mind. Rather, for Harvey knowledge is a social construction that has a relative autonomy from the realities it depicts. As such, Harvey sees all knowledge as in the service of particular constituencies with particular interests by virtue of their social location. This was evident in his early critiques of neo-Malthusian reasoning – where all knowledge was considered to be 'ideological' – and of public policy discourse (Harvey 1974a, 1974d); a decade ago, it was the theme of his pointed discussion of 'globalization talk' (1996b); and, more recently, his essay on 'cartographic knowledges' strongly accents the non-innocence of all geographical imaginations (2001a: ch. 11). But if Harvey (Harvey and Scott 1989f: 215) sees 'the production of knowledge as a political project irreversibly implicated in the organizing of power relations', he also sees it as a basis for resistance. For him, Marxism's special quality as a body of insurgent knowledge is that it is a critique of capitalism rather than of those other systems of social domination with which it intersects. More particularly, I think Neil Smith (1995: 506) is right that Harvey early conceived of his work 'as a form of situated knowledge from the perspective of the working class'. This is clear as far back as *Social Justice* (1973a: 127), where he declared that Marxism 'provides the key to understanding capitalis[m] . . . from the position of those *not* in control of the means of production'. (I want to return to this claim later in the chapter.)

If, then, Harvey sees knowledge as a situationally varied construct he also sees it as a 'material force' in much the way that Marx imagined it to be. For him, all forms of knowledge – particularly those that are hegemonic – enter fully into the constitution of the world they describe, explain or evaluate. Indeed, if he did not believe this he would hardly have spent his career since *Explanation in Geography* (1969a) consciously promulgating Marxism, a body of knowledge that gained purchase in the Anglophone academy precisely through the efforts of Harvey and his generation of historical materialists. As he put it in *Consciousness and the Urban Expe-*

rience: 'the struggle to make Marxian concepts both plain and hegemonic
... [is] as important ... as active engagement on the barricades. That is
why Marx wrote *Capital*. And that is why I can write these words' (Harvey
1985a: xii). This notion that knowledge intervenes rather than merely represents, recalls Marx's oft-cited final thesis on Feuerbach once more. But
that thesis should not be understood too one-sidedly. Commenting on it,
Martin Heidegger (1971: 35) maintained that 'changing the world presup-
poses changing the *representation* of the world, and a representation of
the world can only be obtained when one has sufficiently *interpreted* it'.
Harvey apparently shares the sentiment: 'in order to change the world', he
also wrote in *Consciousness*, ' . . . we [first] have to understand it' (1985a:
xii). In this light, his voluminous writings as a Marxist can be seen as
underpinned by an anxiety: an anxiety that, without proper cognition,
actions to change the world for the better will go awry.

In sum, Harvey's view of knowledge is activist in the double sense that
knowledge is seen as both constructed and consequential. What he said in
Social Justice has, I think, formed a memorable template for his subsequent
work: 'It is irrelevant to ask whether concepts, categories and relationships
are "true" or "false". We have to ask, rather, what it is that produces them
and what they serve to produce' (Harvey 1973a: 298). This two-sided conception of knowledge feeds directly into Harvey's understanding of the
'power' of theory. I noted above that Harvey's publications as a Marxist
have, for the most part, been neither philosophical nor empirical in focus
– notwithstanding some contributions in both areas. 'As a Marxist', he
declared in *The Urbanization of Capital*, 'I am overtly rather than subliminally concerned with rigorous theory building' (Harvey 1985b: xiii).
The Limits to Capital had already testified to this fact, with its three-cut
account of the capitalist mode of production, and texts like *The Condition
of Postmodernity* have subsequently demonstrated Harvey's firm predilec-
tion for theoretical discourse (albeit in a more essayistic mode than *The
Limits*). It may seem odd that in a world suffering so many frighteningly
concrete problems, Harvey continues to insist on 'more rather than less
attention to theory construction' (1989a: 15) – odd because theorizing is
often thought to be an ethereal pursuit rather removed from the grim realities (and joys) of everyday life. Yet for Harvey this is anything but the case.
So why, in his view, can something called 'theory' make good on his aspirations both to understand and to change the world?

The detour of theory

The second part of this question – which speaks to the normative and practical dimensions of theory (my main concern in this chapter) – I'll defer
answering until the third, fourth and fifth sections. For now, it is sufficient
(and much easier) to construct an answer to the first part – which speaks
to the explanatory-diagnostic dimensions of theory. This can be done by
scrutinizing Harvey's scattered comments on theory and theorizing. These
comments have been made, for the most part, in the introductions, prefaces and afterwords of his many books. Studied closely, they indicate that
theory possesses three key characteristics in Harvey's estimation. These
characteristics mark both its specificity and its importance, distinguishing
it from the other possible fruits of intellectual labour.

First, and most obviously, theory allows us to see the wood for the trees in
Harvey's opinion. Marx once famously described social reality as 'the unity
of the diverse' and noted that analysts have only the 'power of abstraction' on hand in order to make that reality intelligible. Harvey feels much
the same. Theory, he insisted in his most conceptually muscular book
(*The Limits*), will not 'procure a full understanding of singular events . . .
The aim, rather, is . . . to grasp the most significant relationships at work'
(1982a: 450). This calls to mind Andrew Sayer's (1995: 5–6) lucid definition of theory as a set of connected abstractions that 'cut into the connective
tissue of the world at different angles . . . spotlight[ing] certain objects while
plunging others into darkness'. In short, one of theory's key attributes for
Harvey is that it allows us to detect the signals in the noise.

Secondly, Harvey values theoretical labour because it makes visible that
which is unseen. Like Marx's later works, Harvey's are peppered with references to 'surface appearances' and 'underlying realities' – most recently
in *The New Imperialism*. This reflects his conviction that capitalism makes
itself apparent by, as it were, hiding itself. The key relations, tendencies and
processes that make capitalism dance a dialectical tune are, Harvey insists,
compelled to appear as something other than themselves. This means that
they are invisibly real and really invisible. The only way they can be understood, then, is *cognitively* not phenomenally or perceptually. As Harvey
argued in the introduction to *The Urban Experience* – one of his most
forthright statements on the matter – theory is a 'way of seeing' in precisely
the former sense. It involves going beyond the actual in order to fathom
that which is virtual. In light of this, it is no surprise that the cognitive
insights provided by theory are very 'hard-won' (Harvey and Scott 1989f:
224) in Harvey's view. There is no royal road to understanding, but Harvey
is adamant that theory can make our journey down that road a good deal

easier by deciphering fugitive impressions and disputing 'common sense' empiricism.

Thirdly, and finally, Harvey values theory for its capacity to identify the commonalities that masquerade in and as differences. The commonalities that concern him are, of course, those of capital reproduction and expansion. The differences that concern him are, to posit an overdrawn distinction, those 'internal' and 'external' to capitalism – principally differences of geography (place and region), of individual and group identity (class, 'race', gender, etc.) and of social structure (culture, politics, etc.).

In reviews of both *The Condition of Postmodernity* (e.g. Deutsche 1991) and *Justice, Nature and the Geography of Difference* (e.g. Braun 1998), Harvey has been accused of reducing difference to commonality and indicted for his 'meta-theoretical' impulses (i.e. supposed cognitive exorbitancy). I don't propose to assess these linked charges here. Suffice to say that in Harvey's view the messenger is here being blamed for the message. If capitalism is an economic system that penetrates every nook and cranny of contemporary life, then any theory of it must necessarily be totalizing and holistic. This, at least, is Harvey's take on things – one articulated forcefully in a co-authored essay with Allen Scott (1989f), in a response to feminist critics of *The Condition* (Harvey 1992b), and in a rejoinder to a trio of commentaries on *Justice, Nature and the Geography of Difference* (Harvey 1998a). If this view is defensible then the necessity for a 'way of seeing' that can identify what conjoins otherwise different and disparate aspects of daily existence becomes clear. This way of seeing shows capitalism not be to an 'economic system' narrowly defined but, rather, a 'way of life' that pushes beyond all geographical and social boundaries. If capitalism's hidden hand appears, at first sight, *not* to be at work in and on all manner of putatively 'non-capitalist' forms of difference then this is only because of what I noted above: namely, that it manifests itself in duplicitous ways that it is the job of Marxist theory to expose.

To summarize, the explanatory-diagnostic power of theory appears to be threefold if we attend to Harvey's comments on the matter. It helps us discern (i) order in apparent confusion, (ii) underlying realities that are hidden from view, and (iii) the ties that bind the apparently dissociated. 'An object', Louis Althusser (1970: 184) once said, 'cannot be defined by its immediately visible or sensuous appearance; it is necessary to make a detour via its concept in order to grasp it'. In all three of the ways identified above, this comment captures well the 'theoretical imperative' (Harvey and Scott 1989f: 223) of Harvey's Marxism. For him the detour of theory is necessary if we are to get to our destination: namely, a rigorous understanding of capitalism in all its creative destructiveness and crafty promiscuity. It is precisely because theory is about a world that is unable to reveal its fundamental character without a major effort of intellectual labour that it is so indispensable and so important for Harvey.

A Critical Theorist?

None of this is unconnected to critique, of course. If it were, then Harvey's numerous theoretical interventions would be most un-Marxist – little more than a positive science devoid of any evaluative force or practical consequence. As Max Horkheimer (1972 [1937]) argued in a now classic statement, the exemplary promise of 'critical' as opposed to what he called 'traditional' theory is that it combines explanation and evaluation without recourse to anything outside its object of analysis. This organic link between the is and the ought is one that Harvey has both recognized and celebrated since his turn to Marxism thirty years ago. In *Social Justice*, for example, he declared that 'the act of observing *is* the act of evaluation' and made a famous distinction between 'revolutionary', 'counter-revolutionary' and 'status quo' theory, arguing that the former 'holds out the prospect for creating truth rather than [merely] finding it' (1973a: 15, 151). Almost a decade later, in *The Limits*, he made an equally forthright declaration about the 'unity of rigorous science and politics' that characterized his own and Marx's theorization of capitalism (Harvey 1982a: 37). And more recently he has invoked the figure of the 'insurgent architect' to describe his intellectual endeavours as a whole (Harvey 2000a). In short, Harvey has consistently maintained that the act of depicting the fundamental attributes of capitalist society – which is what theory, in its three above-mentioned dimensions, aims to do – is, *ipso facto*, an act of judging them.

This said, Harvey (like Marx before him) has rarely gone beyond terse or suggestive statements about why explanation *is* critique. Nor has he really established why the intimate link between cognition and judgement is, apparently, so important. Nor, finally, has he reflected much in print on the problems of burdening theory and the theorist with so great a responsibility – that of being both explainer and evaluater. In the rest of this chapter I want to tackle these issues and, in so doing, answer the simple question posed in my introduction. In what specific ways, and with what consequences, has David Harvey been a critical theorist as opposed to a putatively 'uncritical' one?

What Kind of Evaluation for What Kind of Change?

The answer to the first part of this question, might, at first sight, appear rather straightforward. Harvey's work is littered with judgements about the ills of capitalism's geographies and ecologies. What's more, he has codified many of these claims into full-blooded normative arguments – for instance, about justice (as in *Justice, Nature and the Geography of Difference*) and rights (as in *Spaces of Hope*). So presumably one need only look closely at Harvey's formalized criticisms to understand the link between his rich theorization of how capitalism works and what's wrong with it. But things are not, I think, so straightforward.

In the first place, it's striking that these formalized judgements mostly occur in books and essays that are either philosophical in tenor or where Harvey says little of a substantive theoretical nature about capitalist society. For instance, his well-known retort to the 'postmodern death of justice' involved drawing on Iris Young's (1990) multi-dimensional concept of (in)justice and illustrating its utility by way of a vignette about Hamlet, North Carolina (Harvey 1996a: ch. 12). Secondly, and conversely, where Harvey offers detailed theoretical insights into the dynamics of capitalism – as in *The Limits* – his animadversions are neither codified nor formally justified. Rather, they are thrownout at the reader as if their validity is more-or-less self-evident. If we periodize this, we might say, at the obvious risk of oversimplification, that (i) after *Social Justice* Harvey spent twenty years *explaining how capitalism works* – yet without formally articulating the grounds for his many critical asides, while (ii) devoting many of the works between *The Condition of Postmodernity* and *Spaces of Capital* to *formally evaluating capitalism's ills* – yet without linking evaluation tightly to a substantive analysis of its object.

It may well be that this link can be made convincingly with a little intellectual effort on our part. But I'd offer another interpretation of this apparent disjuncture between Harvey's formal exercises in explanatory and normative argumentation. Marx, on several occasions, made much of the difference between critique and criticism. The former, as we know, has a strong claim to be the favoured and, as it were, official self-description of his work. The latter, he once observed acerbically, 'knows [only] how to . . . condemn the present, but not how to comprehend it' (Marx 1976: 361). Critique, then, was for Marx an act 'not of judging the present but of disclosing its potentiality, of making manifest what is latent and bringing to the surface what is active only in a subterranean way' (McCarney 1990: 109). Critique thus relies on the autocritical nature of its object (in this case capitalism) to do the work that critics must do by bringing extraneous values to bear. It circumvents what Perry Anderson (1980: 86) once called 'the vain intrusion of moral judgements in lieu of causal understanding . . . leading to an "inflation" of ethical terms'.

I'll explain the relevance of this critique–criticism distinction to Harvey's work presently. But let me first trace its general consequences for analysis and evaluation. Critique is meaningless unless the phenomena being analysed are pregnant with possibilities and potentialities that, if realized, would address existing maladies. Criticism, meanwhile, while lacking the immanence of critique, can none the less serve a useful function in situations where the room for progressive change is limited. Though Marx was generally dismissive of criticism, and though the Frankfurt School later declared *both* it and critique impotent in the face of what they saw as a totally administered society, this underestimates its potential utility. For instance, utopian schemes that may have little chance of coming to fruition can none the less usefully highlight the contingency and non-necessity of existing societal or environmental arrangements.

It seems to me that Harvey's writings as a Marxist vacillate between critique and criticism. Rather than condemn him for inconsistency I think it's more productive to understand why the equivocation has arisen in the first place and in what it consists. My sense is that Harvey turned to criticism at that point when he recognized that critique can only be compelling under certain highly restrictive conditions. Let me elaborate.

The attraction of critique, as Harvey recognized in the 'socialist formulations' of *Social Justice*, is that evaluation is located in the object of analysis (capitalism) rather than potentially arbitrary values imposed by the theorist. Yet the theorist still has an important role to play, of course, since it takes a major effort of intellectual labour to expose what is hidden and latent. Harvey realized soon after *Social Justice* that he understood neither Marx's political economy nor, as a consequence, the complexities of capitalism well enough – something he 'needed to straighten . . . out' (Harvey 2000a: 82). His 1970s essays on capitalism, cities and space and *The Limits to Capital* were (and remain) rigorous attempts to 'mirror' in theory the dynamics that bind capitalism and its geographies together dialectically. They differ from the 'liberal formulations' of the first half of *Social Justice* not just in the obvious sense that they are Marxist in character. More than this, these writings are critical of capitalism yet without any of the formal normative argumentation used to attack intra-urban unevenness in *Social Justice*'s early chapters. While it may seem that Harvey simply put normative issues to one side after 1973, I'd suggest instead that his substantive theoretical work through the seventies and into the eighties took the form of *critique*. In other words, Harvey did not puff out his work with learned discussions of equality or justice, or schemes to make these concepts flesh. Instead, in the very act of analysing capitalism he followed the later Marx in thereby evaluating it too.

This is clearly the case in *The Limits*, though it takes a skilled interpreter to see exactly how. More than any of Harvey's books this one sticks close to the spirit and letter of Marx the political economist. Though it seems to be a rather austere dissection of capitalism's temporalities and spatialities, it is also a non-moralistic indictment of this mode of production. Seyla Benhabib's work is my guide here. In *Critique, Norm and Utopia*, (1986) Benhabib usefully outlined the specific ways in which *Capital* is a critique of political economy rather than an economics. Though I don't have the space to justify the claim, I'd suggest that her elucidation of Marxian critique applies almost exactly to *The Limits*. This should be no surprise for the simple and obvious fact that *The Limits* is so deeply grounded in the arguments of *Capital*, as well as ancillary texts like the *Grundrisse*. Benhabib argues that *Capital* is a critique in the following ways. First, it is an *immanent critique* of capitalism because it shows how the values of this society – like equality – are abrogated in its very functioning. Secondly, it is a *defetishing critique* of capitalism because it shows that the system is not, in its fundamentals, what it appears to be on the surface. Finally, Benhabib shows that *Capital* is a *transformatory critique* of capitalism because it shows that system to be crisis-prone and self-negatory. All these elements of critique can readily be found in *The Limits* once one knows to look for them, most obviously in the third case ('critique-as-crisis-theory': Castree 1996).

If *The Limits* is Harvey's most accomplished work of critique – rather than criticism tacked on to a notionally 'neutral' exposé of capitalism's inner geo-temporal dynamics – then it arguably stands as an unrepeated precedent in Harvey's oeuvre post-1989. In many of his writings after *The Condition of Postmodernity* Harvey (re)turned to normative questions with an explicitness not found in his work since *Social Justice*. With the major exception of *The New Imperialism*, this return was coincident with a move away from formal theory construction towards more philosophical, speculative and interpretive writings. Specifically, many of Harvey's 1990s publications were an attempt to adumbrate principles suitable for an attack on capitalism, while recognizing that there's more in the world to criticize than capitalism alone. These principles were intended to be both benchmarks for judging the present and standards that might mobilize broad-based opposition to capitalism at a time when leftists have many targets to consider – such as gender inequality, homophobia and environmental degradation, for example. In addition to laying out these principles with a formality not seen in his work for twenty years, Harvey ended the nineties with a fictional depiction of a postcapitalist society barely incipient in the present – thus contributing to a long and honourable tradition of left utopian thinking (Harvey 2000: Appendix). Together, I'd suggest that these various normative interventions constitute a break with Marxian critique. While they are critical of capitalism, they are not, in my view, put forward with any rigorous reference to Harvey's earlier theoretical studies of this mode of production. Rather, these studies hover in the background. In short, Harvey's belief in the power of critique seems to have given way over the course of his career to a belief that 'criticism' is none the less a useful second best. In saying this, I realize that Harvey would probably reject this reading and insist that he has never once relinquished the weapon of critique.

Why has Harvey's commitment to critique given way to a more explicit but less exacting form of evaluation as the years have gone by? I'd suggest two reasons, both of which are underpinned by the fact that as long as critique remains wedded to theory it cannot, despite its aspirations, lay any serious claim to realism! As Harvey's various comments on theory over the years attest, he acknowledges that while it is indubitably *about* the world it is not, by definition, *coterminous with it*. The distinctiveness and value of theory is that its abstracts from reality in order to reveal key aspects of it. What this means is that while critique can be compelling *at the theoretical level*, it is found wanting when put to the test of conjunctural specifics. This has a 'horizontal' and a 'vertical' dimension. First, because Harvey has theorized capitalism in abstraction from other systems of social domination (like patriarchy), his critique of political economy necessarily assumes 'non-interference' from these other systems. Secondly, because Harvey has theorized capitalism in abstraction from any specific social formations – with the signal exception of the Paris essays in *Consciousness and the Urban Experience* – his critique of political economy has been equally 'unadulterated' by empirical complications. In other words, the limits of critique are those of theory itself.

Harvey, it seems to me, came to realize this by the late eighties, once he had worked through Marx's ideas and created his own distinctive theoretical compages (what he called 'historical-geographical materialism'). What that working through demonstrated – as *The Limits* so richly showed – was that Marx's critique was indeed as 'revolutionary' as Harvey had claimed in 1973a: nothing less than a root-and-branch demonstration of capitalism's internal contradictions and crisis tendencies. *But* after the major economic crisis of the early seventies that shook the Western world, it became all too plain that actually existing capitalism (as opposed to Harvey's theory of capitalism in general) was adapting very well to its own torsions and tensions. In the West, the end of the Keynesian welfare state era, the defeat of the labour movement and the successful installation of neoconservative ideas all indicated that the promise of critique would probably fall short when confronted with these contingent realities. It was surely not for nothing that Harvey, for a time, supplemented his abstract theorization of capitalism with Regulation School ideas (e.g. Harvey 1988a). For these meso-level abstractions helped explain precisely why capitalist societies contain the resources to *prevent* economic crises making flesh the postcapitalist future promised by critique.

If a resilient late twentieth-century capitalism thus drew some of the sting from Harvey's critique of political economy, it was accompanied by a wider 'crisis of Marxism' within the Western academy and the rise of a more heterodox left. I won't rehearse the reasons for this crisis, except to say that by the nineties it appeared to many still committed to Marxist ideas that capitalism was being let off the hook too lightly. As free market ideology was aggressively disseminated worldwide, we might conjecture that some Marxists felt it was pragmatically important to use any and all tools available to indict a globalizing capitalist system. This conjecture might well apply to Harvey who, as his essay 'Postmodern morality plays' (1992a) showed, was frustrated that the academic left was abandoning Marxism at the very moment when capitalism was entering a 'competitive' phase redolent of the time when Marx was writing. In this light, one might see his decision to discuss justice, difference and rights in quite general terms through the nineties the following terms. Not only was it a response to the intrinsic problems of critique. It was also an attempt to keep anticapitalist arguments alive in inhospitable circumstances where intellectual allies seemed to be diminishing in number.

To summarize this section, if one takes Harvey's Marxist writings in their entirety, it seems to me that he has come to recognize the insufficiency of critique when confronted with changing real-world and intellectual circumstances. The detour of a theory of capitalism can, it seems, only get us so far in a context where the system's ills and irrationalities are inextricably linked with all manner of non-capitalist repressions and struggles. Over three decades after the effusions of 'Revolutionary and counterrevolutionary theory in geography', Harvey remains a trenchant critic of capitalism but is now a more considered one. To the extent that capitalism does not exist in a 'pure' state, so Harvey's critique has had to relinquish its rigour and reckon with a more overdetermined world where progressive change is inevitably 'dilemmatic'.

A Rebel without a Subject?

If I'm correct that the 'power' of critique has been attenuated in Harvey's work over time, I'd suggest that this has been coincident with an increasing inability to identify determinate agents capable of effecting meaningful anti-capitalist struggle. Clearly, this inability is problematic for a Marxism aiming to change the world rather than remain a sullen witness to its own impotence. It is this inability I want now to describe and explain.

In section two of this chapter, I noted that Harvey early regarded Marxism as a form of situated knowledge from the perspective of the working class. He reiterated this belief in an apologia for *The Condition of Postmodernity*, where he reminded his critics that wage-labourers were constituted as the prime 'other' of capitalist history (Harvey 1992b). Yet, despite these asseverations, I'd argue that Harvey recognized almost from the start of his turn to Marx that there is no such thing as a specifiable working-class actor at either the theoretical or 'real-world' (empirical) levels. This recognition was forced upon Harvey not by any failings in his work but by realities (to reuse my earlier distinction) both 'internal' and 'external' to capitalism.

The first signs of this are evident in a long footnote early on in *The Limits* and in the 'Afterword' to that book. *The Limits* is an analysis of what sociologists call 'system (dis)integration': it abstracts capitalism from its real-world integument and, from the third-person perspective of a thinker-observer (Harvey), explicates its logic. In a footnote on the Althusserian distinction between mode of production and social formation, Harvey (1982a: 26) acknowledges that the 'neat two class analytics' of *The Limits* are unrealistic. Similarly, in the book's concluding pages he admits that an examination of the lived reality of working-class people 'constitutes a fundamentally different point of departure' in the analysis of how capitalism survives or is overthrown (1982a: 447). Even at the level of theory, I would argue that *The Limits* deconstructs its own seeming identification of a singular working-class actor exploited by a capitalist class. As I have argued elsewhere, the text depicts capitalism as an impersonal mode of domination as much as a system in which the exploitation of one class by another at the site of production is the fundamental issue (Castree 1999). Following Postone (1996), *The Limits* can be read not simply as a critique of capitalism from the standpoint of wage-labourers. Rather, it can be seen as exposing the peculiar fact that in a capitalist world *everyone* touched by the system is subject to a 'quasi-objective form of social mediation' (Postone 1996: 5) that extends well beyond the productive sphere. Here relations between individuals, regardless of who they are or what they do, confront them as invisible forces (e.g. falling profit rates, economic crises) or visible things (commodities, built environments, etc.). Though *The Limits* does say a fair bit about class struggle, it devotes far more time and energy to tracing the various forms in which the products of wage-labour become seemingly foreign, uncontrollable factors standing over against people of all stripes. Indeed, as if to confirm this, Harvey's appendix on value theory (Harvey 1982a: 35–8) stresses that Marx's political economy is an exposé of 'the concatenation of forces and constraints' that serve to discipline people 'as if they are externally imposed necessity' (1982: 27). And in later works – like the essay on money, time and space in *Consciousness and the Urban Experience* (1985a: ch. 5) – this theme of domination by abstractions appears with equal clarity.

Even if I'm wrong here, it *is* clear that Harvey recognized in and after *The Limits* that part of the logic of capitalism is to fragment workers geographically and so tendentially undermine the possibility for the emergence of a wider class consciousness. Capitalism's propensity to produce different cities and regions with a 'structured coherence' – so well explained in *The Urbanization of Capital* – confounds co-operative thought and action among spatially separated working class communities. It follows that there is no such thing as *the* working-class but only ever spatially dissonant, place-based class groupings – unless organizational apparatuses can create translocal forms of solidarity. It is also clear – particularly in *Consciousness* – that Harvey was at pains many years ago not to confuse the identification of an insurgent subject at the *theoretical* level with the realities of working-class agency at the *empirical* level. As the Paris essays of this book showed, even in moments of crisis a coherent working-class actor does not simply step into the breach. These essays – which are inquiries into what sociologists would call 'social (dis)integration' – make clear that working class people exist not as a collective singular constituency but as an empirically complex, disunified one. The mix of class fractions is always such that the abstract class analytics of a text like *The Limits* do not translate cleanly at the level of lived experience.

By the late 1980s, then, it was evident that a subject potentially capable of ushering in socialism existed in Harvey's work at a theoretical level only – and even then there are reasons to believe that this subject was not as central to the analysis as one might suppose or as coherent and self-possessed as it appeared to be. Through the nineties, it seems to me that the identification of *determinate* anti-capitalist actors became something Harvey more-or-less gave up on in his writings. This was not simply a function of the objective weakening of the labour movement worldwide. It was as much a response to the already mentioned crisis of Marxism in the academy and the rise of other left-wing paradigms like feminism. After *The Condition of Postmodernity*, Harvey's attempts to bring non-capitalist forms of 'difference' into his analysis inevitably rendered the notion of a broadly identifiable working-class subject even less plausible. Indeed, it is telling that in *Justice, Nature and the Geography of Difference* Harvey defines class not as a determinate constituency of people but more generally as 'positionality in relation to processes of capital accumulation' (1996a: 359). This ecumenical definition is, I think, Harvey's concession to the fact that all subjects on the ground are 'discerned' in Paul Smith's (1988) sense of the term. That is, all individuals are interpellated into multiple subject-positions that mesh in often contradictory ways such that a person's 'true interests' are anything but clear. Given this, 'class is a question not of identity or coherence . . . but of *composition*' (Thoburn 2003: 63).

This is not to say that Harvey has given up on the idea that class matters as his career has evolved. But it is to say that he now concedes that class consciousness and class action must be understood in relation to non-capitalist forms of identity within and between various 'militant particularisms'. Because he has taken little interest in analysing these forms of identity substantively, his most recent writings on class have inevitably been quite general in character. His ultimately banal observation in *Justice, Nature and the Geography of Difference* that 'agency is everywhere' to the extent that capitalism is now everywhere set the tone. For instance, in the early chapters of *Spaces of Hope* he argues (sensibly enough) that in these neoliberal times wage-workers need to recognize their common interests, even if those workers may be massively differentiated by ethnicity, nation, gender, etc. Similarly, in *The New Imperialism* he usefully identifies what labour movements and the more inchoate 'anti-capitalist' movement prominent 'post-Seattle' have in common. But in both cases, because he lacks an exacting theoretical grasp of non-capitalist forms of power and resistance, his comments about agency lack specificity – even at the theoretical, never mind empirical, level.

In sum, that most talismanic of Marxist ideas – an insurgent working-class actor who is capitalism's gravedigger – has been steadily attenuated in Harvey's work as the years have gone by. It seems to me that, ironically, his is a critical theory that lacks a subject. This is no mere function of temporary historical circumstance – the fact that over the last thirty years the workers' movements have suffered defeats at the local, national and global levels. More profoundly, it is, I'm arguing, a result of an enduring ontological fact: the fact that people's identities are so multiplex within and between places that the development of working-class consciousness and action at any geographical scale is a precarious achievement that is exceedingly hard won.

The Politics of Academic Labour

In the previous two sections I have discussed two ways in which Harvey's theoretical works have aspired to be 'critical'. By placing these works in a wider social and intellectual context, I have suggested their critical bite has yielded to less determinate forms of argumentation over time. My contention has been that, since the early nineties, Harvey's writings have lost some of the theoretical rigour of his earlier work as a result of the failings of both critique and an implausible conception of working-class agency. The result is that Harvey's objections to capitalism have become more explicit but also more abstract and 'moralistic', while his conception of anti-capitalist struggle has become ever less precise. In this final main section of the chapter, I want to turn to a third dimension of the putative power of David Harvey's critical theorization of capitalism. It is one that he has barely ever discussed but which is absolutely vital to any proper evaluation of the impact his writings have had this last thirty-plus years. It concerns the degree to which he has taken steps to ensure that his ideas travel beyond university audiences.

Harvey is an academic who has worked in universities his whole professional life. He began his career at Bristol University in the sixties, became a professor at Johns Hopkins University in the early seventies, took the Halford Mackinder chair of geography at Oxford University in 1987, and then moved back to Hopkins in the nineties before taking up his current (and probably last) post at CUNY in 2000. Though he has been involved in left-wing political struggles in his private life, the bulk of his professional existence has been dedicated to thinking, teaching and writing. This commitment to academia has served him well. The intellectual freedoms afforded by the Western university have allowed him and his generation of Anglophone Marxists to construct a corpus of work that, as I noted in the introduction, was virtually non-existent prior to the seventies.

At whom has this corpus of work been directed though? The obvious answer is other (non-Marxist) academics for the most part, as well as degree students. From *Social Justice* until at least *The Condition of Postmodernity*, Harvey's writings were attempts to demonstrate the perspicuity of Marxist ideas to geographers and urban analysts who had scarcely encountered them until Harvey, Castells and a few others burst on the scene. Important as this paradigm-shifting endeavour was, in recent years Harvey has clearly had his eye on audiences beyond the university. The unexpected success of *The Condition* – which sold among educated sections of the public as much as paid academics – seemed to embolden him to pitch many of his subsequent writings more widely. This is most obviously the case with *The New Imperialism*, which began life as a series of public lectures delivered in Oxford (see Castree 2006). And Harvey has, in other recent works, expressed a belief that his ideas do travel beyond academia. Thus, in *Spaces of Capital* (his 'greatest hits' book) he has described his work as an attempt 'to change ways of thought . . . among the public at large' as much as in the academy (Harvey 2001a: vii). Similarly, in a reissue of *The Limits* he expressed the hope that his work might help 'inform . . . practices on the part of oppositional forces committed to finding an alternative to capitalist hegemony' (Harvey 1999a: xxvii).

Harvey's aspiration to connect with wider constituencies outside the university is, of course, consistent with the Marxist tradition his work has so richly extended. As Anderson (1983: 14) rightly noted, 'Marxist theory, bent on understanding the world, has always aimed at an asymptotic unity with a popular practice seeking to transform it'. If, for argument's sake, we discount the conclusions of the previous section, we can ask how well Harvey has pitched his claims to non-academic, left-wing audiences. In other words, if we assume that during his career a strong labour movement potentially receptive to Marxist ideas had existed in the Anglophone world, then we can speculate as to whether his work might have served as a 'guide to action' on that 'political proving ground . . . [which], in the analysis, is the only one that counts' (Harvey 1989: 15, 16).

Such speculation does not presume that Harvey is entirely responsible for the wider impact of his writings as a theorist. But to the extent that theory cannot represent itself – it must, after all, be represented (by a living theorist, David Harvey) – then the site in and from which theoretical work is undertaken undoubtedly makes a difference to who encounters it. Antonio Gramsci wisely noted that 'the critic's starting point is "knowing thyself" as a product of historical process to date, which has deposited in you an infinity of traces, without leaving an inventory' (cited in Said 2001: 170). Harvey, it seems, has failed to heed this injunction. In none of his attempts at self-explanation (e.g. the *New Left Review* interview of 2000 or the very biographical introduction to *Spaces of Hope*) does he consider how his academic location has materially affected the extent to which his ideas travel beyond academics accustomed to the intellectual difficulties of his work. A considered examination of Harvey's socialization in the academy, I would suggest, might explain why his hopes to have reached non-academic audiences may only have been minimally realized. Let me explain.

Early in the chapter I mentioned Harvey's activist epistemology, but such an epistemology must reckon with the fact that not all knowledges are equally 'active' within the wider society. Academics are, of course, principally producers of new knowledge – philosophical, theoretical and empirical. But where they were once, perhaps, special in this regard, today they are just one of many knowledge producers in late capitalist societies. Broadcasters, computer designers, lawyers, management consultants, policy experts and journalists are some of the many professionals who nowadays create and distribute knowledge rather than, say, material goods. Most of these professionals – like most academics – speak and write in a *lingua franca* largely unintelligible to ordinary people. A few of them, though, are 'organic intellectuals' in Gramsci's expansive but precise sense of the term: that is, people whose ideas aim to 'organize interests, gain more power, get more control' (Said 1994: 4).

Such people have the influence they do by self-consciously writing in accessible ways (which is not the same as 'dumbing down') and disseminating their ideas in media that permit them wide exposure. Judged by these two standards Harvey's work can be found wanting. First, despite the clarity of his best prose, most non-academics would doubtless perceive his work to be forbiddingly difficult. Secondly, the overwhelming majority of his work has been written for academic audiences rather than any other addressees. Yet, to be an effective thought-shaper today – whatever one's political beliefs – one needs exposure in newspapers and magazines, as well as on television. This fact perhaps explains why the most prominent left-wing voices of our age are journalists, like George Monbiot and John Pilger, or a documentary-maker like Michael Moore.[3] Journalists use articles, columns and broadcasts to reach wide audiences, often building up a following in the process. Michael Moore has done the same through his docu-films. This is not to say that book publishing no longer matters. On the contrary, the appetite for book reading in Western societies (fictional and non-) remains undiminished. Norena Hertz and Naomi Klein are two radicals whose books have sold to a very large number of people disenchanted with neoliberalism.[4] The success of their polemics shows that thought fundamentally critical of the current order does not lack a ready audience. But unlike Harvey not only are these two best-selling authors not Marxists; they also have the knack of writing for general audiences. Of course, the price of this is that their books lack analytical rigour and depth. But if there's a lesson here for Harvey it is surely this: to make the Marxist critique of capitalism 'common-sense' once more the tactical use of writing and speaking media is required.

Marxists have long boasted that theirs is not only a theory of society but also one that can explain its own existence – in Anderson's (1983: 11) words, 'it includes, indivisibly and unremittingly, *self*-criticism'. Part of this autocritical sensibility must surely extend to an examination of those institutions that have shaped actually existing Marxism in the early twenty-first century. Like virtually all Marxist thinkers of his generation, Harvey has been the voluntary agent of involuntary determinations bequeathed by the universities he has worked in and for. Yet, as I noted above, the political and moral economy of Western university life has merited virtually no formal discussion in any of Harvey's few attempts to explain his credo biographically.[5] It's as if the conditioning forces of higher education – like the demand to publish research in academic journals rather than in more populist outlets – has had no important bearing on the style of his Marxism. This is, of course, implausible. Like the generation of Marxists to which he belongs, the university environment has afforded Harvey intellectual licence at the cost of wider social relevance. This environment has, indelibly, deposited 'an infinity of traces' that have prevented him from sharing his ideas in ways he might otherwise have had the nous to do. Harvey's detour of theory has, ultimately, had its greatest impact in the academic worlds Harvey inhabits rather than anywhere else.

The (In)Consequences of Theory?

In this chapter I have offered a critical overview of what's actually or potentially 'critical' about David Harvey's theoretical interrogation of capitalism. I have focused on three things, two relating to the content of Harvey's writings, the third to his favoured mode and media of communicating his thinking. If my threefold examination of Harvey's critical theory of capitalism has seemed ultimately mean-spirited let me end on a positive note. David Harvey remains an absolute inspiration – not only to me but to many who do not necessarily share his Marxian worldview. If I have subjected his work to an exacting examination, then it is only because Harvey sets such high standards for himself and thus for those of us who follow in his wake. He has achieved more than most of us could ever hope to emulate. I hope the almost athletic rational energy he has displayed for over three decades continues undiminished for many years to come. If a critical theory of capitalism is to have any consequences at all, then it first needs theorists of Harvey's calibre. It is to be hoped that those of my own and a younger generation can make the detour of Marxist theory a necessity, not only for radical academics but also for capitalism's many discontents in the wider world. If we succeed then it is only because figures like David Harvey have given us the tools to do so.

Notes

1 Jones III's (2005) book is currently the only published attempt to consider the entirety of Harvey's writings, prior to which parts of Derek Gregory's (1995) *Geographical Imaginations* offered the most synoptic account. In the case of geography and the interdisciplinary Marxist community this absence is particularly egregious. Yet it is not surprising. Geography, Harvey's 'native' discipline (despite his current berth in an anthropology department), is a peculiar subject in that it has no history of celebrating its 'intellectual giants' in the way that canonical thinkers in anthropology, sociology, philosophy and the like have been lauded for decades. So even though Harvey's influence has been immense, the discipline has been slow – perhaps through timidity or embarrassment – to undertake extensive appraisals of his glittering career. Meanwhile, Marxists outside geography have been equally slow to recognize Harvey's distinctive contributions to their critical discourse for one sad but understandable reason. His professional status as a 'geographer' no doubt disposed many Marxists located in departments of history, economics, sociology, etc. to overlook his work for many years. Stereotypes of the discipline probably fed the suspicion that its practitioners had little to contribute theoretically since theirs is principally an 'empirical' and 'applied' subject. Though Harvey is now, belatedly, seen as a major figure within an embattled Marxist camp, it remains the case that others of his generation (e.g. Jameson and Eagleton) have had their work evaluated in the round while he has not.

2 Harvey has rarely published programmatic pieces that explain his self-understanding and his politics. The various things he has published in this regard – mostly introductions, prefaces and afterwords to his books – I usually find disappointing because they lack depth. Upon close inspection, they tend to tantalize rather than satisfy. Even his interview with *New Left Review*, where he is very candid about his life's work, yields only superficial insights. The same can be said of his published exchange with Donna Haraway.

3 Intriguingly, Harvey's first book as a Marxist was dedicated to 'all good committed journalists everywhere' (Harvey 1973a: 19). In the early 1990s, Harvey in fact tried his hand in a journalistic medium: radio. He made a series of programmes on modern cities for BBC Radio 4.

4 And Monbiot and Pilger have also enjoyed success as book writers, using their profiles as journalists to gain a wide audience for their critiques.

5 These exercises in self-explanation typically appear in introductions to his many books.

14

Space as a Keyword

David Harvey

If Raymond Williams were contemplating the entries for his celebrated text on *Keywords* today, he would surely have included the word 'space'. He may well have included it in that short list of concepts, such as 'culture' and 'nature', to be listed as 'one of the most complicated words in our language' (Williams 1985). How, then, can the range of meanings that attach to the word 'space' be clarified without losing ourselves in some labyrinth (itself an interesting spatial metaphor) of complications?

'Space' often elicits modification. Complications sometimes arise from the modifications (which all too frequently get omitted in the telling or the writing) rather than from any inherent complexity in the notion of space itself. When, for example, we write of 'material', 'metaphorical', 'liminal', 'personal', 'social' or 'psychic' space (just to take a few examples) we indicate a variety of contexts that so inflect matters as to render the meaning of space contingent upon the context. Similarly, when we construct phrases such as spaces of fear, of play, of cosmology, of dreams, of anger, of particle physics, of capital, of geopolitical tension, of hope, of memory or of ecological interaction (again, just to indicate a few of the seemingly infinite sites of deployment of the term) then the terrain of application defines something so special as to render any generic definition of space a hopeless task. In what follows, however, I will lay aside these difficulties and attempt a general clarification of the meaning of the term. I hope thereby to disperse some of the fog of miscommunication that seems to bedevil use of the word.

The entry point we choose for such an inquiry is not innocent, however, since it inevitably defines a particular perspective that highlights some matters while occluding others. A certain privilege is, of course, usually accorded to philosophical reflection, since philosophy aspires to rise above the various and divergent fields of human practices and partial knowledges, in order to assign definitive meanings to the categories to which we may appeal. I have formed the impression that there is sufficient dissension and confusion among the philosophers as to the meaning of space as to make that anything but an unproblematic starting point. Furthermore, since I am by no means qualified to reflect on the concept of space from within the philosophical tradition, it seems best to begin at the point I know best. I therefore start from the standpoint of the geographer, not because this is a privileged site that somehow has a proprietary right (as some geographers sometimes seem to claim) over the use of spatial concepts, but because that is where I happen to do most of my work. It is in this arena that I have wrestled most directly with the complexity of what the word 'space' might be all about. I have, of course, frequently drawn upon the work of others operating within various branches of the academic and intellectual division of labour as well as upon the work of many geographers (too many to be acknowledged in a brief essay of this sort) who have been actively engaged in exploring these problems in their own distinctive ways. I make no attempt here to build a synthesis of all this work. I give a purely personal account of how my own views have evolved (or not) as I have sought meanings that work, as satisfactorily as possible, for the theoretical and practical topics of primary concern to me.

I began reflecting upon this problem many years ago. In *Social Justice and the City*, published in 1973, I argued that it was crucial to reflect on the nature of space if we were to understand urban processes under capitalism. Drawing upon ideas previously culled from a study of the philosophy of science and partially explored in *Explanation in Geography*, I identified a tripartite division in the way space could be understood:

> If we regard space as absolute it becomes a 'thing in itself' with an existence independent of matter. It then possesses a structure which we can use to pigeon-hole or individuate phenomena. The view of relative space proposes that it be understood as a relationship between objects which exists only because objects exist and relate to each other. There is another sense in which space can be viewed as relative and I choose to call this relational space – space regarded in the manner of Leibniz, as being contained in objects in the sense that an object can be said to exist only insofar as it contains and represents within itself relationships to other objects.
>
> (Harvey 1973a)

I think this tripartite division is well worth sustaining. So let me begin with a brief elaboration on what each of these categories might entail.

Absolute space is fixed and we record or plan events within its frame. This is the space of Newton and Descartes and it is usually represented as a pre-existing and immovable grid amenable to standardized measurement and open to calculation. Geometrically it is the space of Euclid and therefore the space of all manner of cadastral mapping and engineering practices. It is a primary space of individuation – *res extensa* as Descartes put it – and this applies to all discrete and bounded phenomena including you and me as individual persons. Socially this is the space of private property and other bounded territorial designations (such as states, administrative units, city plans and urban grids). When Descartes's engineer looked upon the world with a sense of mastery, it was a world of absolute space (and time) from which all uncertainties and ambiguities could in principle be banished and in which human calculation could uninhibitedly flourish.

The relative notion of space is mainly associated with the name of Einstein and the non-Euclidean geometries that began to be constructed most systematically in the nineteenth century. Space is relative in the double sense: that there are multiple geometries from which to choose and that the spatial frame depends crucially upon what it is that is being relativized and by whom. When Gauss first established the rules of a non-Euclidean spherical geometry to deal with the problems of surveying accurately upon the curved surface of the earth, he also affirmed Euler's assertion that a perfectly scaled map of any portion of the earth's surface is impossible. Einstein took the argument further by pointing out that all forms of measurement depended upon the frame of reference of the observer. The idea of simultaneity in the physical universe, he taught us, has to be abandoned. It is impossible to understand space independent of time under this formulation and this mandates an important shift of language from space *and* time to space-time or spatio-temporality. It was, of course, Einstein's achievement to come up with exact means to examine such phenomena as the curvature of space when examining temporal processes operating at the speed of light (Osserman 1995). But in Einstein's schema time remains fixed while it is space that bends according to certain observable rules (much in the same way as Gauss devised spherical geometry as an accurate means to survey through triangulation on the earth's curved surface). At the more mundane level of geographical work, we know that the space of transportation relations looks and is very different from the spaces of private property. The uniqueness of location and individuation defined by bounded territories in absolute space gives way to a multiplicity of locations that are equidistant from, say, some central city location. We can create completely different maps of relative locations by differentiating between distances measured in terms of cost, time, modal split (car, bicycle or skateboard) and even disrupt spatial continuities by looking at networks, topological relations (the optimal route for the postman delivering mail), and the like. We know, given the differential frictions of distance encountered on the earth's surface, that the shortest distance (measured in terms of time, cost, energy expended) between two points is not necessarily given by the way the legendary crow flies. Furthermore the standpoint of the observer plays a critical role. The typical New Yorker's view of the world, as the famous Steinberg cartoon suggests, fades very fast as one thinks about the lands to the west of the Hudson River or east of Long Island. All of this relativization, it is important to note, does not necessarily reduce or eliminate the capacity for calculability or control, but it does indicate that special rules and laws are required for the particular phenomena and processes under consideration. Difficulties do arise, however, as we seek to integrate understandings from different fields into some more unified endeavour. The spatio-temporality required to represent energy flows through ecological systems accurately, for example, may not be compatible with that of financial flows through global markets. Understanding the spatio-temporal rhythms of capital accumulation requires a quite different framework to that required to understand global climate change. Such disjunctions, though extremely difficult to work across, are not necessarily a disadvantage provided we recognize them for what they are. Comparisons between different spatio-temporal frameworks can illuminate problems of political choice. (Do we favour the spatio-temporality of financial flows or that of the ecological processes they typically disrupt, for example?)

The relational concept of space is most often associated with the name of Leibniz who, in a famous series of letters to Clarke (effectively a stand-in for Newton), objected vociferously to the absolute view of space and time so central to Newton's theories.[1] His primary objection was theological. Newton made it seem as if even God was inside of absolute space and time rather than in command of spatio-temporarality. By extension, the relational view of space holds there is no such thing as space or time outside of the processes that define them. (If God makes the world then He has also chosen, out of many possibilities, to make space and time of a particular sort.) Processes do not occur *in* space but define their own spatial frame. The concept of space is embedded in or internal to process. This very formulation implies that, as in the case of relative space, it is impossible to disentangle space from time. We must therefore focus on the relationality of space-time rather than of space in isolation. The relational notion of space-time implies the idea of internal relations; external influences get internalized in specific processes or things through time (much as my mind absorbs all manner of external information and stimuli to yield strange patterns of thought including dreams and fantasies as well as attempts at rational calculation). An event or a thing at a point in space cannot be understood by appeal to what exists only at that point. It depends upon everything else going on around it (much as all those who enter a room to discuss bring with them a vast array of experiential data accumulated from the world). A wide variety of disparate influences swirling over space in the past, present and future concentrate and congeal at a certain point (e.g. within a conference room) to define the nature of that point. Identity, in this argument, means something quite different from the sense we have of it from absolute space. Thus do we arrive at an extended version of Leibniz's concept of the monad.

Measurement becomes more and more problematic the closer we move towards a world of relational space-time. But why would it be presumed that space-time only exists if it is measurable and quantifiable in certain traditional ways? This leads to some interesting reflections on the failure (perhaps better construed as limitations) of positivism and empiricism to evolve adequate understandings of spatio-temporal concepts beyond those that can be measured. In a way, relational conceptions of space-time bring us to the point where mathematics, poetry and music converge if not merge. And that, from a scientific (as opposed to aesthetic) viewpoint, is anathema to those of a positivist or crudely materialist bent. On this point the Kantian compromise of recognizing space as real but only accessible to the intuitions tries to build a bridge between Newton and Leibniz precisely by incorporating the concept of space within the theory of Aesthetic Judgement. But Leibniz's return to popularity and significance not only as the guru of cyberspace but also as a foundational thinker in relationship to more dialectical approaches to mind–brain issues and quantum theoretical formulations signals some sort of urge to go beyond absolute and relative concepts and their more easily measurable qualities as well as beyond the Kantian compromise. But the relational terrain is an extremely challenging and difficult terrain upon which to work. There are many thinkers who, over the years, have applied their talents to reflecting upon the possibilities of relational thinking. Alfred North Whitehead was fascinated by the necessity of the relational view and did much to advance it.[2] Deleuze likewise made much of these ideas both in his reflections on Leibniz (with reflections on baroque architecture and the mathematics of the fold in Leibniz's work) as well as on Spinoza (Deleuze 1992).

But why and how would I, as a working geographer, find the relational mode of approaching space-time useful? The answer is quite simply that there are certain topics, such as the political role of collective memories in urban processes, that can only be approached in this way. I cannot box political and collective memories in some absolute space (clearly situate them on a grid or a map) nor can I understand their circulation according to the rules, however sophisticated, of relative space-time. If I ask what Tiananmen Square or 'Ground Zero' *mean*, then the only way I can seek an answer is to think in relational terms. This was the problem that I confronted when writing about the Basilica of Sacré-Cœur in Paris (Harvey 1979a). And, as I shall shortly show, it is impossible to understand Marxian political economy without engaging with relational perspectives.

So is space (space-time) absolute, relative or relational? I simply don't know whether there is an ontological answer to that question. In my own work I think of it as being all three. This was the conclusion I reached thirty years ago and I have found no particular reason (nor heard any arguments) to make me change my mind. This is what I then wrote:

> space is neither absolute, relative or relational in itself, but it can become one or all simultaneously depending on the circumstances. The problem of the proper conceptualization of space is resolved through human practice with respect to it. In other words, there are no philosophical answers to philosophical questions that arise over the nature of space – the answers lie in human practice. The question 'what is space?' is therefore replaced by the question 'how is it that different human practices create and make use of different conceptualizations of space?' The property relationship, for example, creates absolute spaces within which monopoly control can operate. The movement of people, goods, services, and information takes place in a relative space because it takes money, time, energy, and the like to overcome the friction of distance. Parcels of land also capture benefits because they contain relationships with other parcels . . . in the form of rent relational space comes into its own as an important aspect of human social practice.
>
> (1979a: 13)

Are there rules for deciding when and where one spatial frame is preferable to another? Or is the choice arbitrary, subject to the whims of human practice? The decision to use one or other conception certainly depends on the nature of the phenomena under investigation. The absolute conception may be perfectly adequate for issues of property boundaries and border determinations but it helps me not a whit with the question of what is Tiananmen Square, Ground Zero or the Basilica of Sacré-Cœur. I therefore find it helpful – if only as an internal check – to sketch in justifications for the choice of an absolute, relative or relational frame of reference. Furthermore, I often find myself presuming in my practices that there is some hierarchy at work among them in the sense that relational space can embrace the relative and the absolute, relative space can embrace the absolute, but absolute space is just absolute and that is that. But I would not confidently advance this view as a working principle let alone try to defend it theoretically. I find it far more interesting in principle to keep the three concepts in dialectical tension with each other and to think constantly through the interplay among them. Ground Zero is an absolute space at the same time as it is relative and relational in space-time.

Let me try to put this in a more immediate context. I give a talk in a room. The reach of my words is bounded by the absolute space of those particular walls and limited to the absolute time of the talk. To hear me people have to be there within that absolute space during that absolute time. People who cannot get in are excluded and those that come later will not hear me. Those who are there can be identified as individuals – individuated – each according to the absolute space, such as the seat occupied, for that time. But I am also in a relative space with respect to my audience. I am here and they are there. I try to communicate across the space through a medium – the atmosphere – that refracts my words differentially. I talk softly and the clarity of my words fades across space: the back row can't hear at all. If there is a video-feed to Aberdeen I can be heard there but not in the back row. My words are received differentially in relative space-time. Individuation is more problematic since there are many people in exactly the same relative location to me in that space-time. All the people in the fourth row are equi-distant from me. A discontinuity in space-time arises between those who can hear and those who cannot. The analysis of what is going on in the absolute space and time of the talk given in the room looks very different when analysed through the lens of relative space-time. But then there is the relational component too. Individuals in the audience bring to the absolute space and time of the talk all sorts of ideas and experiences culled from the space-time of their life trajectories and all of that is co-present in the room: he cannot stop thinking of the argument over breakfast, she cannot erase from her mind the awful images of death and destruction on last night's news. Something about the way I talk reminds someone else of a traumatic event lost in some distant past and my words remind someone else of political meetings they used to go to in the 1970s. My words express a certain fury about what is going on in the world. I find myself thinking while talking that everything we are doing in this room is stupid and trivial. There is a palpable sense of tension in the room. Why aren't we out there bringing the government down? I extricate myself from all these relationalities, retire back into the absolute and relative spaces of the room and try to address the topic of space as a keyword in a dry and technical manner. The tension dissipates and someone in the front row nods off. I know where everyone is in absolute space and time but I have no idea, as the saying goes, 'where peoples' heads are at'. I may sense that some people are with me and some are not but I never know for sure. Yet this is, surely, the most important element of all. That, after all, is where shifting political subjectivities lie. The relationality is elusive if not impossible to pin down, but it is none the less vitally important for all that.

There is, I mean to show by this example, bound to be a liminality about spatiality itself because we are inexorably situated in all three frameworks simultaneously, though not necessarily equally so. We may end up, often without noticing it, favouring one or other definition through our practical actions. In an absolutist mode, I will do one thing and reach one set of conclusions; in a relative mode, I'll construct my interpretations differently and do something else; and if everything looks different through relational filters then I will conduct myself in a quite different way. What we do as well as what we understand is integrally dependent upon the primary spatio-temporal frame within which we situate ourselves. Consider how this works in relation to that most fraught of socio-political concepts we call 'identity'. Everything is clear enough in absolute space and time, but things get a bit more awkward when it comes to relative space-time and downright difficult in a relational world. But it is only in this last frame that we can start to grapple with many aspects of contemporary politics since that is the world of political subjectivity and political consciousness. Du Bois long ago attempted to address this in terms of what he called 'double consciousness' – what does it mean, he asked, to carry within oneself the experience of being both black and American? We now complicate the question further by asking what does it mean to be American, black, female, lesbian and working class? How do all those relationalities enter into the political consciousness of the subject? And when we consider other dimensions – of migrants, diasporic groups, tourists and travellers and those who watch the contemporary global media and partially filter or absorb its cacophony of messages – then the primary question we are faced with is understanding how this whole relational world of experience and information gets *internalized* within the particular political subject (albeit individuated in absolute space and time) to support this or that line of thinking and of action. Plainly, we cannot understand the shifting terrain upon which political subjectivities are formed and political actions occur without thinking about what happens in relational terms.

If the contrast between absolute, relative and relational conceptions of space is the only way to unpack the meaning of space as a keyword, then matters could safely be left here. Fortunately or unfortunately, there are other and equally cogent ways to address the problem. Many geographers

in recent years, for example, have pointed to a key difference in the deployment of the concept of space as an essential element in a materialist project
of understanding tangible geographies on the ground and the widespread
appropriation of spatial metaphors within social, literary and cultural
theory. These metaphors, furthermore, have frequently been used to disrupt
so-called metanarratives (such as Marxian theory) and those discursive
strategies in which the temporal dimension typically prevails. All of this
has provoked an immense debate on the role of space in social, literary
and cultural theory. I do not intend to get into any detailed discussion of
the significance of this so-called 'spatial turn' in general and its relation to
postmodernism in particular. But my own position has been fairly clear
throughout: of course the proper consideration of space and space-time
has crucial effects upon how theories and understandings get articulated
and developed. But this creates absolutely no justification whatsoever for
turning away from all attempts at any kind of metatheory (the end result
would be to take us back to geography as it was practised in the academy
in the 1950s, which is, interestingly where a significant segment of contemporary British Geography seems to be happily, if unwittingly, substantively
headed). The point about grappling with space as a keyword is therefore to
identify how this concept might be better integrated into existing social, literary and cultural metatheories and with what effects.

Cassirer, for example, sets up a tripartite division of modes of human
spatial experience, distinguishing between *organic, perceptual* and *symbolic* spaces (Cassirer 1944; see also Harvey 1973a: 28). Under the first he
arranges all those forms of spatial experience given biologically (hence materially and registered through the particular characteristics of our senses).
Perceptual space refers to the ways we process the physical and biological
experience of space neurologically and register it in the world of thought.
Symbolic space, on the other hand, is abstract (and may entail the development of an abstract symbolic language like geometry or the construction
of architectural or pictorial forms). Symbolic space generates distinctive
meanings through readings and interpretations. The question of aesthetic
practices here comes to the fore. In this domain, Langer, for her part, distinguishes between 'real' and 'virtual space'. The latter, in her view, amounts
to a 'created space built out of forms, colours, and so on' so as to produce
the intangible images and illusions that constitute the heart of all aesthetic
practices. Architecture, she argues, 'is a plastic art, and its first achievement
is always, unconsciously and inevitably, an illusion: something purely imaginary or conceptual translated into visual impression'. What exists in the real
space can be described easily enough but in order to understand the affect
that comes with exposure to the work of art we have to explore the very

different world of virtual space. And this, she holds, always projects us into a distinctively ethnic domain (Langer 1953; see also Harvey 1973a: 31). These were the sorts of ideas I first encountered in *Social Justice and the City*.

It is out of this tradition of spatialized thought that Lefebvre (almost certainly drawing upon Cassirer) constructs his own distinctive tripartite division of material space (the space of experience and of perception open to physical touch and sensation); the representation of space (space as conceived and represented); and spaces of representation (the lived space of sensations, the imagination, emotions and meanings incorporated into how we live day by day) (Lefebvre 1991 [1974]).

If I focus on Lefebvre here it is not because, as so many in cultural and literary theory seem to suppose, Lefebvre provides the originary moment from which all thinking about the production of space derives (such a thesis is manifestly absurd), but because I find it more convenient to work with Lefebvre's categories rather than Cassirer's. Material space is, for us humans, quite simply the world of tactile and sensual interaction with matter, it is the space of experience. The elements, moments and events in that world are constituted out of a materiality of certain qualities. How we represent this world is an entirely different matter, but here too we do not conceive of or represent space in arbitrary ways, but seek some appropriate if not accurate reflection of the material realities that surround us through abstract representations (words, graphs, maps, diagrams, pictures, etc.). But Lefebvre, like Benjamin, insists that we do not live as material atoms floating around in a materialist world; we also have imaginations, fears, emotions, psychologies, fantasies and dreams (Benjamin 1999). These spaces of representation are part and parcel of the way we live in the world. We may also seek to represent the way this space is emotively and affectively as well as materially lived by means of poetic images, photographic compositions, artistic reconstructions. The strange spatio-temporality of a dream, a fantasy, a hidden longing, a lost memory or even a peculiar thrill or tingle of fear as we walk down a street can be given representation through works of art that ultimately always have a mundane presence in absolute space and time. Leibniz, too, had found the whole question of alternate spatio-temporal worlds and dreams of considerable interest.

It is tempting, as with the first tripartite division of spatial terms we considered, to treat of Lefebvre's three categories as hierarchically ordered, but here too it seems most appropriate to keep the three categories in dialectical tension. The physical and material experience of spatial and temporal ordering is mediated to some degree by the way space and time are represented. The oceanographer/physicist swimming among the waves may experience them differently from the poet enamoured of Walt Whitman or the pianist who loves Debussy. Reading a book about Patagonia will probably affect how we experience that place when we travel there even if we experience considerable cognitive dissonance between expectations generated by the written word and how it actually feels upon the ground. The spaces and times of representation that envelop and surround us as we go about our daily lives likewise affect both our direct experiences and the way we interpret and understand representations. We may not even notice the material qualities of spatial orderings incorporated into daily life because we adhere to unexamined routines. Yet it is through those daily material routines that we absorb a certain sense of how spatial representations work and build up certain spaces of representation for ourselves (e.g. the visceral sense of security in a familiar neighborhood or of being 'at home'). We only notice when something appears radically out of place. It is, I want to suggest, the dialectical relation between the categories that really counts, even though it is useful for purposes of understanding to crystallize each element out as distinctive moments to the experience of space and time.

This mode of thinking about space helps me interpret works of art and architecture. A picture, like Munch's *The Scream*, is a material object but it works from the standpoint of a psychic state (Lefebvre's space of representation or lived space), and attempts through a particular set of representational codes (the representation of space or conceived space) to take on a physical form (the material space of the picture open to our actual physical experience) that says something to us about the qualities of how Munch lived that space. He seems to have had some sort of horrific nightmare, the sort from which we wake up screaming. And he has managed to convey something of the sense of that through the physical object. Many contemporary artists, making use of multimedia and kinetic techniques, create experiential spaces in which several modes of experiencing space-time combine. Here, for example, is how Judith Barry's contribution to the Third Berlin Biennial for Contemporary Art is described in the catalogue:

> In her experimental works, video artist Judith Barry investigates the use, construction and complex interaction of private and public spaces, media, society, and genders. The themes of her installations and theoretical writings position themselves in a field of observation that addresses historical memory, mass communication, and perception. In a realm between the viewer's imagination and media-generated architecture, she creates imaginary spaces, alienated depictions of profane reality . . . In the work *Voice Off* . . . the viewer penetrates the claustrophobic crampedness of the exhibition space, goes deeper into the work, and, forced to move through the installation, experiences not only cinematic but also cinemaesthetic impressions. The divided projection space offers the possibility of making

contact with different voices. The use and hearing of voices as a driving force, and the intensity of the psychic tension – especially on the male side of the projection – conveys the inherent strength of this intangible and ephemeral object. The voices demonstrate for spectators how one can change through them, how one tries to take control of them and the loss one feels when they are no longer heard.

Barry, the catalogue concludes, 'stages aesthetic spaces of transit that leave the ambivalence between seduction and reflection unresolved' (Third Berlin Biennial for Contemporary Art 2004: 48–9).

But to grapple fully with this description of Barry's work, we need to take the concepts of space and space-time to a deeper level of complexity. There is much in this description that escapes the Lefebvrian categories but refers back to the distinctions between absolute space and time (the cramped physical structure of the exhibit), relative space-time (the sequential motion of the visitor through the space) and relational space-time (the memories, the voices, the psychic tension, the intangibility and ephemerality, as well as the claustrophobia). Yet we cannot let go of the Lefebvrian categories either. The constructed spaces have material, conceptual and lived dimensions.

I propose, therefore, a speculative leap in which we place the threefold division of absolute, relative and relational space-time up against the tripartite division of experienced, conceptualized and lived space identified by Lefebvre. The result is a three-by-three matrix within which points of intersection suggest different modalities of understanding the meanings of space and space-time. It may properly be objected that I am here restricting possibilities because a matrix mode of representation is self-confined to an absolute space. This is a perfectly valid objection. And in so far as I am here engaging in a representational practice (conceptualization) I cannot do justice to either the experienced or the lived realms of spatiality either. By definition, therefore, the matrix I set up and the way I can use it has limited revelatory power. But with all that conceded, I find it helpful to consider the combinations that arise at different intersections within the matrix. The virtue of representation in absolute space is that it allows us to individuate phenomena with great clarity. And with a bit of imagination it is possible to think dialectically across the elements within the matrix so that each moment is imagined as an internal relation of all the others. I illustrate the sort of thing I have in mind (in a somewhat condensed, arbitrary and schematic form) in Figures 14.1 and 14.2. The entries within the matrices are merely suggestive rather than definitive (readers might enjoy constructing their own entries just to get some sense of my meaning).

I find it helpful to read across or down the matrix of categories and to

Figure 14.1 A matrix of possible meanings for space as a keyword

	Material space (experienced space)	Representations of space (conceptualized space)	Spaces of representation (lived space)
Absolute space	Walls, bridges, doors, stairways, floors, ceilings, streets, buildings, cities, mountains, continents, bodies of water, territorial markers, physical boundaries and barriers, gated communities . . .	Cadastral and administrative maps; Euclidan geometry; landscape description; metaphors of confinement, open space, location, placement and positionality; (command and control relatively easy) – *Newton and Descartes*	Feelings of contentment around the hearth; sense of security or incarceration from enclosure; sense of power from ownership, command and domination over space; fear of others 'beyond the pale'
Relative space (time)	Circulation and flows of energy, water, air, commodities, peoples, information, money, capital; accelerations and diminutions in the friction of distance	Thematic and topological maps (e.g. London tube system); non-Euclidean geometries and topology; perspectival drawings; metaphors of situated knowledges, of motion, mobility, displacement, acceleration, time-space compression and distanciation; (command and control difficult requiring sophisticated techniques) – *Einstein and Riemann*	Anxiety at not getting to class on time; thrill of moving into the unknown; frustration in a traffic jam; tensions or exhilarations of time-space compression, of speed, of motion
Absolute space (time)	Electromagnetic energy flows and fields; social relations; rental and economic potential surfaces; pollution concentrations; energy potentials; sounds, odours and sensations wafted on the breeze	Surrealism; existentialism; psycho-geographies; cyberspace; metaphors of internalization of forces and powers (command and control extremely difficult – chaos theory, dialectics, internal relations, quantum mathematics) – *Leibniz, Whitehead, Deleuze, Benjamin*	Visions, fantasies, desires, frustrations, memories, dreams, phantasms, psychic states (e.g. agoraphobia, vertigo, claustrophobia)

Figure 14.2 A spatio-temporal matrix for Marxian theory

	Material space (experienced space)	Representations of space (conceptualized space)	Spaces of representation (lived space)
Absolute space	Useful commodities, concrete labour processes, notes and coins (local moneys?), private property/state boundaries, fixed capital, factories, built environments, spaces of consumption, picket lines, occupied spaces (sit-ins); storming of the Bastille or Winter Palace . . .	**Use values and concrete labours** Exploitation in the labor process (Marx) vs. work as creative play (Fourier); maps of private property and class exclusions; mosaics of uneven geographical developments	Alienation vs. creative satisfaction; isolated individualism vs. social solidarities; loyalties to place, class, identity, etc.; relative deprivation; injustice; lack of dignity; anger vs. contentment
Relative space (time)	Market exchange; trade; circulation and flows of commodities, energy, labour power, money, credit or capital; commuting and migrating; depreciation and degradation; information flows and agitation from outside	**Exchange-values (value in motion)** Accumulation schemas; commodity chains; models of migration and diasporas; input–output models. theories of spatio-temporal 'fixes', annihilation of space through time, circulation of capital through built environments; formation of the world market, networks; geopolitical relations and revolutionary strategies	Money and commodity fetish (perpetual unfulfilled desire); anxiety/exhilaration at time-space compression; instability; insecurity; intensity of action and motion vs. repose; 'all that is solid melts into air . . .'
Relational space (time)	Abstract labour process; fictitious capital; resistance movements; sudden manifestations and expressive irruptions of political movements (anti-war, 1968, Seattle . . .); 'the revolutionary spirit stirs'	**Money values** Value as socially necessary labour time; as congealed human labour in relation to the world market; laws of value in motion and the social power of money (globalization); revolutionary hopes and fears; strategies for change	**Values** Capitalist hegemony ('there is no alternative'); proletarian consciousness; international solidarities; universal rights; utopian dreams; multitude; empathy with others; 'another world is possible'

imagine complex scenarios of combination. Imagine, for example, the absolute space of an affluent gated community on the New Jersey shore. Some of the inhabitants move in relative space on a daily basis into and out of the financial district of Manhattan where they set in motion movements of credit and investment moneys that affect social life across the globe, earning thereby the immense money power that permits them to import back into the absolute space of their gated community all of the energy, exotic foods and wondrous commodities they need to secure their privileged lifestyle. The inhabitants feel vaguely threatened, however, because they sense that there is a visceral, undefinable and unlocatable hatred for all things American arising in the world out there and its name is 'terrorism'. They support a government that promises to protect them from this nebulous threat. But they become increasingly paranoid about the hostility they sense in the world around them and increasingly look to build up their absolute space to protect themselves, building higher and higher walls, even hiring armed guards to protect the borders. Meanwhile, their profligate consumption of energy to power their bullet-proof humvees that take them into the city every day proves the straw that breaks the back of global climate change. Atmospheric patterns of circulation shift dramatically. Then, in the compelling but rather inaccurate popularized depiction of chaos theory, a butterfly flaps its wings in Hong Kong and a devastating hurricane hits the New Jersey shore and wipes out the gated community. Many residents die because they are so fearful of the outside that they ignore the warnings to evacuate. If this were a Hollywood production, a lone scientist would recognize the danger and rescue the woman he adores but who has hitherto ignored him but she now falls gratefully in love with him . . .

In the telling of a simple story of this sort it proves impossible to confine oneself to just one modality of spatial and spatio-temporal thinking. The actions taken in the absolute space only make sense in relational terms. Even more interesting, therefore, is the situation in which moments in the matrix are in more explicit dialectical tension. Let me illustrate.

What spatial and spatio-temporal principles should be deployed in redesigning the site known as 'Ground Zero' in Manhattan? It is an absolute space that can be materially reconstructed and to this end engineering calculations (informed by Newtonian mechanics) and architectural designs must be made. There is much discussion about retaining walls and the load-bearing capacities of the site. Aesthetic judgements on how the space, once turned into a material artefact of some sort, might be lived as well as conceptualized and experienced also become important (Kant would approve). The problem is to so arrange the physical space as to produce an emotive effect while matching certain expectations (commercial as well as emotive and aesthetic) as to how the space might be lived. Once constructed the experience of the space may be mediated by representational forms (such as guide books and plans) that help us interpret the intended meanings of the reconstructed site. But moving dialectically across the dimension of absolute space alone is much less rewarding than the insights that come from appealing to the other spatio-temporal frames. Capitalist developers are keenly aware of the relative location of the site and judge its prospects for commercial development according to a logic of exchange relations. Its centrality and proximity to the command and control functions of Wall Street are important attributes and if transportation access can be improved in the course of reconstruction then so much the better since this can only add to land and property values. For the developers the site does not merely exist *in* relative space-time: the re-engineering of the site offers the prospect of transforming relative space-time so as to enhance the commercial value of the absolute spaces (by improving access to airports for example). The temporal horizon would be dominated by considerations of the amortization rate and the interest/discount rate applying to fixed capital investments in the built environment.

But there would almost certainly be popular objections, led by the families of those killed at that site, to thinking and building only in these absolute or relative spatio-temporal terms. Whatever is built at this site has to say something about history and memory. There will probably also be pressures to say something about the meanings of community and nation as well as about future possibilities (perhaps even a prospect of eternal truths). Nor could the site ignore the issue of relational spatial connectivity to the rest of the world. Even capitalist developers would not be averse to combining their mundane commercial concerns with inspiring symbolic statements (emphasizing the power and indestructibility of the political-economic system of global capitalism that received such a body blow on 9/11) by erecting, say, a towering phallic symbol that spells defiance. They, too, seek expressive power in relational space-time. But there are all manner of relationalities to be explored. What will we know about those who attacked and how far will we connect? The site is and will have a relational presence in the world no matter what is built there and it is important to reflect on how this presencing works: will it be lived as a symbol of US arrogance or as a sign of global compassion and understanding? Taking up such matters requires that we embrace a relational conception of space-time.

If, as Benjamin has it, history (a relative temporal concept) is not the same as memory (a relational temporal concept) then we have a choice of whether to historicize the events of 9/11 or to seek to memorialize them. If the site is merely historicized in relative space (by a certain sort of monumentality) then this imposes a fixed narrative on the space. The effect will be to foreclose on future possibilities and interpretations. Such closure will tend to constrict the generative power to build a different future. Memory, on the other hand, is, according to Benjamin, a potentiality that can at times 'flash up' uncontrollably at times of crisis to reveal new possibilities (Benjamin 1968). The way the site might be lived by those who encounter it then becomes unpredictable and uncertain. Collective memory, a diffuse but nevertheless powerful sense that pervades many an urban scene, can play a significant role in animating political and social movements. Ground Zero cannot be anything other than a site of collective memory and the problem for the designers is to translate that diffuse sensibility into the absolute spaces of bricks, mortar, steel and glass. And if, as Balzac once put it, 'hope is a memory that desires' then the creation of a 'space of hope' on that spot requires that memory be internalized there at the same time as ways are left open for the expression of desire (Harvey 2003a: ch. 1).

The expressive relationality of Ground Zero in itself poses fascinating questions. The forces that converged over space to produce 9/11 were complex. How, then, can some accounting be given of these forces? Can something experienced as a local and personal tragedy be reconciled with an understanding of the international forces that were so powerfully condensed within those few shattering moments in a particular place? Will we get to feel in that space the widespread resentment in the rest of the world towards the way US hegemony was so selfishly being exercised throughout during the 1980s and 1990s? Will we get to know that the Reagan administration played a key role in creating and supporting the Taliban in Afghanistan in order to undermine the Soviet occupation and that Osama bin-Laden turned from being an ally of the USA into an enemy because of US support for the corrupt regime in Saudi Arabia? Or will we only learn of cowardly, alien and evil 'others' out there who hated the USA and sought to destroy it because of all it stood for in terms of the values of liberty and freedom? The relational spatio-temporality of the event and the site can be exhumed with enough dedicated digging. But the manner of its representation and of its materialization is uncertain. The outcome will clearly depend upon political struggle. And the fiercest battles will have to be fought over what relational space-time the rebuilding will invoke. These were the sorts of issues I encountered when I attempted to interpret the meaning of the Basilica of Sacré-Cœur in Paris against the background of the historical memory of the Paris Commune.

This brings me to some observations on the politics of the argument. Thinking through the different ways in which space and space-time get used as keywords helps define certain conditions of possibility for critical engagement. It also opens up ways to identify conflicting claims and alternative political possibilities. It invites us to consider the ways we physically shape our environment and the ways in which we both represent and get to live in it. I think it fair to say that the Marxist tradition has not been deeply engaged upon such issues and that this general failure (although there are, of course, numerous exceptions) has more often than not meant a loss of possibilities for certain kinds of transformative politics. If, for example, socialist realist art fails to capture the imagination and if the monumentality achieved under past communist regimes was so lacking in inspiration, if planned communities and communist cities often seem so dead to the world, then one way to engage critically with this problem would be to look at the modes of thinking about space and space-time and the unnecessarily limiting and constricting roles they may have played in socialist planning practices.

There has not been much explicit debate about such issues within the Marxist tradition. Yet Marx himself is a relational thinker. In revolutionary situations such as that of 1848 Marx worried that the past might weigh like a nightmare on the brain of the living and forthrightly posed the question as to how a revolutionary poetry of the future might be constructed then and there (Marx 1963). At that time he also pleaded with Cabet not to take his communist-minded followers to the new world. There, Marx averred, the Icarians would only replant the attitudes and beliefs internalized from out of the experience of the old. They should, Marx advised, stay as good communists in Europe and fight through the revolutionary transformation in that space, even though there was always the danger that a revolution made in 'our little corner of the world' would fall victim to the global forces ranged around it (cited in Marin 1984).

Lenin, plainly distressed at Mach's idealist mode of presentation, sought to reinforce the absolute and mechanistic views on space and time associated with Newton as the only proper materialist basis for scientific inquiry. He did so at the very time when Einstein was bringing relative, but equally materialist views of space-time into prominence. Lenin's strict line was to some degree softened by Lukacs's turn to a more pliable view of history and temporality. But Lukacs's constructivist views on the relation to nature were roundly rejected by Wittfogel's assertion of a hard-headed materialism that morphed into environmental determinism. In the works of Thompson, Williams and others, on the other hand, we find different levels of appreciation, particularly of the temporal dimension though space and place are also omnipresent. In Williams's novel *People of the Black Mountains* the relationality of space-time is central. Williams uses it to bind the narrative together and directly emphasizes the different ways of knowing that come with different senses of space-time:

If lives and places were being seriously sought, a powerful attachment to lives and to places was entirely demanded. The polystyrene model and its textual and theoretical equivalents remained different from the substance they reconstructed and simulated . . . At his books and maps in the library, or in the house in the valley, there was a common history which could be translated anywhere, in a community of evidence and rational enquiry. Yet he had only to move on the mountains for a different kind of mind to assert itself; stubbornly native and local, yet reaching beyond to a wider common flow, where touch and breadth replaced record and analysis; not history as narrative but stories as lives.

(Williams 1989: 10–12)

For Williams the relationality comes alive walking on the mountains. It centres a completely different sensibility and feeling than that constructed from the archive. Interestingly, it is only in his novels that Williams seems able to get at this problem. Within the Marxian tradition, with the exception of Lefebvre and the geographers, an expansive understanding of the problematics of space and time is missing. So how then can these perspectives on space and space-time become more closely integrated into our reading, interpretation and use of Marxian theory? Let me lay aside all concern for caveats and nuances in order to present an argument in the starkest possible terms.

In the first chapter of *Capital*, Marx introduces three key concepts of use-value, exchange-value and value. Everything that pertains to use-value lies in the province of absolute space and time. Individual workers, machines, commodities, factories, roads, houses and actual labour processes, expenditures of energy and the like can all be individuated, described and understood within the Newtonian frame of absolute space and time. Everything that pertains to exchange-value lies in relative space-time because exchange entails movements of commodities, money, capital, labour power and people over time and space. It is the circulation, the perpetual motion, that counts. Exchange, as Marx observes, therefore breaks through all barriers of space and time (Marx 1976b: 209). It perpetually reshapes the co-ordinates within which we live our daily lives. With the advent of money this 'breaking through' defines an even grander and more fluid universe of exchange relations across the relative space-time of the world market (understood not as a thing but as continuous movement and interaction). The circulation and accumulation of capital occurs in relative space-time. Value is, however, a relational concept. Its referent is, therefore, relational space-time. Value, Marx states (somewhat surprisingly), is immaterial but objective. 'Not an atom of matter enters into the objectivity of commodities of values.' As a consequence, value does not 'stalk about with a label describing what it is' but hides its relationality within the fetishism of commodities (Marx 1976b: 167). The only way we can approach it is via that peculiar world in which material relations are established between people (we relate to each other via what we produce and trade) and social relations are constructed between things (prices are set for what we produce and trade). Value is, in short, a social relation. As such, it is impossible to measure except by way of its effects (try measuring any social relation directly and you always fail). Value internalizes the whole historical geography of innumerable labour processes set up under conditions of or in relation to capital accumulation in the space-time of the world market. Many are surprised to find that Marx's most fundamental concept is 'immaterial but objective' given the way he is usually depicted as a materialist for whom anything immaterial would be anathema. This relational definition of value, I note in passing, renders moot if not misplaced all those attempts to come up with some direct and essentialist measure of it. Social relations can only ever be measured by their effects.

If my characterization of the Marxian categories is correct, then this shows no priority can be accorded to any one spatio-temporal frame. The three spatio-temporal frames must be kept in dialectical tension with each other in exactly the same way that use-value, exchange-value and value dialectically intertwine within the Marxian theory. There would, for example, be no value in relational space-time without concrete labours constructed in innumerable places in absolute spaces and times. Nor would value emerge as an immaterial but objective power without the innumerable acts of exchange, the continuous circulation processes, that weld together the global market in relative space-time. Value is, then, a social relation that internalizes the whole history and geography of concrete labours in the world market. It is expressive of the social (primarily but not exclusively class) relations of capitalism constructed on the world stage. It is crucial to mark the temporality involved, not only because of the significance of past 'dead' labour (fixed capital including all of that embedded in built environments) but also because of all the traces of the history of proletarianization, of primitive accumulation, of technological developments that are internalized within the value form. Above all, we have to acknowledge the 'historical and moral elements' that always enter into the determination of the value of labour power (Marx 1976b: 275). We then see Marx's theory working in a particular way. The spinner embeds value (i.e. abstract labour as a relational determination) in the cloth by performing concrete labour in absolute space and time. The objective power of the value relation is registered when the spinner is forced to give up making the cloth and the factory falls silent because conditions in the world market are such as to make this activity in that particular absolute space and time value-less. While all of this may seem obvious, the failure to acknowledge the interplay entailed between the different spatio-temporal frames in Marxian theory often produces conceptual confusion. Much discussion of so-called 'global–local relations' has become a conceptual muddle, for example, because of the inability to understand the different spatio-temporalities involved. We cannot say that the value relation causes the factory to close down as if it is some external abstract force. It is the changing concrete conditions of labour in China when mediated through exchange processes in relative space-time that transforms value as a social relation in such a way as to bring the concrete labour process in Mexico to closure.

So far, I have largely confined attention to a dialectical reading of Marxian theory down the left-hand column of the matrix. What happens when I start to read across the matrix instead? The materiality of use-values and concrete labours is obvious enough. But how can this be represented and conceived? Physical descriptions are easy to produce but Marx insists that the social relations under which work is performed are critical also. Under capitalism the wage-labourer is conceptualized (second column) as a producer of surplus-value for the capitalist and this is represented as a relation of exploitation. This implies that the labour process is lived (third column) as alienation. Under different social relations (e.g. those of socialism) work could be lived as creative satisfaction and conceptualized as self-realization through collective endeavours. It may not even have to change materially in order for it to be reconceptualized and lived in a quite different way. This was, after all, Lenin's hope when he advocated the adoption of Fordism in Soviet factories. Fourier, for his part, thought that work should be about play and the expression of desire and be lived as sublime joy and for that to happen the material qualities of work processes would need to be radically restructured. At this point we have to acknowledge a variety of competing possibilities. In his book *Manufacturing Consent*, for example, Burawoy found that the workers in the factory he studied did not generally experience work as alienation (Burawoy 1982). This arose because they smothered the idea of exploitation by turning the workplace into a site for role- and game-playing (Fourier style). The labour process was performed by the workers in such a way as to permit them to live the process in a non-alienated way. There are some advantages for capital in this, since unalienated workers often work more efficiently. Capitalists have therefore acceded to various measures, such as calisthenics, quality circles and the like, to try to reduce alienation and to emphasize incorporation. They have also produced alternative conceptualizations that emphasize the rewards of hard work and produce ideologies to negate the theory of exploitation. While the Marxian theory of exploitation may be formally correct, therefore, it does not always or necessarily translate into alienation and political resistance. Much depends on how it is conceptualized. The consequences for political consciousness and working-class action are wide-ranging. Part of class struggle is therefore about driving home the significance of exploitation as the proper conceptualization of how concrete labours are accomplished under capitalist social relations. Again, it is the dialectical tension between the material, the conceived and the lived that really matters. If we treat the tensions in a mechanical way then we are lost.

While working through matters in this way is helpful, I earlier argued that the 'matrix thinking' offers limited opportunities unless we are prepared to range freely and dialectically over all the moments of the matrix simultaneously. Let me give an example. The primary form of representation of value is through money. This too is an immaterial concept with objective power but it must also take on material form as an actual use-value. This it does in the first instance through the emergence of the money commodity (e.g. gold). The emergence occurs, however, through acts of exchange in relative space-time and it is this that allows tangible money forms to become an active presence in absolute space and time. This creates the paradox that a particular material use-value (such as gold or a dollar bill) has to represent the universality of value, of abstract labour. It further implies that social power can be appropriated by private persons and from this the very possibility of money as capital placed in circulation in relative space-time arises. There are, as Marx points out, many antinomies, antitheses and contradictions in how money is created, conceptualized, circulated and used as both a tangible means of circulation and a representation of value on the world market. Precisely because value is immaterial and objective, money always combines fictitious qualities with tangible forms. It is subject to that reversal Marx describes in the fetishism of commodities such that material relations arise between people and social relations are registered between things. Money as an object of desire and as an object of neurotic contemplation imprisons us in fetishisms while the inherent contradictions in the money form inevitably produce not only the possibility but also the inevitability of capitalist crises. Money anxieties are frequently with us and have their own spatio-temporal locations (the impoverished child who pauses before the vast panoply of capitalist commodities perpetually beyond reach in the window of the store). The spectacles of consumption that litter the landscape in absolute space and time can generate senses of relative deprivation. We are surrounded at every turn with manifestations of the fetish desire for money power as the representation of value on the world market.

For those unfamiliar with Marxian theory, this will all doubtless appear rather mysterious. The point, however, is to illustrate how theoretical work (and I would like to suggest this should be true of all social, literary and cultural theory) invariably and necessarily entails at the very minimum moving dialectically across all points within the matrix and then beyond. The more we move the greater the depth and range of our understandings. There are no discrete and closed boxes in this system. The dialectical tensions must not only be kept intact. They must be continuously expanded.

I end, however, with some cautionary remarks. In recent years many academics, including geographers, have embraced relational concepts and ways of thinking (though not very explicitly with respect to those of space-time). This move, as crucial as it is laudable, has to some degree been associated with the cultural and postmodern turn. But in the same way that traditional and positivist geography limited its vision by concentrating exclusively on the absolute and relative and upon the material and conceptual aspects of space-time (eschewing the lived and the relational), so there is a serious danger of dwelling only upon the relational and lived as if the material and absolute did not matter. Staying exclusively in the lower right part of the matrix can be just as misleading, limiting and stultifying as confining one's vision to the upper left. The only strategy that really works is to keep the tension moving dialectically across all positions in the matrix. This is what allows us better to understand how relational meanings (such as value) are internalized in material things, events and practices (such as concrete labour processes) constructed in absolute space and time. We can, to take another example, debate interminably all manner of ideas and designs expressive of the relationality of Ground Zero, but at some point something has to be materialized in absolute space and time. Once built, the site acquires a 'permanence' (Whitehead's term) of physical form. And while it is always open to reconceptualize the meaning of that material form so that people can learn to live it differently, the sheer materiality of construction in absolute space and time carries its own weight and authority. By the same token, political movements that aspire to exercise some power in the world remain ineffectual until they assert a material presence. It is all fine and good, for example, to evoke relational conceptions such as the proletariat in motion or the multitude rising up. But no one knows what any of that means until real bodies go into the absolute spaces of the streets of Seattle, Quebec City and Genoa at a particular moment in absolute time. Rights, Don Mitchell perceptively observes, mean nothing without the ability to concretize them in absolute space and time:

> If the right to the city is a cry and a demand, then it is only a cry that is heard and a demand that has force to the degree that there is a space

from and within which this cry and demand is visible. In public space – on street corners or in parks, in the streets during riots and demonstrations – political organizations can represent themselves to a larger population and through this representation give their cries and demands some force. By claiming space in public, by creating public spaces, social groups themselves become public.

Public space, Mitchell (2003: 129–35) correctly insists, 'is material' and it 'constitutes an actual site, a place, a ground within which and from which political activity flows'. It is only when relationality connects to the absolute spaces and times of social and material life that politics comes alive. To neglect that connectivity is to court political irrelevance.

Gaining some sense of how space is and how different spatialities and spatio-temporalities work is crucial to the construction of a distinctively geographical imagination. But space turns out to be an extraordinarily complicated keyword. It functions as a compound word and has multiple determinations such that no one of its particular meanings can properly be understood in isolation from all the others. But that is precisely what makes the term, particularly when conjoined with time, so rich in possibilities.

Notes

1 I reviewed some of this in Harvey (1996a) particularly ch. 10.
2 Fitzgerald (1979); I tried to come to terms with Whitehead's views in Harvey (1996a).

David Harvey

List of Publications

Books

2006 *Cosmopolitanism and the Geographies of Freedom*. New York: Columbia University Press (forthcoming).

2005a *A Brief History of Neo-liberalism*. Oxford: Oxford University Press.

2005b *Towards a Theory of Uneven Geographical Development*. Heidelberg: Franz Steiner Verlag.

2003a *Paris, Capital of Modernity*. New York: Routledge (translated into Korean).

2003b *The New Imperialism*. Oxford: Oxford University Press (translated into German, Italian, Japanese, Korean, Norwegian, Portuguese, Rumanian, Spanish and Turkish).

2001a *Spaces of Capital: Towards a Critical Geography*. Edinburgh: Edinburgh University Press and New York: Routledge.

2000a *Spaces of Hope*. Edinburgh: Edinburgh University Press and Berkeley, CA: University of California Press (translated into Chinese and Spanish).

2000b *Possible Urban Worlds*, Megacities Lecture 4, Twynstra Gudde Management Consultants, Amersfoort, Netherlands.

1996a *Justice, Nature and the Geography of Difference*. Oxford: Blackwell.

1993a *The Factory in the City: The Story of the Cowley Automobile Workers in Oxford* (edited with Teresa Hayter). Brighton: Mansell.

1989a *The Urban Experience*. Oxford: Blackwell and Baltimore, MD: Johns Hopkins University Press (translated into Italian).

1989b *The Condition of Postmodernity*. Cambridge, MA and Oxford: Blackwell (translated into Arab, Italian, Japanese, Korean, Portuguese, Romanian, Spanish, Turkish).

1985a *Consciousness and the Urban Experience*. Oxford: Blackwell and Baltimore, MD: Johns Hopkins University Press.

1985b *The Urbanization of Capital*. Oxford: Blackwell and Baltimore, MD: Johns Hopkins University Press (translated into Japanese).

1982a *The Limits to Capital*. Oxford: Blackwell and Chicago, IL: University of

Chicago Press (translated into Korean, Japanese, Portuguese, Spanish); reissued with a new introduction, London: Verso, 1999a.

1973a *Social Justice and the City.* London: Edward Arnold and Baltimore, MD: Johns Hopkins University Press (translated into Italian, Korean, Japanese, Spanish).

1972a *People, Poverty and Wealth* (with Marcia Merry). Glasgow: Collins Certificate Topics in Geography.

1969a *Explanation in Geography.* London: Edward Arnold and New York: St Martin's Press (translated into Chinese, Japanese, Portuguese, Russian, Spanish).

Articles, Book Chapters, Interviews and reports

2004a Geographical knowledges/political powers, in J. Morrill (ed.) *The Promotion of Knowledge* (*Proc. British Academy* 122, 96–112).

2004b Retrospect on *The Limits to Capital, Antipode* 36: 544–9.

2004c A geographer's perspective on the new American imperialism: an interview with David Harvey [interviewer: Harry Kreisler], University of California at Berkeley, March 2004, at http://globetrotter.berkeley.edu/people4/Harvey/harvey-con0.html.

2003c City future contained in city past: Balzac in Paris, in J. Ramon (ed.) *After-Images of the City.* Ithaca, NY: Cornell University Press, 23–48.

2003d New imperialism: accumulation by dispossession, in L. Panitch and C. Leys (eds.), *Socialist Register 2004.* London: Merlin, 63–87.

2003e The city as a body politic, in J. Schneider and I. Susser (eds.) *Wounded Cities.* Oxford: Berg, 25–46.

2002a The art of rent: globalization, monopoly and the commodification of culture, *Socialist Register.* London: Merlin, 93–110.

2002b Memories and desires, in P. Gould and F. Pitts (eds.) *Geographical Voices: Fourteen Autobiographical Records.* Syracuse, NY: Syracuse University Press, 149–88.

2002c Cracks in the edifice of the Empire State, in M. Sorkin and S. Zukin (eds.) *After the World Trade Center.* New York: Routledge, 57–67.

2001b The spaces of utopia, in D. Goldberg, M. Mushenyo and L. Bower (eds.) *Between Law and Culture.* Minneapolis, MN: University of Minnesota Press, 95–121.

2001c The cartographic imagination: Balzac in Paris, in V. Dharwadker (ed.) *Cosmopolitan Geographies.* London and New York: Routledge, 63–87.

2001e Globalization and the spatial fix. *Geographische Revue* 2: 23–30.

2000c Cosmopolitanism and the banality of geographical evils, *Public Culture* 12, 2: 529–64. Reprinted in J. Comaroff and J. L. Comaroff (eds.) *Millennial Capitalism and the Culture of Neoliberalism.* Durham, NC: Duke University Press, 2001d, 271–309.

2000d Reinventing geography [interviewer: Perry Anderson], *New Left Review,* August, 75–97.

1999b Social movements and the city: a theoretical positioning, in Giok Ling (ed.) *Urban Best Practices,* vol. 2. Singapore: Urban Redevelopment Authority and the Institute of Policy Studies, 104–115

1999c Frontiers of insurgent planning. *Plurimondi* 2: 269–86

1999d The work of postmodernity: the body in global space, in J. Davis (ed.) *Identity and Social Change*. New Brunswick, NJ: Transaction Press, 27–52.

1999e On fatal flaws and fatal distractions, *Progress in Human Geography* 23, 4: 557–66.

1999f The body as referent, *The Hedgehog Review* 1: 41–6.

1999g Considerations on the environment of justice, in N. Low (ed.) *Global Ethics and Environment*. London: Routledge, 109–30.

1998a The Humboldt connection, *Annals of the Association of American Geographers* 88: 723–30.

1998b Spaces of insurgency, in J. Beverly, P. Cohen and D. Harvey *Subculture and Homogenization*. Barcelona: Fundacio Antoni Tapies.

1998c Perspectives urbanes per el segle XXI, in *La ciutat: visiones, analisis i reptes*. Ajuntamente de Girona.

1998d The body as an accumulation strategy, *Environment and Planning D: Society and Space* 16, 3: 401–21.

1998e An anniversary of consequence and relevance, *Environment and Planning D: Society and Space* 16, 3: 379–85.

1998f What's green and makes the environment go round?, in F. Jameson and M. Miyoshi (eds.) *The Cultures of Globalization*. Durham, NC: Duke University Press, 27–55.

1998g Retrospective on postmodernism, *Architecture and the Public Sphere*, Architectural Review at the University of Virginia: 38–51.

1998h Marxism, metaphors and ecological politics, *Monthly Review* 49, 11 (April): 17–31.

1998i The restless analyst: an interview with David Harvey [interviewers: Linda Peake and Peter Jackson], *Journal of Geography in Higher Education* 12, 1: 5–20.

1997a David Harvey: the politics of social justice, interview with R. Baruffalo and C. Staddon, *Disclosure: A Journal of Social Theory* 6: 125–43.

1997b The new urbanization and the communitarian trap, *Harvard Design* Winter/Spring, 68–9.

1996b Globalization in question, *Rethinking Marxism* 8, 4: 1–17.

1996c On architects, bees and possible urban worlds, in C. Davidson (ed.) *Anywise*, Cambridge, MA: MIT Press.

1996d The environment of justice, in A. Merrifield and E. Swyngedouw (eds.) *The Urbanization of Injustice*. London: Lawrence and Wishart

1996e Poverty and greed in American cities, in W. Saunders (ed.) *Reflections on Architectural Practices in the Nineties*, New York: Princeton Architectural Press, 104–12.

1995a Militant particularism and global ambition: the conceptual politics of place, space and environment in the work of Raymond Williams, *Social Text* 42: 69–98.

1995b Cities or urbanization? *City* 1, 2: 38–61.

1995c Entrevista: David Harvey, *Geographikos: Una Revista de Geographia* 6: 55–66. Reprinted in *Boletim Paulista de Geografia* 74: 67–82, 1996f.

1995d Nature, politics and possibilities: a debate with David Harvey and Donna Haraway, *Environment and Planning D: Society and Space* 13: 507–27.

1995e A geographer's guide to dialectical thinking, in N. Thrift and A. Cliff (eds.) *Diffusing Geography*. Oxford: Blackwell, 3–21.

1994 The invisible political economy of architectural production, in O. Bouman and R. van Torn (eds.) *The Invisible in Architecture*. London: Academy Editions, 420–7.

1993b From space to place and back again: reflections on the condition of postmodernity, in J. Bird, B. Curtis, T. Putnam, G. Robertson and L. Tickner (eds.) *Mapping the Futures: Local Cultures, Global Change*. London: Routledge, 3–29.

1993c Corporations and communities (with E. Swyngedouw), in T. Hayter and D. Harvey (eds.) *The Factory in the City*. London: Mansell, 11–25.

1993d Class relations, social justice and the politics of difference, in J. Squires (ed.) *Principled Positions: Postmodernism and the Rediscovery of Value*. London: Lawrence and Wishart, 85–120. Reprinted in M. Keith and S. Pile (eds.) *Place and the Politics of Identity*, London: Routledge, 41–66, 1993e.

1993f The nature of environment: the dialectics of social and environmental change, in L. Panitch (ed.) *Socialist Register*, London: Merlin, 1–51.

1993g Towards reclaiming our cities: experience and analysis, an interview with David Harvey, *Regenerating Cities* 1, 5: 4–10 and 1, 6: 3–9.

1992a The view from Federal Hill, in E. Fee, L. Shopes and L. Zeidman (eds.) *The Baltimore Book: New Views on Local History*. Philadelphia, PA: Temple University Press, 232–47.

1992b Postmodern morality plays, *Antipode* 24, 3: 300–26.

1992c Social justice, postmodernism and the city, *International Journal of Urban and Regional Research* 16: 588–601.

1992d Capitalism: the factory of fragmentation, *New Perspectives Quarterly* 9: 42–5.

1991a Flexibility: threat or opportunity? *Socialist Review* 21: 65–78.

1991b The urban face of capitalism, in J. F. Hart (ed.) *Our Changing Cities*. Baltimore, MD: Johns Hopkins University Press, 227–49.

1990 Looking backwards on postmodernism, in A. C. Papadakis (ed.) *Architectural Design Profile*. London: Academy Editions, 10–12.

1989c From managerialism to entrepreneurialism: the transformation in urban governance in late capitalism, *Geografiska Annaler* 71B: 3–17.

1989d Between space and time: reflections on the geographical imagination, *Annals of the Association of American Geographers* 80: 418–34.

1989e From models to Marx, in B. Macmillan (ed.) *Remodelling Geography*. Oxford: Blackwell, 211–16.

1989f The practice of human geography: theory and empirical specificity in the transition from Fordism to flexible accumulation (with A. Scott), in B. Macmillan (ed.) *Remodelling Geography*. Oxford: Blackwell, 217–29.

1988a The geographical and geopolitical consequences of the transition from Fordist to flexible accumulation, in G. Sternlieb and J. Hughes (eds.) *America's New Market Geography*. Rutgers, NJ: Center for Urban Studies, 101–34.

1988b The production of value in historical geography, *Journal of Historical Geography* 14: 305–6.

1988c Forward to S. Zukin, *Loft Living: Capital and Culture in Urban Change*. Baltimore, MD : Johns Hopkins University Press and London: Radius Editions.

1988d Urban places in the 'global village': reflections on the urban condition in late twentieth century capitalism, in L. Mazza (ed.) *World Cities and the Future of the Metropolis*, Milan: Electa, 21–31.

1987a Flexible accumulation through urbanisation: reflections on postmodernism in the American city, *Antipode*, 19, 1: 1–42.

1987b Three myths in search of a reality in urban studies, *Environment and Planning D: Society and Space* 5: 367–86.

1987c The representation of urban life, *Journal of Historical Geography* 13, 3: 317–21.

1987d The world systems trap, *Studies in Comparative International Development* 22: 42–7.

1987e Urban housing entry, in *New Palgrave Dictionary*. London: Macmillan.

1986 The essential and vernacular landscapes of J. B. Jackson, *Design Book Review* Fall: 12–17.

1985c The geopolitics of capitalism, in D. Gregory and J. Urry (eds.) *Social Relations and Spatial Structures*. London: Macmillan, 128–63.

1984a On the history and present condition of geography: an historical materialist manifesto, *The Professional Geographer* 36: 1–11. Reprinted in J. Agnew et al. (eds.) *Human Geography: An Anthology*. Oxford: Blackwell, 95–107, 1996g.

1984b Geography and Urbanisation entries, in A *Dictionary of Marxist Thought*, ed. T. Bottomore. Oxford: Blackwell.

1984c Geography: From capitals to capital (with Neil Smith), in B. Olman and E. Vermelya (eds.) *The Left Academy*, vol. 2. New York: Praeger, 99–121

1983 Owen Lattimore: A memoire, *Antipode* 15, 3: 3–11.

1982b Marxist geography and Mode of production, entries in R. J. Johnston et al. (eds.) *The Dictionary of Human Geography*. Oxford: Blackwell.

1982c The space-economy of capitalist production: a Marxian interpretation, *International Geographical Union, Latin American Regional Conference, Symposia and Round Tables*, vol. 2, Rio de Janeiro.

1981a The spatial fix: Hegel, von Thunen and Marx, *Antipode* 13, 3: 1–12.

1981b Rent control and a fair return, in J. Gilderbloom (ed.) *Rent Control: A Source Book*. San Francisco, CA: Foundation for National Progress.

1979a Monument and myth, *Annals of the Association of American Geographers* 69, 3: 362–81.

1978a The urban process under capitalism: a framework for analysis, *International Journal of Urban and Regional Research* 2. Reprinted in M. Dear and A. Scott (eds.) *Urbanization and Planning in Capitalist Society*. London: Methuen, 1981c.

1978b On planning the ideology of planning, in J. Burchall (ed.) *Planning for the '80s: Challenge and Response*. New Brunswick, NJ: Rutgers University Press.

1978c On countering the Marxian myth – Chicago style, *Comparative Urban Research* 6, 1: 28–45.

1977a Labor, capital and class struggle around the built environment, *Politics and Society* 7, 2: 265–95. Reprinted in K. Cox (ed.) *Urbanisation and Conflict in Market Societies*. Chicago, IL: Maaroufa Press, 9–37, 1978d; in A. Giddens and D. Held (eds.) *Classes, Power and Conflict*. Berkeley, CA: University of California Press, 545–61, 1982d; and in L. Bourne (ed.) *The Internal Structure of the City*. Oxford: Oxford University Press, 137–49, 1979b.

1977b Government policies, financial institutions and neighborhood change in U.S. cities, in M. Harloe (ed.) *Captive Cities*. Chichester: John Wiley, 123–39.

1976a The Marxian theory of the state, *Antipode* 8, 2: 80–9.

1975a The geography of capitalist accumulation: a reconstruction of the Marxian theory, *Antipode* 7, 2: 9–21. Reprinted in R. Peet (ed.) *Radical Geography*. Chicago, IL: Maaroufa Press, 263–92, 1977c.

1975b Some remarks on the political economy of urbanism, *Antipode* 7, 1: 54–61.

1975c Class structure and the theory of residential differentiation, in M. Chisholm and R. Peel (eds.) *Bristol Essays in Geography*. London: Heinemann.

1975d The political economy of urbanism in advanced capitalist societies: the case of the United States, *Urban Affairs Annual* 9: 119–63. Translated into French as L'économie politique de l'urbanisation aux Etats Unis, *Espaces et Sociétés* 7: 5–41, 1976b.

1974 Population, resources and the ideology of science, *Economic Geography*, 50: 256–77.

1974a What kind of geography for what kind of public policy? *Transactions of the Institute of British Geographers* 63: 18–24.

1974b Class-monopoly rent, finance capital and the urban revolution, *Regional Studies* 8: 239–55. Reprinted in S. Gale and E. Moore (eds.) *The Manipulated City*. Chicago, IL: Maaroufa Press, 145–67, 1975e.

1974c Absolute rent and the structuring of space by governmental and financial institutions (with Lata Chatterjee), *Antipode* 6, 1: 22–36. Reprinted in L. Bourne (ed.) *The Internal Structure of the City*. Oxford: Oxford University Press, 85–98, 1979b.

1974d Population, resources and the ideology of science, *Economic Geography*, 50: 256–77. Reprinted in R. Peet (ed.) *Radical Geography*. Chicago, IL: Maaroufa Press, 213–42, 1977c; and in S. Gale and G. Olsson (eds.) *Philosophy in Geography*. Dordrecht: Reidel, 155–85, 1979c.

1974e Discussion with Brian Berry, *Antipode* 6, 2: 145–9.

1974f PHA policies and the Baltimore City housing market (with L. Chatterjee and L. Klugman), The Urban Observatory Inc., City Planning Department, Baltimore.

1972b Revolutionary and counter-revolutionary theory, *Antipode* 4, 2: 1–25.

1972c Revolutionary and counter-revolutionary theory in geography and the problem of ghetto formation, in *Perspectives in Geography*, vol. 2, Chicago, IL: Northern Illinois University Press.

1972d Social justice and spatial systems, in R. Peet (ed.) *Geographical Perspectives on Poverty and Social Well Being*, *Antipode* Monographs in Social Geography 1. Worcester, MA: Clark University Geography Department, 12–25, Reprinted in M. Albaum (ed.) *Geography and Contemporary Issues*. Chichester: John Wiley, 565–84, 1973b; in D. Weir (ed.) *The City in Britain*. London: Fawcett Books, 15–27, 1975e; and in S. Gale and E. Moore (eds.) *The Manipulated City*. Chicago, IL: Maaroufa Press, 106–20, 1975f.

1972e On obfuscation in geography; a comment on Gale's heterodoxy, *Geographical Analysis* 41, 3: 323–30.

1972f The role of theory, in N. Graves (ed.) *New Movements in the Study and Teaching of Geography*. Philadelphia, PA: Temple Smith, 29–41.

1972h The housing market and code enforcement in Baltimore (with L. Chatterjee, M. Wolman and J. Newman), The Baltimore Observatory Inc. City Planning Department, Baltimore.

1972i A commentary on the comments, *Antipode* 4, 2: 36–41.

1971 Social processes, spatial form, and the redistribution of real income in an urban system, in M. Chisholm (ed.) *Regional Forecasting*. London: Butterworth Scientific Publications, 267–300. Reprinted in M. Stuart (ed.) *The City: Problems of Planning*. Harmondsworth: Penguin, 288–306, 1972g.

1970a Social processes and spatial form: an analysis of the conceptual problems of urban planning, *Papers of the Regional Science Association* 25: 47–69. Reprinted in E. Jones (ed.) *Readings in Social Geography*. Oxford: Oxford University Press, 76–96, 1975g.

1970b Behavioral postulates and the construction of theory in human geography, *Geografica Polonica* 18: 27–45.

1969b Conceptual and measurement problems in the cognitive behavioral approach to location theory, in K. Cox and R. Golledge (eds.) *Behavioural Problems in Geography: A Symposium*. Evanston, IL: Northwestern University Press, 16–28.

1968a Pattern, process and the scale problem in geographical research, *Transactions of the Institute of British Geographers* 45: 1–8.

1968b Some methodological problems in the use of the Neyman Type A and negative binomial probability distributions for the analysis of spatial point patterns, *Transactions of the Institute of British Geographers* 44: 85–95.

1968c Geographical processes and the analysis of point patterns: testing models of diffusion by quadrat sampling, *Transactions of the Institute of British Geographers* 44: 85–95.

1967a Models of the evolution of spatial patterns in human geography, in R. J. Chorley and P. Haggett (eds.) *Models in Geography*. London: Methuen, 549–608.

1967b The problem of theory construction in geography, *Journal of Regional Science* 7, 2 (Supplement): 1–6.

1966 Theoretical concepts and the analysis of agricultural land use patterns, *Annals of the Association of American Geographers* 56, 3: 361–74. Reprinted in F. Dohrs and L. Sommers *Economic Geography: Selected Readings*, New York: Crowell, 1970c.

1965 *Monte Carlo Simulation Models*, Uppsala: Forskningsrapnorter Kulturgeografiska Insitutionen Uppsala University 1.

1964 Fruit growing in Kent in the nineteenth century, *Archaeologia Cantiana* 7: 95–108.

1963 Locational change in the Kentish hop industry and the analysis of land use patterns, *Transactions of the Institute of British Geographers* 33: 123–40. Reprinted in E. J. Taafe, L. J. King and R. H. T. Smith (eds.) *Readings in Economic Geography*. London: McGraw Hill, 79–93, 1968d; and in A. Baker et al. (eds.) *Geographical Interpretations of Geographical Sources*. New York: Barnes and Noble, 243–65, 1970d.

1962 'Aspects of agricultural and rural change in Kent, 1815–1900', PhD thesis, Cambridge University.

Other Activities

BBC News and Current Affairs (Radio Four): 'City Lights/City Shadows'. Three Radio Broadcasts, 10 October, 17 October and 24 October 1993h, produced by Sallie Davies, scripted and narrated by David Harvey.

Bibliography

Abu-Lughod, J. L. (1988) Book reviews, *Economic Development and Cultural Change* 36: 411–15.

Alliez, E. (1999) Tarde et le problème de la constitution, in G. Tarde *Monadologie et Sociologie*. Paris: Institut Synthelabo, 9–32.

Althusser, L. (1970) *For Marx* B. Brewster (trans.). London: Verso.

Althusser, L., and Balibar, E. (1969) *Reading Capital*. London: New Left Books.

Althusser, L. and Balibar, E. (1969) *Reading Capital* B. Brewster (trans.). London: Verso.

Altvater, E. (1991) *The Future of the Market: An Essay on the Regulation of Money and Nature after the Collapse of 'Actually Existing Socialism'* P. Camiller (trans.). London: Verso.

Anderson, P. (1976) *Considerations on Western Marxism*. London: New Left Books.

Anderson, P. (1980) *Arguments within English Marxism*. London: Verso.

Anderson, P. (1983) *In the Tracks of Historical Materialism*. London: Verso.

Anderson, P. (1998) *The Origins of Postmodernity*. London: Verso.

Ansell Pearson, K. (1999) *Germinal Life: The Difference and Repetition of Deleuze*. London: Routledge.

Aronson, R. (1995) *After Marxism*. New York: Guilford Press.

Arrighi, G. (1994) *The Long Twentieth Century*. London: Verso.

Arthur, C. (1979) Dialectic of the value-form, in D. Elson (ed.) *Value: The Representation of Labour in Capitalism: Essays*. London: CSE Books, 67–81.

Arthur, C. (2002) *The New Dialectic and Marx's 'Capital'*. Leiden: Brill Academic Publishers.

Aydalot, P. (1976) *Dynamique spatiale et développement inégal*. Paris: Economica.

Badiou, A. (2000) *Deleuze: The Clamor of Being* L. Burchill (trans.). Minneapolis, MN: University of Minnesota Press

Bakker, I. (2001) Neoliberal governance and social reproduction. Presented at conference on Gender, Political Economy, and Human Security, York University, Toronto, Ontario, 5 October.

Bales, K. (1999) *Disposable People*. Berkeley, CA: University of California Press.

Barnes, T. (1996) *Logics of Dislocation: Models, Metaphors, and Meanings of Economic Space.* New York: Guilford Press.

Barnes, T. J. (2000) Local knowledge, in R. J. Johnston, D. Gregory, G. Pratt and M. Watts (eds.) *The Dictionary of Human Geography* (4th edn.). Oxford: Blackwell, 452–3.

Barnes, T. J. (2001) Retheorizing economic geography: from the quantitative revolution to the 'cultural turn', *Annals of the Association of American Geographers* 91: 546–65.

Barnes, T. J. (2004) Placing ideas: heterotopias, genius loci, and geography's quantitative revolution, *Progress in Human Geography* 28, 5: 565–96.

Barrett, M. (1991) *The Politics of Truth: From Marx to Foucault.* Cambridge: Polity Press.

Bataille, G. (1985) The notion of expenditure, in *Visions of Excess: Selected Writings 1927–1939.* Minneapolis, MN: University of Minnesota Press, 116–29.

Bataille, G. (1988) Sacrifices and the wars of the Aztecs, in *The Accursed Share: An Essay on General Economy, vol. 1: Consumption.* New York: Zone Books, 45–61.

Battersby, C. (1998) *The Phenomenal Woma:. Feminist Metaphysics and the Patterns of Identity.* Cambridge: Polity Press.

Baudrillard, J. (1975) *The Mirror of Production* M. Poster (trans.). St Louis, MO: Telos.

Baudrillard, J. (1981) *For a Critique of the Political Economy of the Sign* C. Levin (trans.). St Louis, MO: Telos.

Baudrillard, J. (1990) *Seduction* B. Singer (trans.). London: Macmillan.

Baudrillard, J. (1994) *Simulation and Simulacra* S. Glaser (trans.). Ann Arbor, MI: University of Michigan Press.

Baudrillard, J. (1996) *The Perfect Crime* C. Turner (trans.). London: Verso.

Baudrillard, J. (1998) *The Consumer Society: Myths and Structures* C. Turner (trans.). London: Sage.

Bauman, Z. (1987) *Legislators and Interpreters: On Modernity, Post-Modernity, and Intellectuals.* Cambridge: Polity Press.

Benhabib, S. (1986) *Critique, Norm, and Utopian.* New York: Columbia University Press.

Benjamin, W. (1973) *Charles Baudelaire: A Lyric Poet in the Era of High Capitalism* H. Zohn (trans.). London: New Left Books.

Benjamin, W. (1968) *Illuminations.* New York: Schocken.

Benjamin, W. (1999) *The Arcades Project* H. Eiland and K. McLaughlin (eds.). Cambridge, MA: Belknap Press.

Benton, T. 1989: Marxism and natural limits, *New Left Review* 178: 51–86.

Berger, J. (1985) Manhattan, in *The Sense of Sight.* New York: Pantheon, 61–7.

Berlant, L. (2003) Uncle Sam needs a wife: citizenship and denegation, in R. Castronovo and D. D. Nelson (eds.) *Materializing Democracy: Toward a Revitalized Cultural Politics.* Durham, NC: Duke University Press, 144–74.

Berman, M. (1982) *All That Is Solid Melts into Air: The Experience of Modernity.* New York: Simon and Schuster and London: Verso.

Berry, B. J. L. (1993) Geography's quantitative revolution: initial conditions. A personal memoir, *Urban Geography* 14: 434–41.

Best, S. and Kellner, D. (1991) *Postmodern Theory.* London: Macmillan.

Bhabha, H. (1992) Double visions, *Artforum* January, 85–9.

Bidet, J. and Kouvelakis, E. (eds.) (2001) *Dictionnaire Marx Critique.* Paris: Presses Universitaires de France.

Bois, Y.-A. and Krauss, R. (1997) *Formless: A User's Guide.* New York: Zone.

Bottomore, T. (ed.) (1983) *A Dictionary of Marxist Thought.* Oxford: Blackwell.

Bourdieu, P. (1984) *Distinction: A Social Critique of the Judgment of Taste* R. Nice (trans.). Cambridge, MA: Harvard University Press.

Braun, B. (1998) A politics of possibility without the possibility of politics? Thoughts on Harvey's troubles with difference, *Annals of the Association of American Geographers* 88, 4: 712–23.

Braun, B. (1998) A politics of possibility without the possibility of politics, *Annals of the Association of American Geographers* 88, 4: 712–18.

Braun, B. (2000) Producing vertical territory: geology and governmentality in late-Victorian Canada, *Ecumene.* 7, 1: 7–46.

Brennan, T. (2000) *Exhausting Modernity: Grounds for a New Economy.* London: Routledge.

Breugel, I. (2000) No more jobs for the boys? *Capital and Class* 71: 27–40

Bridge, G. (2000) The social regulation of resource access and environmental impact: production, nature and contradiction in the US copper industry, *Geoforum* 31: 237–56.

Brown, A., Fleetwood, S. and Roberts, J. (eds.) (2001) *Critical Realism and Marxism.* London: Routledge.

Burawoy, M. (1982) *Manufacturing Consent: Changes in the Labor Process under Monopoly Capitalism.* Chicago, IL: University of Chicago Press.

Burbach, R. (1998) The (un)defining of postmodern Marxism: on smashing modernization and narrating new social and economic actors, *Rethinking Marxism* 10, 1: 52–65.

Butler, J. (1993) *Gender Trouble: Feminism and the Subversion of Identity.* London: Routledge.

Callinicos, A. (1985) Anthony Giddens: a contemporary critique, *Theory and Society* 15: 133–66.

Callinicos, A. (2001) Periodizing capitalism and analysing imperialism, in R. Albritton et al. (eds.) *Phases of Capitalist Development.* Houndmills: Palgrave, 230–45.

Callinicos, A. (2002) Marxism and global governance, in D. Held and A. McGrew (eds.) *Governing Globalization.* Cambridge: Polity Press, 249–66.

Callon, M. (1998) Introduction, in M. Callon (ed.) *The Laws of the Market.* Oxford: Blackwell.

Casarino, C. (2002) *Modernity at Sea: Marx, Melville, Conrad in Crisis.* Minneapolis, MN: University of Minnesota Press

Carling, A. (1986) Rational choice Marxism, *New Left Review* (I) 160: 24–62.

Caro, R. (1974) *The Power Broker.* New York: Vintage.

Cassirer, E. (1944) *An Essay on Man.* New Haven, CT: Yale University Press.

Castells, M. (1976) Is there an urban sociology? in C. Pickvance (ed.) *Urban Sociology: Critical Essays.* London: Tavistock, 33–59.

Castells, M. (1996) *The Information Age, vol. 1: The Rise of the Network Society.* Oxford: Blackwell.

Castells, M. (1997) *The Information Age, vol. 2: The Power of Identity.* Oxford: Blackwell.

Castells, M. (1998) *The Information Age, vol. 3: End of Millennium.* Oxford: Blackwell.

Castells, M. (2000) *Th Power of Identity.* Oxford: Blackwell.

Castree, N. (1995) The nature of produced nature: materiality and knowledge construction in Marxism, *Antipode* 27, 1: 12–48.

Castree, N. (1996) Birds, mice and geography, *Transactions of the Institute of British Geographers* 21, 3: 342–62.

Castree, N. (1999) Envisioning capitalism, *Transactions of the Institute of British Geographers* 24, 2: 137–58.

Castree, N. (2002) False antithesis? Marxism, nature and actor-networks *Antipode* 34, 1: 111–46.

Castree, N. (2002) From spaces of antagonism to spaces of engagement, in A. Brown, S. Fleetwood and J. M. Roberts (eds.) *Critical Realism and Marxism.* London: Routledge, 187–214.

Castree, N. (2003) Commodifying what nature? *Progress in Human Geography* 27, 3: 273–97.

Castree, N. (2006) David Harvey's symptomatic silence, *Historical Materialism* (forthcoming).

Castronovo, R. and Nelson, D. D. (2003) *Materializing Democracy: Toward a Revitalized Cultural Politics.* Durham, NC: Duke University Press.

Catephores, G. (1989) *An Introduction to Marxist Economics.* Basingstoke: Macmillan.

Chatterjee, L. and Harvey, D. (1974) Absolute rent and the restructuring of space by governmental and financial institutions, *Antipode* 6, 1: 22–36.

Chorley, R. J. (1995) Haggett's Cambridge: 1957–66, in A. D. Cliff, P. R. Gould, A. G. Hoare and N. J. Thrift (eds.) *Diffusing Geography: Essays for Peter Haggett.* Oxford: Blackwell, 355–74.

Christopherson, S. (1989) On being outside 'the project', *Antipode* 21, 2: 83–9.

Cohen, G. A. (1978) *Karl Marx's Theory of History.* Oxford Clarendon.

Corbridge, S. (1998) Reading David Harvey: entries, voices, loyalties, *Antipode* 30, 1: 43–55.

Corlett, W. (1993) *Community without Unity: A Politics of Derridean Extravagance.* Durham, NC: Duke University Press.

Cottereau, A. (1980) Étude Prealable, in D. Poulot (ed.) *Le Sublime.* Paris: Maspero, 62–80.

Cronon, W. (1995) The trouble with wilderness: or, getting back to the wrong nature, in W. Cronon (ed.) *Uncommon Ground: Toward Reinventing Nature.* New York: W. W. Norton.

Daniell, A. (2002) Preface, in C. Keller and A. Daniell (eds.) *Process and Difference: Between Cosmological and Poststructural Postmodernisms.* Albany, NY: SUNY Press.

Darwin, C. (1974) *Charles Darwin and T. H. Huxley, Autobiographies* G. de Beer (ed.). London: Oxford University Press.

Davis, S. (1995) Touch the magic, in William Cronon (ed.) *Uncommon Ground: Toward Reinventing Nature.* New York: W. W. Norton, 204–32.

Dear, M. (1988) The postmodern challenge: reconstructing human geography, *Transactions of the Institute of British Geographers* 13: 262–74.

DeLanda, M. (1999) Deleuze, diagrams, and the open-ended becoming of the world, in E. Grosz *Becomings: Explorations in Time, Memory and Futures.* Ithaca, NY: Cornell University Press, 29–41.

DeLanda, M. (2002) *Intensive Science and Virtual Philosophy.* London: Continuum.

Delaney, D. and Leitner, H. (1997) The political construction of scale, *Political Geography* 16, 2: 93–7.

Deleuze, G. (1988) *Spinoza: Practical Philosophy* R. Hurley (trans.). San Francisco, CA: City Lights Books.

Deleuze, G. (1990a) *Negotiations.* New York: Columbia University Press.

Deleuze, G. (1990b) *The Logic of Sense,* M. Lester and C. Stivale (trans.). New York: Columbia University Press.

Deleuze, G. (1992) *The Fold: Leibniz and the Baroque.* Minneapolis, MI: Minnesota University Press.

Deleuze, G. (1993 [1988]) *The Fold: Leibniz and the Baroque.* Minneapolis, MI: University of Minnesota Press.

Deleuze, G. (1994 [1968]) *Difference and Repetition.* New York: Columbia University Press.

Deleuze, G. and Guattari, F. (1987) *A Thousand Plateaus: Capitalism and Schizophrenia.* Minneapolis, MN: University of Minnesota Press.

Deleuze, G. and Guattari, F. (1994) *What is Philosophy?* Hugh Tomlinson and Graham Burchell (trans.). New York: Columbia University Press.

Deleuze, G. and Parnet, C. (1987) *Dialogues,* H. Tomlinson and B. Habberjam (trans.). London: Athlone Press.

Dennis, R. (1987) Review article: faith in the city? *Journal of Historical Geography* 13, 3: 310–16.

Derrida, J. (1981) *Positions* A. Bass (trans.). Chicago, IL: University of Chicago Press.

Derrida, J. (1983) *Margins of Philosophy* A. Bass (trans.). Hemel Hempstead: Harvester Wheatsheaf.

Derrida, J. (1992) *Given Time: vol. 1. Counterfeit Money* P. Kamuf (trans.). Chicago, IL: University of Chicago Press.

Derrida, J. (1994) *Specters of Marx: The State of the Debt, the Work of Mourning, and the New International* P. Kamuf (trans.). London: Routledge.

Derrida, J. (1991 [1982]) From 'Différance', in P. Camuf (ed.) *A Derrida Reader: Between the Blinds.* Oxford: Blackwell, 59–79.

Derrida, J. (1991 [1983]) Letter to a Japanese friend, in P. Camuf (ed.) *A Derrida Reader: Between the Blinds.* Oxford: Blackwell, 270–6.

Di Chiro, G. (1995) Nature as community: the convergence of environment and social justice, in W. Cronon (ed.) *Uncommon Ground: Toward Reinventing Nature.* New York: W. W. Norton, 298–320.

Doel, M. A. (1999) *Poststructuralist Geographies: The Diabolical Art of Spatial Science.* Edinburgh: Edinburgh University Press.

Duell, J. (2000) Assessing the literary: intellectual boundaries in French and American literary studies, in M. Lamont and M. Thevenot (eds.) *Rethinking*

Comparitive Cultural Sociology: Repertoires of Evaluation in France and the United States. Cambridge: Cambridge University Press, 94–124.

Duménil, G. (1978) *Le Concept de loi économique dans 'le Capital'.* Paris: Maspero.

Duncan, R. and Wilson, C. (eds.) (1987) *Marx Refuted: The Verdict of History.* Bath: Ashgrove.

Eagleton, T. (1995) Jacques Derrida: specters of Marx, *Radical Philosophy* 73: 35–7.

Eagleton, T. (1997) Spaced out: David Harvey's *Justice, Nature and the Geography of Difference, London Review of Books* 24 April, 19: 22–3.

Eagleton, T. (2001) *The Gatekeeper.* London: Allen Lane.

Ehrlich, P. (1968) *The Population Bomb.* New York: Ballantine Books.

Engels, F. (1946 [1888]) *Ludwig Feuerback and the End of Classical German Philosophy.* Moscow: Progress Publishers.

Engels, Frederick (1978 [1883]) Speech at the graveside of Karl Marx, in Robert Tucker (ed.) *The Marx–Engels Reader.* New York: Norton.

Escobar, A. (2001) Culture sits in places: reflections on globalism and subaltern strategies of localization, *Political Geography* 20, 2: 139–74.

Esteva, G. and Prakash, M. S. (1992) Grassroots resistance to sustainable development: lessons from the banks of the Narmada, *Ecologist* 22: 45–51.

Fields, B. (2001) Whiteness, racism, and identity, *International Labor and Working Class History* 60: 48–56.

Fitzgerald, J. (1979) *Alfred North Whitehead's Early Philosophy of Space and Time.* New York: Rowman and Littlefield.

Foucault, M. (1977) *Discipline and Punish.* New York: Vintage.

Foucault, M. (1980) *Power/Knoweldge.* New York: Vintage.

Fritzsche, P. (1996) *Reading Berlin 1900.* Cambridge, MA: Harvard University Press.

Gale, S. (1972) On the heterodoxy of explanation: a review of David Harvey's *Explanation in Geography, Geographical Analysis* 4: 285–332.

Gandy, M. (2002) *Concrete and Clay: Reworking Nature in New York City.* Cambridge, MA: MIT Press.

Gibson-Graham, J. K. (1996) *The End of Capitalism (As We Know It).* Oxford: Blackwell.

Gibson-Graham, J. K. (2003) An ethics of the local, *Rethinking Marxism* 15, 1: 49–74.

Giddens, A. (1981) *A Contemporary Critique of Historical Materialism.* London: Macmillan.

Gieryn, T. (2002) Three truth spots, *Journal of the History of the Behavioral Sciences* 38: 113–32.

Gleick, J. (2003) *Isaac Newton.* New York: Pantheon.

Gregory, D. (1994) *Geographical Imaginations.* New York: Blackwell.

Gregory, D. and Urry, J. (eds.) (1985) *Social Relations and Spatial Structures.* London: Methuen.

Grossman, H. (1977) Marx, classical political economy, and the problem of dynamics. Part Two, *Capital and Class* 3: 67–99.

Grosz, E. (1994) *Volatile Bodies.* Bloomington, IN: Indiana University Press.

Guattari, F. (2000) *The Three Ecologies.* London, Athlone Press.

Gutenschwager, G. (1976) A Marxian perspective on urbanism, *Monthly Review* May: 44–9.

Hacking, I. (2002) *Historical Ontology*. Cambridge, MA: Harvard University Press.

Haggett, P. (1965) *Locational Analysis in Human Geography*. London: Edward Arnold.

Hannigan, J. (1998) *Fantasy Cities*. London: Routledge.

Hansen, M. (2000) Becoming as creative involution? Contextualizing Deleuze and Guattari's Biophilosophy, *Postmodern Culture* 11.1.

Haraway, D. (1990) A manifesto for cyborgs: science, technology and socialist feminism in the 1980s, in L. Nicholson (ed.) *Feminism/Postmodernism*. London: Routledge, 123–35.

Haraway, D. (1991) Situated knowledge: the science question in feminism and the privilege of partial perspective, in *Simians, Cyborgs and Women: The Reinvention of Nature*. London: Routledge, 183–202.

Haraway, D. (1997) *Modest_Witness@Second_Millennium.Female Man©_Meets_OncoMouse™*. New York: Routledge.

Haraway, D. and Harvey, D. (1995) Nature, politics and possibilities: a debate with David Harvey and Donna Haraway, *Environment and Planning D: Society and Space* 13, 4, 507–27.

Harding, S. (1986) *The Science Question in Feminism*. Ithaca, NY: Cornell University Press.

Hardt, M. (1993) *Gilles Deleuze: An Apprenticeship in Philosophy*. Minneapolis, MN: University of Minnesota Press.

Hardt, M. and Negri, A. (2000) *Empire*. Cambridge, MA: Harvard University Press.

Hardy, F. G. (1998) It's necessary to talk about trees, *Antipode* 30, 1: 6–13.

Hartsock, N. (1984) *Money, Sex, and Power: Toward a Feminist Historical Materialism*. New York: Longman and Boston: Northeastern University Press.

Hartsock, N. (1987) Rethinking Marxism: minority vs majority theories, *Cultural Critique* 7: 187–206.

Hartsock, N. (1989) Postmodernism and political change: issues for feminist theory, *Cultural Critique* 14, 3: 15–33.

Hartsock, N. (1998a) Moments, margins, and agency, *Annals of the Association of American Geographers* 88, 4: 707–12.

Hartsock, N. (1998b) *The Feminist Standpoint Revisited and Other Essays*. Boulder, CO: Westview Press.

Hayden, D. (1982) *The Grand Domestic Revolution*. Cambridge, MA: MIT Press.

Hayden, P. (1997) Gilles Deleuze and naturalism: a convergence with ecological theory and politics, *Environmental Ethics*, 19: 184–204.

Heidegger, M. (1971) Martin Heidegger: an interview, *Listening* Winter, 6: 35–8.

Henderson, (1999) *California and the Fictions of Capital*. Oxford: Oxford University Press.

Hess, D. J. (1997) *Science Studies: An Advanced Introduction*. New York: New York University Press.

Hesse, M. B. (1980) *Revolutions and Reconstructions in the Philosophy of Science*. Brighton: Harvester Wheatsheaf.

Hirschmann, N. (1997) Feminist standpoint as postmodern strategy, in S. J. Kenney and H. Kinsella (eds.) *Politics and Feminist Standpoint Theories/Women and Politics* 18, 2: 73–92.

hooks, b. (1990) *Yearning: Race, Gender and Cultural Politics.* London: Turnaround.

Horkheimer, M. (1972 [1937]) Traditional and critical theory, in M. Connell et al. (eds.) *Critical Theory.* New York: Herder and Herder, 188–214.

Horkheimer, M. and Adorno, T. (1972) *Dialectic of Enlightenment* J. Cumming (trans.). New York: Herder and Herder.

Howard, M. and King, J. (1985) *The Political Economy of Marx* (3rd edn.). Harlow: Longman.

Howitt, R. (1998) Scale as relation: musical metaphors of geographical scale, *Area* 30, 1: 49–58.

Jacobs, J. (1961) *The Death and Life of Great American Cities.* New York: Vintage.

Jameson, F. (1979) Reification and ideology in mass culture, *Social Text* 1: 130–48.

Jameson, F. (1984) Postmodernism, or the cultural logic of late capitalism, *New Left Review* July–August, 146: 53–93.

Janik, A. and Toulmin, S. (1973) *Wittgenstein's Vienna.* New York: Simon and Schuster.

Jessop, B. (2002) *The Future of the Capitalist State.* Cambridge: Polity Press.

Jessop, B. (2004) On the limits of *Limits to Capital, Antipode* 36, 3: 480–96.

Jones, A. (1999) Dialectics and difference: against Harvey's dialectical 'post-Marxism', *Progress in Human Geography* 23, 4: 529–55.

Jones, J.-P. III (2004) *David Harvey.* London: Continuum.

Katz, C. (1996) Towards minor theory, *Environment and Planning D: Society and Space* 14: 487–99.

Katz, C. (1998) Political and intellectual passions: engagements with David Harvey's *Justice, Nature and the Geography of Difference, Annals of the Association of American Geographers* 88, 4: 706–7.

Katz, C. (2001a) On the grounds of globalization: a topography for feminist political engagement, *Signs: Journal of Women in Culture and Society* 26, 4: 1213–34.

Katz, C. (2001b) Vagabond capitalism and the necessity of social reproduction, *Antipode* 33, 4: 709–28.

Katz, C. (ed.) (1998) Political and intellectual passions: engagements with Harvey's *Justice, Nature and the Politics of Difference, Annals of the Association of American Geographers* 88, 4: 706–30.

Kearns, G. (1984) Making space for Marx, *Journal of Historical Geography* 10, 4: 411–17.

Keller, C. and Daniell, A. (2002) *Process and Difference: Between Cosmological and Poststructural Postmodernisms.* Albany, NY: SUNY Press.

Kelly, P. F. (1999) The geographies and politics of globalization, *Progress in Human Geography* 23, 3: 379–400.

Klein, N. (1999) *No Logo.* New York: Picador.

Krätke, M. (1998a) Wie politisch ist Marx' politische Ökonomie? (I), *Zeitschrift Marxistische Erneuerung* 33: 114–28.

Krätke, M. (1998b) Wie politisch ist Marx' politische Ökonomie? (II), *Zeitschrift Marxistische Erneuerung* 34: 146–61.

Kuhn, T. S. (1962) *The Structure of Scientific Revolutions*. Chicago, IL: Chicago University Press.

Lambert, G. (2002) *The Non-Philosophy of Gilles Deleuze*. London: Continuum.

Langer, S. (1953) *Feeling and Form: A Theory of Art*. New York: Prentice Hall.

Latour, B. (1993) *We Have Never Been Modern*. Cambridge, MA: Harvard University Press.

Latour, B. (1998) To modernise or ecologise? That is the question, in B. Braun and N. Castree (eds.) *Remaking Reality: Nature at the Millennium*. New York: Routledge, 221–42.

Latour, B. (2002) Gabriel Tarde and the end of the social, in P. Joyce (ed.) *The Social in Question: New Bearings in History and the Social Sciences*. London: Routledge, 117–50.

Latour, B. (2003) Is re-modernization occurring – and, if so, how to prove it? *Theory Culture and Society* 20: 35–48.

Latour, B. (2004) *Politics of Nature: How to Bring the Sciences into Democracy*, C. Porter. (trans.). Harvard, MA: Blackwell.

Lebowitz, M. (1986) Capital reinvented, *Monthly Review* June, 33–41.

Lefebvre, H. (1991 [1974]) *The Production of Space* D. Nicholson-Smith (trans.). Oxford: Blackwell.

Leitner, H. (1990) Cities in pursuit of economic growth, *Political Geography Quarterly* 9, 2: 146–70.

Ley, D. and Samuels, M. (eds.) *Humanistic Geography*. Chicago, IL: Maroufa Press.

Leyshon, A. (1998) Geographies of finance III, *Progress in Human Geography* 22, 3: 433–46

Livingstone, D. N. (2003) *Putting Science in Its Place*. Chicago, IL: University of Chicago Press.

Logan, J. and Molotch, H. (1986) *Urban Fortunes*. Berkeley and Los Angeles, CA: University of California Press.

Longino, H. (2002) *The Fate of Knowledge*. Princeton, NJ: Princeton University Press.

Luxemburg, R. (1951) *The Accumulation of Capital* Agnes Schwarz Child (trans.). New York.: Routledge and Kegan Paul.

Lyotard, J.-F. (1984) *The Postmodern Condition*. Minneapolis, MN: University of Minnesota Press.

Lyotard, J.-F. (1993) *Libidinal Economy* I. Hamilton Grant (trans.). London: Athlone.

Lyotard, J.-F. (1998) *The Assassination of Experience by Painting—Monory* R. Bowlby (trans.). London: Black Dog.

Malcolm, N. (1958) *Ludwig Wittgenstein: A Personal Memoir*. Oxford: Oxford University Press.

Mandel, E. and Freeman, A. (eds.) (1984) *Ricardo, Marx, Sraffa: The Langston Memorial Volume*. London: Verso.

Marin, L. (1984) *Utopics: A Spatial Play*. Atlantic Heights, NJ: Humanities Press.

Marston, S. (2000) The social construction of scale. *Progress in Human Geography* 24, 2: 219–42.

Martin, G. (1987) Foreword, in M. Kenzer (ed.) *Carl O. Sauer: A Tribute*. Corvalis, OR: University of Oregon Press, ix–xvi.

Martinez-Alier, J. (1987) *Ecological Economics: Energy, Environment, and Society*. Oxford: Blackwell.

Marx, K. (1946 [1845]) Theses on Feuerback, in F. Engels, *Ludwig Feuerback and the End of Classical German Philosophy*. Moscow: Progress Publishers, 61–5.

Marx, K. (1954 [1886]) *Capital: A Critique of Political Economy*, vol. 1 F. Engels (ed.), S. Moore and E. Aveling (trans.). London: Lawrence and Wishart.

Marx, K. (1963) *The Eighteenth Brumaire of Louis Bonaparte*. New York: International Publishers.

Marx, K. (1964) *Economic and Philosophical Manuscripts of 1844* Dirk Struik (trans.). New York: International Publishers.

Marx, K. (1967 [1867]) *Capital*, vol. 1 S. Moore and E. Aveling (trans.). London: Lawrence and Wishart.

Marx, K. (1970) *Capital*, vol. 1. London: Lawrence and Wishart.

Marx, K. (1973a) *Grundrisse: Foundations of the Critique of Political Economy*, New York: Vintage Books and Harmondsworth: Penguin.

Marx, K. (1973b [1859]) *Grundrisse* Martin Nicolaus (trans.). Harmondsworth: Penguin.

Marx, K. (1975) Early economic and philosophical manuscripts, in L. Colletti (ed.) *Karl Marx: Early Writings*. Harmondsworth: Pelican.

Marx, K. (1975 [1881]) Notes on Adolph Wagner's 'Lehrbuch der politischen Ökonomie', in Terrell Carver (ed.) *Karl Marx: Texts on Method*. Blackwell: Oxford.

Marx, K. (1976a [1867]) *Capital*, vol. 1 B. Fowkes (trans.). Harmondsworth: Penguin.

Marx, K. (1976b) *Capital*, vol 1. New York: Viking Press.

Marx, K. (1977 [1847]) Die Weiterentwicklung der Theorie, in *Marx-Engels Collected Works*, vol. 20. London: Lawrence and Wishart.

Marx, K. (1983 [1857–8]) Grundrisse der Kritik der Politischen Ökonomie, in Institut für Marxismus-Leninismus beim Zentralkommittee der SED (ed.) *Karl Marx, Friedrich Engels: Werke*. Berlin: Dietz Verlag, 47–768.

Marx, K. and Engels, F. (1975 [1881]) *Collected Works*, vol. 5. London: Lawrence and Wishart.

Marx, K. and Engels, F. (1976) *Collected Works*, vol. 5. New York: International Publishers.

Marx, K. and Engels, F. (1986 [1848]) *Manifesto of the Communist Party*. Moscow: Progress Publishers.

Massey, D. (1984) *Spatial Divisions of Labour*. London: Macmillan

Massey, D. (1991a) Flexible sexism, *Environment and Planning D: Society and Space* 9, 1: 31–57.

Massey, D. (1991b) A global sense of place, *Marxism Today*: 24–9.

Massey, D. (1994) *Space, Place and Gender*. Minneapolis, MN: University of Minnesota Press.

Massey, D. (1999) Space-time, 'science' and the relationship between physical and human geography, *Transactions of the Institute of British Geographers* 24, 3: 261–76.

Massey, D. and Thrift, N. J. (2003) The passion of place, in R. J. Johnston and M. Williams (eds.) *A Century of British Geography*. Oxford: Oxford University Press, 275–99.

May, J. and Thrift, N. (eds.) (2001) *Timespace: Geographies of Temporality*. London: Routledge.

McCarney, J. (1990) *Social Theory and the Crisis of Marxism*. London: Verso.

McDowell, L. (1992) Multiple voices: speaking from inside and outside 'the project', *Antipode* 24, 1: 56–72.

McDowell, L. (1998) Some academic and political implications of *Justice, Nature and the Geography and Difference, Antipode* 30, 1: 3–5.

McDowell, L. (ed.) (1998) *Special Issue: Justice, Nature and the Politics of Difference. Antipode* 30, 1: 1–55.

McDowell, L. (2000) Learning to serve? Young men's labour market aspirations in an era of economic restructuring, *Gender, Place and Culture* 7: 389–416.

Meadows, D., et al. (1972) *The Limits to Growth*. New York: Universe Books.

Merrifield, A. (2003) *Metromarxism: A Marxist Tale of the City*. London: Routledge.

Mies, M. (1986) *Patriarchy and Accumulation on a World Scale*. London: Zed Press.

Millet, J. (1970) *Gabriel Tarde et la philosophie de l'histoire*. Paris: Vrin.

Mitchell, D. (2003) *The Right to the City: Social Justice and the Fight for Public Space*. New York: Guilford Press.

Mitchell, K., Marston, S. A. and Katz, C. (eds.) (2004) *Life's Work: Geographies of Social Reproduction*. Oxford: Blackwell.

Mitchell, T. (2002) *The Rule of Experts: Egypt, Techno-politics, Modernity*. Berkeley, CA: University of California Press.

Mohanty, C. T. (2003) 'Under western eyes' revisited: solidarity through anti-capitalist struggles, in *Feminism without Borders: Decolonizing Theory, Practicing Solidarity*. Durham, NC: Duke University Press, 221–51.

Molotch, H. (1976) The city as a growth machine, *American Journal of Sociology* 82: 309–32.

Monk, R. (1990) *Wittgenstein: The Duty of Genius*. London: Vintage.

Moorcock, M. (2003) Firing the cathedral, in P. Crowther (ed.) *Cities*. London: Gollancz, 155–246.

Morris, M. (1992) The man in the mirror, *Theory, Culture, and Society* 9: 253–79.

Nancy, J-L. (1996) The Deleuzian fold of thought, in P. Patton (ed.) *Deleuze: A Critical Reader*. Oxford: Blackwell, 107–13.

Naples, N. and Desai, M. (eds.) (2002) *Women's Activism and Globalization*. New York: Routledge.

Ollman, B. (1971) *Alienation*. Cambridge: Cambridge University Press.

Ollman, B. (1976) *Alienation: Marx's Conception of Man in Capitalist Society*. Cambridge: Cambridge University Press.

Ollman, B. (1993) *Dialectical Investigations*. New York: Routledge.

Olsson, G. (1991) *Lines of Power/Limits of Language*. Minneapolis, MN: University of Minnesota Press.

Olsson, G. (2000) From a = b to a = a, *Environment and Planning A* 32: 1235–244.

Osserman, R. (1995) *The Poetry of the Universe*. New York: Doubleday.

Peet, R. (1981) Spatial dialectics and Marxist geography, *Progress in Human Geography* 5: 105–10.

Peterson, V. Spike (2003) *A Critical Rewriting of Global Political Economy.* New York: Routledge.

Pinchbeck, I. (1969 [1930]) *Women Workers and the Industrial Revolution: 1750–1850.* London: Frank Cass.

Poovey, M. (1995) The production of abstract space, in *Making a Social Body: British Cultural Formation, 1830–186).* Chicago, IL: University of Chicago Press, 76–92.

Postone, M. (1996) *Time, Labor and Social Domination.* Cambridge: Cambridge University Press.

Poulantzas, N. (1979) *State, Power, Socialism.* London: Verso.

Prigogine, I. and Stengers, I. (1984) *Order out of Chaos.* New York: Bantam Books.

Probyn, E. (1996) *Outside Belongings: Disciplines, Belongings and the Place of Sex.* London: Routledge.

Putnam, H. (1981) *Reason, Truth, and History.* Cambridge: Cambridge University Press.

Rae, D. (2003) *City: Urbanism and Its End.* New Haven, CT: Yale University Press.

Rediscovering Geography Committee (1997) *Rediscovering Geography: New Relevance for Science and Society.* Washington, DC: National Academy Press.

Reineke, Y. 197. Positioning bodies for justice, *Gender, Place, and Culture* 4, 3: 367–9.

Rescher, N. (1979) *Leibniz: An Introduction to His Philosophy,* Totawa, NJ: Opus.

Richards, S. (1987) *Philosophy and the Sociology Sciences* (2nd edn.) Oxford: Blackwell.

Rose, G. (1993) *Feminism and Geography: The Limits of Geographical Knowledge.* Minneapolis, MI: University of Minnesota Press.

Rosenberg, J. (1994) *The Empire of Civil Society.* London: Verso.

Rothschild, E. (1973) *Paradise Lost.* New York: Vintage.

Rouse, J. (1987) *Knowledge and Power: Towards a Political Philosophy of Science.* Ithaca, NY: Cornell University Press.

Rubin, I. (1973 [1928]) *Essays on Marx's Theory of Value* M. Samardzija and F. Perlman (trans.). Montreal: Black Rose.

Ryan, M. (1982) *Marxism and Deconstruction: A Critical Articulation.* Baltimore, MD: Johns Hopkins University Press.

Said, E. (1994) *Representation of the Intellectual.* New York: Vintage.

Said, E. (2001) *Power, Politics and Culture.* New York: Vintage.

Saunders, P. and Williams, P. (1986) The new conservatism: some thoughts on recent and future developments in urban studies, *Environment and Planning D: Society and Space* 4: 393–9.

Sayer, A. (1995) *Radical Political Economy: A Critique.* Oxford: Blackwell.

Sayer, A. (2000) *Realism and social science.* Thousand Oaks, CA: Sage.

Schmidt, A. (1971) *The Concept of Nature in Marx.* London: New Left Books.

Scott, J. W. (1988) *Gender and the Politics of History.* New York: Columbia University Press.

Shapin, S. (1994) *A Social History of Truth: Civility and Science in Seventeenth Century England*. Chicago, IL: University of Chicago Press.

Shapin, S. (1998a) Placing the view from nowhere: historical and sociology problems in the location of science, *Transactions of the Institute of British Geographers* 23, 1: 5–12.

Shapin, S. (1998b) The philosopher and the chicken: the dietetics of disembodied knowledge, in C. Lawrence and S. Shapin (eds.) *Science Incarnate: Historical Embodiments of Natural Knowledge*. Chicago, IL: University of Chicago Press, 21–50.

Sheppard, E. (1979) Geographic potentials. *Annals of the Association of American Geographers* 69, 4: 438–47.

Sheppard, E. (1987) A Marxian model of the geography of production and transportation in urban and regional systems, in C. Bertuglia, G. Leonardi, S. Occelli et al. (eds.) *Urban Systems: Contemporary Approaches to Modelling*. London, Croom Helm, 189–250.

Sheppard, E. (1990) Modeling the capitalist space economy: bringing society and space back, *Economic Geography* 66: 201–28.

Sheppard, E. (2002) The spaces and times of globalization: place, scale, networks, and positionality, *Economic Geography* 78, 3: 307–30.

Sheppard, E. (2004) The spatiality of *The Limits to Capital*, *Antipode* 36, 3: 470–79.

Sheppard, E. and Barnes, T. J. (1990) *The Capitalist Space Economy: Geographical Analysis after Ricardo, Marx and Sraffa*. London: Unwin Hyman.

Sheppard, E. and McMaster, R. (eds.) (2004) *Scale and Geographic Inquiry*. Oxford: Blackwell.

Sheppard, E. and Nagar, R. (2004) From east–west to north–south, *Antipode* 36, 4: 557–63.

Smith, N. (1979) Toward a theory of gentrification: a back to the city movement by capital not people, *Journal of the American Planning Association* 45: 538–48

Smith, N. (1981) Degeneracy in theory and practice: spatial interactionism and radical eclecticism, *Progress in Human Geography* 5: 111–18.

Smith, N. (1984) *Uneven Development: Nature, Capital and the Production of Space*. Oxford: Blackwell.

Smith, N. (1992) Contours of a spatialized politics: homeless vehicles and the production of geographical space. *Social Text* 33: 54–81.

Smith, N. (1995) Trespassing on the future, *Environment and Planning D: Society and Space* 13, 3: 505–6.

Smith, N. (1996) The production of nature, in G. Robertson, M. Mash, L. Tickner, J. Bird, B. Curtis, and T. Putnam (eds.) *Future Natural: Nature, Science, Culture*. London: Routledge, pp. 35–54.

Smith, N. (2001) New geographies, old ontologies: optimism of the intellect, *Radical Philosophy* 106: 21–30.

Smith, P. (1998) *Discerning the Subject*. Minneapolis, MN: University of Minnesota Press.

Smith, R. J. and Doel, M. A. (2001) Baudrillard unwound: the duplicity of post-Marxism and deconstruction, *Environment and Planning D: Society and Space* 19, 2: 137–59.

Soja, E. (1980) The socio-spatial dialectic, *Annals of the Association of American Geographers* 70, 3: 207–25.

Soja, E. (1989) *Postmodern Geographies: The Reassertion of Space in Critical Social Theory*. London: Verso.

Soja, E. (1996) *Thirdspace: Journeys to Los Angeles and other real-and-imagined places*. Oxford: Blackwell.

Soja, E. (2000) *Postmetropolis: Critical Studies of Cities and Regions*. Oxford: Blackwell.

Sorkin, M. and Zukin, S. (eds.) (2002) *After the World Trade Center*. New York: Routledge.

Spivak, G. (1985) Scattered speculations on the question of value, *Diacritics* 15, 4: 73–93.

Spivak, G. (1995) Ghostwriting. *Diacritics* 25, 2: 65–84.

Sraffa, P. (1960) *The Production of Commodities by Means of Commodities*. Cambridge: Cambridge University Press.

Stahel, A. W. (1999) Time contradictions of capitalism. *Culture, Nature, Society*, 10, 1: 101–32.

Steedman, I., et al. (1979) *The Value Controversy*. London: New Left Books.

Stengers, I. (2002) *Penser avec Whitehead: Une libre et sauvage création de concepts*. Paris Gallimard

Stiglitz, J. (2002) *Globalization and Its Discontents*. New York: W. W. Norton.

Sweezy, P. (1968) *The Theory of Capitalist Development: Principles of Marxian Political Economy*. London: Modern Reader.

Swidler, A. (2001) *Talk of Love: How Culture Matters*. Chicago, IL: University of Chicago Press.

Swyngedouw, E. (1997) Neither global nor local: 'glocalization' and the politics of scale, in K. Cox (ed.) *Spaces of Globalization: Reasserting the Power of the Local*. New York: Guilford Press.

Swyngedouw, E. (1999) Modernity and hybridity: Nature, *Regeneracionismo*, and production of the Spanish waterscape, 11890–1930, *Annals of the Association of American Geographers*. 89, 3: 443–65

Tarde, G. (1999 [1898]) *Les Lois sociales: equisse d'une sociologie*. Paris: Institut Synthelabo.

Théret, B. (1992) *Régimes économiques de l'ordre politique*. Paris: Presses Universitaires de France.

Third Berlin Biennial for Contemporary Art (2004) *Catalogue: Judith Barry, Voice Off*. Berlin: Biennale, 48–9.

Thoburn, N. (2003)) The hobo anomalous, *Social Movement Studies* 2, 1: 61–84.

Thompson, E. P. (1963) *The Making of the English Working Class*. New York: Vintage Books.

Thrift, N. J. (2003) Space, in S. Holloway, S. Rice and G. Valentine (eds.) *Key Concepts in Geography*. London: Sage.

Thrift, N. J. (2004a) Summoning life, in P. Cloke, P. Crang and M. Goodwin (eds.) *Envisioning Geography*. London: Edward Arnold.

Thrift, N. J. (2004b) A geography of unknown lands, in J. S. Duncan and N. Johnson (eds.) *The Blackwell Companion to Cultural Geography*. Oxford: Blackwell.

Thrift, N. J. (2004c) Intensities of feeling: towards a spatial politics of affect. *Geografiska Annaler* 86, 1: 57–68.

Thrift, N. J. (2004d) *Knowing Capitalism*. London: Sage.

Toews, D. (2003) The new Tarde: sociology after the end of the social. *Theory Culture and Society* 20: 81–98.

Topalov, C. (1973) *Capital et propriété foncière: contribution à l'étude des politiques foncières urbaines*. Paris: Centre de Sociologie Urbaine.

Tsing, A. (2001) The global situation, in J. W. Scott and D. Keates (eds.) *Schools of Thought: Twenty-Five Years of Interpretive Social Sciences*. Princeton, NJ: Princeton University Press, 104–38.

Virilio, P. (1991) *The Aesthetics of Disappearance* P. Beitchman (trans.). New York: Semiotext(e).

Vogel, S. (1996) *Against Nature: The Concept of Nature in Critical Theory*. Albany, NY: SUNY Press.

Walker, R. (2004) The spectre of Marxism, *Antipode* 36, 3: 424–35.

Watts, M. (2001) 1968 and all that, *Progress in Human Geography* 25, 2: 157–88.

Webber, M. (1996) Profitability and growth in multiregional systems: theory and a model, *Economic Geography* 72, 3: 335–52.

Whatmore, S. (1999) Human geographies: rethinking the 'human' in human geography, in D. Massey, J. Allen and P. Sarre (eds.) *Human Geography Today*. Cambridge: Polity Press, 22–39.

Whatmore, S. (2002) *Hybrid Geographies: Natures, Cultures, Spaces*. London: Sage.

Whitehead, A. (1929) *Process and Reality: An Essay in Cosmology*. New York: Macmillan.

Whitehead, A. (1948) *Science and Philosophy*. New York: Philosophical Library.

Williams, R. (1980) *Problems in Materialism and Culture*. London: Verso.

Williams, R. (1985) *Keywords: A Vocabulary of Culture and Society* (rev. edn.). Oxford: Oxford University Press.

Williams, R. (1989) *People of the Black Mountains: The Beginnings*. London: Chatto and Windus.

Wittgenstein, L. (1953) *Philosophical Investigations* G. E. M. Anscombe and R. Rhees (eds.). Oxford: Blackwell.

Wittgenstein, L. (1961) *Tractatus Logico-Philosophicus* D. F. Pears and B. F. McGuinness (trans.), first published in German in 1918, and translated into English in 1922 by C. K. Ogden and F. P. Ramsey. London: Routledge.

Wright, M. W. (2004) From protests to politics: sex work, women's worth, and Ciudad Juárez modernity, *Annals of the Association of American Geographers*, 94, 2: 369–87.

Yeung, H. (2002) Deciphering citations. *Environment and Planning A* 34: 2093–102.

Young, I. M. (1990) *Justice and the Politics of Difference*. Princeton, NJ: Princeton University Press.

Young, I. M. (1998) Harvey's complaint with race and gender struggles: a critical response. *Antipode* 30, 1: 36–42.

Young, I. M. (1990) *Justice and the Politics of Difference*. Princeton: University of Princeton Press.

Zournazi, M. (ed.) (2002) *The Politics of Hope*. New York: Routledge.

Zukin, S. (1982) *Loft Living: Capital and Culture in Urban Change*. Baltimore, MD: Johns Hopkins University Press.

Zukin, S. (1991) *Landscapes of Power: From Detroit to Disney World*. Berkeley and Los Angeles, CA: University of California Press.

Zukin, S. (1995) *The Cultures of Cities*. Oxford: Blackwell.

Index

Antipode
A Radical Journal of Geography

Antipode

A Radical Journal of Geography

Edited by Noel Castree and Melissa W. Wright

For more than 30 years *Antipode* has published dissenting scholarship that explores and utilizes key geographical ideas like space, scale, place and landscape. It aims to challenge dominant and orthodox views of the world through debate, scholarship and politically-committed research, creating new spaces and envisioning new futures. *Antipode* welcomes the infusion of new ideas and the shaking up of old positions, without being committed to just one view of radical analysis or politics.

In addition to publishing academic papers, *Antipode* publishes short polemical interventions and longer, more reflective, explorations of radical geography in particular fields or locations.

* Essential reading for critical social scientists

* Publishes cutting-edge radical theory and research

* The only left-wing journal dedicated to exploring the geographical constitution of power and resistance

* Explores how space, place and landscape both shape and are shaped by unequal social relations

Visit the *Antipode* home page for up-to-date contents listings, editorial details, submission guidelines and ordering information:
www.blackwellpublishing.com/journals/anti

Blackwell
Publishing

ISSN: 0066-4812

9600 Garsington Road, Oxford OX4 2DQ, UK | 350 Main Street, Malden, MA 02148, USA